To build a button

1. Create the button:
   - Choose the Button tool.
   - Select New Button from the Objects menu.
2. Customize the button:
   - Double-click on the new button (or select Button Info... from the Objects menu).
   - Type a name for the button (optional).
   - Choose the button style (for invisible button, click Transparent with Show Name clicked off).
   - Click on Icon... if desired, select an icon, and click OK.
   - Drag the corner of the button to change its shape; drag the center to move it.
3. Assign tasks:
   - Double-click on the button; click on Tasks....
   - Click on the Go to Destination icon.
   - If linking to the stack's first or last card, click on First Card or Last Card.
   - If linking with a logical link (see page 88) to next or previous card, click on Next Card or Previous Card.
   - If linking to a new card with the same background, select New Card from the Edit menu, and click on Current Card.
   - If linking to a new card with a different background, select New Background from the Objects menu, and click on Current Card.
   - If linking to a new card with a previously used background, go to a card with that background, select New Card from the Edit menu, and click on Current Card.
   - Click on the Visual Effect icon; select visual effect and speed (optional).
   - If button is to play a sound, click on Sounds task icon, and select sound from list (optional).
   - Click on Assign Tasks.
4. Script the button (optional):
   - Double-click on the button again; click on Script... button.
   - Add to or modify existing script.
   - Click the close box of the script window.

To build a field to contain editable text

1. Create the field:
   - Choose the Field tool.
   - Select New Field from the Objects menu.
2. Customize the field:
   - Double-click on the new field (or select Field Info... from the Objects menu).
   - Type a name for the field.
   - Choose the field style (Transparent for invisible).
   - Drag the corner of the field to change its shape; drag the center to move it.
   - Click on Font...; select desired font and style (use a common font such as Geneva if your stack will be used on other computers).
3. Fill the field:
   - Select the Browse (hand) tool (*not* the *A*), position it over the field, and type text.
   - Use standard editing techniques, including Cut Text, Copy Text, and Paste Text.

HyperCard® 2.3 in a Hurry

The Fast Track to Multimedia

George Beekman
Oregon State University

INTEGRATED MEDIA GROUP

An Imprint of Wadsworth Publishing Company
I(T)P® An International Thomson Publishing Company

Belmont · Albany · Bonn · Boston · Cincinnati · Detroit · London · Madrid · Melbourne
Mexico City · New York · Paris · San Francisco · Singapore · Tokyo · Toronto · Washington

Editor: *Kathy Shields*
Assistant Editor: *Tamara Huggins*
Print Buyer: *Karen Hunt*
Compositor: *Scratchgravel Publishing Services*
Printer: *Malloy Lithographing, Inc.*

Printed in the United States of America
1 2 3 4 5 6 7 8 9 10—02 01 00 99 98 97 96

For more information, contact Wadsworth Publishing Company:

Wadsworth Publishing Company
10 Davis Drive
Belmont, California 94002, USA

International Thomson Publishing Europe
Berkshire House 168-173
High Holborn
London, WC1V 7AA, England

Thomas Nelson Australia
102 Dodds Street
South Melbourne 3205
Victoria, Australia

Nelson Canada
1120 Birchmount Road
Scarborough, Ontario
Canada M1K 5G4

International Thomson Editores
Campos Eliseos 385, Piso 7
Col. Polanco
11560 México D.F. México

International Thomson Publishing GmbH
Königswinterer Strasse 418
53227 Bonn, Germany

International Thomson Publishing Asia
221 Henderson Road
#05-10 Henderson Building
Singapore 0315

International Thomson Publishing Japan
Hirakawacho Kyowa Building, 3F
2-2-1 Hirakawacho
Chiyoda-ku, Tokyo 102, Japan

ISBN 0-534-51300-X

To my family, whose love, support, and patience serve as a constant reminder that some things are better when you're *not* in a hurry.

Contents

Session 5
Behind the Buttons: Introducing HyperTalk 142

Preface

This book is designed to deliver what it promises: *HyperCard 2.3 in a Hurry: The Fast Track to Multimedia.* Rather than exhaustively describing every feature and nuance of HyperCard and HyperTalk, *HyperCard 2.3 in a Hurry* systematically introduces the fundamentals of HyperCard, version 2.3 and beyond, through a series of self-study, hands-on sessions. The first two sessions introduce HyperCard as a tool for information storage and retrieval. The five remaining sessions illustrate essential techniques and tricks for building a variety of HyperCard stacks.

HyperCard 2.3 in a Hurry is not *Instant HyperCard.* Learning a complex and powerful tool takes time. But by focusing on the essentials of HyperCard and stack design, *HyperCard 2.3 in a Hurry* minimizes the amount of time it takes to become a competent, confident HyperCard stack designer. After a few hours with this book, even if you're a beginner, you should be able to design, build, and customize visually impressive and conceptually complex stacks to perform a variety of tasks. This statement says as much about HyperCard as it does about this book. Before HyperCard, it simply wasn't possible for a computer neophyte, with an investment of a dozen hours, to build sophisticated graphic presentations with complex logical structures. With HyperCard, beginners turn into programmers every day. This book is designed to facilitate that process.

Previous editions of this book have been tested by thousands of students, instructors, hobbyists, and multimedia enthusiasts. Many of the first users of this book were university students in a freshman computer literacy class, where they learned how to use computers mostly through hands-on experience with Microsoft Works and HyperCard. Junior high students in two-week summer math camps sponsored by the American Indian Science and Engineering Society provided the greatest inspiration in shaping the book. After being led through an abridged version of the Dungeon project in Session 4, these students applied what they learned to produce visual recreations of classic native American legends. Their creations, completed in just a few hours, should convince even the most jaded skeptic that HyperCard *can* be learned in a hurry.

From Zero to HyperCard in Seven Sessions

This book can be used by anyone interested in learning HyperCard. It assumes minimal Macintosh experience but provides time-saving shortcuts and bypasses for Mac veterans. Each session guides you step by step through the process of using or creating stacks, pointing out important concepts along the way. Projects are drawn from a variety of subject areas, so readers with different backgrounds and interests can see by example how they can put HyperCard to work in practical and provocative ways.

Each session adds another layer to your understanding of HyperCard. It's not necessary to complete all seven sessions to learn HyperCard. You may find everything you're looking for in the first few sessions.

Sessions 1 and 2 lay the groundwork for the rest of the book by providing a guided tour of HyperCard from the user's point of view. Session 1 focuses on HyperCard fundamentals. Session 2 shows how to use HyperCard as a personal database. It includes a short section on modifying an existing database stack, providing a preview of HyperCard's authoring tools.

In Sessions 3 and 4, you'll learn the basics of stack construction in the process of creating a dynamic multilayer map/display and a complex maze game. Graphic tools, cards, buttons, links, and backgrounds are introduced gradually as these projects unfold. At the same time they introduce HyperCard's most important tools, these sessions explain and illustrate aesthetic and technical design principles that apply to those tools.

Sessions 5 and 6 explore HyperTalk, the programming language that hides under HyperCard's friendly point-and-click interface. Session 5 uses sound effects and animation in a presentation graphics stack. Session 6 builds a nonlinear hypertext reference. Both sessions emphasize the design process that precedes the actual hands-on construction work. These sessions provide the background you'll need to explore and learn from scripts created by others.

Session 7 introduces several supplementary stacks and features that make HyperCard a popular multimedia authoring tool. This session shows you how to add color, a custom soundtrack, digitized speech, and video clips to your stacks *without scripting*. The session also shows you how to save any stack as a stand-alone, double-clickable application.

Just in case you aren't satisfied with what you learn in these seven sessions, Appendix A provides links to other sources and resources, including books, software, and hardware. This section is designed to provide answers to such questions as "What's a good way to learn more about HyperTalk?" and "What hardware and software tools make HyperCard even easier to use?"

The remaining appendices are designed to make this book a useful reference tool. These appendices answer the most common HyperCard questions, organize and annotate all the important HyperCard menu and keyboard commands, and define the essential HyperTalk terms.

In the process of writing four editions of this book and giving countless *HyperCard in a Hurry* workshops, I've become even more convinced of the importance of HyperCard as a tool for educators, students, multimedia authors, and others whose communication needs go beyond the conventional. HyperCard unlocks the door that used to say, "Programmers only beyond this point!" There's an exciting world full of creative computing behind that door. *HyperCard 2.3 in a Hurry* is a guidebook to that world.

Acknowledgments

This book would not be what it is without the mental, physical, and spiritual contributions of many, many people. To all of you who helped me with a kind word, a thoughtful suggestion, an open ear, and/or a warm heart, I thank you—you know who you are, even if you don't find your name here. I owe a *special* thank you to Ben Beekman for the many hours of hard work he put in helping me organize, write, illustrate, and test the new material in this and the previous edition of this book. In addition, I'm offering a heartfelt thank you to Kathy Shields, Tamara Huggins, Hal Humphrey, Roslyn Bullas, Martha Steffen, Gail McDonald Jordan, Joanne Clapp Fullagar, Steve Stansel, Susan Jane Riley, Chuck Boody, Adam Ray, Miles Oden, Lori Carlson, Lucy McDonald, Frank Ruggirello, Carol Carreon, Rhonda Gray, Anne Draus, Greg Draus, Meg Korones, Mark Dinsmore, Delores Dinsmore, Casey Dinsmore, Danny Goodman, Walter Rudd, Rebecca Smith, Larry Beekman, charles chesney, Alice Trinka, Sarah Richards, Brian Crissie, Rajeev Pandey, Jeannie Holmes, Mary Ann Dengler, Jeff Hino, Mike Quinn, Kevin Hurst, Pam Meyer, Ken Tubbs, Paul Ritter, Gail Sanders, Shannon Whitmore, Bryan Miller, Phil Brown, Jack Dymond, Phil Russell, Neal Gladstone, Don Poole, Mike Massey, Linda Fernandes, Liza Weiman, Loretta Reilly, Bernie Feyerheim, Clara Knutsen, Sheryl Parker, the OSU Computer Science Department office staff, Shoobedebop, SMILE, the students and staff of the 1989 OSU/AISES Math Camp, the hundreds of CS 101 students who beta-tested this material, the consultants and support technicians in the CS Department, and the representatives of Apple, Claris, and the other hardware and software companies who provided invaluable information and advice throughout the process of putting together this book. I am also grateful to the following educators who reviewed the material while it was still in manuscript form: Sherry Francis, University of Akron; Paul W. Ross, Millersville University of Pennsylvania; Mary Anderson, Gonzaga University; Susan Wilkins, California State Polytechnic University; and Scott Kronick. Most of all, thanks to my family—Ben, Johanna, and Susan—whose sacrifices and support made this book possible.

Introduction

> If you're *really* in a hurry to get started with HyperCard, you may safely bypass the first two sections of this introduction, skipping directly to "HyperCard Essentials." But if you're totally unfamiliar with HyperCard, the material in those two sections will provide you with a background for understanding the ideas behind HyperCard.

What Is HyperCard?

HyperCard is one of the most interesting and influential pieces of software to be released in recent years. It's also one of the most difficult to describe. The question "What is HyperCard?" has several answers:

- **HyperCard is a tool for accessing information.** There's no shortage of information in today's world; the problem is finding the right piece of information when you need it. It's easy to spend hours scanning reference books for an elusive fact, quote, or idea, following footnotes and bibliographies that may lead toward other promising sources. There's no easy way to seek out particular facts quickly with conventional printed references.

  When you're looking for facts with HyperCard, it's easier to cut your own trails through the information. Unlike a conventional book or article, a typical HyperCard document contains links that can lead you quickly to other parts of the document—or to other related documents. If you're researching logging practices in the Pacific Northwest, you might choose to jump from reading a card about the Douglas fir to perusing a detailed entry on the spotted owl that lives in old-growth canopies, perhaps clicking a button that plays a recording of the owl's call. The possibilities are nearly limitless.

- **HyperCard is a tool for managing information.** Like a standard database, HyperCard allows you to store all kinds of information, from phone numbers to phonetic spellings, in organized packages that can be expanded and changed to meet your needs. But because HyperCard documents can be linked, it's possible to jump instantly from a calendar reminder of a friend's birthday to a phone book that can automatically dial your friend's phone number for you.

  Many people use HyperCard simply to access "canned" information; others use it to store their own personal information in an easy-to-access form.

- **HyperCard is a software construction kit.** The Macintosh has long held a reputation for being the most user-friendly of computers. With its intuitive, graphic user interface and its consistent command structure, the Macintosh has become the computer of choice for millions of people who don't want to be bothered with memorizing cryptic commands like CHDIR SYS3825 or DEL *.BAS.

  Ironically, the user-friendly interface makes the Macintosh programmer-hostile when compared with less friendly machines. Traditional Macintosh programming is incredibly difficult, in large part because the programmer has to anticipate the needs of the user in so many ways.

  HyperCard has changed all that. With HyperCard, it's possible for nonprofessional programmers to create original working software applications in hours rather than months. In the same way that applications like ClarisWorks make child's play of computer graphics, HyperCard can make a game of building software applications. Bill Atkinson, HyperCard's creator, calls it a "software erector set."

  Like any programming tool, HyperCard has strengths and weaknesses. Although it's not designed for building industrial-strength word processors or spreadsheets, it's well-suited for building customized personal information managers, educational tutorials, multimedia presentations, and user interfaces to other, less friendly programs.

- **HyperCard is a medium for publishing information in nonsequential form.** By simplifying the program-construction process, HyperCard has opened up the world of programming to thousands of people who consider themselves nonprogrammers. Most of these nonprofessional programmers are creating programs that are more like documents than applications. Engineers, teachers, and other professionals are using HyperCard as a medium for making their expertise available to others in a dynamic, interactive form.

- **HyperCard is a gateway to multimedia computer applications.** The user interface is often the weak link in a new piece of hardware or software. Because HyperCard shines as a user interface construction kit, it is often used to create friendly "front ends" for other software packages, hardware peripherals, and multimedia devices. With a well-constructed HyperCard front end, an otherwise complex technological device like a videodisc player or a CD-ROM drive can become as easy to control as a child's toy.

HyperCard, Hypertext, and Hypermedia: Beyond Books

Although HyperCard is a relatively new software product, it's based on ideas that go back to the earliest days of computing. In 1945, Vannevar Bush, science advisor to President Roosevelt, wrote about his vision of a system for tracking and using scientific literature. The **memex**, as he called it, would link together articles, sketches, and photographs in a comprehensive, cross-referenced research tool.

The technology of the time made it difficult, if not impossible, to actually create a memex. But over the years, Bush's ideas inspired Doug Engelbart, Ted Nelson, Alan Kay, and other computer visionaries to push the technology toward that end. The results of these early efforts were generally referred to as **hypertext** because they allowed mostly textual information to be linked in nonlinear ways. Conventional text media such as books are linear, or sequential: They are designed to be read from beginning to end in one particular order. **Hypermedia**—which can include graphics and other media in addition to text—invite readers to cut their own trails through information.

If you're reading about Beethoven's life, for example, you might want to learn more about his hometown, the disease that caused his deafness, the composers who most inspired him, or the culture that spawned him. If you decide to explore the culture of the time, you might be fascinated by a discussion of religious festivals and decide to focus on those. That might start you wondering about the primitive rituals that predated those festivals, and so on. With a large, all-encompassing hypertext reference, you can follow your curiosity wherever it might lead you.

You're not likely to find HyperCard documents that give you the kind of absolute intellectual freedom hinted at here; that kind of multidimensional, cross-disciplinary information source requires an investment of time and hardware that goes beyond what most of us would consider reasonable. But because HyperCard is the first software tool to popularize the concepts of hypermedia, it's rapidly pushing us toward the visions of Vannevar Bush.

HyperCard Essentials

When you work with a Macintosh, or any computer, you use **applications**—software tools—such as word processors and graphics programs to create **documents** such as letters, research papers, and posters. In the same way, you'll use HyperCard to create documents. A HyperCard document is known as a **stack**, and it's made up of identically-sized **cards**.

Like a 3 × 5 note card, a HyperCard card can contain any combination of graphics or text. Depending on the size of the card and the size of your monitor screen, a card might occupy a window on your screen, exactly fill the screen, or be so large that it's only partially visible on your screen.

It's possible to **browse** through the cards in a stack in sequential order, from the first card to the last. But in most stacks you aren't restricted to this kind of sequential access. **Buttons** on each card are **linked** to other related cards or stacks so that you can jump to another information location with a click of the mouse. As you'll see, it's a simple process to create a button that links one card to another.

Buttons can do far more than take you to another screen. HyperCard buttons can play music, open dialog boxes, launch other applications, rearrange information, perform menu operations, dial telephones, send messages to hardware devices—do just about anything that you can do with your Macintosh. Programming a button to perform many of these tasks generally requires some knowledge of **HyperTalk**, HyperCard's built-in programming language, or some other scripting language. But as you'll see in Sessions 3, 4, and 7 of this book, it's possible to accomplish a surprising amount without learning a word of HyperTalk or any other programming language. In Sessions 5 and 6 you'll see how HyperTalk scripts can enhance the stacks that you create.

Charting a Path through This Book

Learning HyperCard is like learning to ride a bicycle: Reading isn't enough. This book is designed to give you hands-on experience so that you can start using HyperCard productively as quickly as possible. It's divided into seven sessions. Each session provides a new way of working with HyperCard. The more sessions you complete, the deeper your understanding of HyperCard. This kind of layered structure is possible because of HyperCard's multileveled nature. HyperCard can be just about as powerful a tool as you choose to make it.

To clarify, let's compare HyperCard to television. When you read an instruction manual for a new TV set, you learn how to turn it on, adjust the volume, and navigate the channels—but not how to make your own TV shows. In Session 1 of this book, you'll use HyperCard like a TV set: as a medium for receiving information packages created by others. Session 2 treats HyperCard more like a VCR; you'll learn how to capture and customize information sources. In Sessions 3 and 4, you'll master HyperCard as a video camera so that you can actually create your own programs. In the remaining sessions you'll learn to work with HyperCard scripts created by you and by others. These scripts have no analogy in the world of consumer video today. It's as if you could teach your video camera or television to do things that they couldn't do when they left the factory.

> During a typical session of *HyperCard 2.3 in a Hurry*, you'll use HyperCard to solve a real-world problem, learning several new concepts and techniques as you do. Each session can be completed in somewhere between one and three hours. (If you're a rank beginner and/or very thorough, some sessions may take longer. If you have lots of experience, you can probably zip through two sessions in the time it takes a neophyte to complete one.)
>
> With a couple of exceptions, each session assumes you've mastered the material in the previous session, so resist the temptation to skip ahead. There may be times, though, when skipping ahead is the right thing to do. This book is designed to meet the needs of a widely diversified audience: seasoned Macintosh users, experienced programmers, and (especially) rank beginners—in short, anyone who wants to learn HyperCard in a hurry. Because different readers have different needs, this book has road signs in boxes like this to steer you around material that may be unnecessary or inappropriate for you.

In each session, you'll be asked to perform a number of tasks to complete a project. A typical task might look like the following:

Resetting the User Level

The steps to perform a given task are preceded by check boxes, like this:

☐ **Point to the button labeled Cancel and click the mouse.**

Follow each instruction *carefully,* checking it off when you complete it. The paragraphs that precede and/or follow the instructions give you more details about why you're doing what you're doing. If you skip a step or don't do exactly what it tells you to do, you may take a wrong turn and stray from the path described in this guidebook.

Illustrations along the way show you what your screen should look like. Don't worry if your screen doesn't *exactly* match the ones in the book; when you're working in HyperCard's visual environment, there are all kinds of variations that have no effect on the end result.

Starting late in Session 2, you'll be regularly switching back and forth between HyperCard's transparent card layer and opaque background layer. Because these two layers often look alike, it's easy to forget where you are and perform some operation in the wrong layer. HyperCard reminds you that you're in the background by putting candy stripes on the menu bar. Similarly, this book includes a striped bar next to all instructions that apply to the background layer, just like the bar you see here.

Even if you follow every instruction, check every screen shot, and monitor every background switch, you may feel hopelessly lost at some point when things don't match. When that happens, you can either (1) panic or (2) accept your disorientation as an opportunity to do some creative detective work. If you're here to learn, go with the second approach. Retrace your steps looking for the wrong turn. Read ahead to see if you made any incorrect assumptions about where the book is leading you. Uncertainty is a wonderful catalyst for learning; make the most of it!

Break Point

You may want to take a break in the middle of a session. This icon will let you know when it's a good time to quit. If you have to quit before completing a session, be sure to (1) quit HyperCard, (2) back up the files you have created or modified, and (3) shut down the computer. When you return, (1) start up the computer and (2) open the stack you were working on.

As you proceed through a session, don't try to memorize every step of every process. If a piece of information is crucial, this book will tell you.

> Boxes like this one contain facts, concepts, and pointers worth remembering. It's not necessary to memorize every detail in these boxes. They're easy to scan when you're reviewing a session or looking for a piece of important information later. In effect, this book has already been highlighted with a see-through marker.

Like anything else, HyperCard has a vocabulary that includes terms you may not recognize. When a new term is introduced in this book, it's printed in **boldface** so it's easy to spot. At the end of each session, you'll find all of the new terms collected in a list of key words. Exercises and projects at the end of each session will help you test your knowledge and understanding and further develop your HyperCard skills.

If you forget a detail and can't remember where you saw it, use the inside covers and the appendices at the end of the book. You'll find summaries of menu and keyboard commands, a short cookbook of essential HyperCard procedures, a troubleshooting guide to answer common questions, and an annotated list of references to help you find answers to questions that aren't covered in this book.

One final word: *HyperCard 2.3 in a Hurry* is intended to get you up and running with HyperCard quickly. But that doesn't mean you should rush through the material. You'll learn more and learn faster if you take your time and relax while working through these examples. HyperCard is fun—*enjoy it!*

Key Words

application
browse
button
card
document
hypermedia
HyperTalk
hypertext
memex
link
stack

HyperCard® 2.3 in a Hurry

The Fast Track to Multimedia

Session 1

By the end of this session you should be able to

- Begin a HyperCard session
- Open a HyperCard stack from the Home stack
- Use HyperCard buttons, menu commands, keyboard shortcuts, and palettes to navigate a HyperCard stack and return to the Home stack
- Terminate a HyperCard session

HyperCard for Browsers

Making Tracks through Stacks

The Problem

You've contracted a serious case of information anxiety. You're sitting in the middle of an information explosion, and the gap between what you know and what you think you *should* know is getting wider every day. Traditional information-gathering tools don't seem to help anymore. Books take too long to read, and they're often obsolete by the time they become widely available. Magazines and newspapers are timely, but the information they contain is almost impossible to find when you need it. Radio provides no practical tool for sifting the relevant from the repetitive. And TV, which promises so much and delivers so little, is probably the worst time waster of all. Computers helped create this rapidly expanding sea of information. Can they help keep you from drowning? Perhaps HyperCard can help.

Introduction

This first session will introduce you to the basics of exploring HyperCard stacks. You'll learn how to navigate in HyperCard using menu commands, buttons, and keyboard shortcuts. Take your time, take notes on things that aren't clear, and take breaks when the spirit moves you. Have fun!

Preliminary Questions

We'll start pressing buttons as soon as we deal with a few necessary questions.

Which System?

HyperCard 2.3 requires System 6.05 or later, but it's easier to learn, easier to use, and more versatile with System 7. For these reasons, *HyperCard 2.3 in a Hurry* assumes you're using System 7. If you're using System 6, you'll need to make minor adjustments to the procedures in this book that involve assigning tasks to buttons, as described in the *HyperCard* documentation. Whatever system you're using, the HyperCard installer will install all the necessary files on your hard disk.

What about Memory?

With System 6, HyperCard requires a minimum of 2 megabytes of memory; with System 7, it requires at least 4 MB of memory—5 MB if you're using the Color Tools described in Session 7. For large, complex projects or projects that include video, sound, speech, and other memory-intensive features, you'll probably need more than the minimum memory requirements.

In some situations HyperCard won't allow you to complete an operation because there's not enough internal memory (RAM) available. Sometimes it will tell you explicitly; other times it simply won't let you perform the operation. (If you suspect a memory shortage, check your computer's memory by choosing About this Macintosh... from the Apple menu when you have no applications open. A window shows you how much total memory your machine has and how much memory is available for applications. Even if there's plenty of available memory, HyperCard may not take advantage of that memory unless you give it permission. To reset HyperCard's preferred memory allocation, locate the HyperCard icon, choose Get Info... from the File menu, type a number into the Preferred Size box, and close the window. The number you type determines how much of the computer's available memory will be used by HyperCard the next time you launch it.)

Which HyperCard?

HyperCard evolved through several versions before Version 2.3 was released in 1995. Since Version 1 of HyperCard can't open stacks created with later versions, it is rarely used today. Versions 2.0, 2.1, and 2.2 are still widely used, but they lack many features found in Version 2.3. If you're using an older version of HyperCard, you'll find occasional differences between the instructions and illustrations in this book and what you see on your screen. For best results, upgrade to the latest version of HyperCard.

The HyperCard Player

The **HyperCard Player** that comes with most Macintoshes allows you to view and add data to existing HyperCard stacks but not create or modify stacks in other ways. (Most of the material in Sessions 1 and 2 of this book can be completed with the HyperCard Player.) If your friends have Macintoshes, they almost certainly have the HyperCard Player. That means you can share your stacks with them even if they don't have HyperCard. If you have HyperCard installed on your hard disk, you don't need the HyperCard Player. In fact, it's better if you *don't* have both HyperCard and the HyperCard Player on your hard disk; having both can cause unnecessary confusion for you and your computer. When you install HyperCard 2.3 (or later) on your hard disk, copy the HyperCard Player onto a backup floppy disk and delete it from your hard disk.

What If I'm Working in a School or Public Lab?

You may be sharing hardware and software resources with many other users. These tips will help minimize conflicts and make your HyperCard experience easier:

- If you're new to the Macintosh, familiarize yourself with the basics of the Mac before you proceed. Specifically, you should know how to initialize and back up disks, how to work with windows and icons on the desktop, and how to do basic file organization and manipulation. If you can, start with the Guided Tour that Apple provides with every Macintosh.
- Learn the specifics of working with the hardware and software in your lab. What are the access rules? Where are public files stored? Are any special procedures necessary for using the lab software and hardware?

- If you have a password-accessible storage area on the file server or hard disk, keep your password private.
- If you're working in a public lab with shared copies of HyperCard and its stacks, remember that others will be following in your footsteps. Don't leave the hard disk or network file server littered with your personal files, and don't change or delete any files that aren't yours.
- To protect public files from accidental changes, create a disk that contains personal copies of the Home stack and the other stacks you'll be using. For example, in Session 2 you'll use the Addresses stack. Rather than using the original, copy the stack onto your personal work disk along with the Home stack. Always work with your own personal copies of stacks rather than the public originals. You'll automatically use your Home copy if you double-click on it to start HyperCard.
- For faster performance, especially when working with sound, color, and video, store your stacks on the hard disk while creating and editing them. At the end of each session, copy your stacks to floppy disks and delete the hard disk copies.
- Some older Macintoshes can't read modern high-density disks. If your lab has any of these machines, you may want to use 800K disks for your work. They hold less data, but they're compatible with almost all Macintoshes.

> If you're an experienced Macintosh user, you should be able to move quickly through this session. If you've used HyperCard before, you may be able to skip the hands-on part altogether, reading only the reminder boxes. But beware: Some aspects of HyperCard run counter to conventional Mac wisdom. Pay attention! If you miss something along the way, feel free to go back, or consult the reference sections in the appendices at the end of this book.

Hello, HyperCard

Ready to go? Let's start up HyperCard.

Launching HyperCard

☐ **Locate the HyperCard icon. Double-click on it to open it.**

You can launch HyperCard by double-clicking on the HyperCard icon or on the icon for any HyperCard stack, including Home. Opening a stack icon on the desktop tells the Macintosh to do three things:

- Launch HyperCard (or the HyperCard Player, if it's available).
- Locate the Home stack (even if that's not the stack that was double-clicked).
- Locate and open the stack that was double-clicked.

When you launch HyperCard, you're transported to the **Home stack**—your HyperCard base of operations. The first card of the Home stack, sometimes called the **Home card**, should look something like this:

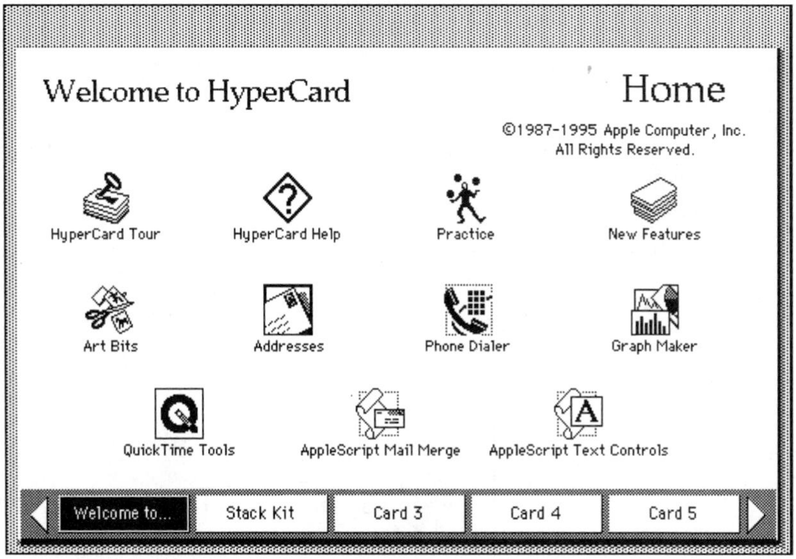

If you're using a small-screen Macintosh, the Home card may fill the entire screen below the menu bar. On larger screens, it just fills a window on the screen.

If, instead of this Home card, you see one that says "HyperCard Player," the HyperCard Player was launched instead of HyperCard. To prevent this from happening, save a backup copy of the HyperCard Player and delete the original from the computer's hard disk. If you need to keep the HyperCard Player on your hard disk, you'll need to double-click on the HyperCard icon rather than the Home icon when launching HyperCard.

The menu bar includes the Apple, File, and Edit menus that are found in virtually all Macintosh applications. Many of the menu commands are similar to commands you've seen in other applications. For example, HyperCard's File menu contains an **Open Stack...** command that works like the Open... command found in other applications: It displays a dialog box that allows you to locate and select a HyperCard document—a stack—to open. But **buttons**, rather than menus, are HyperCard's primary navigation tools.

Taking a Tour

The Home card is populated with icons. Each of these icons is a HyperCard button waiting to perform some operation when you click it with the mouse.

> HyperCard buttons, like all Macintosh buttons, respond when clicked *once* with the mouse. This is always true—even when the buttons look like icons.

HyperCard Tour

☐ **Click once on the icon/button labeled HyperCard Tour.**

This click transports you to the **HyperCard Tour**, a stack that will introduce you to the basics of HyperCard. (If you see a dialog box that says "Where is HyperCard Tour?" locate the HyperCard Tour stack. If you can't find the stack, click Cancel and simply read along for the remainder of this section.)

> **Where is _____?**
>
> When you're working through this and future sessions, you may see a dialog box that asks you "Where is XYZ?" where XYZ is the name of a particular HyperCard stack. Except for that question, this dialog box looks and works like the Open Stack... dialog box. Respond by locating the missing file, remembering the Open... and Save... dialog box navigation rules:
>
> - Clicking the Desktop button (System 7) takes you to the Desktop (highest) level of the hierarchy, allowing you to select from all available drives.
> - Clicking the Drive button (System 6) switches to the next drive (or file server). Repeatedly clicking Drive cycles through all available drives.

- Clicking the Eject button ejects the disk currently displayed in the box. (This button is dimmed if the current drive is a file server or hard disk, or if there is no disk in the other drive.) It's useful if you need to insert another disk.
- Double-clicking a folder opens that folder and takes you into that folder.
- Dragging down from the current folder icon reveals a pop-up menu that takes you out of that folder.

Once you've located the missing file, HyperCard will remember where you found it so it doesn't need to ask again (unless the stack is moved or deleted).

Notice that the menu bar has disappeared; many HyperCard stacks hide the menu bar. Buttons are also often hidden in HyperCard. A **hidden button** can respond to mouse clicks even though you can't see it. In this case a hidden button fills this entire card; clicking that button transports you to the next card.

☐ **Click anywhere on the card to proceed to the next card in the stack.**

This screen appears:

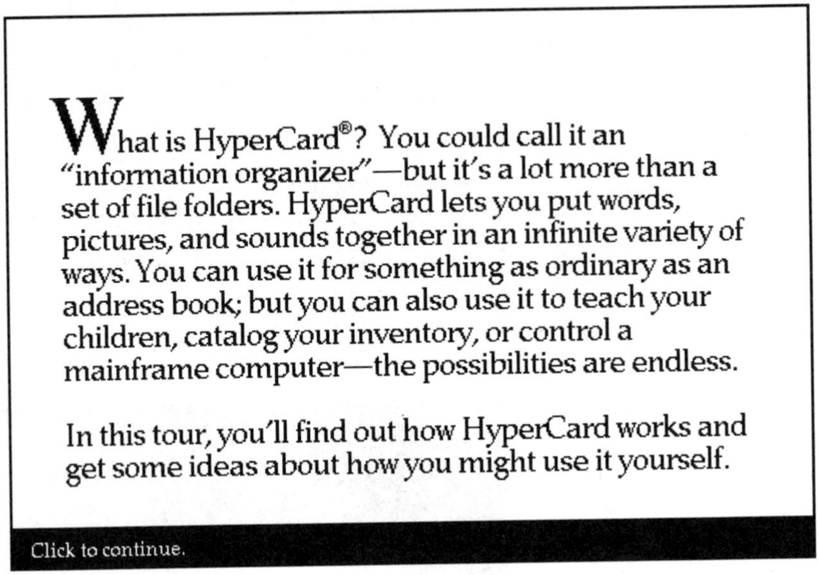

What is HyperCard®? You could call it an "information organizer"—but it's a lot more than a set of file folders. HyperCard lets you put words, pictures, and sounds together in an infinite variety of ways. You can use it for something as ordinary as an address book; but you can also use it to teach your children, catalog your inventory, or control a mainframe computer—the possibilities are endless.
In this tour, you'll find out how HyperCard works and get some ideas about how you might use it yourself.
Click to continue.

☐ **Click anywhere on the screen to continue.**

A hidden button takes you to the next card.

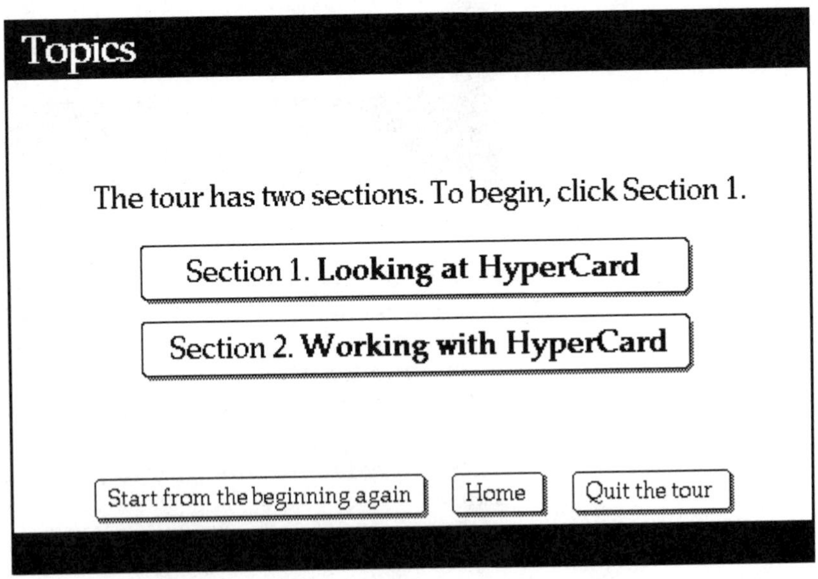

This screen contains several visible buttons for navigating.

☐ **Click on the first button: Section 1. Looking at HyperCard.**

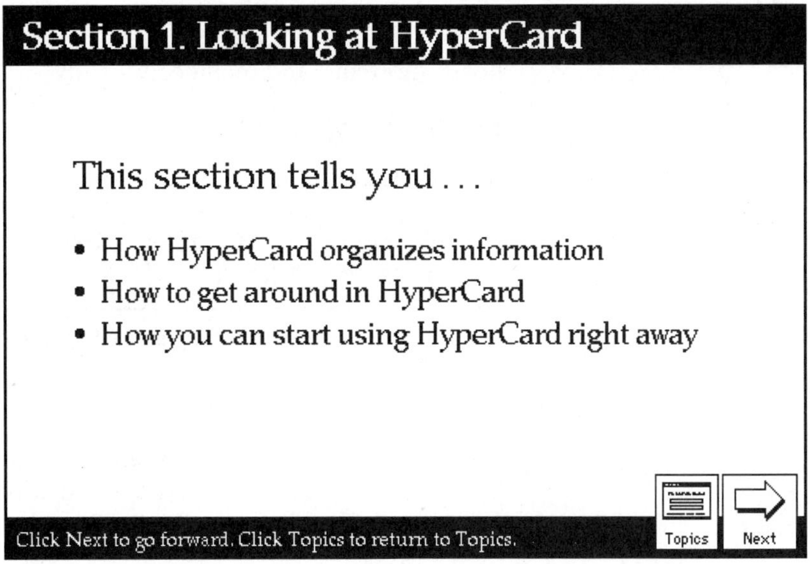

Section 1. Looking at HyperCard
This section tells you . . .
• How HyperCard organizes information
• How to get around in HyperCard
• How you can start using HyperCard right away
Click Next to go forward. Click Topics to return to Topics.
Topics
Next

This card also contains several buttons, including one with a standard meaning in most HyperCard stacks.

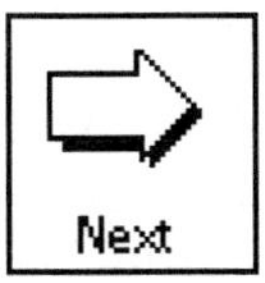

☐ **Click on the right-arrow button to go to the next card in the stack.**

The next card has two arrow buttons: one for moving forward through the stack, and another for going back to the previous card.

☐ **Click on the left-arrow button to go back one card.**

☐ **Proceed through the tour by repeatedly clicking on the right-arrow button on each card.**

The HyperCard Tour provides an excellent overview of HyperCard. Take your time exploring it; you'll be able to apply what you learn as you proceed through this book.

During this tour you'll see that buttons can take a variety of shapes and perform a variety of operations. The last card contains another "standard" HyperCard button: the **Home button.**

☐ **Click on the Home button to return to the Home stack.**

HyperCard Navigation Tips

HyperCard offers several navigation options, including buttons, keyboard shortcuts, and menu commands.

Browsing with Buttons

If your Home card has arrow buttons, you can use those buttons to move to other cards in the stack. Navigation buttons are all you need to explore most HyperCard stacks. Here's a summary of the most common navigation buttons:

Common HyperCard Navigation Buttons

Go to the Home card.

Go to the next card in the stack. If you're at the end of the stack, go to the first card.

Go to the previous card in the stack. If you're currently at the beginning of the stack, go to the end.

Go to the first card in the stack.

Go to the last card in the stack.

Return to a previously visited card. The **return-arrow button** always takes you back, but how far back depends on the stack. It might take you back to the stack from which you came; it might take you back to a title page; it might take you back to a higher level card containing a menu.

Tell me more. The **asterisk** is generally used in the same way it's used in books—to let the reader know that there's more to say on a subject.

Tell me about it. The **cartoon balloon** and the **light bulb** usually indicate sources of background information about the current stack or card.

Give me an overview of the stack. This button provides the big picture.

Help me. The **? button** provides **on-line help** for users who are having trouble navigating or using the stack.

Find a keyword in the stack. Next session you'll see how to use the Find command; this icon is sometimes used as a shortcut to that command or a variation.

Navigating with the Go Menu

There are other ways to get around in HyperCard. The **Go menu** contains several commands for quickly moving within and between stacks.

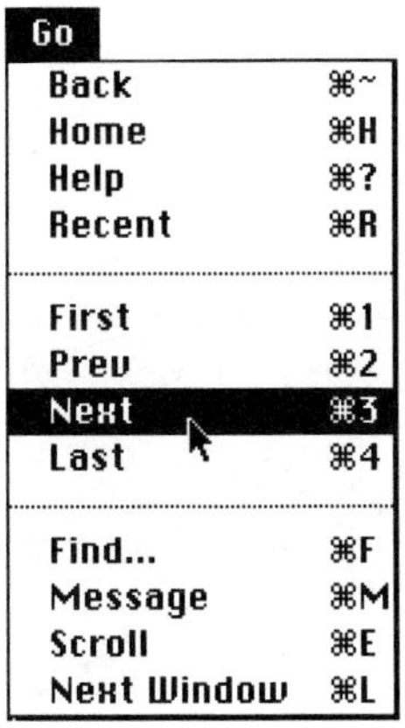

☐ **Select the Next command from the Go menu.**

This command has the same effect as clicking on a right-arrow button, but it works even if the current card has no right-arrow button.

☐ **Select the Prev command from the Go menu.**

This is the command equivalent of the left-arrow button.

☐ **Select the Last command from the Go menu.**

This command takes you to the last card in the stack. We'll return to this card soon.

☐ **Select the First command from the Go menu.**

This command takes you back to card 1 from any point in the stack.

Navigating by Keyboard

If you're a Macintosh veteran, you know that the symbols to the right of each command in the Go menu represent **keyboard shortcuts** for those commands. For example, Command-H is the keyboard shortcut for **Go Home**; pressing this keyboard combination will transport you to the Home stack from almost anywhere in HyperCard.

> If you find yourself selecting the same menu command over and over, you'll save time and energy if you memorize and use the keyboard shortcut.

Let's browse through the Home stack using keyboard shortcuts.

☐ **Press Command-3 (Next) repeatedly to flip sequentially through all the cards in the Home stack.**

When you reach the last card in the stack, Next takes you back around to the first card.

☐ **Press Command-2 (Prev) repeatedly until you return to the first card.**

This has just the opposite effect; it goes backward through the stack, one card at a time, wrapping around to the back when it reaches the first card.

☐ **Press Command-4 (Last).**

This takes you to the last card in the stack.

☐ **Press Command-1 (First).**

An especially useful navigation key is the **Tilde** (~). (If you have an **Esc** key, it's functionally equivalent.) This key, with or without the Command key, takes you back one step in your HyperCard journey each time you press it.

☐ **Press the Tilde (~) or Esc key to go back one card. Press it several times, observing where it takes you.**

> Pressing the **Go Back** key (~ or Esc) retraces your steps through the cards, reversing the order in which you viewed them. This is *not* the same as going backward through the stack.
>
> *Note*: When you're working with HyperCard's paint tools, this key becomes an "undo" key when used by itself. When used with the Command key, it *always* means go back.

If you have to retrace more than a few steps, there's an easier way.

☐ **Select Recent from the Go menu (or press Command-R).**

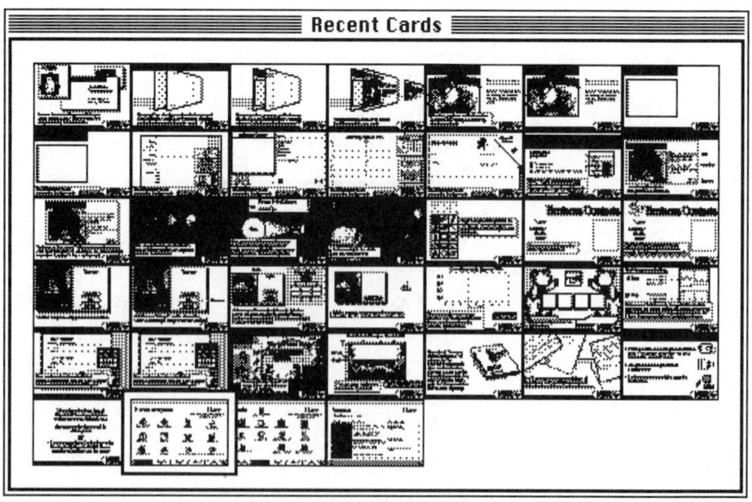

You're looking at tiny pictures of HyperCard screens that you've seen. It's as if you took one snapshot each time you visited a card for the first time. Those snapshots are arranged here in the order you took them. The number of screens you see depends on how many cards you've visited this session.

> Recent (Command-R) displays the last 42 cards of the session in the order they were visited, not necessarily in the order they appear in the stack(s). (If you visited a card more than once, it still appears only once here.) Clicking on a card's image transports you to that card.

☐ **Click on any of the small cards to go to that card; from that card, go Home.**

You can also use the arrow keys on your keyboard to navigate. The left- and right-arrow keys work the same as left- and right-arrow buttons on the screen; the down-arrow is another Go Back key (like ~), and the up-arrow retraces your steps forward through cards you've gone back through with the down-arrow.

☐ **Try navigating through this stack using the arrow keys. End your explorations on the first card.**

Using the Navigator Palette

If you don't think you'll be able to memorize all of these commands and keyboard shortcuts, here's a way you can have instant access to almost all the navigation tools you've seen so far. The catch is that you have to actually *type* a command to make it happen. Here's how.

☐ **Select Message from the Go menu (or press Command-M) to open the message box.**

The long window at the bottom of the screen, called the message box, allows you to send messages to HyperCard.

☐ **Type "nav".**

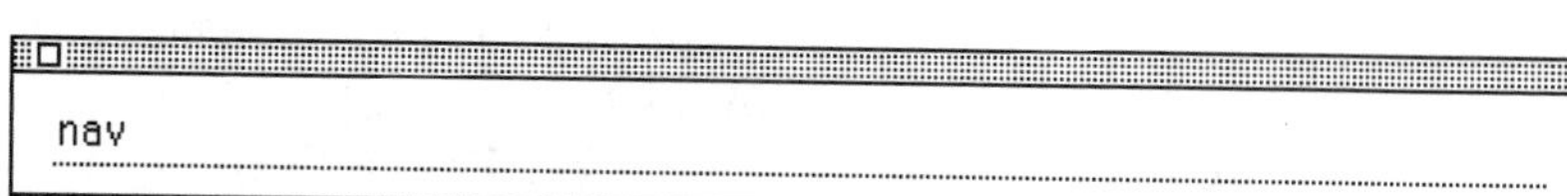

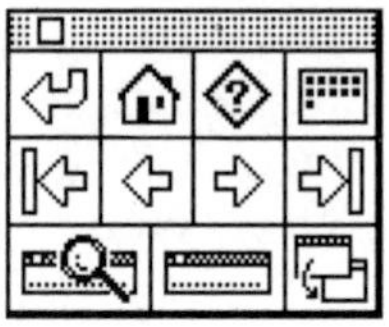

When you press Return, you should see this tiny window floating above the stack. (If you don't, your Home stack has probably been modified so that it no longer recognizes the shorthand command. Try typing "palette navigator" followed by Return.)

The Navigator Palette

The **navigator palette** appears when you type "nav" or "palette navigator" in the message box. It provides one-touch access to HyperCard's most important controls in the same way a VCR's remote control device provides VCR controls. Here's a summary of the palette control buttons and their menu bar command equivalents:

Button	Function	Go Menu Command
	Go to the Home stack.	Home
	Go to the Help stack (if available).	Help
	Go to the first card in the stack.	First
	Go to the last card in the stack.	Last
	Go to the card before the current card.	Prev
	Go to the card after the current card.	Next
	Go back to the last card visited, wherever it is.	Back
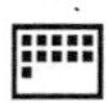	Show 42 most recently visited cards.	Recent
	Go to the next HyperCard window if others are open.	Next Window
	Show/Hide the message box.	Message
	Show/Hide the message box with the Find command (see Session 2).	Find...

Note: The navigator palette is an *external* tool—that is, it's not one of the standard tools built into HyperCard; it's an add-on accessory that's provided with the software. The distinction, important to programmers, is generally of little consequence from the user's point of view. In Session 7 you'll learn more about HyperCard externals.

☐ **Try navigating through the Home stack with the navigator palette controls. When you're finished, click in the close box (the small square at the top) to put it away.**

Using the Scroll Window

If you're working on a nine-inch compact Mac screen, you may not be aware that the Home stack is actually a window on your screen. The title bar is hidden behind your menu bar and the window has no scroll bars or size box. Nonetheless, it's a window that can be resized and moved so that you can view other windows. Changing a HyperCard window's size is different than resizing a standard Macintosh window; it requires a special **scroll window**.

☐ **Select Scroll from the Go menu (or press Command-E) to open the scroll window.**

This window represents the shape of the currently visible stack.

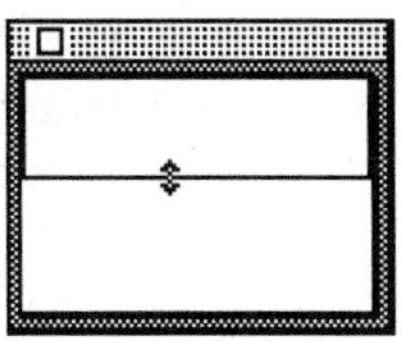

☐ **Move the pointer to the bottom edge of the white box in the scroll window.**

It turns into a double-headed arrow, indicating that it can be moved up or down. Since you're at the bottom of the box, the only way to go is up.

☐ **Drag up to about the center of the scroll window.**

You'll see a horizontal line rising in the box like the bottom of a window shade. At the same time, a horizontal line rises in the Home stack window. When you release the mouse button, the part of the Home card below the line vanishes. The bottom half of the card is still there; you just have to scroll to see it.

☐ **Move the pointer over the top half of the white box (the part above the line).**

It turns into a hand, waiting to push the picture around.

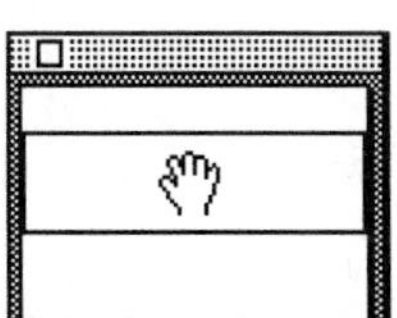

☐ **Drag the hand pointer down, then up, watching the Home card as you do.**

You're controlling which part of the Home card is visible. You can reduce the horizontal size of the window by dragging the left or right edge of the box. By dragging a corner you can change both dimensions of the window at once.

☐ **Reduce the vertical and horizontal size of the Home window and try scrolling in all directions.**

The scroll window makes it possible to work with a stack whose cards are bigger than your screen. It also makes it easy to view partial contents of several stacks at one time, memory permitting. Changing the size of a stack's window with the scroll window does not change the size of the cards in the stack. It's possible to resize the cards using the Stack Info dialog box, which will be discussed later, but all cards in a given stack must be the same size.

☐ **Return the Home window to full size.**

You may do this by double-clicking in the scroll window, or you may use the zoom box on the right side of the Home window's title bar. If you can't see the title bar, that's because it's hidden behind the menu bar. Here's how to look behind the menu bar.

Hiding and Showing the Menu Bar

☐ **Press the Command key and the Space bar at the same time.**

Notice how the menu bar disappeared. (If it didn't disappear, the most likely culprit is a popular system utility called SCSI Probe. This utility uses **Command-Space** as a default key combination for one of its commands. You can easily resolve this conflict by opening the SCSI Probe Control Panel, found in Control Panels in the Apple menu, clicking Options, and typing in a new Mount Key combination.)

☐ **Press Command-Space again.**

The menu bar is back. When you're learning HyperCard, it's best to keep that bar visible. But because many stacks hide the menu bar without your permission, it's important to know how to get it back when you need it.

Finding Hidden Buttons

As you've seen, not every button has an icon. How can you know where buttons are hiding on a card? There's one almost sure-fire technique for exposing hidden buttons.

☐ **Hold down the Command and Option keys at the same time (Command-Option).**

Every button on the card is outlined as long as you hold those two keys down. (The only exceptions are buttons that have been specially programmed to remain hidden.) This is an important trick to remember when you're working with stacks that don't use icons for buttons.

Asking for Help

If you're wondering how you're going to remember all of this information, you'll be interested in learning about HyperCard's on-line help facility. By pressing **Command-?** or selecting **Help** from the Go menu, you can transport yourself to HyperCard's detailed **Help stack.**

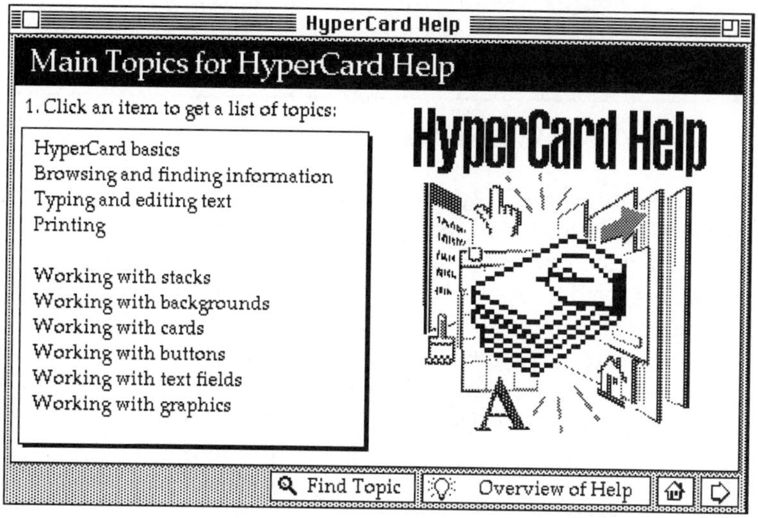

Besides providing its own menu and the interactive table of contents shown above, the three-stack HyperCard Help set includes options for navigating in a variety of ways, as outlined on this card. The Help stack is an excellent example of the kind of nonlinear reference document sometimes called hypertext or hypermedia. Take some time to explore it.

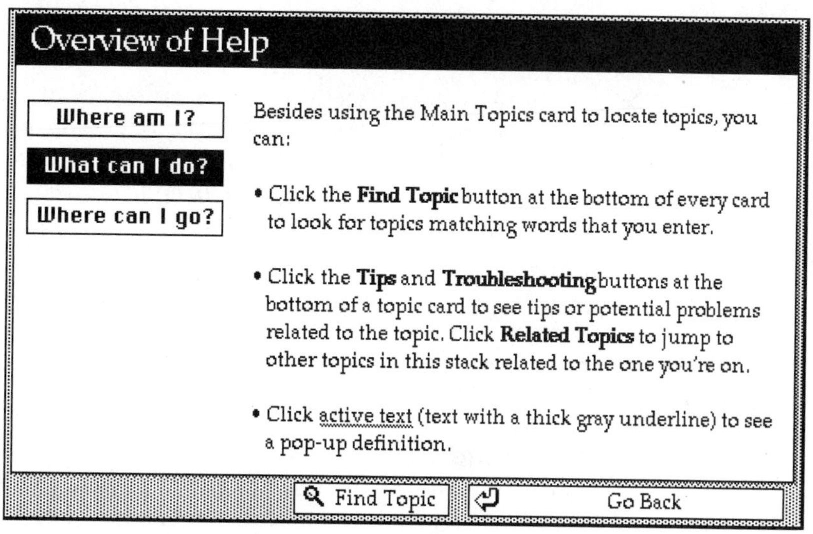

When you're using the Help stack, or any other stack, remember that Command-H will take you back Home.

Ending a HyperCard Session

☐ **Press Command-Q (or Select Quit HyperCard from the File menu) to return to the desktop.**

There are many other keyboard commands in HyperCard. Here's a summary of the HyperCard keyboard commands you've seen so far, plus a couple of new ones in boldface type:

Keyboard Commands (and Their Menu Equivalents) for Browsers

Go to the last card visited.	(Command-)~ or down-arrow	Go: Back
Go forward through retraced cards.	up-arrow	
Go to the previous card in the stack.	Command-2 or left-arrow	Go: Prev
Go to the next card in the stack.	Command-3 or right-arrow	Go: Next
Go to the first card in the stack.	Command-1 or up-arrow	Go: First
Go to the last card in the stack.	Command-4 or down-arrow	Go: Last
Go to the next open HyperCard window.	**Command-L**	Go: **Next Window**
Go to the Help stack (if available).	Command-?	Go: Help
Go to the Home stack.	Command-H	Go: Home
Open the scroll window.	Command-E	Go: Scroll
Show most recent 42 cards visited.	Command-R	Go: Recent
Open a new stack.	Command-O	File: Open Stack...
Open a new stack in a new window.	**Command-Shift-O**	
Show (peek at) outlines of most buttons.	Command-Option	
Show or hide the menu bar.	Command-Space	
Cancel current action.	**Command-Period**	
Quit HyperCard, and return to the Finder.	Command-Q	Quit HyperCard

As you can see, there are many ways to accomplish the same task in HyperCard. It's not necessary to memorize all the different commands, shortcuts, and tricks to make the most of HyperCard as a tool. Use the ones that work best for you, adding new tricks to your repertoire as you need them.

Summary

After just one session, you're on your way to HyperCard literacy. You've learned how to launch HyperCard and navigate through stacks using on-screen buttons, menu commands, and keyboard shortcuts.

Session 2 will show you how HyperCard stacks can be used to keep track of text and numerical information. You'll learn how to store, organize, and retrieve that information efficiently. Then the real fun begins: In Session 3, you'll learn how to build your own HyperCard stacks.

Key Words

? button
asterisk
button
cartoon balloon
Command-? (help)
Command-Option (show buttons)
Command-Period (cancel current action)
Command-Shift-O (open new stack in new window)
Command-Space (show/hide menu bar)
Esc
First command (Command-1, Go menu)
Go Back (~ or Command-~)
Go Home (Command-H)
Go menu
Help command (Command-?, Go menu)
Help stack
hidden button
Home button
Home card
Home stack
HyperCard Player
HyperCard Tour
keyboard shortcuts
Last command (Command-4, Go menu)
left-arrow button
light bulb
message box
Message command (Command-M, Go menu)
navigator palette
Next command (Command-3, Go menu)
Next Window command (Command-L, Go menu)
on-line help
Open Stack command (Command-O)
Prev command (Command-2, Go menu)
Quit HyperCard command (Command-Q)
Recent command (Command-R, Go menu)
return-arrow button
right-arrow button
Scroll command (Command-E, Go menu)
scroll window
Tilde

Exercises

1. What is the difference between the Back command and the Prev command? Under what circumstances will they produce different results?
2. What is the difference between the Next command and the right-arrow button? Under what circumstances will they produce different results?

3. List several different things that can happen when you click a button in HyperCard.
4. What happens when you double-click a button in HyperCard?
5. List three ways to go to the next card in a stack.
6. What is the usual meaning for each of these icons in HyperCard?

   a. 

   b. 

   c. 

   d. 

   e. 

   f. 

   g. 

7. What is the keyboard shortcut for each of the following commands?
   a. Quit HyperCard
   b. Go to the first card in the stack
   c. Go Home
   d. Go Back
8. Consider this picture:

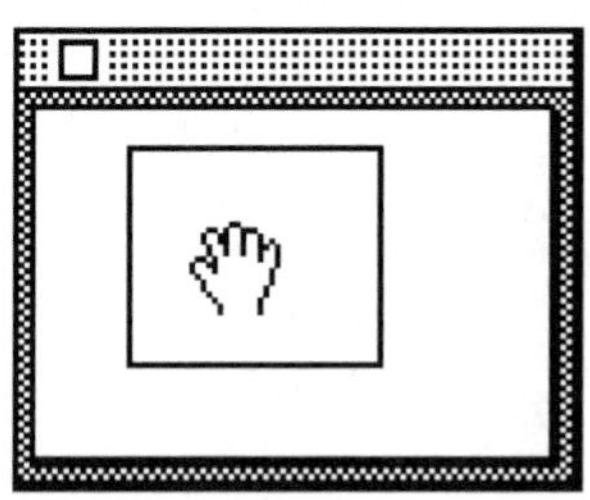

   a. Describe what's happening.
   b. What is this window called?
   c. How can you make it appear?

9. Consider this picture of the navigator palette:

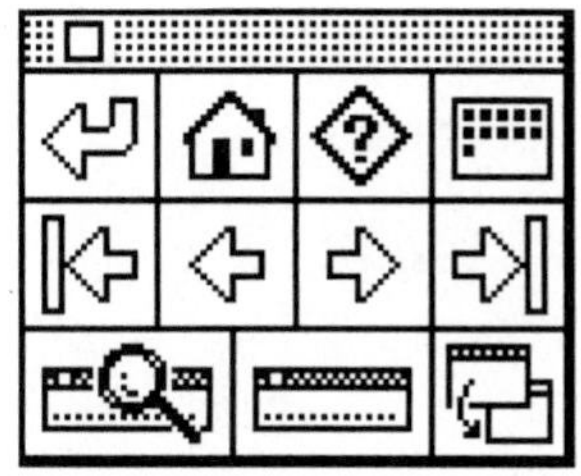

a. How can you make the navigator palette appear?

b. Describe the functions of each of the buttons on the navigator palette.

Session 2

By the end of this session you should be able to

- Use HyperCard to manage your personal information
- Enter text and numeric information into HyperCard fields
- Edit text in a field
- Use the Clipboard to copy and move text from one field to another
- Add a card to a stack
- Delete a card from a stack
- Sort cards into alphabetical order
- Use the Find command to locate a card with a specific piece of information
- Customize a stack by rearranging fields

The Dynamic File Cabinet

Information Storage and Retrieval

The Problem

Your work space is a mess. You haven't paid your bills for two months because you can't find them on your desk. You need to call your brother, but you lost his new phone number. You have an appointment with the head of your department sometime next week, but you can't remember where you wrote down the time. You're within two days of the final deadline for an important project, and your notes are scattered everywhere. If only you could organize all these bits of information in your life. Perhaps HyperCard can help.

Introduction

In Session 1 you explored HyperCard as a window shopper, browsing but never touching or changing anything. Now it's time to learn how to personalize HyperCard stacks by adding new information, changing old information, and rearranging existing information.

Many of the tasks we'll be asking HyperCard to do in this session would normally be done in the business world by a **database** program—a program designed for the organized storage and retrieval of information. In a typical database, a **data file** (like the library's card catalog) is made up of many identically structured **records** (the cards in that catalog), each of which is divided into **fields** of information (author's name, book title, and so on).

At first glance, HyperCard has a similar structure: Stacks are made up of cards, each of which can have fields. In fact, this similarity is no accident; HyperCard performs many common database functions with ease. But as you'll see, HyperCard's buttons allow it to be used in ways that you wouldn't think of using a conventional database.

Home Base

For this session you'll need another stack besides HyperCard and Home: the Addresses stack that comes with HyperCard. In the process of working through this session, you'll make changes to this stack and to the Home stack. Because HyperCard saves changes automatically as you work, the changes you make can be difficult to undo. But if you work with *copies* in this session, the original will remain unchanged. This is especially important if you're working with a computer that's used by others.

Whether you're working with your own computer or a shared computer, this session assumes you want to work with a copy of the Home and Addresses stacks so that the originals can be left unchanged. Depending on your situation, you may want to store your temporary working stacks on a floppy disk or in a separate folder on your hard disk. These instructions will show you how to do either.

Creating Working Copies

☐ **If you want to work with a floppy disk: Locate the Home stack and the Addresses stack on your hard disk. To copy these files onto a floppy disk, drag their icons onto the icon of an empty or blank floppy disk.**

☐ **If you want to work from the hard disk: Type Command-N or select New Folder from the File menu. Type "Session 2 files" to name the folder. Select the icons for the Home stack and the Addresses stack. Hold down the Option key while you drag these icons onto the new folder icon. The files will be copied, rather than moved, into the folder.**

Whether you're working with floppy disk or hard disk copies, there's one more thing you need to do to make sure HyperCard doesn't find the originals and open them rather than your copies.

☐ **If the original Addresses stack is stored in the same folder as HyperCard, move it into another folder.**

Now you're ready to go Home.

Starting at Home

☐ **Double-click on the duplicate Home icon you just created.**

You're looking at the Home card—the top card in the HyperCard Home stack. As you learned last session, there are several other cards hidden behind this one.

Changing the User Level and Name

It's time to reset the user level so that you can do some typing.

☐ **Press Command-4 (or select Last from the Go menu) to go to the last card in the stack.**

In addition to having a space for your name, this card allows you to set the **user level**.

☐ **Click on the Typing button.**

Typing user level allows you to type new information into HyperCard stacks and change existing information while still maintaining your rights and privileges as a browser. It won't let you accidentally modify pictures or buttons. To test your new typing privileges, change the user name.

☐ **If there's no name entered in the "Your Name" blank, position the pointer over that blank and click. If there's already a name on the card, select it by dragging the mouse from the first character to the last character, and press the Delete key.**

You should see a flashing vertical line at the beginning of the blank line.

☐ **Type your name.**

Your Name: Mark Twain

If you make any typing errors, use the Delete (Backspace) key to erase the offending characters.

☐ **Click on the right-arrow button to return to the first card.**

Changing the Home Memory

If you'll be using the disk you created as a working disk, you need to take care of one more piece of business to make sure your Home stack doesn't outsmart you later.

> HyperCard uses the Home stack to keep track of where you store your other stacks. When you click on a button to open a stack, HyperCard looks for that stack in the folders where it has found other stacks in the past. If it can't find the stack in those places, HyperCard asks you to locate the stack. When you find the stack in a folder, HyperCard adds that folder to its list of stack storage places.

Here's the problem: The Home stack that you copied may remember where the *originals* of all your copied files are stored, so it will go to those originals, rather than your copies, when you click on their icons. You can prevent that by erasing that part of your Home stack's memory. Here's how.

☐ **Press Command-3 (or select Next from the Go menu) repeatedly until you reach a card with the title "Search Paths" and a black "Stacks" button.**

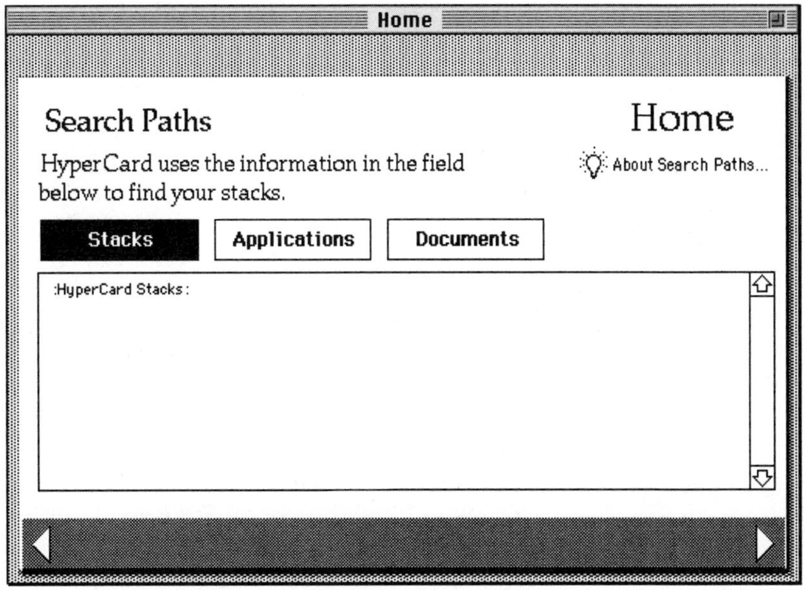

- ☐ **Click on the light bulb icon.**

  You'll see an explanation of search paths and their uses. Although it looks like a different card, this explanation is really a **pop-up field** that can be made visible—or invisible—at the click of a button.

- ☐ **When you've seen enough, click anywhere in the pop-up field to hide this explanation.**

  Your card's list of search paths may not look like the one shown here, but it serves the same function. The next step is to delete the list.

- ☐ **Drag the mouse from the beginning of the first item in the search path list to the end of the last item in the list.**

  All of the text you selected should be highlighted in black.

- ☐ **Press the Delete (Backspace) key.**

  Everything that was highlighted in black should be gone, so Hyper-Card won't automatically look in those folders for stacks. You're about to teach it where to look for the files instead.

- ☐ **Press Command-1 (or select First from the Go menu) to go to the first card in the stack: the Home card.**

Locating a Stack

Each icon on the Home card is a button that will take you to a stack when you click once on it.

☐ **Click on the Addresses icon on the Home card.**

If you see a "Where is Addresses?" dialog box, locate your working copy and open it. You won't need to repeat this every time you open a stack because your Home stack will remember where it found this stack. When the Addresses stack opens, your Home stack will probably close, but that isn't always the case.

> HyperCard 2 does not always close the window for one stack when you open another stack. If you are working on a machine with limited memory, it's a good idea to close windows of stacks you aren't using.

Browsing through the Addresses Stack

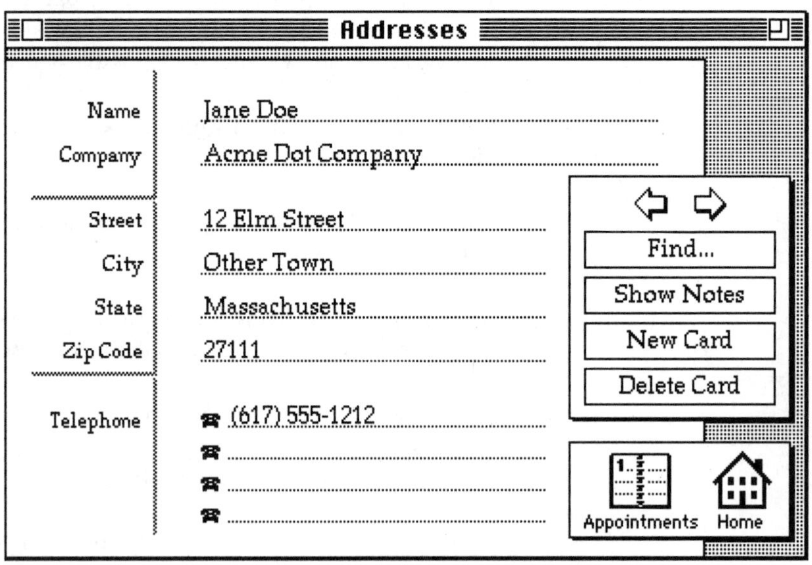

There are several navigation buttons on this card, including the familiar Home button. Of course, it's also possible to navigate with keyboard commands or the Go menu. But this stack has additional navigation commands hidden under the Utilities menu.

☐ **Select Stack Overview from the Utilities menu.**

> Although many stacks use standard HyperCard menus (or no menus at all), some stacks change the menu bar by adding their own specialized menus.

You're transported to a card that provides instructions and help for using the stack. In spite of its different look, the Stack Overview card is still part of the Addresses stack.

> When you're working with HyperCard, the name and boundaries of the current stack aren't always apparent. Going to a card with a different background doesn't necessarily mean that you've gone to a new stack.

☐ **Scroll through the text in the Stack Overview card, skimming it to get an idea of what's there.**

☐ **Click on the button that says "Return to Addresses."**

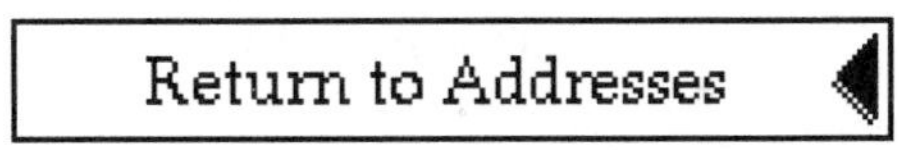

HyperCard's Text Fields

Now let's try modifying the stack by adding some text.

Entering Text into a Field

Each address card has ten editable fields: one each for name, company, street, city, state, and ZIP code, and four for phone numbers. Entering information in these fields involves the same kind of text-editing techniques you use in Macintosh word processors and databases.

☐ **Move the pointer over the last phone field at the bottom of the card.**

Notice how the pointer turns from a hand into an **I-beam** as you move it over a lined field.

☐ **Position the I-beam at the beginning of the phone field and click once.**

As you move the I-beam away, you leave behind a flashing **insertion bar** (sometimes called a **cursor**, for CURrent poSition indicatOR). That's the spot where you will type.

☐ **Type your phone number. When you're done, click outside the field somewhere.**

> Don't confuse the I-beam with the insertion bar. The I-beam is for positioning the insertion bar. But until you click, the insertion bar remains where you left it.

Editing Text

There's another field for longer notes on this card.

☐ **Click on the Show Notes button.**

A pop-up field appears. It's a **scrolling field**, equipped with standard Macintosh scroll bars. If you click in this field, the flashing insertion bar appears, waiting to leave a trail of text when you type.

☐ **Try typing a sentence or two in the Notes field. Edit your note using standard Macintosh text editing tools and techniques. When you have finished, click on the Hide Notes button to see the card in its normal form.**

> **Text Editing Reminders**
>
> You can insert text, delete text, or replace text in any field using standard Macintosh text editing techniques.
>
> As in most word processors, HyperCard fields automatically wrap text around to the next line. The only time you need to press Return is when you want to force something to go to the next line before the current line is full.
>
> To change or delete text, you'll need to **select** it first, using one of these five methods:
>
> - Drag the pointer from the beginning to the end (or from the end to the beginning) of the text to be selected. If the text crosses several lines, move directly down to the end of the selection without crossing all the characters on each line.

- Double-click on a word to select only that word.
- **Double-click-drag** the pointer to some other word; both (whole) words will be selected, as well as everything between them.
- Click on one end of the area to be selected and Shift-click on the other end; this has the same effect as dragging between those two points. As you'll see later, this method is especially handy when part of the text to be selected is scrolled off the screen.
- Type Command-A to select all the text in the field.

The all-important **Undo** command (**Command-**Z) will *usually* restore your work as it was before you executed your last command or did your last round of typing. Undo can take you back only one step, so it won't help if you've done anything since your last error. And it's not always clear what "back only one step" means. For example, HyperCard doesn't always recognize that you've completed a step when you're typing information in a field until you start working outside of that field.

If you've ever lost work when something went wrong in the middle of a computing session, you're probably in the habit of saving your work often with the Save command. You may already have noticed that HyperCard doesn't have a Save command.

HyperCard regularly saves changes to a stack *automatically*, but it doesn't automatically save backups. If you're about to do something that you think might cause irreparable damage, or if you want to make a backup of the current stack on another disk, you can use the **Save a Copy...** command.

Basic Database Operations with HyperCard

If you have no interest in using HyperCard as a database, skim this section without performing all the operations. Don't skip the section on adding and deleting cards, though, if you plan to do any of the later operations.

Adding and Deleting Cards

For an address book to be useful, it must allow you to add and remove pages. There's a **New Card button** on this card, but let's use the standard HyperCard command for doing the same thing.

☐ **Select New Card from the Edit menu (or press Command-N).**

> **New Card (Command-N)** creates a copy of the current card and locates it immediately after that card. If the current card contains text in fields, the text is *not* copied onto the new card.

☐ **Position the insertion point at the beginning of the name field and type "Roger Rabbit".**

> In name-and-address stacks, it's important that the names be entered in the same order (for example, Firstname Lastname) on every card if you want to be able to alphabetize them later.

☐ **Press Tab twice to skip past the company field. Type "123 Toon Terrace" in the street field, press Tab, type "Toontown", press Tab, type "California", press Tab twice, and type "987/555-4321".**

> The **Tab key** generally advances the insertion bar automatically to the next editable field in the card. If the field contains text, the text is highlighted, so anything you type will replace it. Tabbing from the last field takes you to the first field. **Shift-Tab** moves you *backward* through the fields of a card.

You'll need to create several more cards before you can use this stack as a database.

☐ **Add cards to the Addresses stack for each of the following names. For our purposes, it's necessary to fill in only the name and city/state fields. Use the New Card button on the card, the New Card command, or the keyboard shortcut (Command-N) to create new cards. Remember to use the Tab key to move between fields.**

NAME	CITY	STATE
Donald Duck	Eugene	Oregon
Daisy Duck	Columbia	Missouri
Huey Duck	Tampa	Florida
Dewey Duck	Berkeley	California

Louie Duck	**St. Paul**	**Minnesota**
Scrooge McDuck	**New York**	**New York**
Benny Beaver	**Corvallis**	**Oregon**
Mickey Mouse	**Bend**	**Oregon**
Minnie Mouse	**Ashland**	**Oregon**
Porky Pig	**Washington**	**D.C.**
Daffy Duck	**Boston**	**Massachusetts**
Homer Simpson	**Springfield**	**USA**

The last one really doesn't belong, so let's delete it.

☐ **Press Command-Delete (Command-Backspace).**

This is the keyboard shortcut for the **Delete Card** command in the Edit menu. There's also a Delete Card button on this card.

If you need to move a card to another location rather than just delete it, you'll want to use the Macintosh **Clipboard.**

Using the Clipboard in HyperCard

If you're a seasoned Macintosh user, you're familiar with the Clipboard—the part of memory that can be used to temporarily store a chunk of information so it can be easily moved, duplicated, or reused. As you might expect, HyperCard has versions of the basic Clipboard commands:

- **Copy (Command-C)** copies the selected text, picture, or object to the Clipboard, leaving the original unchanged (but replacing anything else that was already in the Clipboard).
- **Cut (Command-X)** places the selected text, picture, or object in the Clipboard, deleting the original *and* anything already in the Clipboard.
- **Paste (Command-V)** places a copy of the contents of the Clipboard in the current position. Paste does *not* empty the Clipboard.

In HyperCard, the Clipboard commands in the Edit menu change, depending on what's selected. For example, if text is selected, the Copy command is Copy Text. HyperCard also has two other commands—**Copy Card** and **Cut Card**—that place a card in the Clipboard. (As usual, Cut removes the original whereas Copy leaves the original in place.) When there is a card in the

Clipboard, the Paste command in the Edit menu becomes Paste Card. Selecting Paste Card places the contents of the Clipboard after the current card in the stack.

(You can't try Copy Card or Cut Card at this point because your user level is set to typing. HyperCard doesn't allow you to use the Clipboard for cards unless the user level is set to authoring or scripting.)

Sorting a Stack

Using Cut Card and Paste Card might be a good way to rearrange the cards in alphabetical order. It might be, but it isn't, because there's a much more convenient way: The **Sort commands** in the Utilities menu allow you to arrange the cards in order using any of five different fields as a key.

☐ **Select Sort Preferences from the Utilities menu.**

☐ **Click on the buttons labeled "First name first," "Sort by last name," and "Return to Addresses."**

These preferences apply to all future sorts until you change them.

☐ **Select Sort by Name from the Utilities menu.**

Almost instantly, the stack of names is rearranged in order by last name. Flip through them to check, if you like.

☐ **Select Sort by State.**

☐ **Flip through the cards to check the order.**

The cards should be grouped by state. Within each state, they should be in alphabetical order by name.

Sorting Hierarchy

For multiple-level sorts, perform the sorts in reverse order of importance: The last sort performed takes precedence over the others.

Now that the cards are in order, it should be easy to find any card in the stack by flipping through the cards. But there's a better way.

Using the Find Command

☐ **Click the Find button.**

A dialog box appears:

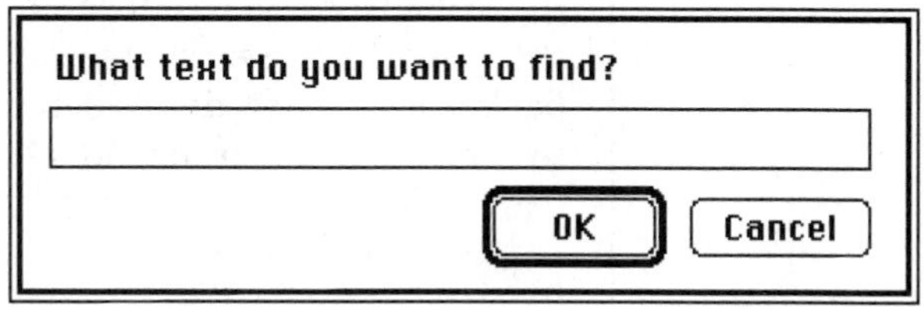

☐ **Type "Benny Beaver" and press Return.**

Faster than you could type it, HyperCard will find the first card in the stack with that name. If it finds a card for somebody else with the same name, just press Return again to restart the search.

This dialog box is not unique to the Addresses stack; you'll see it if you use the Find button in other stacks too. But there's another tool for finding text that works in almost any HyperCard stack.

☐ **Select Find from the Go menu (or type Command-F).**

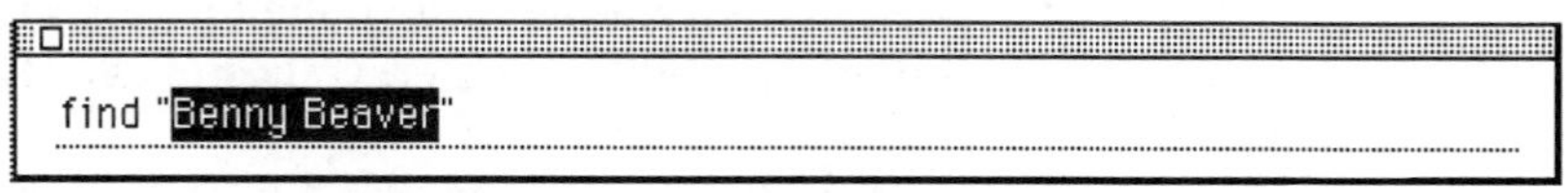

The message box appears with an already typed message: the **Find command**. Later you'll learn how to type other messages to HyperCard in this box, but for now all you need to do is fill in the space between the quotation marks.

☐ **Type something. Whatever you type will replace "Benny Beaver".**

☐ **Type "Minn" and press Return.**

You don't need to type a complete word into the Find command; you just need to type enough characters so that the term you're searching for can be identified uniquely. In this case "Minn" wasn't quite enough to uniquely identify *Minnie;* it's also part of *Minnesota.*

☐ **Press Return again.**

Find Tips

When you use the Find command (Command-F), each time you press Return you're taken to the next word in a searchable field that begins with the characters you have typed. If you type more than one word, you're taken to the next card that contains both those words in searchable fields. (Some text fields, cards, and backgrounds are defined in such a way that they can't be searched. Paint text, introduced in the next session, also can't be searched.)

Two cautionary notes:

- You get what you asked for, even if it's not what you wanted.
- Conversely, you don't get what you don't ask for, so make sure you ask for exactly what you want. (The one exception: Case is irrelevant, so you might find "BASIC" if you look for "basic".)

Examples: If you type "cath", you might find "Cathy" or "cathedral" or "cathode" but not "Kathy".

The moral: Choose your search patterns carefully!

Using the Phone Dialer

Once you locate the card you're looking for, what can you do with it? If there's a phone number, you can have HyperCard dial the number.

☐ **Type a phone number into the first phone field.**

☐ **Click on the phone icon next to that phone number.**

You should hear a series of beeps. If you happen to have your phone properly connected to the computer's sound jack, or if you hold the phone's handset close to the computer's speaker, those beeps will dial the selected number for you. The dialing is done by the Phone Dialer stack. You can customize the dialer with that stack.

Marking Cards

The more names you add to your database, the more useful it can be as a quick reference tool. You can add the names and addresses of frequently called businesses, community organizations, long-distance correspondents, government agencies, and so on. But a large, diverse database presents new challenges for organizing information so that it can be easily retrieved. HyperCard allows you to **mark cards** in large databases so they can be quickly accessed or grouped for printing.

☐ **Click on the upper right corner of the white part of one of the address cards.**

There's a hidden button there that marks the card, at the same time changing its appearance so that it looks as if the corner of the card is folded over.

☐ **Click once again on the folded-over corner.**

The card is no longer marked. For larger databases it's much more efficient to mark and unmark cards in groups.

☐ **Select Mark Cards from the Utilities menu.**

You'll see the following dialog box.

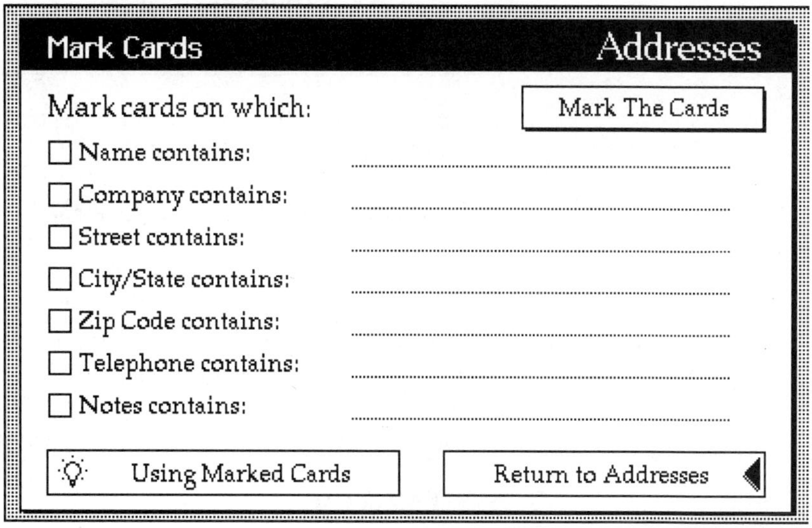

☐ **Click on the "Name contains:" check box.**

☐ **Type "duck".**

☐ **Click on the Mark The Cards button.**

You'll be asked whether you want to unmark all currently marked cards before proceeding.

☐ **Click Yes.**

Another dialog box asks if you want to go to the first marked card.

☐ **Click Yes.**

☐ **Flip through the cards, watching the upper right corner of each card.**

Those cards that contain ducks have turned-down corners, indicating that they've been marked. (Notice that McDuck is marked, too. If we didn't want this one included, we should have typed a space before "duck" when we indicated the cards to be marked.)

☐ **Hold down the Shift key and click the right-arrow button. Try it several times.**

> The **Shift key** generally acts as a constraint key in HyperCard and other Macintosh applications. When used with a tool or command, it constrains that tool or command so it has a more specific meaning.

In this case, the Shift key is telling HyperCard to go not to the next card but to the next *marked* card.

☐ **Hold down the Shift key and click the left-arrow button.**

As you've probably guessed, this takes you *backward* through the stack to the previous marked card.

Suppose you want to mark every card satisfying one of two criteria. To be marked, a card should have (1) "duck" in the name field *or* (2) "Oregon" in the state field. We already have all the duck names marked, so we just need to add the Oregon cards to the list.

☐ **Select Mark Cards.**

☐ **Click on the "State contains:" check box and type "Oregon".**

☐ **Click on the "Name contains:" check box to unselect it (remove the X).**

☐ **Click on the Mark The Cards button.**

☐ **When you're asked whether you want to unmark already marked cards, click No.**

Remember, we want to retain the marks on the duck cards.

☐ **Flip through the marked cards to see if they're marked correctly.**

Now suppose you decide that what you really want is to select only ducks from Oregon; that is, cards that contain (1) "duck" in the name field *and* (2) "Oregon" in the city/state field.

- ☐ **Select Mark Cards.**

- ☐ **Click on the check box for "Name contains:" to put the X back in it.**

There should already be an X in the "City/State contains:" check box. We're narrowing the selection criteria by adding a second check.

- ☐ **Click on Mark The Cards.**

- ☐ **When you're asked whether you want to unmark already marked cards, click Yes.**

- ☐ **Click OK to go to the first marked card.**

- ☐ **Check the results.**

You've just extracted three different subsets of cards from the set of cards that form the Addresses stack. In the process, you've put to work the basics of **Boolean algebra**. Here's a summary of those basic principles.

Boolean Algebra and Marked Addresses

When you select multiple criteria for marking cards in the Addresses stack, you're applying the principles of Boolean algebra. Here are the specific selection rules:

- To select the **intersection** of two subsets (the set of cards that belongs to both group A and group B—for example, cards with "Texas" in the State field *and* "Beaver" in the Name field), mark both criteria in the same pass.
- To select the **union** of two subsets (the set of cards that includes cards that belong to Group A, Group B, or both groups—for example, cards with either "New York" or "New Jersey" in the state field), mark one set first, then mark the second without unmarking the first.

Note: Not all HyperCard stacks have automated card-marking capability. If you don't know HyperTalk, you may need to mark individual cards in other stacks by clicking Card Marked in the Card Info dialog box or by typing "Mark Card" in the message box.

The tools for selecting marked cards in the Addresses stack, while useful, are fairly primitive when compared with the selection tools in more powerful database programs. For instance, most database programs allow you to use relational operators for selecting cards. (Example: Select all records with income less than $10,000.) If you need this kind of capability in a HyperCard stack, you'll need to build it yourself using HyperTalk.

Printing Card Images

HyperCard is handy for recording and looking up addresses . . . as long as you're sitting in front of the computer. But if you use HyperCard to store names, phone numbers, and other essential information, you need to have a way of making a **hard copy** so you can take the information with you when your computer stays home.

> The **Print Card** command (Command-P) prints an image of the current card—nothing more, nothing less. The **Print Stack...** command allows you to print images of every card in the stack (or, if you prefer, every *marked* card in the stack).

☐ **Select Print Stack... from the File menu.**

The dialog box that appears allows you to customize your printout in a number of ways.

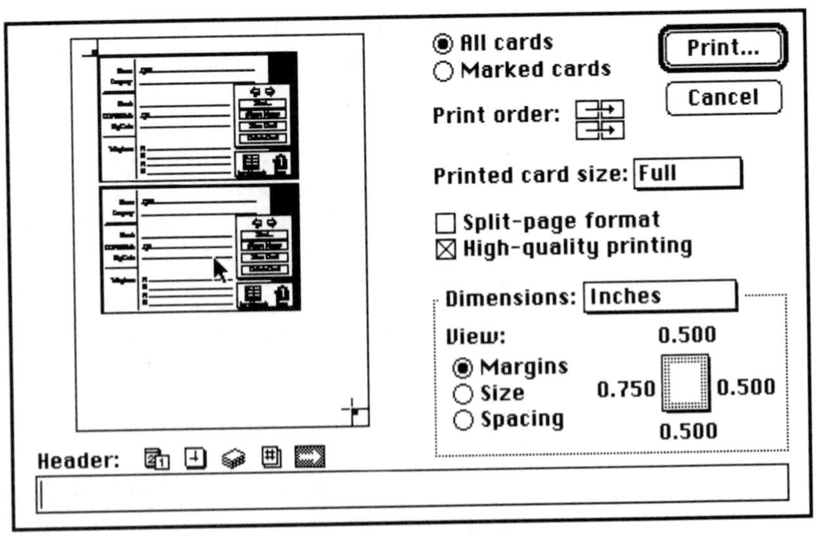

In the interest of saving paper, we'll print just the marked cards.

☐ **Click on the Marked cards button.**

We'll also save paper by reducing the size of the printed images so that more can be printed on each page.

☐ **Hold the mouse button down while pointing to the Printed card size (probably Full). A pop-up menu reveals several other card size choices; select Half.**

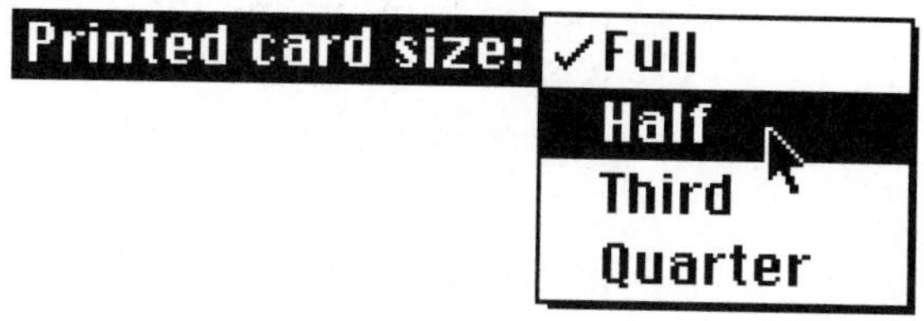

We don't need split page format (a format designed for printouts that will be folded in half) or high-quality (slow) printing.

☐ **If there is an X in either check box, click to remove it.**

You can control the size of the card images, the spaces between images, and the page margins by dragging on corners and handles in the picture on the left side of the dialog box. For more exact adjustments, you can monitor the numbers in the Dimensions box while you drag.

☐ **Drag the margin handle in the lower right corner of the page image to change the margins to .750 on all sides.**

☐ **Click on the Spacing button in the Dimensions box so you can view changes in the spacing between images.**

☐ **Drag the lower right card image so that its edges come close to the new margins.**

The bottom of the dialog box allows you to create a customized **header** that appears at the top of each page of the printout. The icons allow you to insert page number, date, and time into the header; the arrow allows you to tab to the center and again to the right of the header between items. You'll use some of the icons now to create a header that contains the date on the left, the page number in the center, and your name on the right.

☐ **Click on the calendar icon, the arrow (tab) icon, the page number (#) icon, and the arrow icon again. Type your last name.**

☐ **If you don't want to print the report, click Cancel. Otherwise click Print... and respond to the next dialog box by clicking OK.**

If nothing happens, your computer may not be properly connected to a working printer.

> Before printing anything, you might need to use the **Chooser** in the Apple menu and the **Page Setup** command in the File menu to select a printer and control the layout of the page.

Printing a Report

In many situations it's useful to print part of the information from your stack without reproducing complete card images.

> The **Print Report...** command can be used to print database-style **reports**, mailing labels, address book pages, or other custom printouts. This command allows you to control which fields will be printed, how they will be arranged, and what information will appear in the header at the top of each page.

☐ **Select Print Report... from the File menu.**

The Addresses stack allows you to create several different reports using prefabricated **report templates**—one for mailing labels, one for address book pages, and one for creating a name and address list. The **Reports menu** allows you to choose a report template.

☐ **Select Address Book from the Reports menu.**

The picture in the dialog box shows you the page layout for the report and allows you to adjust it if necessary.

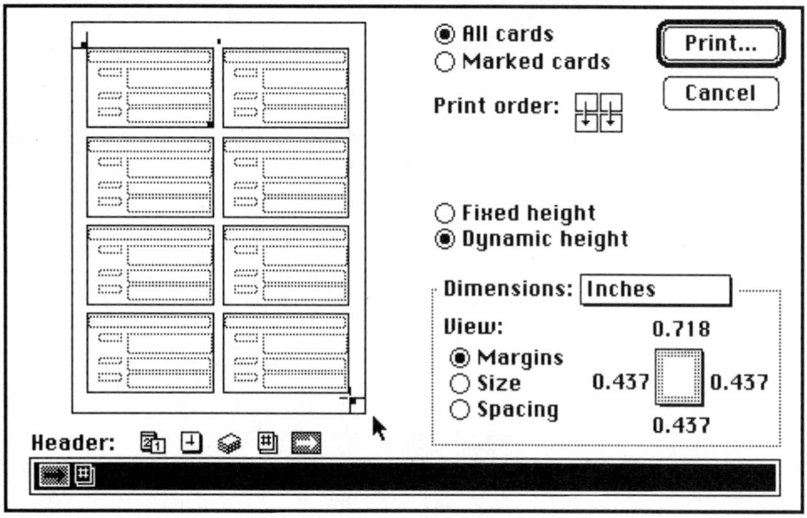

☐ **If you don't want to print the report, click Cancel. Otherwise click Print... and respond to the next dialog box by clicking OK.**

Creating a Report Template

If none of the existing templates meets your needs, you can easily create your own. Let's create a simple phone list.

☐ **Select Print Report... from the File menu.**

☐ **Select New Report from the Reports menu.**

☐ **Type "Phone List" to name the report.**

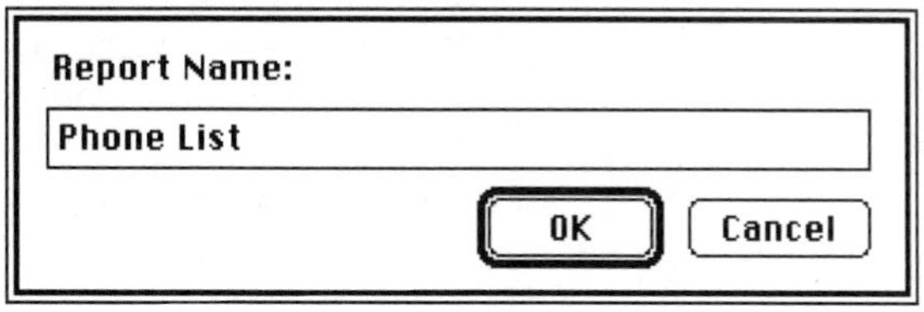

First you'll need to change the layout of the report so that the cells aren't shaped like mailing labels.

- [ ] **Point the handle on the lower right corner of the upper left cell and drag it up and to the right, as shown here:**

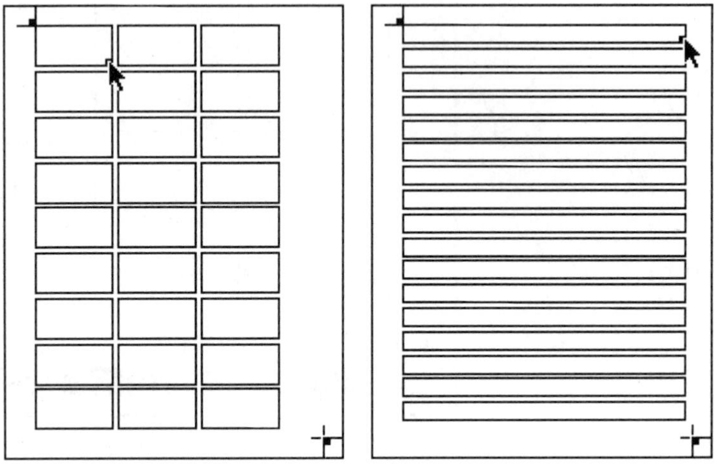

These cells don't contain anything yet; it's time to specify which fields will appear in each of them.

- [ ] **Double-click on one of the cells (or select Report Items... from the Edit menu, or press Command-E).**

The next dialog box shows a closeup of one cell.

- [ ] **Select New Item from the Items menu.**

- [ ] **Double-click on the dotted box that appears in the cell (or select Item Info... from the Items menu, or press Command-I).**

The dialog box allows you to specify what, exactly, will appear in each cell. You could type the item in the dialog box, but it's easier to just select the items you want from the scrolling list of available fields.

- [ ] **Scroll through the list of background fields; select Name and click OK.**

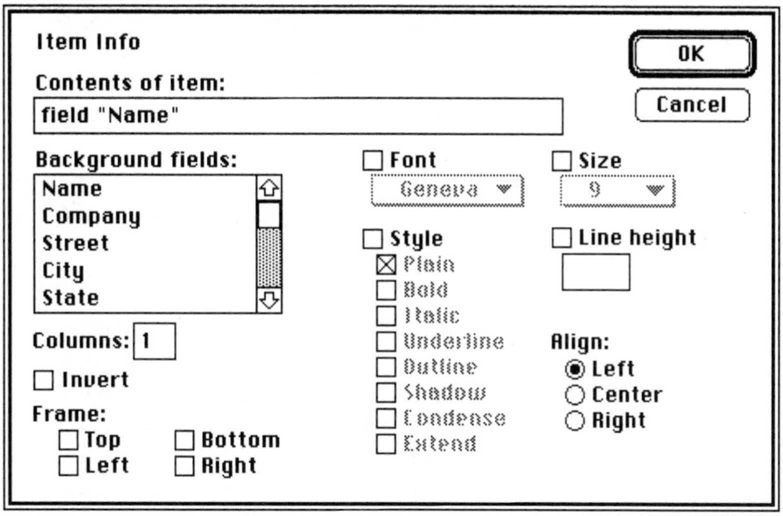

(This dialog box also allows you to control font, style, and other aspects of the printed field; you'll learn about these topics in later sessions.)

☐ **Drag the corner of the new report item so that it's big enough to show a long name.**

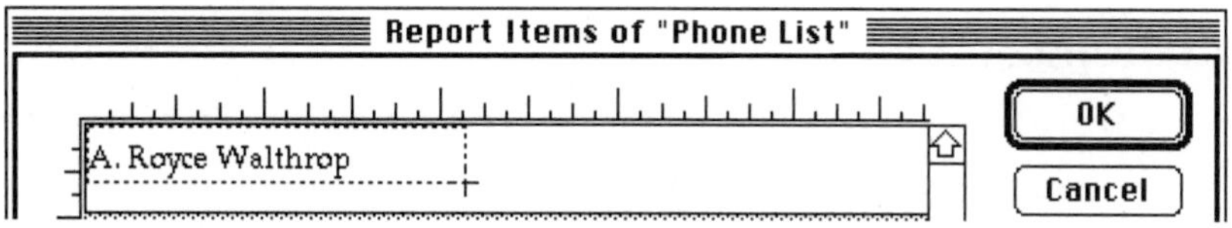

Now we need to add the phone number to the cell.

☐ **Select New Item again; choose Phone 1 from the scrolling list of fields, and click OK.**

The new field image should appear right on top of the old one.

☐ **Point to the center of the new report item and drag it to the right. Drag its corner to enlarge it so it can show a whole phone number.**

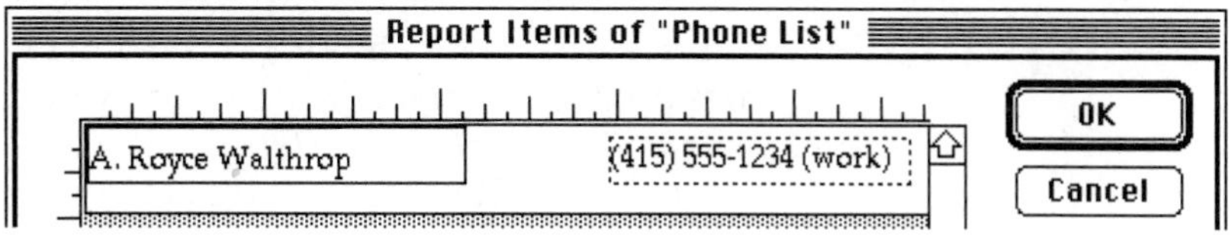

☐ **Click OK to return to the Print Report dialog box.**

☐ **Refine your layout if you aren't happy with it; then click Print... or Cancel.**

You'll be asked whether you want to save changes to the new report. If you decide to save, remember to choose your own disk in the Save dialog box.

> Report templates are saved with stacks, so it's not necessary to create templates each time you print a report. A stack can have up to 16 associated templates. Once you've created a report template for one stack, it's possible to copy the template and paste it into another stack.

Break Point

This is a good time to take a break if you need one.

Customizing Cards

> If you're content using HyperCard stacks just they way they come out of the box, you can stop here. But if you want to learn how to modify those stacks so they more closely meet your personal needs, this section is essential. The techniques you'll see here will be covered in more detail in future sessions, so don't worry if some of the concepts seem foreign now.

The Addresses stack is a good example of the kind of stacks that are available to make HyperCard a useful office tool. If we think of computer software as an extension of the human mind, then canned stacks such as these are designed to extend the *average* computer user's mind. But the concept of "average" often has little to do with reality; a person with one foot in ice and the other in fire is not, on the average, comfortable. Programs written for average people aren't written for real people. Fortunately, HyperCard makes it easy to customize existing stacks or create brand new stacks that can meet the exact needs of individual users.

Suppose, for example, you want to modify the Addresses stack by deleting two of the four phone buttons and replacing the corresponding phone number fields with a field for recording the person's birthday (or electronic mail address, or whatever). The procedure is straightforward if you understand the basics of HyperCard. These buttons and fields are stored in the **background** shared by all cards in the stack. When you add, delete, or change a field in the background, you're affecting every card in the stack. So to delete or modify the buttons and fields, it's necessary to go into the background layer.

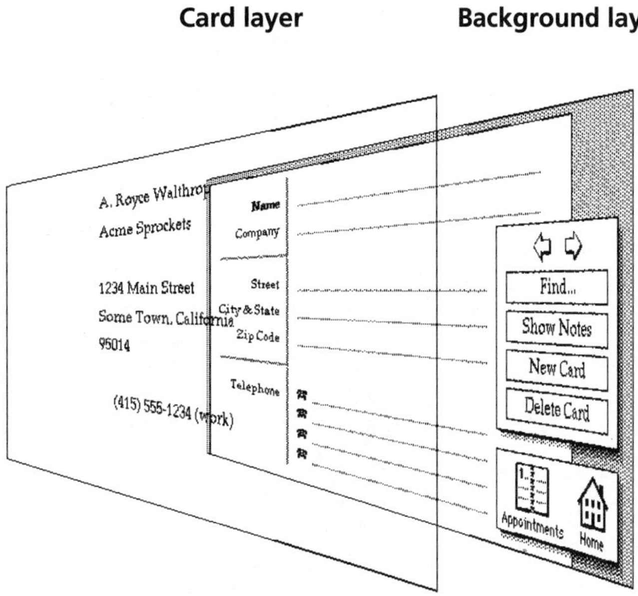

There are two kinds of fields in the background of the Addresses stack's cards: editable fields that contain different information on each card, and locked fields that share the same text on all cards. HyperCard's **Field tool** is used for working with both kinds of fields. We'll use the Field tool to delete one of the phone number fields and reposition another so it's appropriate for birthdays. Then we'll duplicate one of the locked labels, unlock the duplicate, type a new name in it, relock it, and position it. In addition, we'll remove the two extra phone buttons with the **Button tool**. Ready?

Resetting the User Level

At the beginning of this session, you reset the user level to level 2, typing, so that you could modify stacks by adding cards, deleting cards, and editing text in fields—things you couldn't do at the **browsing** level. HyperCard's browsing and typing user levels are designed to protect your stacks from being accidentally modified by untrained users. It's time to set your user level to level 4, authoring.

(Level 3 is painting; we're skipping that level because it doesn't allow us to create new buttons, cards, or stacks.) The **authoring** user level gives you access to all of HyperCard's tools except scripts, which will be introduced in Session 5.

☐ **Press Command-H (or select Home from the Go menu) to go Home.**

☐ **Press Command-4 (or select Last from the Go menu) to go to the last card of the Home stack.**

☐ **Click on the Authoring option.**

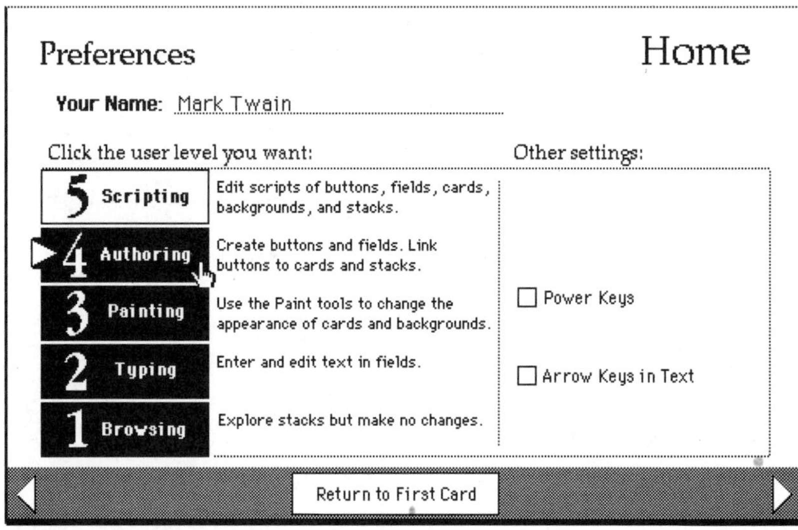

Saving a Copy

☐ **Press Command-R (or select Recent from the Go menu).**

☐ **Click on the image of any card from the Addresses stack to go to that card.**

☐ **Select Save a Copy... from the File menu.**

You're preserving a duplicate before you make any changes.

☐ **When the dialog box appears, check the destination disk to make sure the copy is going where you want it to and press Return.**

The saved copy will remain unchanged regardless of what you do to the original.

Going into the Background

Now you're ready to modify the Addresses stack. Because you want the changes to affect every card, the first step is to go to their shared background.

☐ **Select Background from the Edit menu (or press Command-B).**

You're now looking at the background that's shared by every address card in the stack. (The **striped menu bar** always indicates that you're in the background. So does the striped margin bar in this text.)

Deleting Buttons and Fields

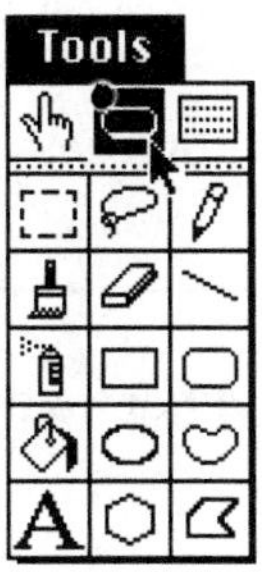

☐ **Select the Button tool from the top row in the center of the Tools menu.**

All the buttons on the card should be clearly outlined, including the four phone buttons.

☐ **Click on the third phone button from the top of the card.**

Because the Button tool is selected, clicking on the button selects it without activating it.

☐ **Press the Delete (Backspace) key to delete the selected button.**

☐ **Select and delete the bottom phone button.**

Now it's time to work with fields.

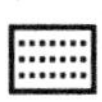

☐ **Select the Field tool from the upper right corner of the Tools menu.**

Every field in the background should be outlined with solid lines, including the four phone number fields.

☐ **Click on the third phone field to select it and press the Delete (Backspace) key.**

A dialog box will ask if you want to delete the field, warning that if you do you'll wipe out everything that's stored in that field for every card in your stack.

☐ **Click Delete.**

Copying a Field

We could delete the fourth field, too, but then we'd have to create a new birthday field. It's simpler just to give this field a new label and function. We'll need to create a label field like the ones for name, company, and the rest. We could use the New Field command, but then we'd have to tweak the field quite a bit to make it match the other labels. It makes more sense to make a copy of one of those fields, position the copy where we want it, and put "Birthday" in it.

☐ **Hold down the Option key and drag the field with "telephone" in it down toward the bottom of the card.**

This is a labor-saving shortcut for copying the field.

> **Option-drag** creates a *copy* of the field (or button), leaving the original behind while the copy is moved.

☐ **Position the new field so that it's below the original field and next to the lowest field on the card.**

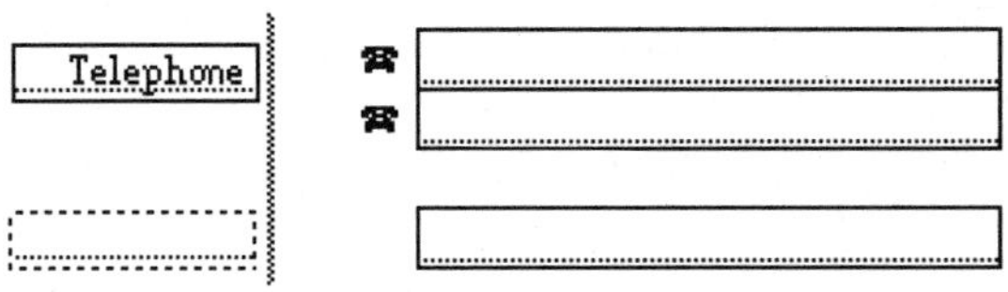

Labeling the Field

Now we just need to put "Birthday" in the new field. But we can't do that until we unlock the field so we can type in it.

☐ **Double-click on the new field.**

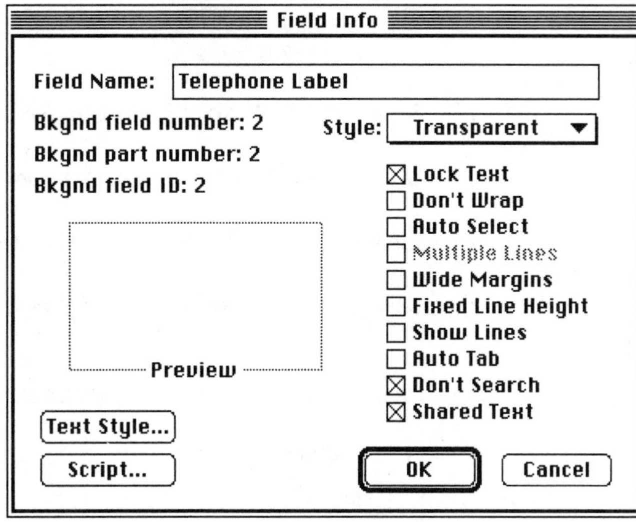

The dialog box that appears provides a complete profile of the field. We can ignore most of the options for now; they'll be covered in later sessions as we need them. These two concern us here:

> If the **Shared Text** option is checked, text in a background field is shared by every card with that background.
>
> The contents of a field cannot be changed as long as the **Lock Text** option is checked.

☐ **Type "Birthday Label" to rename the field.**

☐ **Click on the Lock Text check box to unlock the text and click OK.**

☐ **Select the Browse tool (the pointing hand) from the Tools menu.**

The pointer should turn back into a hand.

☐ **Position the pointer over the new field and click.**

The pointing hand becomes an I-beam, which places an insertion bar in the field.

☐ **Type "Birthday".**

Now we need to lock the field again so we don't inadvertently change our label later.

☐ **Select the Field tool from the Tools menu.**

☐ **Double-click on the Birthday Label field.**

☐ **Click on the Lock Text check box to lock the text; then click OK.**

☐ **Select the Browse tool from the Tools menu.**

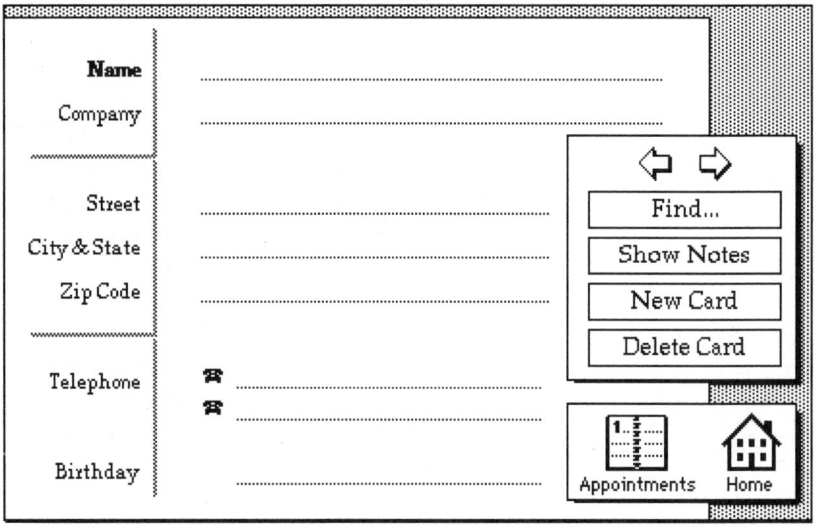

If your card looks like this one, you're ready to leave the background and try it out.

☐ **Press Command-B or select Background from the Edit menu.**

The stripes should vanish from the menu bar as you return to the card layer.

Finishing Up

As you flip through the cards, they'll all reflect the changes you made in the background.

☐ **Test the modified field by typing in birthdays on some of the cards.**

We could spend more time exploring HyperCard's information management tools. But you've seen the basics now, and the exercises and projects will give you a chance to apply the principles you've learned in a variety of interesting ways.

☐ **Select Quit HyperCard from the File menu.**

Summary

You've accomplished quite a bit in this session. You learned how to enter and edit text in HyperCard fields. You learned how to add cards, delete cards, sort cards, and find particular items on those cards using character string pattern matches. Finally, you got a feel for what's involved in customizing stacks by working with the Field and Button tools.

You're a certified HyperCard user now, prepared to browse and type your way through all kinds of HyperCard stacks. If you have no intention of creating your own stacks, you can quit now. But be forewarned: The best is yet to come.

Key Words

authoring (user level)
background
Boolean algebra
Browse tool
browsing (user level)
Button tool
Chooser
Clipboard
Copy command (Command-C)
Copy Card command
cursor
Cut command (Command-X)
Cut Card command
data file
database
Delete Card command (Command-Delete, Command-Backspace)
double-click-drag
field (database and HyperCard)
Field tool
Find command (Command-F)
hard copy
header
I-beam
insertion bar
intersection
locked text (field)
Mark Cards command
marking cards
New Card button
New Card command (Command-N)
Option-drag
Page Setup command
Paste command (Command-V)
phone icon
pop-up field

- Print Card command (Command-P)
- Print Report... command
- Print Stack... command
- record (database)
- report
- Reports menu
- report template
- Save a Copy... command
- scrolling field
- selecting text
- shared text (field)
- Shift key
- Shift-Tab
- Sort commands
- striped menu bar
- Tab key
- typing (user level)
- Undo command (Command-Z)
- union
- user level

Exercises

1. There's no Save command in HyperCard. Is it necessary to use the Save a Copy... command to save your work? Explain.
2. Give three examples illustrating *different* reasons the Find command might not take you to the sought-after card.
3. Why is it important to make sure all of the names in an address book stack are listed with the first and last names arranged in the same order?
4. Explain the difference between deleting and cutting a card.
5. What is the difference between printing a stack and printing a report? Describe situations in which each is appropriate.
6. What are the advantages of using HyperCard as a personal address book rather than using a conventional paper address book? What are the disadvantages?

Projects

Note: Some of these projects involve modifying standard HyperCard stacks that accompany HyperCard. If you're working in a public lab with shared files, use copies of these files. In order to make sure you open *your* copy, rather than the public copy, use the Open Stack... command to locate each file on your disk.

1. Open the Addresses stack and save a copy. Delete all but one of the cards from your copy and build a new Addresses stack that includes the addresses of your friends and relatives. Sort the stack in alphabetical order by last name. Mark the cards that contain names of people you call frequently. Print an address book of all of the names in the stack and a phone list containing only names and phone numbers from marked cards.

2. Use the Find command in the Art Bits stack to answer the following questions:

   a. Which page contains pictures of the planets?

   b. How many pages include the word *sun* in the index?

   c. How many pages include the word *drum* in the index?

3. Use the Graph Maker stack to create the following charts:

   a. A column chart illustrating the median income for men by level of education using the figures shown here (from 1986):

Men with four or more years of college	$33,304
Men with one to three years of college	23,738
Men with high school diplomas	9,772
Men with less than four years of high school	13,401

   b. A bar chart comparing the median income of men and women with four or more years of college education, using these figures:

Men with four or more years of college	$33,304
Women with four or more years of college	18,065

   c. A pie chart showing the occupational breakdown of the population completing four years or more of college, using the following figures:

Professional and managerial	68%
Technical, sales, and administrative	24%
Service	3%
Blue collar	5%

4. Open the Stack Templates stack (probably accessible from a button on the Stack Kit card of your Home stack). Following the instructions in the stack overview, create and customize a stack from one or more of the templates.

5. There are thousands of HyperCard stacks in existence. If you have access to a library of HyperCard stacks, locate and explore several stacks in your area of interest. Pay attention to how these stacks work; compare their similarities and their differences.

Session 3

By the end of this session you should be able to

- Create and name a new HyperCard stack and save a copy of that stack
- Use the Rectangle tool, the Oval tool, the Straight Line tool, the Pencil tool, the Paint Bucket, and the Patterns palette to create a drawing
- Use the Paint Text tool to add different styles of text to a stack
- Use the Eraser, the Undo command, and other editing tools to edit the graphics in the stack
- Create a button with a labeled icon and link it to a new card in the stack
- Copy a portion of a picture and paste it on another card
- Copy a button and paste it on another card

Stacks from Scratch

Building with Buttons

The Problem

Your local museum is preparing an exhibit on the seven wonders of the ancient world. They've asked you to prepare an interactive display on Egypt's Great Pyramid that will (1) show a cross section of the pyramid revealing passages and rooms; (2) provide close-up views of the King's Chamber and other rooms; and (3) be interactive and self-explanatory, so anyone can explore it. You don't have the time or money to create physical models, and you don't have the wall space to hang drawings or photos. Perhaps HyperCard can help.

Introduction

So far we've focused on using HyperCard as a tool for storing and accessing information. We've explored some professionally designed HyperCard stacks, modifying one so that it can be used in a slightly different way than the designer envisioned. As you'll see in this session, it's almost as easy to create your own stacks as it is to browse through or modify stacks created by others. HyperCard does such a good job of breaking down the distinction between computer *user* and computer *programmer* that you might not even notice when you cross that line in this session. Programming has never been easier.

Stack Construction Toolbox

Creating a New Stack

☐ **Start HyperCard by double-clicking on the Home Stack.**

☐ **Select New Stack... from the File menu.**

(If the New Stack... command is dimmed in the menu, double-check to make sure your user level has been set to authoring, as explained in the "Customizing Cards" section of Session 2.)

You'll see this:

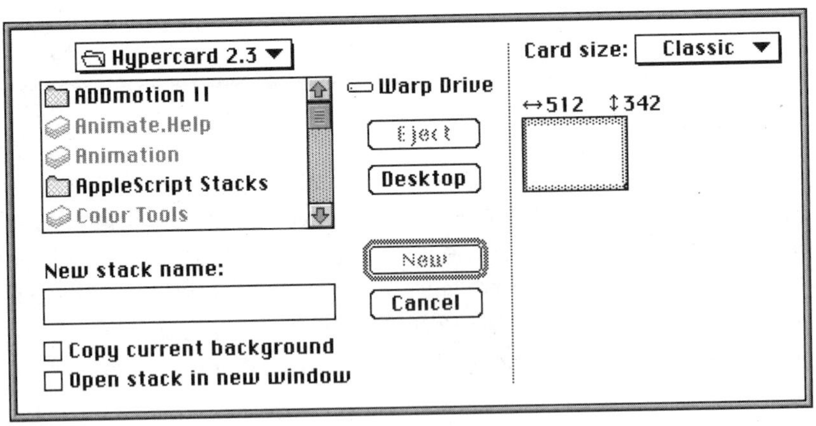

New Stack Dialog Box Options

In addition to the usual disk and folder selection options, the New Stack dialog box offers several choices:

- Copy current background: Check this box if you want your new stack to use the current stack's background. Backgrounds are discussed in more detail in the next session.
- Open stack in new window: Check this box if you want to keep the current stack open when the new stack is created. This is a good choice if you'll be switching back and forth between stacks, but it requires more memory.
- Card sizes: This pop-up menu allows you to choose between several common sizes or create your own. Here's what the Help stack says about it:

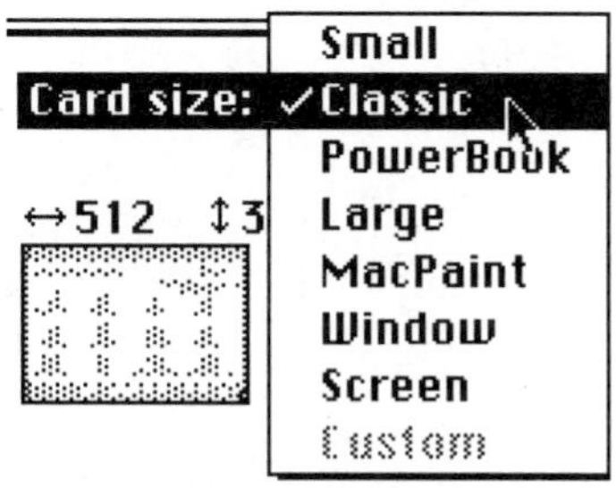

In this book we'll consistently choose the "Classic" size because that size is completely visible on every Mac screen.

☐ **Make sure that both check boxes are turned off and that "Classic" is the selected card size.**

☐ **Make sure the disk shown above the Eject button is the appropriate disk for saving the stack.**

☐ **Type "Pyramid".**

This is the name you're assigning to your about-to-be-created stack.

Naming a Stack

You can choose any name you like for a stack, as long as

- It is less than 32 characters long and contains no colons (:)
- It is not the same as the names of any other files in the same folder on the disk

It's usually a good idea to choose a name that describes the stack contents, so you don't need to actually open the stack to remember what it does.

We're starting with a plain white background with no buttons, which is what you get if you don't copy the background from the current stack. You'll learn more about how backgrounds work in the next session.

☐ **Click New.**

You're looking at the first (and only) card in your new stack. It's totally empty now, but it's still saved on disk. HyperCard will automatically save this stack on this disk regularly as you work on your stack.

Tearing Off the Tools Menu

You'll be heavily using the **Tools menu** for a while, so let's put it where it's more accessible.

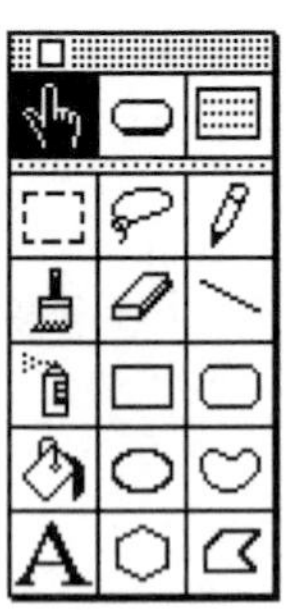

☐ **Drag your mouse (with the button held down) from the title of the Tools menu down past the bottom of that menu. Drag the dotted outline of that menu to the right side of the screen near the top.**

As you can see, Tools is a **tear-off menu**. You can now select tools from the Tools menu (it's still there) or from the **Tools palette** that you just created. The top three tools in the Tools menu/palette are **general tools** that allow you to choose between browsing, working with buttons, and working with fields; all of the remaining tools are **paint tools** specifically designed for painting. Notice that the Browse tool—the pointing hand—is highlighted. That means that it's the selected tool—the one that's currently being controlled by the mouse. When you select any of the paint tools, you tell the computer you want to paint on the screen or you want to modify something that's already painted on the screen.

Painting in HyperCard is really just the process of telling the computer which **pixels** (picture elements or dots) in the card should be black and which should be white. Those are the only two choices; shades of gray are made of different black and white patterns. Technically, this is called **bit-mapped graphics**, because each pixel is controlled by one **bit**, or binary digit of the computer's memory. HyperCard has many sophisticated tools to make it easy to paint complex shapes, lines, words, and patterns, but all these tools are doing the same thing: telling HyperCard to display some card pixels white and others black. (In Session 7 you'll see how to add color to your HyperCard stacks.)

Drawing Lines

☐ **Click on the Pencil tool to select it.**

Three menus disappear from the menu bar, only to be replaced by three other menus. These new menus are used for painting, so they aren't visible when you aren't using paint tools.

☐ **Move the pointer over the HyperCard card—the white screen below the menu bar (inside the window if you're using a large screen).**

Notice how the pointer turns into a pencil.

☐ **Hold down the mouse button and drag the Pencil tool around on the screen.**

☐ **Try signing your name, remembering that you can pick up the mouse and move it if you run out of desk space. Then underline your signature.**

As you can see, it's easy to draw with the mouse, but not very easy to draw *well*. Straight lines are particularly difficult. Fortunately, there's another tool designed to make that easier.

☐ **Select the Straight Line tool.**

The pointer turns into cross hairs, ready to draw.

☐ **Drag the mouse with the button held down between any two points in the window.**

Notice how a straight line stretches like a rubber band between those two points. Wherever you let go, that's where the line stays. Draw a few more lines if you like. When your window becomes hopelessly cluttered, you can erase anything you don't like.

Using the Eraser

☐ **Select the Eraser tool from the palette by clicking on it. (If you prefer, you can select the Eraser in the Tools *menu*.)**

Notice how the pointer turns into a square when you move it over the white card.

☐ **Drag the Eraser through part of your scribbles with the mouse button held down.**

The parts you erase disappear without a trace. But erasing like this can be tedious if you want to clear the entire screen. Fortunately, there's a shortcut.

☐ **Double-click on the Eraser tool.**

> Double-clicking on the Eraser clears everything that's painted on the card. This is a handy—and potentially costly—trick. If you ever do it by mistake, remember Command-Z, the Undo command.

By this time, you're probably anxious to do some serious doodling. If so, take a few minutes to experiment. When you're done playing, double-click on the Eraser to clear the screen and we'll build a pyramid.

Drawing Polygons

☐ **Select the Polygon tool.**

This tool works like the Straight Line tool, except that it draws a series of connected lines. Each successive mouse click forms another angle and another new line; the lines stop forming when you click on the starting point or somewhere outside the window or when you double-click.

- ☐ **Draw a triangle with the Polygon tool by clicking on three different points on the screen. Complete the triangle by clicking once more on the starting point.**

If your triangle doesn't look like a pyramid, never mind. You already know one way to remove it: You can double-click on the Eraser to clear the window. But Undo will work here, too:

- ☐ **Press Command-Z (or select Undo from the Edit menu).**

If you haven't clicked the mouse button anywhere else since you drew the last triangle, the triangle will vanish.

- ☐ **Draw two more overlapping triangles. Press Command-Z *three times* after you draw the second one. Watch how the picture changes each time you select Undo.**

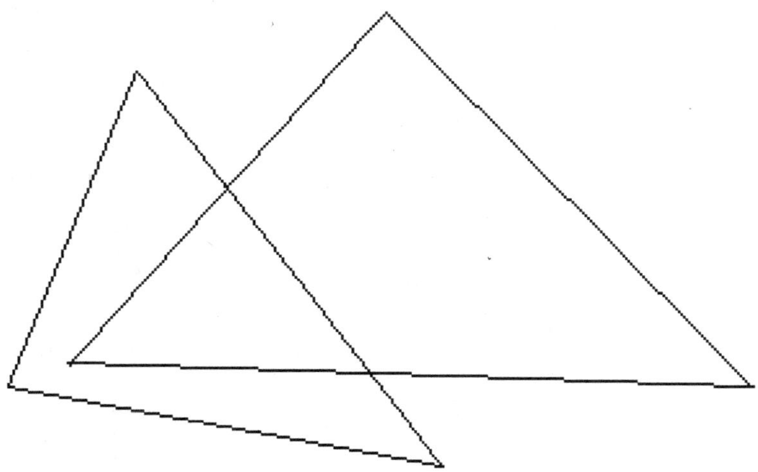

Since Undo can't take you back more than one step, you'll never be able to remove that first triangle with it. That's why it's important to check your work after each step before doing any more typing, clicking, or dragging.

Graphics Insurance

When you're working with paint tools, it's easy to spoil a work in progress with an accidental slip of the mouse. You can avoid serious, irreversible damage by remembering and using these insurance commands:

- The Go Back key (~ or Esc) backtracks one step when you have a paint tool selected. (To go back to the last card when you have a paint tool selected, press Command-~ or Command-Esc.)
- Undo (Command-Z) backtracks exactly one step.
- **Keep** (in the Paint menu, or **Command-K**) tells HyperCard to save the current picture.
- **Revert** (in the Paint menu) tells HyperCard to go back to the last saved version of the picture.

When you're painting in HyperCard, your picture is saved to disk when you do any of the following:

- Switch to another card.
- Switch to or from the background layer.
- Select any of the three general tools at the top of the Tools palette.
- Select Keep (Command-K).

When you're painting, make a habit of selecting Keep (or pressing Command-K) every few minutes. If you make an error, try to erase it using Undo, ~, or Esc. If that doesn't take you back far enough, use Revert.

☐ **Double-click on the Eraser to clear the window.**

If you've been trying to make your triangles look like pyramids, you've probably noticed that it's not easy to make the two sides exactly the same length. Here's a trick that might help.

☐ **Hold down the Shift key while drawing the triangle with the Polygon tool.**

When you're using many of the paint tools, the Shift key serves as a **constraint key**, temporarily constraining the tool in some helpful way.

In this case, it constrains the Polygon tool so that every line is either horizontal or a multiple of 15 degrees from horizontal. It's much easier to draw true horizontal lines and equal angles when the tool is constrained this way; you can be sure you will hit the horizontal or the vertical right on the mark. Even with this constraint, you'll probably have to try a few times to get the pyramid to come out right. If it doesn't work, just erase and try again. Your goal is to produce a triangle with two equal sides that fills about the top three-fourths of the window, like this:

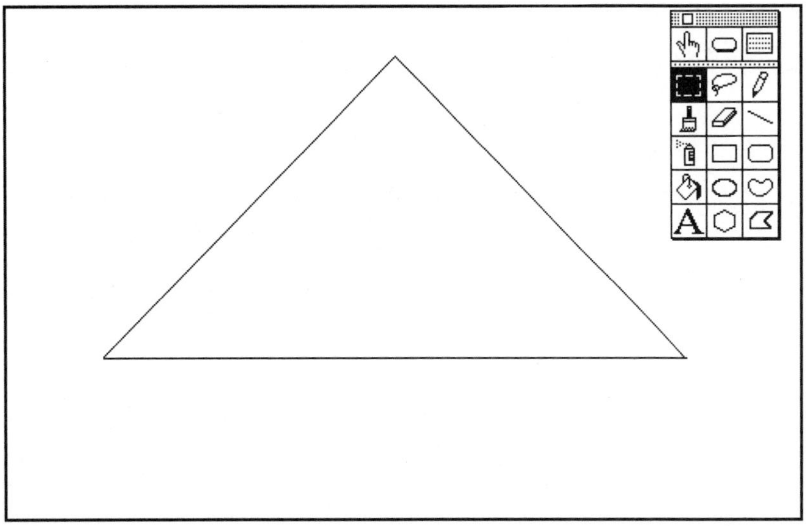

(Your local Egyptologist might tell you that this pyramid doesn't exactly match the geometry of the Great Pyramid. Never mind; he just lacks perspective.)

Pouring Paint Patterns

Shape notwithstanding, the pyramid doesn't look authentic because it lacks texture. The Great Pyramid was built with gigantic granite blocks (enough blocks to stretch three-fourths of the way around the planet if laid end to end). We can simulate the granite blocks by painting our pyramid. Unlike real-world paint, HyperCard paint comes in patterns rather than colors. A selection of these patterns is available in the **Patterns menu**, which can be torn off and made into a portable **Patterns palette**.

☐ **Drag the Patterns menu down from the menu bar and over to the right side of the screen so it's below the Tools palette.**

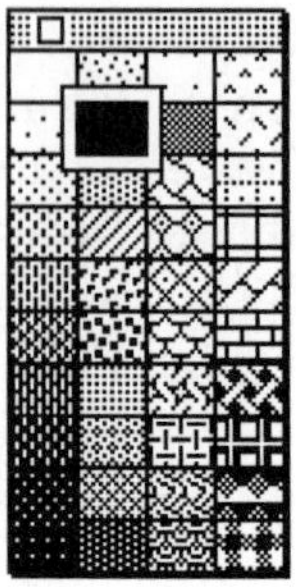

Notice that black paint is selected when you first open the palette.

☐ **Click to select the pattern that looks like bricks.**

This is the paint we'll use on the pyramid.

☐ **Select the Paint bucket tool from the Tools palette. The pointer should turn into a paint bucket.**

The Paint Bucket tool allows you to pour paint into any white area that's completely enclosed by black (or into a black area that's enclosed by white).

☐ **Position the Paint Bucket so that the dripping paint is somewhere inside the triangle and press the button to pour the paint.**

Your triangle should fill with bricks. If the whole screen fills with bricks, your triangle has a leak.

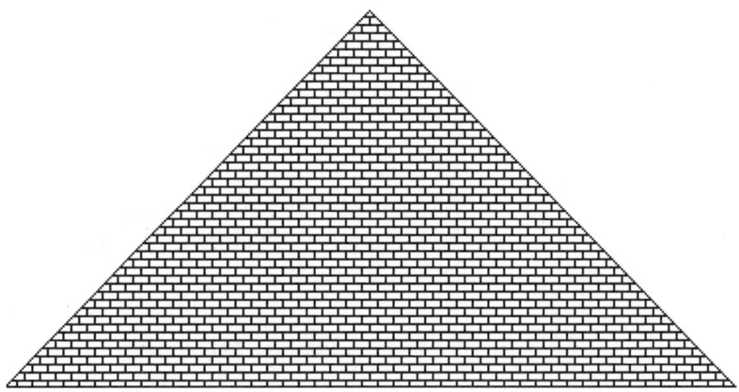

> The area to be filled with poured paint must be completely surrounded by black (or by white if you're pouring into a black area). Even the tiniest pinhole in the boundary will allow paint to leak out to fill a larger area. If your paint ever leaks unexpectedly, select Undo *immediately*, locate and correct the leak with the Pencil (or redraw the shape), and pour the paint again.

We have a pyramid; let's add the desert.

☐ **Use the Pencil tool to draw a line from the left edge of the bottom of the pyramid to the left edge of the screen. Make sure that there are no gaps at either end of the line. Repeat on the right side of the pyramid. (If necessary, drag the Patterns palette out of the way using the bar at the top of the palette.)**

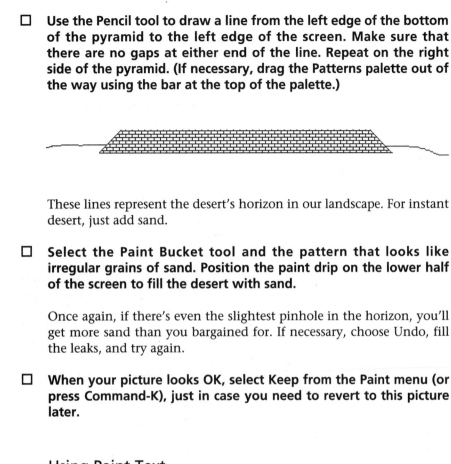

These lines represent the desert's horizon in our landscape. For instant desert, just add sand.

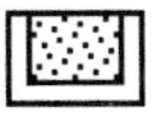

☐ **Select the Paint Bucket tool and the pattern that looks like irregular grains of sand. Position the paint drip on the lower half of the screen to fill the desert with sand.**

Once again, if there's even the slightest pinhole in the horizon, you'll get more sand than you bargained for. If necessary, choose Undo, fill the leaks, and try again.

☐ **When your picture looks OK, select Keep from the Paint menu (or press Command-K), just in case you need to revert to this picture later.**

Using Paint Text

Even though you may have no trouble identifying the Great Pyramid in your picture, others might need a hint. So let's add a title. You worked with text fields in Session 2, but for this job there's another kind of text that's more appropriate.

Two Kinds of Text in HyperCard

- **Paint text**, after it's typed, blends into the whole painting, becoming just another pattern of black and white dots on the screen. Consequently, it can't be edited later using the standard editing techniques. (Nor can it be found with the Find command.)
- **Field text** remains text forever. Unless a field is locked (see Session 5), you—or any user—can always edit it using the usual editing techniques.

Since we don't want casual users of our stack to mess with the title, we're better off using paint text.

☐ **Select the Paint Text tool (the letter *A*).**

The pointer turns into an I-beam. As you saw in the last session, the I-beam is used to position the cursor for typing.

☐ **Position the I-beam just below the bottom of the pyramid in the center and click.**

A flashing cursor appears, beckoning you to type.

☐ **Type "The Great Pyramid".**

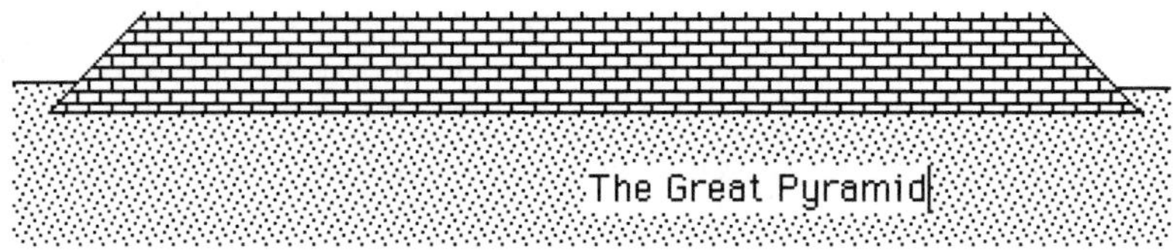

The words are there, all right, but they lack style. We can fix that.

☐ **Double-click on the Paint Text tool.**

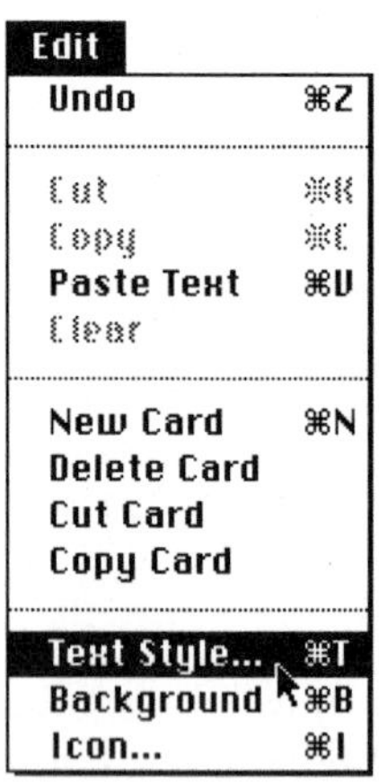

This is a shortcut to save time. The alternative is to select **Text Style...** from the Edit menu (or press **Command-T**).

You'll see a dialog box that looks something like this one:

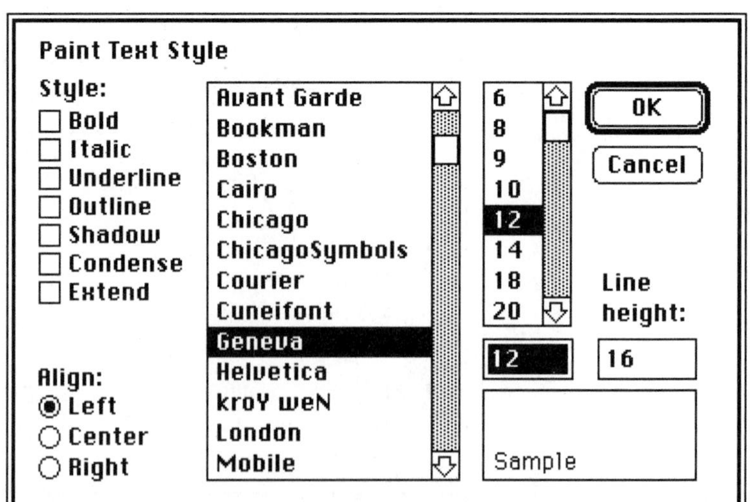

This crowded dialog box gives you control over the way the text looks, rather than what it says. If you haven't clicked anywhere since you typed your title, you can change the style of the title text by simply clicking on different options. But first, a brief explanation of the available options is in order.

The Text Styles Dialog Box

The text **styles** listed on the left side of the dialog box—bold, underline, and the rest—can be used to draw attention to text and add visual pizzazz to a screen. But beware: It's easy to overuse these styles and make your stack look like a reject from a supermarket tabloid.

The names in the center of the box represent **fonts**—basic typefaces—that are stored in your System. Different fonts have different looks; compare this text with the text of the instruction below this box. The font names that you see on your screen probably don't match those shown here; you have different fonts stored in your System file. There are hundreds of fonts available for Macintosh users: Some come free with the System; others must be purchased; still others are available free in the public domain. Consequently, it's rare for two computer systems to have the same set of fonts.

You can also control the **size** of the text by clicking on different sizes. (Sizes are measured in **points**; a point is a typographer's unit of measure.) Once again, the sizes that are available are determined by the fonts that are stored in your System. What's more, different fonts may have different available sizes. You can type in sizes that aren't stored with the system for a particular font, but, depending on how your System is configured, you may end up with lumpy, hard-to-read letters on the screen. The sample text shown in the lower right corner of the dialog box can be used to preview the options.

Finally, the dialog box lets you control **alignment** of the text. Typically, text is aligned to the left, but you can also specify right alignment or automatic centering around the insertion point.

- ☐ **Experiment with the sample text in the lower right corner of the dialog box by choosing different combinations of fonts, styles, and sizes.**

- ☐ **When you're done experimenting, click on styles Bold, Shadow, and Extend, on font Geneva, on size 24 point (if it's visible; otherwise click on the largest available number), and on align Center.**

Then click on the OK button to apply all these changes to your title.

The Great Pyramid

If the title didn't change, it's probably because you clicked somewhere else on the window before choosing Text Style.... Remember, paint text "dries" as soon as you let go of it.

From an aesthetic point of view, these letters leave something to be desired. (Outline and shadow characters generally do.) But they'll serve our purposes because they stand out even when surrounded by sand.

Because the text cleared a path in the sand, we need to do some touch-up work with the Paint Bucket.

☐ **With the Paint Bucket and the sand pattern selected, position the paint drip over part of the area whited out by the text and click to pour.**

☐ ***Carefully* position the end of the paint drip inside the opening in the *P* and pour; fill the *d* the same way.**

If you make any mistakes, remember to select Undo before you click anywhere else.

If your screen looks like this, you've completed the artwork on your first card:

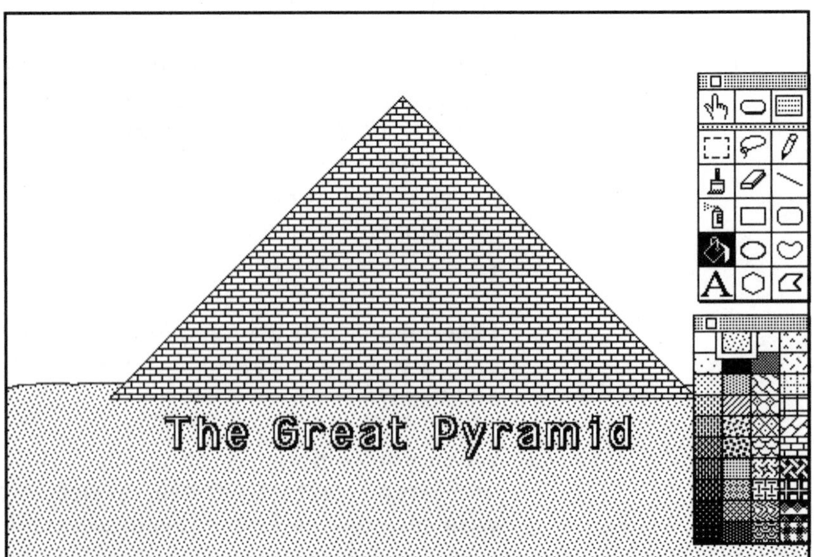

Instant Buttons, Instant Cards

Creating a Button

☐ **Click on the Button tool in the top row of the Tools palette.**

The Paint, Options, and Patterns menus are replaced by three other menus, and the pointer turns into the familiar arrow.

☐ **Select New Button from the Objects menu.**

This is the generic HyperCard button. It's up to us to make it look and act the way we want it to. Let's start by making the button bigger.

☐ **Place the pointer at the corner of the button and drag it away from the button's center.**

If you found the right spot, the button should stretch as you drag. If it doesn't, reposition the mouse and try again.

☐ **Drag the corner until the button is about twice its original length.**

This button is inconveniently located right on top of our pyramid, but it's easy enough to move.

☐ **Place the pointer in the middle of the button and drag it down between the bottom of the card and the title.**

What does this button do?

☐ **Try clicking once on this button to see what it does.**

Nothing happens.

> HyperCard buttons work only when clicked by the Browse hand tool; the Button tool is used to create and change buttons, not to click them.

But in this case, switching to the Browse tool wouldn't help, because we haven't told the button what to do when it's clicked. We're ready to do that now.

☐ **Double-click on the New Button button.**

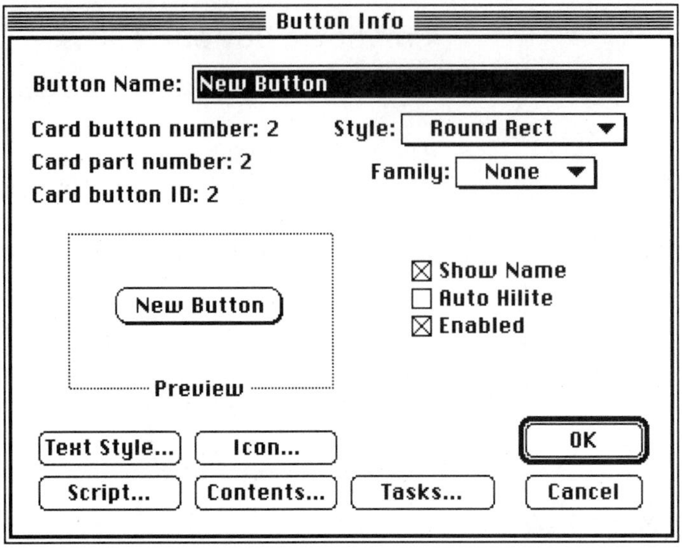

This dialog box is packed with buttons and options you'll use to determine what your button looks like and to "program" it. You'll explore most of the options first-hand in this and future sessions, starting with the button you just created. But before you customize your button, take a minute to get an overview of this important box.

The Button Info Dialog Box

The Button Info dialog allows you to name the button, determine its appearance, and establish what will happen when the button is clicked. The Preview box shows how the selected features look in a sample button.

The **Button Name** you type appears in the button if the **Show Name** check box is checked; it can be used to provide instructions for the user.

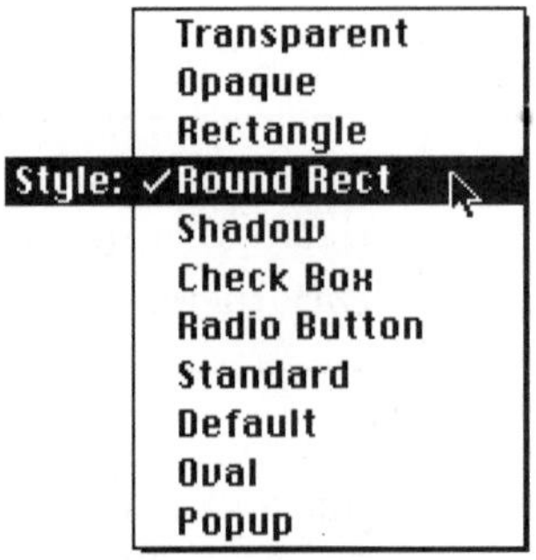

Several styles of button are available via pop-up menu:

- **Transparent** and **Oval** buttons are invisible; they allow paint and other objects to show through.
- **Opaque** buttons are white and borderless; they're used for hiding paint and other objects. Rectangle, Round Rect, and Shadow are styles for borders that frame the button name.
- Standard, Default, Check Box, Radio Button, and Popup have specific meanings according to Macintosh user interface guidelines; they should generally be used only for their designated purposes. Except for Standard, they all require some HyperTalk scripting to behave according to the guidelines, so they're described only briefly here. Standard and Default perform actions in dialog boxes; the Default button is surrounded by a thick black line indicating that pressing Return has the same effect as pressing this button. (The OK button in this dialog box is a Default-style button; the other seven buttons at the bottom of the box are Standard-style buttons.) Check boxes and Radio buttons adjust settings rather than perform actions. Check boxes are on/off toggle switches that allow the user to make several independent choices at once. (There are three examples in this dialog box.) Radio buttons are grouped in families (using the other pop-up menu in this dialog box) so that only one per family can be selected at a time. Popup allows you to create pop-up menus similar to the one you're using right now; the menu options are typed in using the Contents... button below.

Auto Hilite determines whether the button will give visual feedback when clicked; it's generally appropriate except for transparent, opaque, and oval buttons that don't appear to the user to have clearly defined boundaries.

Enabled means that the button works and it is not grayed out; it should generally be checked.

Two buttons at the bottom of the dialog box, Text Style... and Icon..., allow you to change the appearance of the text in the button and add an icon. The remaining buttons allow you to program the actions that will be performed when the button is clicked.

Let's start by changing the name of the button.

☐ **Type "Click here to see inside".**

Since the original name of the button, New Button, was highlighted, that name is replaced by your typing.

We have several choices of button styles; for this button, the already-selected round rectangle is just fine. But it might be nice if we could have the button flash black when clicked, like official Macintosh dialog box buttons do.

☐ **Click on Auto Hilite.**

Assigning a Task

Now that you've determined the button's appearance, you're ready to program it with an assigned task: transporting the viewer to a new card showing a cross section of the pyramid. You'll **link** the button to that cross-section card so the card appears when the button is clicked.

☐ **Click on Tasks...**

A new **Tasks window** appears in the center of the screen:

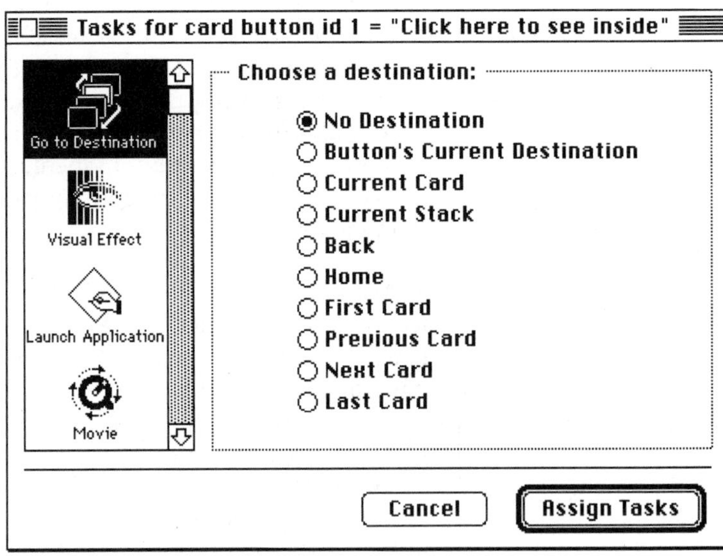

This window, new to HyperCard 2.3, allows you to assign a variety of tasks to a button automatically. The scrolling box on the left represents several types of common button tasks as icons. When you click on an icon in this box, you specify a general task type; the box on the right allows you to program the details of the button's task.

☐ **If it's not already highlighted in black, click on the icon labeled Go to Destination.**

The Go to Destination choice offers several destination options, most of which are identical to commands found in the Go menu. You'll have a chance to experiment with these options soon enough. For now, we'll just choose the one that makes the most sense for this button.

☐ **Click on the Next Card option (either the radio button or the phrase "Next Card").**

Of course, there's a problem: We don't have a next card in this one-card stack. We'll fix that shortly. First let's assign another task to the button: a visual effect.

Adding a Visual Effect

Well-chosen **visual effects** can enhance the look and feel of your stack as it moves from card to card.

Visual Effect

☐ **Scroll down through the task icons until you see the Visual Effect icon; click on it.**

The right side changes to a list of visual effects and a choice of speeds.

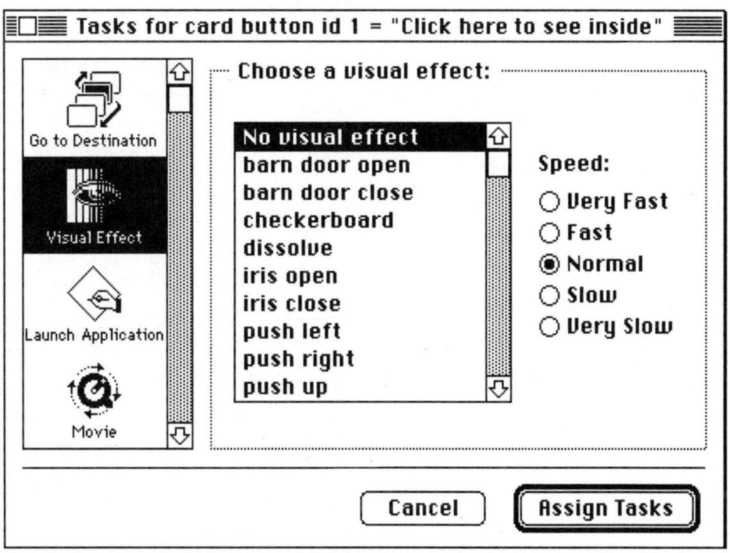

☐ **Scroll through the list of visual effects until you see "shrink to top". Click on that one.**

You've selected two tasks for this button: Go to the next card, and display a visual effect. It's time to assign those tasks.

☐ **Click on Assign Tasks.**

The dialog box disappears. You can test the button as soon as you create another card.

Adding the Next Card

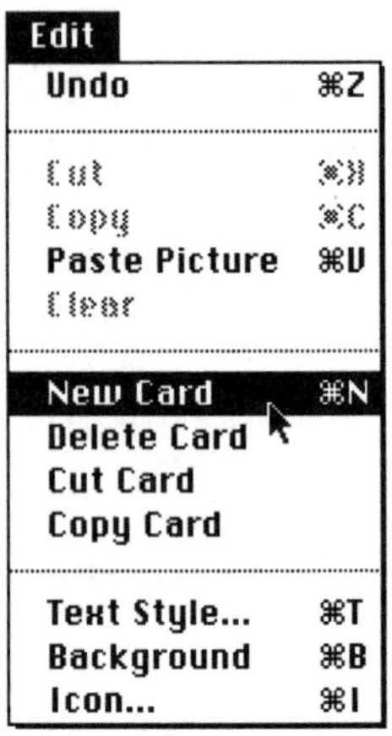

☐ **Select New Card from the Edit menu (or press Command-N, the keyboard equivalent).**

You're looking at a brand-new, all-white card, located right behind the first card in your stack. So when you click on the button on card 1, it should take you to this card—the next card in the stack. Let's try it.

☐ **Type Command-1 (or select Go First) to go to the first card in the stack.**

☐ **Press Command-Tab.**

This is the keyboard equivalent of selecting the Browse tool (the hand) from the Tools palette.

☐ **Click on the button you created.**

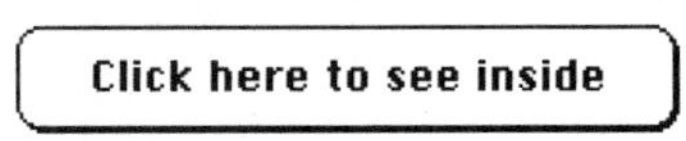

If it worked properly, the button flashed black and the entire scene shriveled up until it vanished at the top of the window. You've been transported to your new, all-white card. The Tools palette is still visible; it travels with you until you put it away. (If you're not on the new white card, you didn't link the button properly. You can remedy the situation by choosing the Button tool, double-clicking on the button, clicking on Tasks..., clicking on Go to Destination, selecting Last Card, and clicking on Assign Tasks.)

Using the Clipboard

Now return to the first card so we can borrow from our previous artwork to decorate this card.

☐ **Press Command-1 (or select First from the Go menu).**

We'll copy this picture to the Clipboard so we can use it as raw material for our next card. But before a graphic can be copied to the Clipboard, it must be selected. There are many ways to select a graphic in HyperCard.

HyperCard Graphic Selection Techniques

- To select the entire card's graphics including the white spaces between them, double-click on the **Selection rectangle** *or* use the **Select All command (Command-A)** with any graphic tool selected.

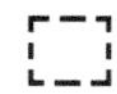

- To select all the graphic objects on the card without selecting surrounding white spaces, double-click on the **Lasso** *or* use the **Select command (Command-S)** with the lasso selected.

- To select the most recently painted object (before you click anywhere else), do nothing (it's automatically selected) unless you want to move it; in that case, use the Select command (Command-S).
- To select a rectangular area, use the Selection rectangle.
- To select an irregularly shaped area, use the Selection rectangle with the Option key held down, *or* use the Lasso, *or* use the Select command after selecting an object with the rectangle.

Note: We'll modify this list next session when we work with backgrounds.

We'll use the Selection rectangle momentarily and the Lasso in the next session. For our current job, the most appropriate tool is the Select All command.

☐ **Click on any of the paint tools and choose Select All from the Paint menu (or press Command-A).**

A dotted line should be moving around the edge of the screen, indicating that the whole picture is selected.

☐ **Press Command-C (or select Copy Picture from the Edit menu).**

You can't see it, but you just placed a copy of the entire drawing in the Clipboard.

☐ **Press Command-~ (Go Back) to return to the blank card.**

When you're using the paint tools, pressing the ~ (Tilde) key by itself will undo the last step. To use it to go back one card, press the Command key with it. (This combination always takes you back, whether you're painting or not.)

☐ **Press Command-V (Paste Picture).**

The entire pyramid portrait should appear on the card, ready to be revised into a cross-section view. (Notice that the button did not copy with the artwork.)

The first thing we want to do is eliminate the title from this page so we have room for our subterranean passages.

☐ **Choose the Selection rectangle (the dashed rectangle) from the Tools palette.**

When you drag a diagonal with the Selection rectangle, you're selecting the rectangular area determined by that diagonal.

☐ **Drag a diagonal from the top right corner of the title to the bottom left corner, making sure to include the whole title in the rectangle. If you miss, click outside the selected area and try again.**

You should see a moving dashed line around the area you've selected. (Because of these moving dashes, the Selection rectangle has been nicknamed the marquee, or more informally, marching ants.)

☐ **Press the Delete (Backspace) key to delete the selected portion of the picture.**

That leaves a white space, because you deleted some sand, too.

☐ **With the sand pattern selected, select the Paint Bucket and click once in the white rectangle to fill it with sand paint.**

Painting Passages

☐ **Double-click on the Straight Line tool.**

This is the shortcut equivalent of selecting **Line Size...** from the Options menu. You're going to be drawing some underground passages, and you'll need a line that's thicker than the one you've been using.

☐ **Click on the fourth line in the dialog box:**

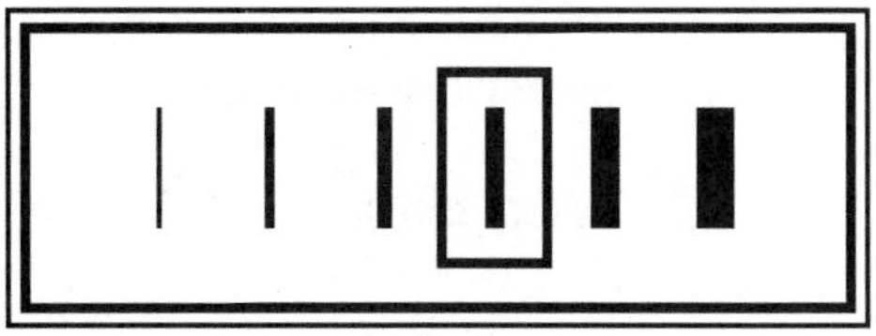

☐ **Select the Straight Line Tool and drag a line that looks like this:**

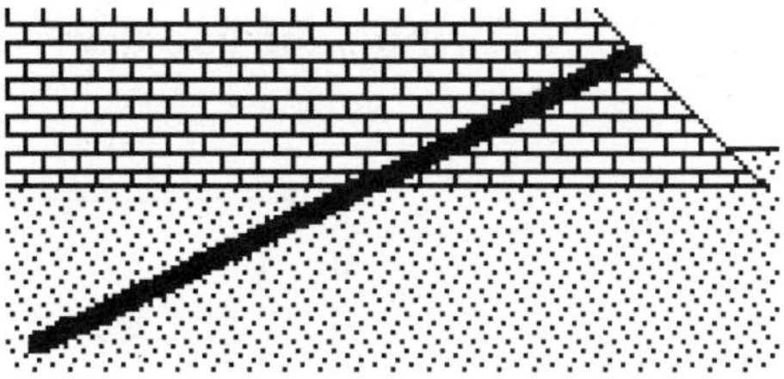

☐ **Now add another:**

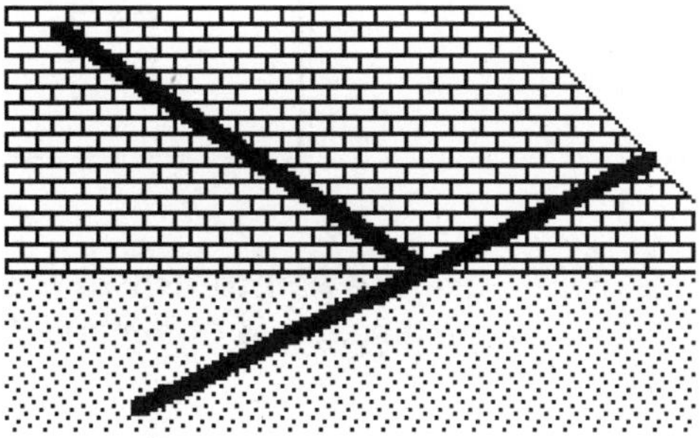

☐ **Hold down the Shift key to constrain the Straight Line tool and draw two horizontal lines:**

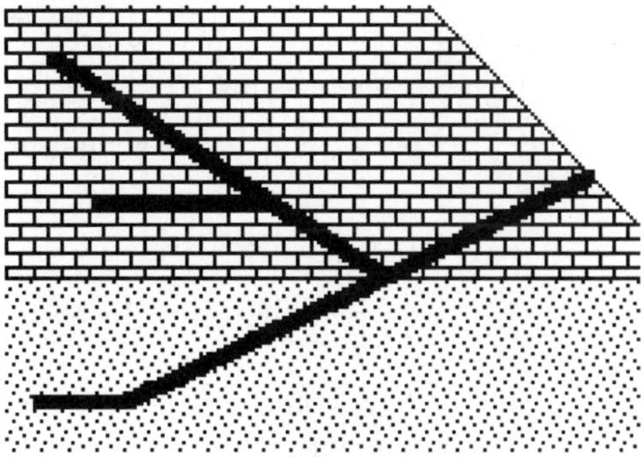

With the straight passages drawn, you're ready to draw the crooked escape passage.

☐ **Select the Paintbrush tool.**

☐ **Select black paint from the Patterns palette.**

Double-click on the Paintbrush tool. Another keyboard shortcut, this one has the same effect as choosing **Brush Shape...** from the Options menu.

☐ **Select a brush shape from the dialog box (you *must* select one, even if it's the one that's already selected).**

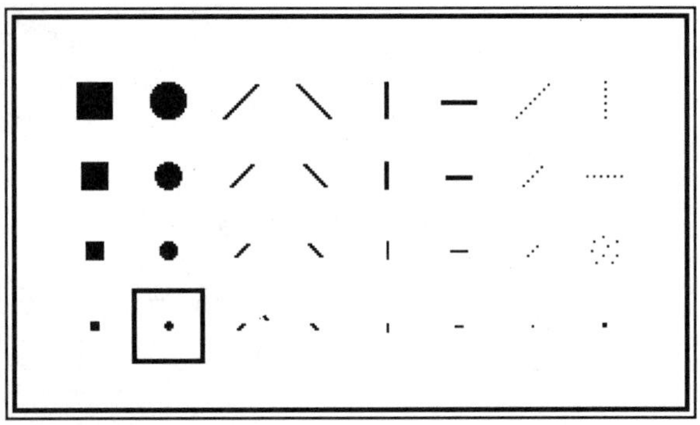

☐ **Use the Paintbrush to draw the curved passage. If you make a mistake, press Command-Z (Undo) and try again.**

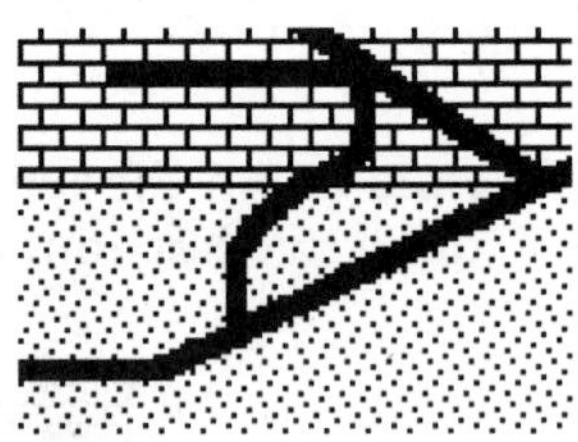

Now we can add the chambers.

Drawing Rooms

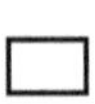

☐ **Select the Rectangle tool from the palette.**

When you drag between two points with this tool, you create a rectangle with those two points as opposite vertices.

☐ **Draw a rectangular-shaped chamber under the pyramid like this:**

Notice that the sides of the rectangle are the line thickness that we selected earlier; that thickness applies to all shape tools until we specify otherwise.

To be consistent with the black passages, we should paint the subterranean chambers black, too.

☐ **Select the Paint Bucket and the black paint.**

☐ **Place the paint drip *inside* the rectangle and click to pour.**

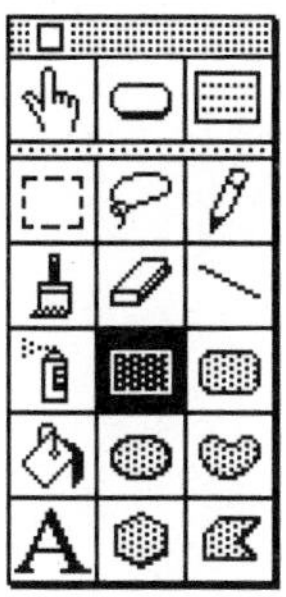

You can combine those two steps—creating a shape and filling it—by telling HyperCard that you want to draw filled shapes.

☐ **Double-click on the Rectangle tool.**

This is the same as selecting **Draw Filled** from the Options menu. Notice how the shape tools in the palette are now filled.

☐ **Select the Rectangle tool and draw two rectangles inside the pyramid, like this:**

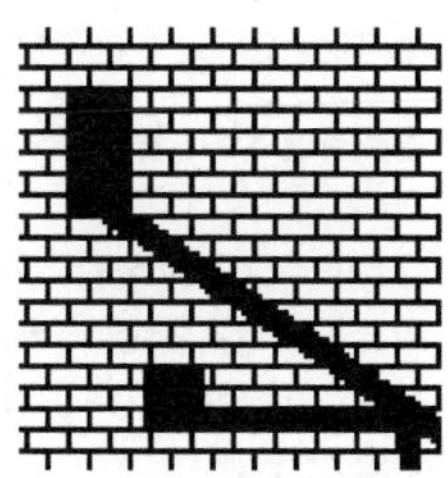

The Polygon tool also draws filled.

☐ **Double-click on the Straight Line tool and select the thinnest line width.**

☐ **Select the Polygon tool.**

☐ **Draw a parallelogram like the one shown here by clicking around its vertices in order, starting and ending at the same corner.**

Notice how the shape fills with the selected paint when you complete it.

☐ **Add triangular peaks to the two internal chambers by clicking around the triangles with the Polygon tool.**

This is a good time to save your work, just in case.

☐ **Press Command-K (or select Keep from the Paint menu).**

This picture clearly needs some labels.

Drawing Labels

☐ **Select the Rounded Rectangle tool.**

This tool works like the Rectangle tool except that the corners of the drawn shapes are rounded. We'll use it to create labels. The labels should be filled with paint to obscure the pyramid bricks, but black paint would not be appropriate.

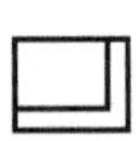

☐ **Select white paint from the Patterns palette.**

Even with the benefit of the HyperCard shape tools, it's difficult to make two shapes the same height. We can ensure that all of our labels are the same height, though, by forcing their edges to fall into some invisible grooves on the screen.

☐ **Select Grid from the Options menu.**

You'll notice the effect of the invisible grid as soon as you move the mouse around the card. Notice how the cross hairs jump from point to point rather than gliding smoothly across the screen.

> The grid is more effective than the human eyeball for aligning objects on the screen. When you turn on the grid with the Grid command, it stays on until you turn it off by selecting Grid again.

☐ **Draw four rounded rectangles like these:**

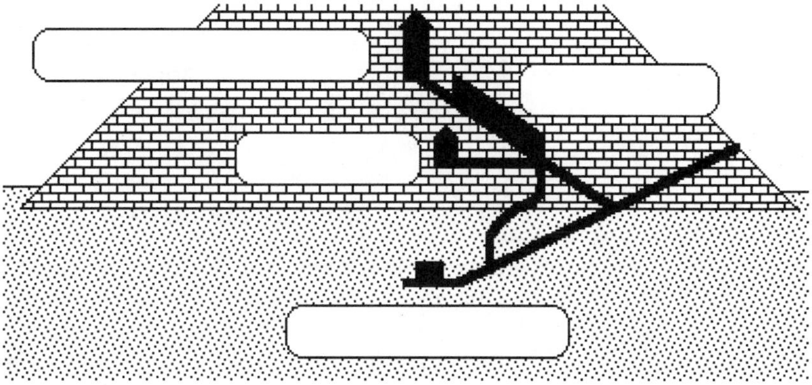

In addition to noticing the effect of the grid, note how the white paint fill obscures the pyramid bricks and the sand.

> There's a critical difference between white paint and no paint when it comes to filling a shape: A shape filled with white paint hides what it covers; an unfilled shape is transparent.

Now we can fill those shapes with text.

☐ **Double-click on the Paint Text tool (the letter *A*) to bring up the Text Styles dialog box.**

☐ **Select centered, 9-point, Geneva with all other styles turned off. Click OK.**

This combination will apply to all of the text you type until you change it.

☐ **Select the Paint Text tool, move the I-beam to the center of one of the rounded rectangles, click to position the pointer, and type. Repeat for the other labels in the following picture:**

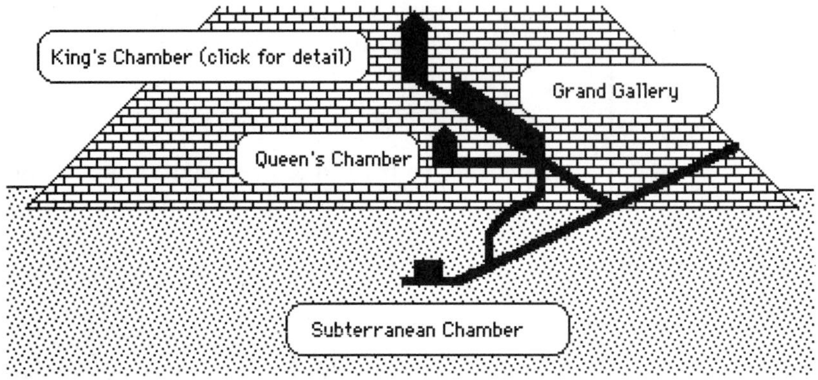

Creating an Invisible Button

Now let's provide our audience with a closer view of the King's Chamber.

☐ **Click on the Button tool in the Tools palette.**

☐ **Select New Button from the Objects menu.**

☐ **Drag this button so that it sits right on top of the King's Chamber.**

☐ **Stretch the corner so that it covers the chamber and the corresponding label completely.**

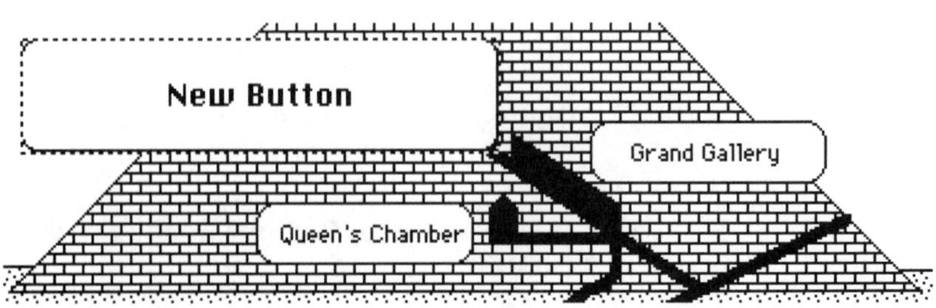

☐ **Double-click on the button to bring up the Button Info dialog box.**

We want the button and its name to be invisible.

☐ **Change the button style to Transparent.**

☐ **Click to turn *off* Show Name option.**

Because the button's name won't show up on the screen, it's not strictly necessary to change its name. Do it anyway.

> It's a good idea to name buttons and other objects, even if those names won't be visible to the user. Those names just might make it easier for you to figure out what's going on if you decide to change something later.

☐ **Type "King's Chamber".**

Before we tell this button where to go, let's specify a visual effect.

☐ **Click on the Tasks... button in the Button Info... dialog box.**

☐ **Scroll to the Visual Effect task icon and click on it.**

☐ **Scroll to "zoom open" and click on it.**

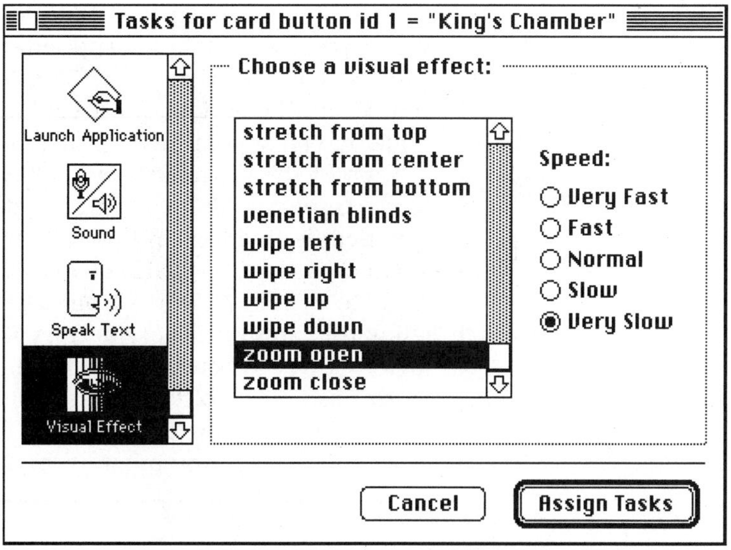

☐ **Click on Very Slow.**

Now it's time to link the button to another card.

☐ **Scroll back up through the icons until you see Go to Destination; click on it.**

We *could* just tell the button to go to the Next Card, the same way we did with our first button. That makes sense if we know that the King's Chamber card will always be the next card in the stack. But what if we later insert cards for the Queen's Chamber and the Grand Gallery? Those cards can't *all* be the card that immediately follows this card. To play it safe, we should create an absolute **link** between the button and the King's Chamber card. That way, even if the card moves or others are inserted in the stack, the button will always take the viewer to the King's Chamber card. Linking the button to the card is easy; it's just a matter of finding (or creating) the card and selecting "Current Card" as the destination.

Absolute and Logical Links

A button with "next card" as a destination uses a **logical reference** to transport the viewer to the next card, whatever it might be. A button linked to a card using the "current card" destination is hard-wired to the card by an **absolute reference**. Computer spreadsheet users deal with a similar distinction every day when working with formulas in cells. So do you, unconsciously, when a stranger asks you, "Where is the office for the local newspaper?" The absolute answer, "435 Madison Street," is helpful if your questioner wants to send letters that will reach the editor from any mailbox in town. The logical answer, "six blocks south" or "the end of the street," is more helpful if the questioner has an appointment to meet with the editor today.

Each of these reference types has advantages and disadvantages. Absolute links (Go to this card; Go Home) take you to the specified destination card no matter how many or which cards are in between. Logical links (Go Next, Go Last) allow you to add cards to or remove cards from a sequence without having to relink the cards on either side. As you'll see in the next session, a logical "Go Next" button installed in the background can replace many absolute "Go to this card" buttons installed on the card layer. You'll see how each of these button types can be used in other situations as you progress through this book.

Before we can link this button to a card, we have to create that card.

☐ **Select New Card from the Edit menu.**

Another white card will appear; this is the future home of the King's Chamber. Now you can finish assigning the button tasks by telling HyperCard that this card—the *current card*—is the absolute destination of the button.

☐ **Click on the button labeled Current Card in the dialog box.**

The link between the button and the card will be completed as soon as you officially assign the task.

☐ **Click on Assign Tasks.**

When you return to the cross-section card, your button is visible only in outline form.

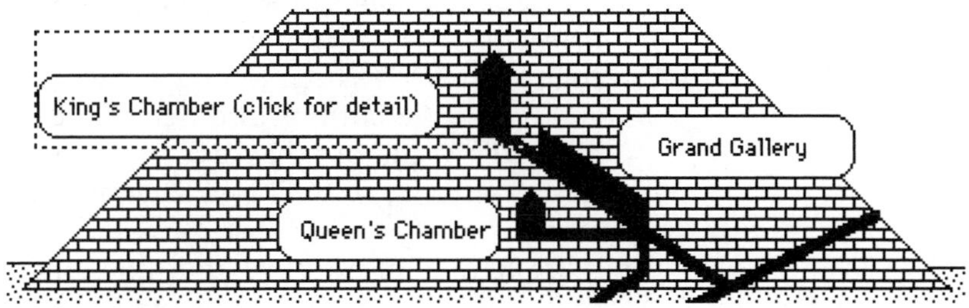

When you choose the Browse tool, the button will disappear altogether, but you'll know it's there because it will transport you to the new card when you click on it.

☐ **Press Command-Tab (or click on the Browse tool) and click on the King's Chamber.**

Drawing One Last Card

Now you need to fulfill the promise of the previous card by drawing a close-up view of the King's Chamber. Here's a sketch of what it might look like.

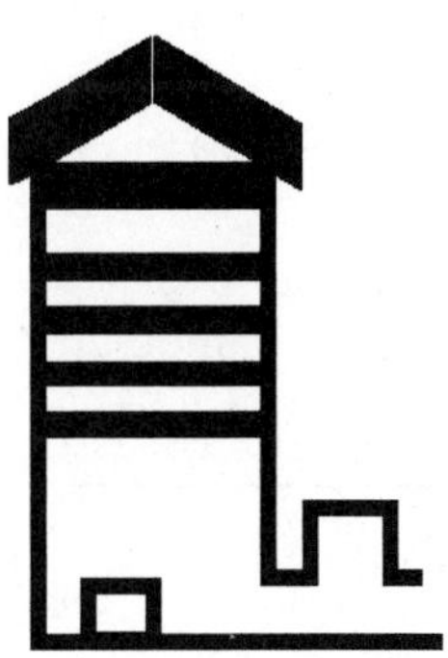

☐ **Use the Rectangle tool, the Polygon tool, the Straight Line tool, and the Eraser to draw a rough facsimile of this sketch on the blank card.**

Introducing Stackware Engineering

Software Engineering Simplified

Software engineering is a branch of computer science that concerns itself with applying the design principles of engineering to the art and science of computer programming. When an engineer designs a bridge, we can generally assume that it won't fall down if we walk across it; when an engineer designs a TV set, it's probably going to be easy enough to operate that we won't need to read a 300-page manual to use it. Similarly, if a computer program is well engineered, we should be able to assume that it works reliably and that it has a **user interface** that's easy to understand.

Unfortunately, much software isn't well designed when measured against these criteria. But there's no reason we can't apply some basic software engineering principles to the stacks we create to make them reliable and easy to understand.

The surest way to determine the reliability of the stack's performance is to test it thoroughly while you're building it and after it's completed. We've been testing as we go, but you should still go back and try all the buttons in different orders when the project is completed. This kind of exhaustive testing isn't always possible with large, complex stacks, so we'll look later at other ways to ensure stack reliability.

Designing an intuitive and functional user interface is a process that generally begins long before you sit down in front of the computer. But for this stack we'll simply look at the existing design and ask ourselves the question, "If I were a naive user with little or no HyperCard experience, what problems would I encounter with this stack?"

Adding Emergency Exits

Of course, we'll want to look at the screens as we answer this question. But it's also helpful to examine a flowchart or **map** of the stack:

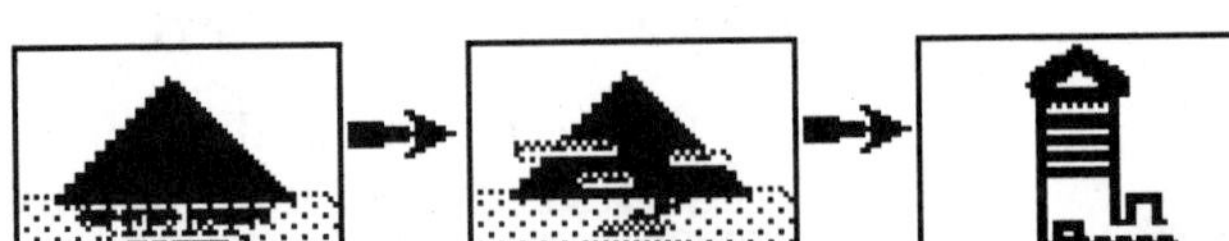

This diagram reveals a major design flaw: The stack is like a one-way street with a dead end; buttons lead you into the King's Chamber, but there's no button to take you out.

> Always give the user at least one exit from each card.

Let's add a button to return to the first card in the stack.

- ☐ **Select the Button tool.**
- ☐ **Select New Button from the Objects menu.**
- ☐ **Double-click on the button.**
- ☐ **Type "Click here to return".**
- ☐ **Click on the Tasks... button and select Go to Destination.**
- ☐ **Select the First Card destination.**

This provides a logical link to the first card. Like the Go First menu command, it will always go to the first card of the current stack.

Next we'll add a visual effect.

- ☐ **Scroll down to the Visual Effect icon and click on it.**
- ☐ **Select "zoom open" and click on Very Slow.**
- ☐ **Click on Assign Tasks.**
- ☐ **Finally, change the shape and location of the button so it looks like this:**

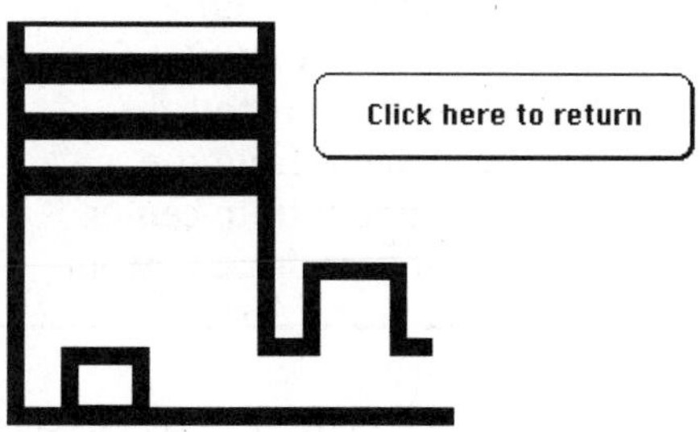

Now let's test the button.

- ☐ **Select the Browse tool (Command-Tab).**
- ☐ **Click on the new button.**

You should be back outside the pyramid on card 1.

You've used two different visual effects so far. Following is a complete list of the available effects:

HyperCard Visual Effects

Effect	*Suggested Use*
dissolve	for gradual transitions
iris open	go to a card providing more detail
iris close	return after an iris open
zoom open (or zoom out)	go to a card providing more detail
zoom close (or zoom in)	return after zoom open
wipe left	go to next card
wipe right	go to previous card
wipe up	go to next card
wipe down	go to previous card
scroll left	go to next card
scroll right	go to previous card
scroll up	go to next card
scroll down	go to previous card
push left	go to next card
push right	go to previous card
push up	go to next card
push down	go to previous card
barn door open	introduce a topic
barn door close	end a topic
checkerboard	use between cards with high contrast
venetian blinds	use between cards with high contrast
shrink to top	flip to next card
shrink to center	flip to next card
shrink to bottom	flip to next card
stretch from top	flip to previous card
stretch from center	flip to previous card
stretch from bottom	flip to previous card

Of course, these effects can be used in other ways; it pays to experiment. Changing the speed can change the impact of an effect, too.

Borrowing a Button

We're almost through; all that remains is to provide the naive user with a graceful way to exit the stack and go Home. We need another button, but we won't create this one from scratch.

☐ **Press Command-H (Go Home).**

Addresses

Home

☐ **Click on the Addresses icon to open the Addresses stack.**

☐ **Select the Button tool from the Tools palette.**

☐ **Click on the Home button to select it.**

☐ **Press Command-C (or select Copy Button from the Edit menu).**

Because the Button tool is selected, the Copy command now says Copy Button instead of Copy Picture. You now have a copy of the Home button on the Clipboard.

☐ **Press Command-~ twice to go back two cards, so you're looking at the pyramid again.**

☐ **Press Command-V (or select Paste Button).**

A shimmering copy of the Home button, complete with icon, should appear.

☐ **Drag this button to the lower right corner of the window.**

This is not just a lookalike button; it comes complete with instructions to make it do exactly what the original did: Take you home. Let's test it.

☐ **Select the Browse tool (Command-Tab).**

☐ **Click the new Home button.**

You're home! Now let's go back and install similar buttons on the other cards in the stack so our users have a convenient exit at any level.

☐ **Press Command-~ to return to your stack.**

☐ **Select the Button tool.**

☐ **Select the Home button you just added and press Command-C to copy it to the Clipboard.**

Actually, we already had a copy of the button in the Clipboard, but not in the right position.

> When a button is copied from a card to the Clipboard and pasted on another card, it appears in the same relative location on both cards (until you move it).

☐ **Press Command-3 to go to the next card in the stack.**

☐ **Press Command-V to paste another copy of the Home button onto this card.**

It should appear in just the right spot. You still have one card in your stack without a Home button.

☐ **Press Command-3 to go to the next (and last) card in the stack.**

☐ **Paste another Home button here.**

Here's a map of the stack as it now stands:

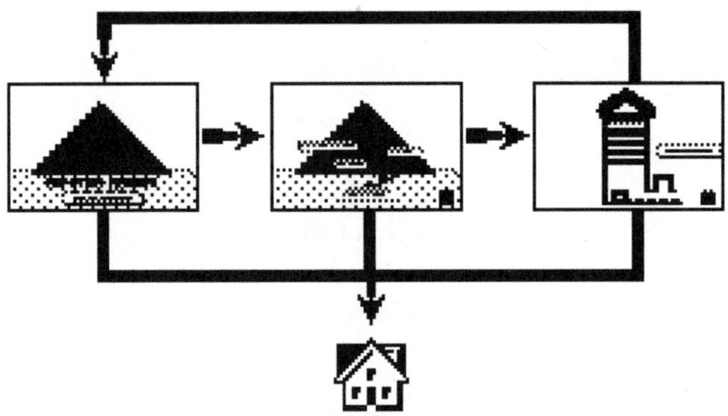

There's plenty more we could do to this stack: We could use the Eraser, the Paint Bucket, and the Pencil to soften the lines at the base of the pyramid; we could use the Spray Can with a sand-patterned paint to give the pyramid a weathered look; we could add buttons to the first card to reveal interesting facts, theories, and mysteries concerning the pyramid; we could add buttons to the cross section to zoom in on the other chambers of the pyramid—the possibilities are limited only by our creativity and time.

But that's enough for now. Take a couple of minutes to try out the stack, making sure that you understand what it's doing each time you click a button.

We've covered a lot of ground in this session. The tools and procedures you've used to build this stack can be used to build dynamic business charts, educational presentations, interactive tutorials, multilevel maps, and all kinds of other stacks. The exercises at the end of this session will suggest several projects that you might want to try on your own to practice your new skills. In the next session you'll learn more HyperCard tricks that will make it even easier to build your own stacks.

Summary

In this session we've focused on the fundamentals of stack construction. You learned how to create new stacks and new cards. You used the Pencil tool, the Straight Line tool, various shape tools, the Paint Bucket, the Paintbrush, and the Patterns palette to draw pictures on cards. You used the Clipboard, the Undo command, and the Eraser to edit those pictures. You practiced using paint text in a variety of styles, sizes, and alignments. You learned how to create buttons, label them, size them, position them, add visual effects, and link them to other cards. Finally, you learned how to copy buttons from other stacks into your own stack. Nice work!

Key Words

absolute reference (link)
alignment (text)
Auto Hilite (button)
bit
bit-mapped graphics
Brush Shape... command
Button Name
constraint (Shift) key
Copy Button command (Command-C)
Copy Picture command (Command-C)
Draw Filled command
Eraser tool
field text
font
general tools
Grid command
Keep command (Command-K)
Lasso
Line Size... command
link
logical reference (link)
map
New Button command
New Stack... command
Objects menu
Opaque (button style)
Oval (button style)
Paintbrush tool
Paint Bucket tool
paint text
Paint Text tool
paint tools
Paste Button command (Command-V)
Paste Picture command (Command-V)
Patterns menu
Patterns palette
Pencil tool
pixel
point (size)
Polygon tool
Rectangle tool
Revert command
Rounded Rectangle tool
Select All command (Command-A)
Select command (Command-S)
Selection rectangle
Show Name (button)
size (text)
software engineering
Straight Line tool
style (text)

Tasks... command	Tools menu
Tasks window	Tools palette
tear-off menu	Transparent (button style)
Text Style... command (Command-T)	user interface
	visual effect

Exercises

1. Under what conditions are the Paint and Objects menus visible?
2. What's the best way to draw a perfect square in HyperCard?
3. While putting the finishing touches on your drawing of Mom, you sneeze and make her ear way too big. Name two ways you can erase the offending line.
4. What's the fastest way to erase everything you've painted on the current card?
5. Describe how you can use the Clipboard to duplicate a button on a different card and to duplicate a portion of a picture on a different card.
6. List three visual effects, what they do, and suggested uses for each one.
7. What do each of these standard HyperCard tool icons represent?

   a. 

   b. 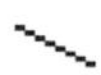

   c. 

   d. 

   e. 

   f. A

   g. 

   h. 

   i. 

   j. 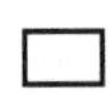

   k. 

8. Many of the tools shown in exercise 7 have a special meaning when double-clicked. Which special meanings can you remember?
9. Describe the difference between relative reference and absolute reference to another card. Under what circumstances would each of these be the most appropriate way to assign a button's destination?

Projects

1. Draw a tree chart showing the organization of the top levels of government. Your chart should contain a box labeled U.S. Constitution with three subordinate boxes representing the three government branches (executive, legislative, judicial). Create buttons for each of these subordinate boxes and link those buttons to cards that illustrate, describe, or subdivide those branches. Add a return button to each new card and a Home button to the main chart card.

2. Draw a map of a baseball field with buttons on each fielder's position linked to "baseball cards" for each of these fielders on your favorite team. Include return buttons on each card and a Home button on the baseball field card.

3. Draw a chart representing at least three generations of your family tree. Add a button to each node and link each button to a card containing a description of that family member. Include a return button on each card and a Home button on the main tree card.

4. Draw a flowchart representing the major components of a computer (input, CPU, output, storage device). Add buttons to each of the boxes and link those buttons to cards describing and illustrating those components. Include return buttons on each card and a Home button on the main card.

5. Draw a hyper-greeting card. On the first card of the stack, draw the outside of the card, complete with graphics and the first part of the message. Add a button with a "click here" message and link it to the inside of the card containing the punch line and signature. Now go back and modify the original button's message and add a second button to the outside of the card offering the recipient an alternative message ("click here if you're male" on one, "click here if you're female" on the other; "click here if you're over/under 40"; "click here if you want a plausible excuse/the truth," etc.). The two buttons should link to different inside cards with different messages; both of these cards should have Home buttons on them.

6. Draw a map of your house, school, or dorm. Place a transparent button on your room that will reveal a close-up view of your room. Add a return button to the close-up and a Home button to the original map. Variations: Draw expandable maps of your city, your state, your country, the world, the solar system, or the galaxy.

Session 4

By the end of this session you should be able to

- Use all the HyperCard paint tools and understand how the effects of many of these tools can be modified by menu commands and various keystroke combinations
- Use HyperCard's background layer to give cards in your stack a consistent look
- Create a stack with multiple backgrounds
- Design and build a complex network of cards to simulate a real-world environment

HyperCard's Hidden Layers

Backgrounds and Backtracking

The Problem

Your cousin Andy—the smart one—is spending tomorrow afternoon at your house. You have no time for playing games with him; you're busy learning HyperCard. But you expect he'll leave you little choice unless you provide him with something interesting to do. What you'd like to do is throw Andy in a dungeon that's full of so many rooms and passages that it would take him all afternoon to find his way back to you. Perhaps HyperCard can help.

Introduction

You know how to build stacks now, but you still haven't learned about some of HyperCard's most impressive and useful stack-building tools. The paint box is full of surprises, both fun and practical. And all of the paint tools become doubly useful once you learn how to take advantage of HyperCard's multiple layers.

Every card has two layers—a transparent **card layer** and a **background layer**—and you can put text, graphics, and buttons on either layer. This simple idea is one of HyperCard's most powerful concepts. Unfortunately, many beginners also find it to be among HyperCard's most puzzling concepts. But as you work through this session's project, you'll find that those layers are crystal clear—and convenient, too.

This session's project is more complex than the last one. Consequently, there are more ways things can go wrong. So we'll spend some time looking at ways we can design the stack that will minimize the chances of errors.

Some Background on Backgrounds

Let's start by looking behind the scenes at Home to see how backgrounds work in a familiar environment.

Examining Home's Backgrounds

☐ **Double-click on your Home stack icon to open HyperCard.**

☐ **Choose Background from the Edit menu.**

(If your Edit menu doesn't have a Background command, your user level is probably not set at authoring; change that on the last card of the Home stack as before.)

You should see two changes:

1. The text and icons have vanished from the Home card, leaving some buttons at the bottom of the window and the word Home at the top.

2. The menu bar has grown candy **stripes**.

The stripes are there to remind you that you're looking not at a card but at a background.

- ☐ **Use the right-arrow key to browse through the stack while in background mode.**

You'll see the background for each card in the stack. In this stack each card has a unique background, but all the backgrounds have common design elements. Contrast this with the Addresses stack used in Session 2, in which almost all the cards share a common fill-in-the-blanks background.

- ☐ **Select Background from the Edit menu again, or use the keyboard shortcut, Command-B, to return to the card (foreground) layer.**

The Benefits of Backgrounds

In most stacks, the same background is shared by several, sometimes all, of the cards. There are practical and aesthetic advantages to designing a stack this way:

- It saves stack creation time because you don't need to create or copy common elements on many different cards; you can build them once in the common background.
- It saves space on disk and in memory because the stack isn't filled with redundant elements.
- It usually results in a more consistent user interface, which helps the user to find her way around.
- It gives the stack a more consistent, appealing look.

When we built the Pyramid stack, we left the background plain white and focused on the card layer. In this session we'll create a stack with several different backgrounds to maximize efficiency.

A HyperCard Adventure

Let's build a HyperCard dungeon to occupy cousin Andy. The dungeon will have all kinds of rooms linked together by doors, windows, and secret passages . . . and only one way out.

This is one variation on a popular kind of computer game known as the **adventure game.** An adventure game is a computer **simulation** of a real or not-so-real environment and situation. Early adventure games were text-based **interactive fiction** in which the reader typed commands telling the main character what to do. Most modern adventure games are more like interactive movies, using graphics instead of text to show the setting and develop the plot of the game.

A graphic adventure game is a perfect project for HyperCard; each room can be represented on one or more cards in a stack; hidden buttons can transport the player to other rooms. To save time and minimize duplication, we can create generic rooms in the background layer and fill in the details on the card layer.

Starting a Stack

> This session is more time-consuming than any that have come before. You'll spend much of your time in this chapter working with HyperCard's graphics tools in the card layer and the background layer. If you're in a hurry and not particularly interested in HyperCard graphics, you might want to skim through this session, skipping the hands-on material and focusing on the reminder boxes. If the concepts seem clear (especially the concept of layered objects), you should be able to jump right into the next session.
>
> If you decide to proceed with this session, be forewarned: Creating a maze can be as confusing as navigating a maze. If you don't pay attention and carefully follow every step of this process, you may become as lost as your intended audience. Check each step with a pencil as you complete it so you can be sure that you don't skip any steps. Focus on understanding the structure of the stack more than on making the graphics perfect. If you're working on a complex graphic, use the Keep command (Command-K) regularly to save your work in progress, so you don't risk losing your train of thought while you reconstruct a spoiled picture. Pay attention to whether you're in the card layer or the background layer throughout the session (the striped bar in the margin of this text indicates work in the background). If you don't understand why you're doing something, read ahead to find out. If you lose your bearings, backtrack through the steps until you find the point where you wandered off the path. If, in spite of everything, your stack becomes hopelessly botched, don't despair. If you don't have time to start fresh, simply read through the rest of the session, focusing on understanding the underlying concepts.

☐ **Select New Stack... from the File menu.**

Navigate to an appropriate disk and folder for saving a stack. Also, make sure neither of the check boxes is marked—you don't want your new stack to use the Home card's background, and you don't need to keep Home open in a separate window.

☐ **Type "Dungeon" and press Return.**

We now have the simplest stack of all: one card with a transparent card layer and an all-white background. Let's gather our tools and go to work on the background.

☐ **Tear off the Tools menu and place it in the upper right corner of the screen.**

☐ **Click on any paint tool to make the paint menus (Paint, Options, Patterns) appear.**

☐ **Drag the Patterns menu to the left side of the screen directly opposite the Tools palette.**

Drawing in the Background

☐ **Press Command-B (or select Background from the Edit menu).**

Every good adventure game needs an enticing introduction, preferably scrawled on a tattered scroll. So let's create a scroll in the background.

> It's easy to forget to change to the background layer, so always check the menu for stripes to make sure you are working in the background.

All of the paint tools work in the background just as they do in the card layer. Let's start by drawing one edge of our scrolled message:

☐ **Select the Pencil and draw a three-inch squiggly line something like the one shown at the left.**

If you don't get it right the first time, remember Command-Z, the Undo command.

☐ **Use the Selection rectangle to select the line and drag it until it's close to the Patterns palette but not hidden by it.**

That's the left side of the scroll; we need another line just like this one for the other side. We *could* copy and paste one, but we'll use the Option key to clone it instead.

☐ **Hold down the Shift and Option keys and drag the selected line until it's near, but not touching, the Tools palette.**

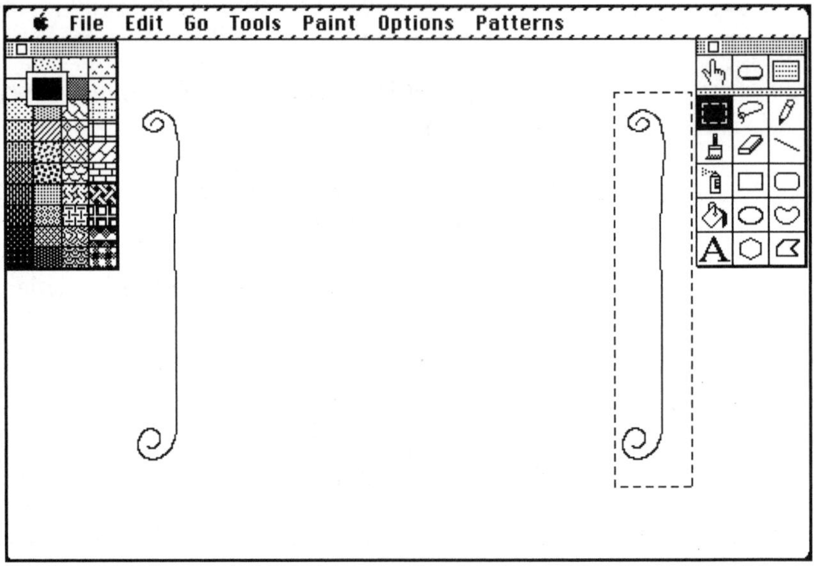

When Dragging a Selected Graphic Object

- The Shift key constrains the movement to horizontal or vertical only.
- The Option key leaves a copy behind.
- If you hold down the Command key and drag the *edge* of the object, the object doesn't move; it stretches or shrinks.
- If you hold down the Command and Shift keys and drag the *corner* of the object, the object stretches or shrinks while maintaining its original proportions.

Note: **Stretching** or **shrinking** bit-mapped graphics usually results in distortion, especially if you don't maintain proportions.

We have the sides; now let's draw the top and bottom of the scroll.

☐ **Use the Straight Line tool to connect the tops of the two lines.**

Remember the trick from the last session: If you hold down the Shift key when you drag between two points, you'll find that it's a cinch to draw perfectly horizontal (or vertical) lines.

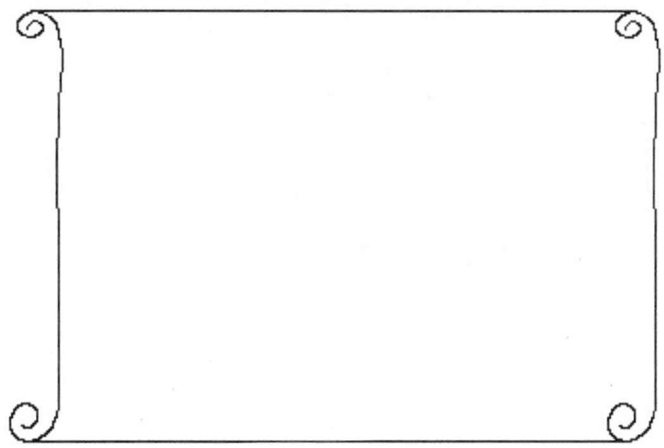

It's a start, but it's still not a scroll.

☐ **Add straight lines to the two left scroll corners, like this:**

Now we need to eliminate the curls from the right side of the scroll using the Eraser and the Pencil. The Eraser's large, square shape makes it awkward for that kind of fine detail work. We can't make the Eraser smaller, but we can make the details of the picture bigger.

☐ **Select the Pencil tool, hold down the Command key, and click once on the upper right corner of your scroll.**

You're telling HyperCard to zoom in for a close-up view of that part of the picture. You can also zoom in for a magnified view by first clicking on the target spot and then double-clicking on the Pencil tool.

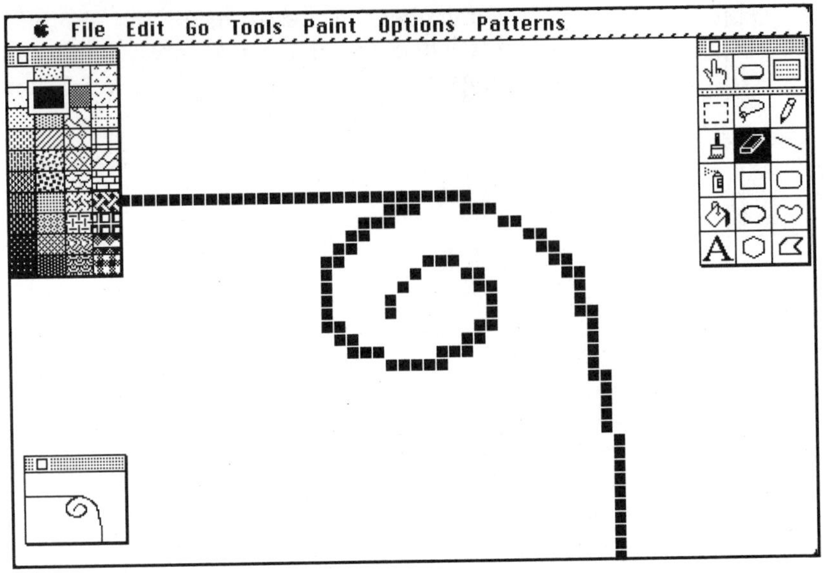

The Options menu command for doing the same thing is called **FatBits**. It's easy to see why, if you remember that each pixel (dot) on HyperCard's bit-mapped screen is represented by a bit in the computer's memory. In FatBits each of these bits is exactly eight times fatter than normal. The small window in the corner of the screen displays a normal magnification view of the same portion of your picture.

☐ **Use the Pencil and/or the Eraser to remove the unwanted curl from the picture.**

☐ **Hold down the Option key and use the Hand tool to drag the magnified picture up so that you can follow the scroll edge down to the curl in the lower right corner.**

☐ **Remove the unwanted curl in the lower right corner of the scroll.**

☐ **If necessary, use FatBits to touch up the other two corners of your scroll, making sure that all the lines connect.**

☐ **Exit FatBits by clicking in the small normal view window (or select FatBits from the Options menu).**

FatBits Tips

- The Pencil is probably the most useful FatBits tool because it allows you to turn each pixel on or off with just a touch. As usual, the Pencil draws black if you start on a white pixel and white if you start on black.

- The Eraser is also helpful because in FatBits it is much smaller relative to a pixel than it is in normal magnification.
- The other paint tools work in FatBits, but some may seem unwieldy at that magnification level.
- If you hold down the Option key while in FatBits, the pointer turns into a hand that you can use to drag the magnified picture so the FatBits window reveals a different part of the picture.
- The picture is shown actual size in the small window.
- You can return to normal magnification by clicking on the small normal view window or by selecting FatBits again or by holding down the Command key and clicking anywhere in the window.

Let's add a background pattern to this background layer.

☐ **Select a medium gray pattern.**

☐ **Use the Paint Bucket tool to paint the area surrounding the scroll.**

Before you do anything else, check to make sure that only the area around the scroll was painted. If part of the scroll changed, you'll need to select Undo, fix the leak, and repaint the areas.

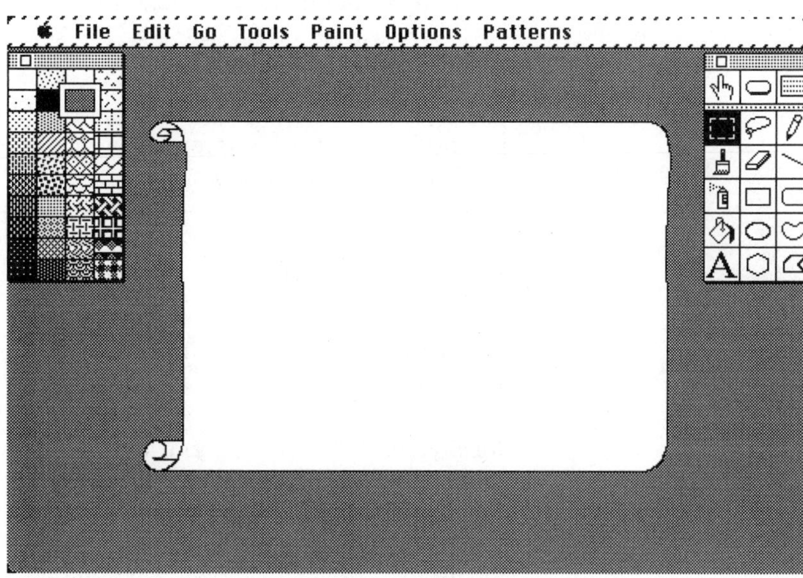

If you like, you can return to this background layer later to add some weathering and shading around the edges with the Spray Can and other tools. For now, let's leave the background and add words and a button to the card layer.

☐ **Press Command-B (or select Background from Edit).**

The only change you should notice is that the candy stripes vanished in the menu bar. We're now working in the card layer, but everything looks the same because *the card layer is transparent until you put something on it.*

If you missed the warnings at the beginning of this section, you might have just realized that you were drawing in the wrong layer. Don't worry; it happens to everybody, and it's easy to fix.

Oops! Wrong Layer!

If you create a drawing on the card layer that should have been in the background, you can move it like this:

1. In the card layer, double-click on the lasso to select everything that's drawn in that layer.

2. Press Command-X (Cut Picture).
3. Press Command-B (Background).
4. Press Command-V (Paste Picture).

In general, any graphic, button, or field can be moved from the card layer to the background (or vice versa) by selecting, cutting, changing layers, and pasting.

Creating Titles

☐ **Double-click on the Paint Text tool to bring up the Text Styles dialog box.**

Ideally, we'd like to use a font that looks as if it was drawn by a medieval scribe. Such fonts exist, but not in the standard system package. We'll use London, but you can choose any font in your System in a large size. (Remember that the sizes available to your System for a font are listed in the dialog box when you select that font.)

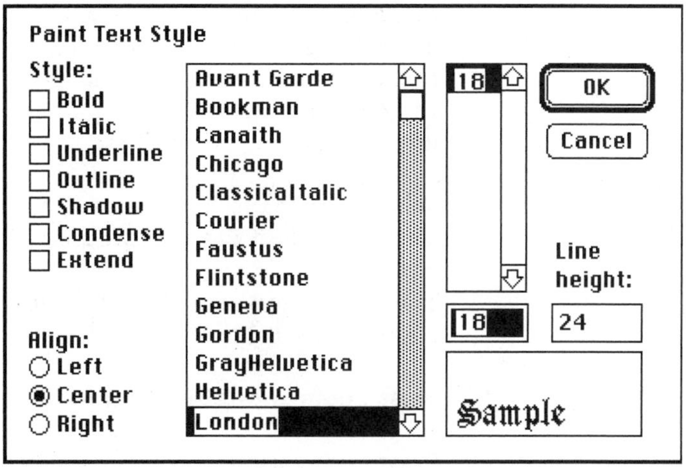

- ☐ **Select a font; then select the largest available size for your chosen font.**

- ☐ **Select Center alignment and click OK.**

When you put away this dialog box, you'll find that the Paint Text tool is automatically selected; HyperCard is anticipating your needs.

- ☐ **Click about a half-inch from the top of your scroll near the center.**

- ☐ **Type something like this, pressing Return at the end of each line:**

Since you're working with paint text, you don't have access to all of the conveniences of field text. Specifically, you can't assume that the text will automatically wrap around to the next line when one line is full, and you don't have the wealth of text-editing tools that we used in Session 2. If you make an error, your only recourse is to backspace to the offending characters and retype the remainder of the text. Once you reposition the insertion point or select another tool, your text is dried paint.

☐ **When you have typed your text, press Command-B to take another look at the background.**

The background doesn't contain any of the words you typed; it's still clean and available for use on your next card.

☐ **Press Command-B to return to the card layer.**

☐ **Press Command-N to create a new card.**

You're whisked out of the background layer and onto a new card that looks just like the old one, except that this one contains no text.

> When you create a new card with the New Card command (Command-N), the new card shares a background with the current card and is positioned directly after it in the stack.

Let's add some text to this card.

☐ **Double-click on the Paint Text tool, select Left alignment, and click OK.**

☐ **Position the insertion bar near the upper left corner of the scroll and type the following, pressing Return after each line:**

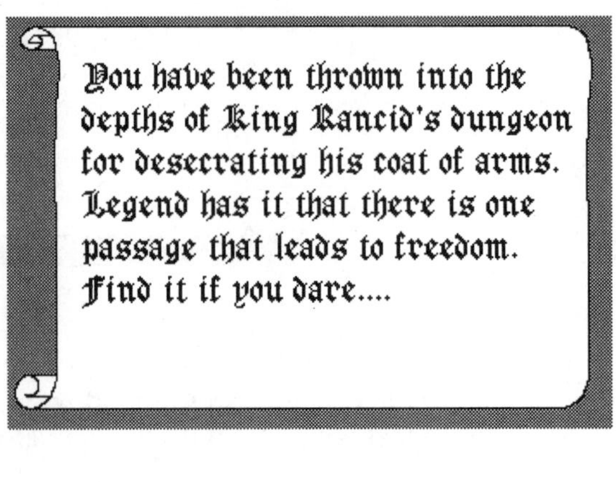

You have been thrown into the
depths of King Rancid's dungeon
for desecrating his coat of arms.
Legend has it that there is one
passage that leads to freedom.
Find it if you dare....

Borrowing a Background Button

We have two introductory cards, but no buttons to link the cards to each other and to the game. We *could* put a button on each card specifically linked to the following card, just as we did in the last session. But since these two cards share a background, it makes more sense to install one "Go to the next card" button in the background layer that will service both cards.

☐ **Press Command-B to go to the background.**

☐ **Select the Button Tool.**

☐ **Choose New Button from the Objects menu.**

☐ **Drag the button to a position near the bottom center of the scroll.**

We'll use a nameless, borderless icon to give this button a medieval look.

☐ **Double-click on the button to open the Button Info dialog box.**

☐ **Choose Transparent style and turn off the Show Name option.**

☐ **Name the button "Next Page". (This step is optional.)**

☐ **Click on the Icon... button in the dialog box.**

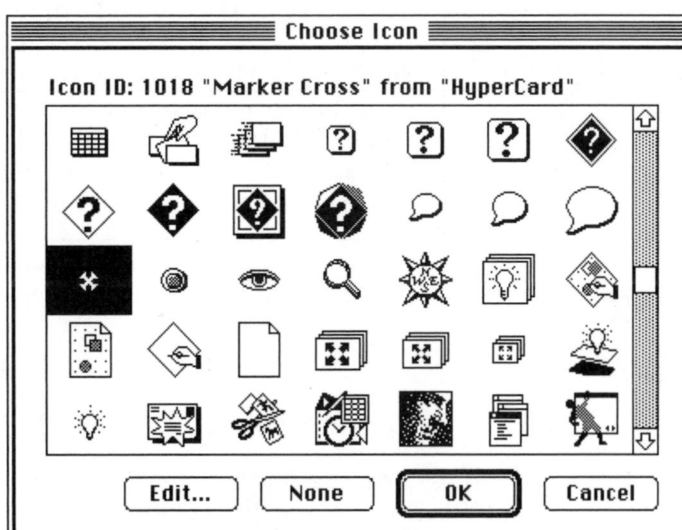

☐ **Scroll through the icons, select an appropriate icon for the period, and click OK.**

☐ **Click on Tasks....**

☐ **Scroll to the Visual Effect task icon and click on it.**

☐ **Select stretch from center and slow.**

The transition effect is set; now we need a destination.

☐ **Scroll up through the icons and select Go to Destination.**

☐ **Select Next Card.**

☐ **Click on Assign Tasks.**

☐ **Click on OK to close the Button Info dialog box.**

This button should now take you to the next card in the stack no matter where you are. Let's try it.

☐ **Press Command-B to leave the background.**

☐ **Press Command-Tab to select the Browse tool (the pointing hand).**

☐ **Click on the button to try it.**

Logical Links in the Background

Recall that a button created with the Go to Next Card procedure is not hard-wired to a particular card by an absolute reference; it uses a logical reference to go to the next card, whatever it happens to be. A logical "Go Next" button in the background, like this one, can replace many buttons on the card layer.

Break Point

Creating a New Background

Our next card will be the first room of the dungeon. If we simply select New Card, the card we create will have the scroll background. We need to tell HyperCard to create a new card with a new background.

- ☐ **Go to the last card in the stack by pressing Command-4.**

- ☐ **Select New Background from the Objects menu.**

The menu bar is striped to indicate that we're working in the background—a new background that we'll use for the next few cards. We want to create a sort of generic dungeon room that can be customized in the card layer for different rooms in the dungeon.

> The **New Background** command creates a new card with a new background directly after the current card.

- ☐ **Select the Rectangle tool.**

- ☐ **Double-check the menu bar to make sure you're in the background. Then draw a rectangle like this in the center of the screen:**

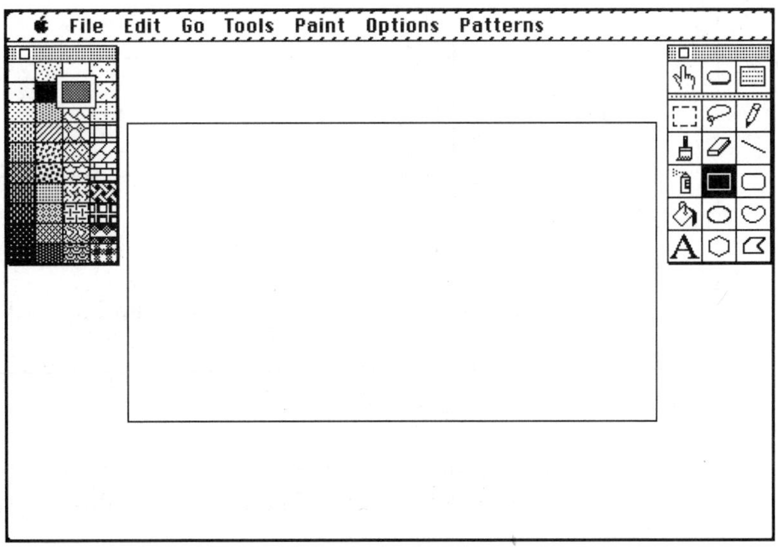

Use the Patterns palette and the Tools palette as guides when you're creating your rectangle. The exact size isn't important, as long as you do your best to center it.

- ☐ **Use the Straight Line tool to draw lines from each corner of the rectangle to the corresponding corner of the window.**

For the top two corners on small-screen Macs, you'll need to drag the line behind the menu bar to the absolute corner of the screen.

> The top of a card may be obscured by the menu bar, but it's still there. You can press Command-Space to temporarily hide the menu bar so you can see what you're painting.

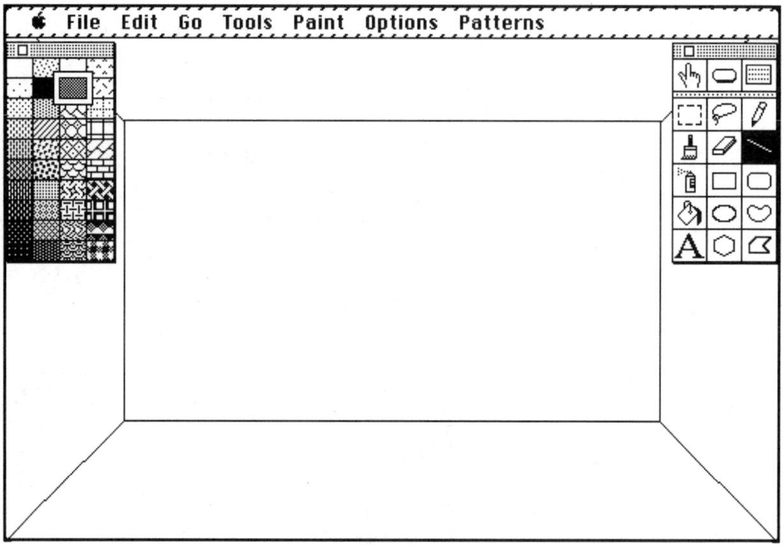

We now have three walls, a ceiling, and a floor, but they need paint.

- ☐ **Select the Paint Bucket tool and a medium gray paint pattern.**

- ☐ **Pour that paint into the bottom (floor) and top (ceiling) sections of your picture.**

- ☐ **Select an irregular dot pattern or a light gray pattern and paint the three remaining sections with the Paint Bucket.**

It's tempting to use the brick paint for the walls, but if we use that or any other regular pattern on the side walls, the illusion of perspective we've created will be shattered.

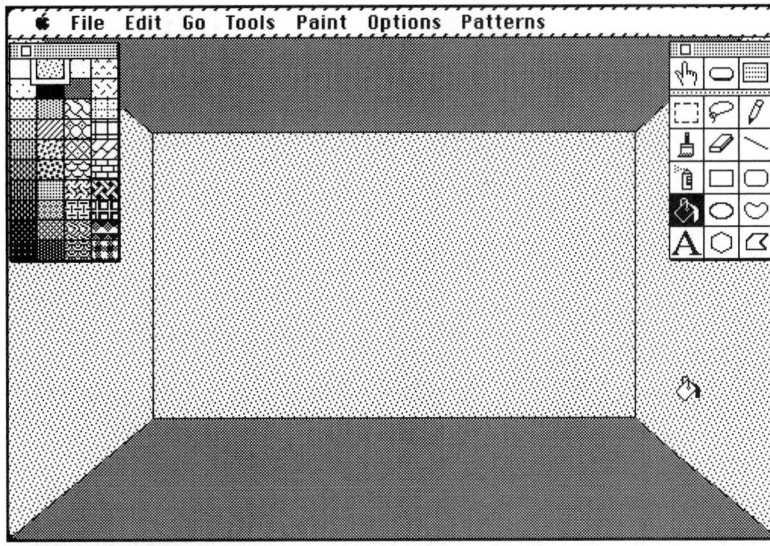

The generic room background is finished and ready to be customized on the card layer.

☐ **Press Command-B to leave the background.**

Shaping Doors and Windows

Let's start with a door.

☐ **Double-click on the Rectangle tool (or choose Draw Filled from the Options menu).**

☐ **Select a likely-looking pattern for the door.**

☐ **Select the Rectangle tool.**

☐ **Draw a door in the far wall of the room, like this:**

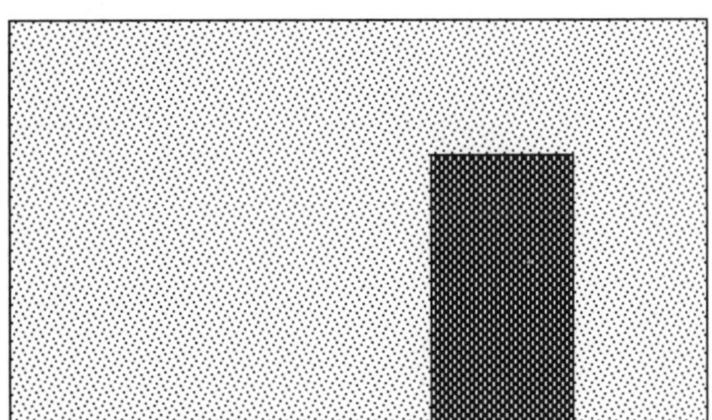

Notice how the door obscures the background.

> Objects drawn on the card layer hide anything behind them in the background layer (unless you specify that the object is transparent).

If this is truly a dungeon, it should have a barred window on the door. We could draw a window and then draw bars, but we can do a better job faster by creating a bar pattern.

☐ **Double-click on the black pattern in the Patterns palette (or choose Edit Pattern... from the Options menu).**

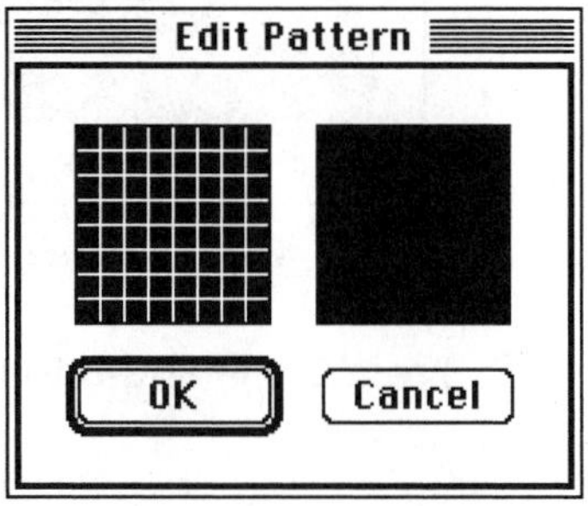

The box on the left shows you the currently selected pattern close-up; the one on the right shows it at normal size.

You can edit this pattern by clicking or dragging on the pixels in the left box; the results are immediately reflected on the right.

☐ **Draw the pattern shown here and then click OK:**

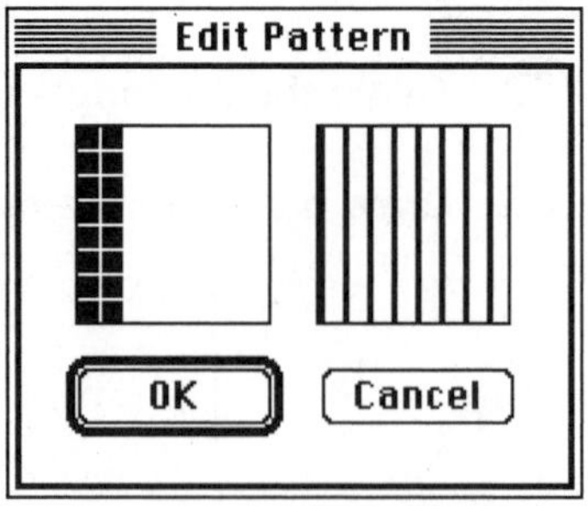

Notice how the original pattern has been replaced in the palette.

☐ **Select the new pattern and draw a rectangle in the center of the door like this:**

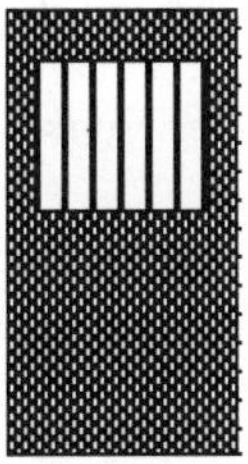

Now, in the spirit of covering our tracks, we should put that pattern back the way we found it.

☐ **Double-click on the bar pattern and edit it so it's all black again. Click OK.**

Let's add one more door to the side wall.

☐ **Drag the Patterns palette below the Tools palette.**

☐ **On the left wall draw a black rectangle that's taller and thinner than the first door.**

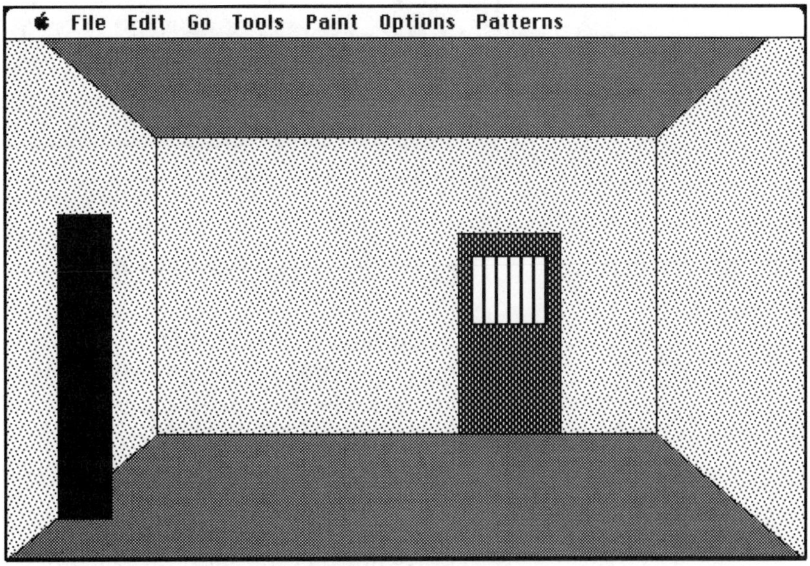

☐ **Use the Selection tool (the dashed rectangle) to select the black rectangle. (Make the marquee as close to the actual size and door as you can make it without leaving any part of the door out of the selection.)**

Now we can apply a special paint effect to the selected area.

☐ **Select Perspective from the Options menu.**

The corners of the selected rectangle should have handles.

☐ **Drag the upper right corner of the rectangle down and the lower right corner up, changing the shape of the rectangle into a parallelogram, like this:**

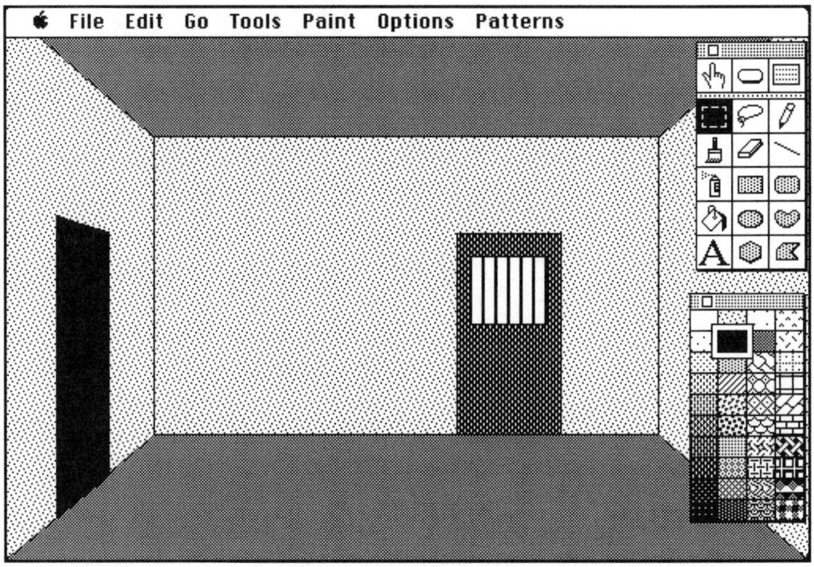

The **Rotate**, **Slant**, **Distort**, and **Perspective** commands in the Options menu can be applied to any area of a picture selected with the Selection tool. Each command produces handles on the selected rectangle; the handles can be dragged to produce the desired effect. Because HyperCard graphics are bit-mapped, the effect may take considerable time to appear and any text or fine graphics in the area may be distorted. **Rotate Right** and **Rotate Left** (Paint menu) quickly rotate any selected graphic, rectangular or not, 90 degrees.

Note: To simulate three-dimensional space in two-dimensional drawings, artists must follow certain rules of perspective. The Perspective command will not produce realistic three-dimensional perspective unless you also follow those rules.

This will be the door into the other chamber of our luxury dwelling. We need a button to take us there.

Creating a Two-Way Link

☐ **Select the Button tool.**

☐ **Select New Button from the Objects menu.**

☐ **Drag and reshape the button so that it covers the door on the left wall:**

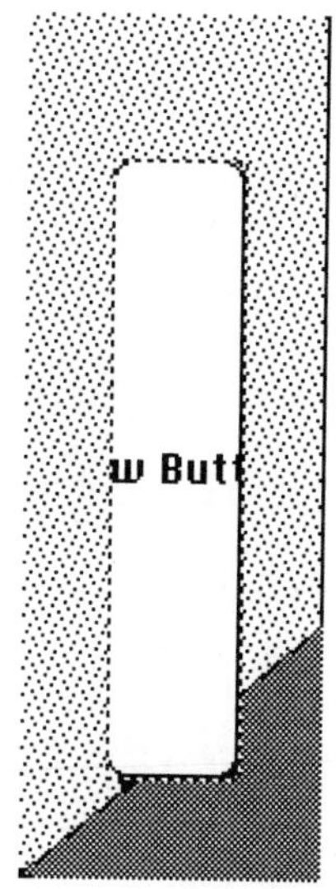

☐ **Double-click on the button.**

Follow these familiar steps to fill in the dialog box:

☐ **Click on the Show Name check box to turn it off.**

☐ **Choose Transparent from the Style pop-up menu.**

☐ **Type "room 1 door". (This step is optional.)**

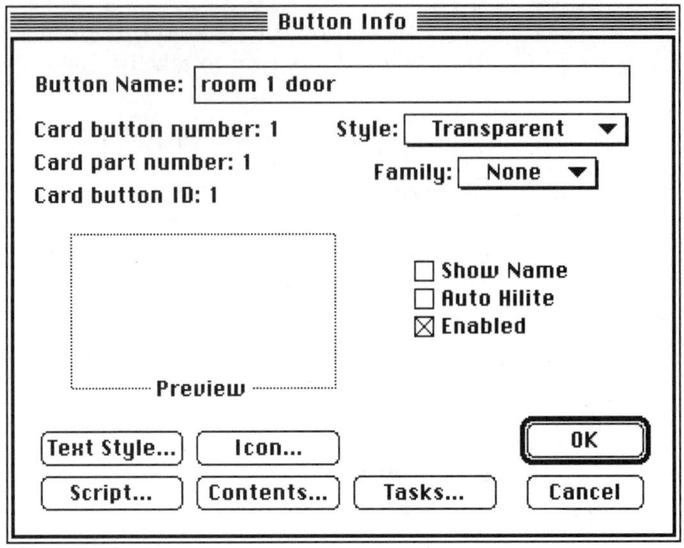

- ☐ **Click on Tasks... and scroll down to Visual Effect.**

- ☐ **Select scroll right.**

All that remains is to link the button.

- ☐ **Select the Go to Destination task icon.**

- ☐ **Press Command-N (or select New Card from the Edit menu).**

The new card has the generic room background and is located after the starting room card in the stack.

- ☐ **Click on the Current Card radio button to link the button to this new card.**

- ☐ **Press Return to close the dialog box.**

You're back in the starting room. As long as we're back in this room, let's borrow the black door so we can make it visible in the new room.

- ☐ **Hold down the Command key while dragging the selection rectangle around the black door.**

Holding down the Command Key forces the Selection rectangle to select only the door.

- ☐ **Press Command-C (Copy Picture).**

☐ **Press Command-3 (Next).**

☐ **Press Command-V (Paste Picture).**

We've put the door into the next room, but it's backward.

☐ **Choose Flip Horizontal from the Paint menu.**

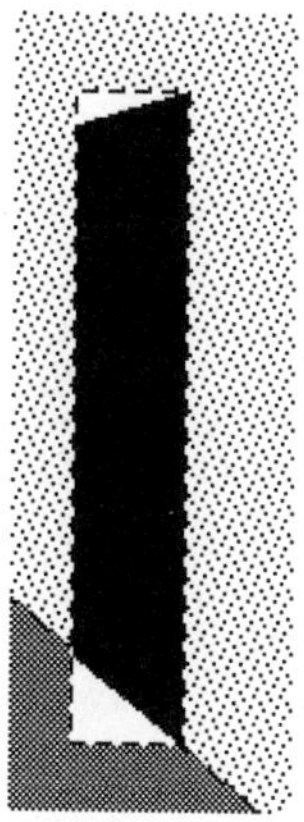

☐ **Move the Tools and Patterns palettes out of the way and drag the door until it's positioned in the center of the right wall.**

The white areas are there because the selected picture is opaque; you can't see the background through it.

☐ **Select Transparent from the Paint menu.**

> The **Transparent** command allows the background to show through the nonblack portions of the selected graphic; **Opaque** turns those portions white so they hide the background. Neither command has any effect on buttons or fields.

Now the door is visible from both sides of the wall. But as it stands now, it's a one-way trip. We need to place an invisible button on the back side of the door that links back to the first room.

☐ **Click on the Button tool.**

☐ **Select New Button from the Objects menu.**

☐ **Drag and reshape the new button so that it covers the door.**

☐ **Double-click on the button to bring up the Button Info dialog box.**

☐ **Click on Show Name in the dialog box to turn it off.**

☐ **Select Transparent style.**

☐ **Type "room 2 door". (This step is optional.)**

☐ **Click on Tasks... and select Visual Effect.**

☐ **Click on scroll left.**

☐ **Select the Go to Destination task icon.**

This time you won't create a new card. This button should take you back to the card right before this one in the stack.

☐ **Press Command-2 (Go Prev).**

☐ **Click on the Current Card button and press Return.**

☐ **Press Command-Tab (Browse tool) and test the door both ways.**

Break Point

Building Portable Furniture

No good dungeon is complete without a secret passage. Let's build a bed and hide our passage underneath. We'll start by drawing a pillow.

☐ **Go to the last card in the stack (the room with only one door).**

☐ **Choose a pattern for the pillow.**

☐ **Select the Curve tool.**

The Curve tool works pretty much like the Pencil, except that the drawn shape fills automatically if Draw Filled is selected.

☐ **Draw a pillow anywhere, as long as it doesn't touch the door.**

(We're in the card layer, and the door is the only other painted object on this layer. As long as we don't put the pillow on the door, we can move it where we want later.)

If you can see the background pattern through your pillow, HyperCard thinks you want everything on this card layer to be transparent. Here's how to fix that.

☐ **Double-click on the Lasso to select all graphics in this layer.**

☐ **Select Opaque from the Paint menu.**

(If you had double-clicked on the Selection rectangle instead of the Lasso, the entire area inside the rectangle, including the area between graphic objects, would become opaque, hiding the background completely.)

Now let's draw the bed.

- ☐ **Choose a pattern for the ends of the bed.**

- ☐ **Use the (filled) Rectangle tool to create a rectangle in the corner of the room, like the top one in this picture.**

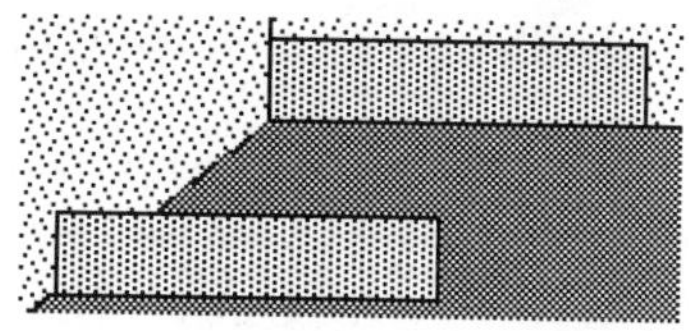

- ☐ **Choose Select from the Paint menu to select the new rectangle.**

- ☐ **Option-drag the rectangle to create the other end of the bed.**

- ☐ **Select the Polygon tool.**

- ☐ **Choose a pattern for the bedspread.**

- ☐ **Click around the corners of the top of the bed ends to create the shape for the top of the bed.**

  When you click on the first point a second time, the shape should fill.

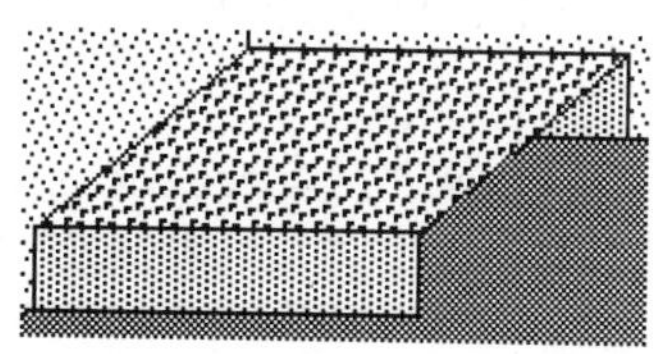

- ☐ **Click on the corners of the side of the bed to define its shape.**

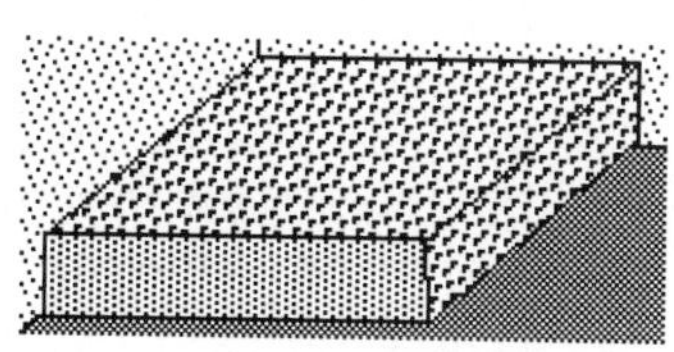

- ☐ **Select the Lasso tool.**

- ☐ **Drag a line around the outside of the pillow without actually touching the edge of it.**

  You don't need to drag all the way around the pillow; if you go most of the way and let go, the two ends of your curve will be connected automatically. When you let go, every painted object that's within the Lasso line in the card layer is selected, but none of the empty space between the objects or around the pillow is selected. The Lasso is a shrink-to-fit tool.

☐ **Drag the selected pillow onto the bed.**

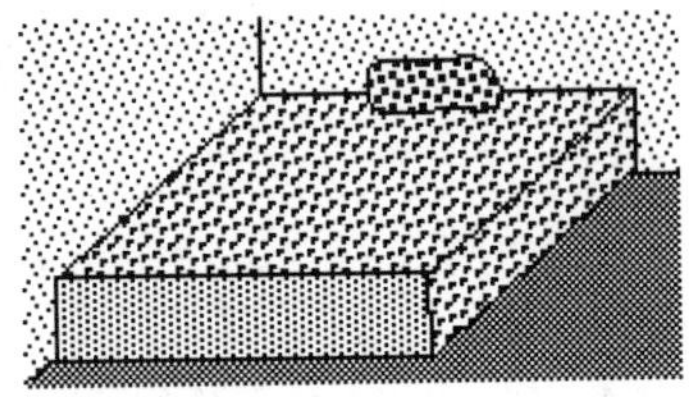

The Lasso is a particularly useful tool for selecting irregularly shaped objects, but it's not the only way. Let's revise the list of selection techniques we started in the last session:

HyperCard Graphic Selection Techniques

Most of the commands in the Paint and Options menus work only when part or all of a graphics layer is selected. There are many tricks for selecting particular kinds of graphics. Here are the most important:

- To select the entire graphics layer of the card or background, double-click on the Selection rectangle *or* use the Select All command (Command-A).
- To select all of the graphic objects in the card or background layer without selecting the whole layer, double-click on the Lasso *or* use the Select command (Command-S).
- To select the most recently painted object (before you click elsewhere), do nothing (it's automatically selected) unless you want to move it; in that case, use the Select command (Command-S).
- To select a rectangular area of the current layer, use the Selection rectangle. Hold down the Command key to make the selected rectangle shrink to the edges of the graphic objects inside it.
- To select an irregularly shaped area in the current layer, use the Selection rectangle with the Option key held down, *or* use the Lasso, *or* use the Select command after selecting an object with the Selection rectangle.

Moving Furniture

If the secret passage is under the bed, we want to be able to move the bed with a click. We'll do that by linking a bed-sized button to a new card just like the current card, but with the bed in a different location. Repeat the now familiar steps for creating a linked button.

☐ **Select the Button tool.**

☐ **Select New Button from Objects.**

☐ **Drag and stretch the new button so it covers the bed, more or less.**

☐ **Double-click on the button to open the Button Info dialog box.**

☐ **Select Transparent style.**

☐ **Click on Show Name to turn off that option.**

☐ **Type "bed" (optional).**

☐ **Click on Tasks... and select Visual Effect.**

☐ **Click on wipe right.**

☐ **Select Go to Destination.**

☐ **Press Command-N (New Card).**

☐ **Click on Current Card, then press Return to assign the tasks.**

☐ **Double-click on the Lasso to select all the objects in this layer.**

You can easily copy them all to the new card.

☐ **Press Command-C (Copy Picture).**

☐ **Press Command-3 (Next).**

☐ **Press Command-V (Paste Picture).**

This card now looks just like the other one. It should, except that the bed must be moved to reveal the secret passage.

☐ **Lasso the bed and drag it to the right a couple of inches.**

Where's the secret passage?

☐ **Select black paint and the Oval tool.**

☐ **Draw a black oval where the bed was originally.**

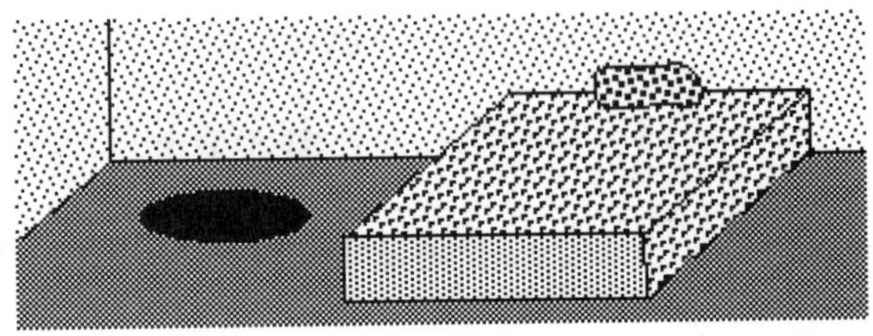

There's the secret opening, waiting for a button to link it to a new room or passage. Until that button is installed, the door is the only exit.

☐ **Press Command-Tab (Browse) and click on the door.**

That won't take us out because we haven't installed a button *on this card*. We can fix that.

☐ **Press Command-2 (Back).**

☐ **Select the Button tool.**

☐ **Click on the Door button.**

☐ **Press Command-C (Copy Button).**

☐ **Press Command-3 (Next).**

☐ **Press Command-V (Paste Button).**

This button is an identical copy of the button from the previous card, so it should do just what the other was trained to do: Take us back to room 1. Try it.

☐ **Press Command-Tab (Browse).**

☐ **Click on the door.**

You're back in the first room.

☐ **Try clicking on the black door to reenter room 2.**

Stackware Engineering Revisited

Uncovering a Bug

At this point you might notice a minor flaw, or **bug**, in our simulated dungeon: The bed has moved back to its original position. Of course, that's because the Door button was linked to the card with the bed in the corner. If we had anticipated this problem, we could have set it up so that moving the bed blocked the door; then the bed would have to be moved back (via another button) before we could go through the door again.

Since this is only a game, we'll sidestep the problem by assuming that either the bed is an enchanted homing bed or this dungeon has incredible room service. And we'll make a note of one of the most important principles of stack design:

> Time spent planning a stack is almost always less than the time wasted repairing an unplanned stack.

Planning a Network

A late plan is better than no plan at all, so let's diagram what we've done so far and figure out where we're going from here. Here's our basic map:

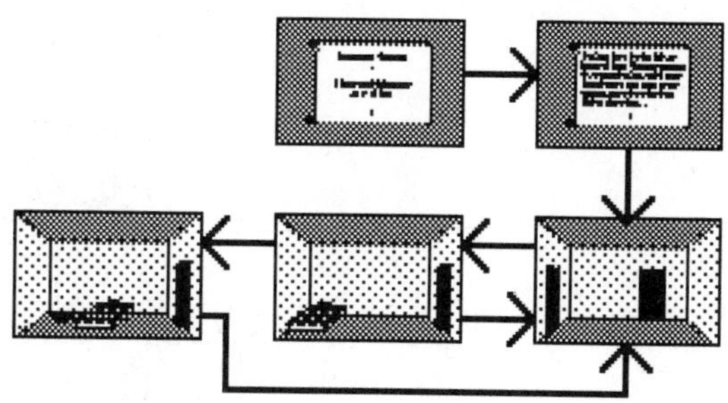

> **Map Tips**
>
> - When you're creating a complex stack, minimize errors by mapping the stack first.
> - Show all possible links between cards on the map with arrows.
> - Label the arrows with button names so the connections are obvious.

- Number the cards on the map to represent the order in which they'll be arranged in the stack.
- When you're constructing the stack, use the map as a visual checklist, checking off cards, links, and sections as you complete them.

One thing is clear from our map: This game, so far, isn't very interesting. We need more passages and pathways. We can start by adding a room with several exits: a couple of doors, a hidden passage, and a pit. Each of these exits will lead to other cards.

In the spirit of a good maze, some of these paths should be dead ends. We can, for example, have the Pit button link to a "Sorry, but you just fell into a pit of starving alligators" card. Other paths should wind back into rooms we've already seen. The two doors in the current room might connect to each other via a secret passage. Still other buttons will branch into multiple paths, only one of which ultimately leads to freedom.

We don't have time to develop a complete, lose-yourself-for-an-afternoon maze in this session, but our next diagram might look like this:

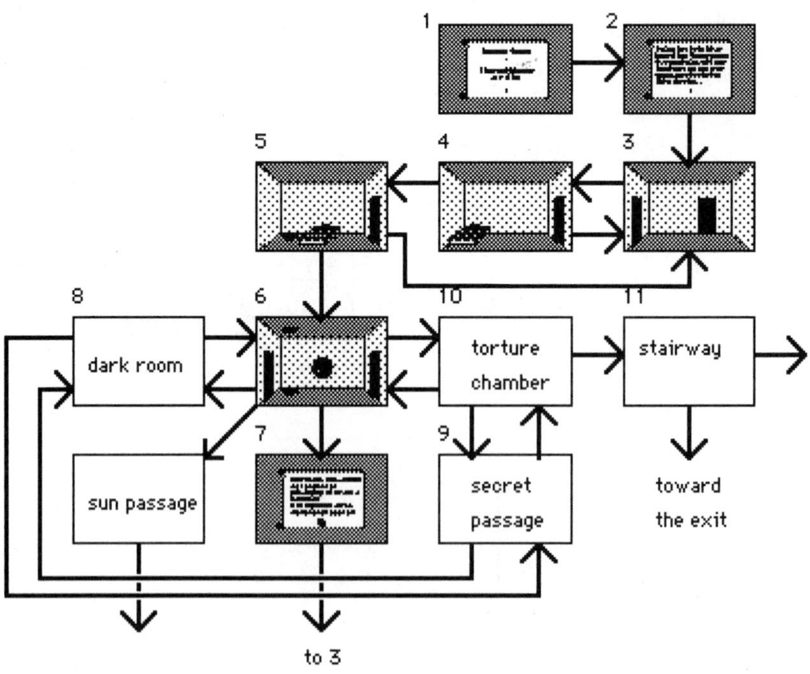

This kind of free-form structure is called a **network**. Network structures tend to be more error-prone than the sequences and loops we've worked with so far, because there are no real rules about the way they should be put together, and because there are so many loose ends to take care of. It's easy to leave things unconnected or to accidentally connect them incorrectly. That's why a map is so important.

Remembering the User

When we discussed software engineering in the last session, we focused on the user interface, developing guidelines to help users find their way around in a stack. Have we applied those guidelines this time around? We've provided the user with no Home or Quit buttons on any of the maze cards, and we've hidden all of the buttons; this stack is almost user-hostile by our earlier standards.

Of course, that's the point. If the buttons were all labeled "this way out" and "dead end" it wouldn't be much of a game. Still, a large, well-designed adventure game allows the player to quit before finishing, often allowing the player to save the current position so he or she can return at a later time. We're not equipped to do that in this session, but we can generalize the idea to an important principle that will make all of our stacks better:

> Always look at your stack design from the user's point of view.

Break Point

Secondhand Art

Since we're using the same backgrounds for so many rooms, it's important to add embellishments so that each room doesn't look like the last one. Embellishing dungeons can be time-consuming, especially for nonartists. But we can always borrow.

Copying a Card

Let's start by borrowing a whole card, the one we just created.

☐ **If you aren't already there, go to the last card in the stack. Then select Copy Card from the Edit menu.**

A copy of this card—graphics, buttons, and all—is in the Clipboard, waiting to be pasted. We'll paste it as soon as we create a new button for the secret passage, using *almost* the same procedure we've done many times.

- ☐ **Select the Button tool.**
- ☐ **Select New Button from the Objects menu.**
- ☐ **Drag and stretch the new button so it covers the hole.**
- ☐ **Double-click on the button to open the Button Info dialog box.**
- ☐ **Choose Oval style to create an oval transparent button.**
- ☐ **Click on Show Name to turn off that option.**
- ☐ **Type "hole under bed" (optional).**
- ☐ **Click on Tasks... and select Visual Effect.**
- ☐ **Click on scroll up.**
- ☐ **Select Go to Destination.**
- ☐ **Press Command-N (New Card).**
- ☐ **Click on Current Card, then press Return to assign the tasks.**

As usual, you're carried back where you came from, but this time it's hard to tell, because the two cards look identical—for now.

- ☐ **Press Command-3 (Next).**

Deleting and Rearranging Graphics

It's easy to forget where we are—these two cards look so much alike. Let's change that.

- ☐ **Use the Lasso to select the bed.**
- ☐ **Press the Delete (Backspace) key to delete the selected bed.**
- ☐ **Select the black hole and Shift-Option-drag it straight up to the ceiling, leaving a copy behind.**

The top hole is the bottom of our secret passage; the bottom hole is a pit.

- ☐ **With the Option key held down, select the door with the Selection rectangle.**

This causes the Selection rectangle to shrink around the door like the Lasso.

- ☐ **Option-drag it to make a copy while leaving the original.**

- ☐ **Select Flip Horizontal and position the new door on the left wall.**

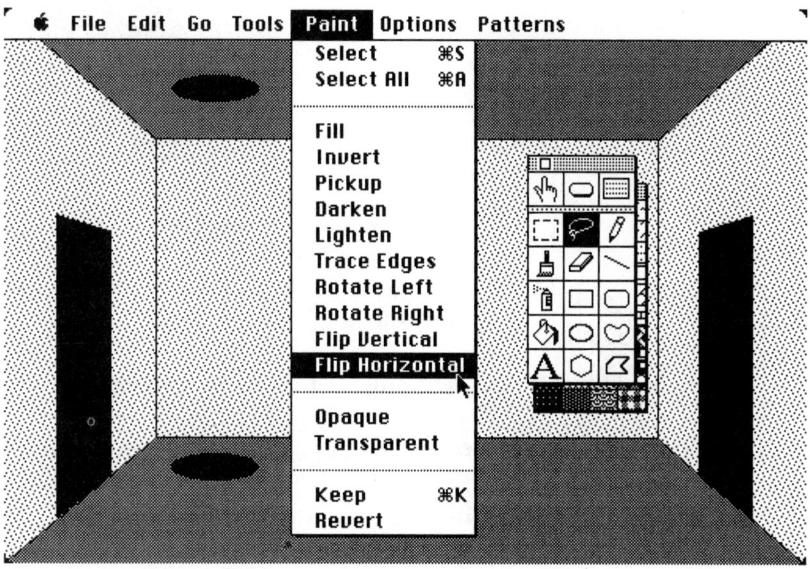

Borrowing Clip Art

If you don't have the Art Bits stack, read through the next few steps to the "Using Clip Art" box. At that point, use the paint tools to paint your own version of this sun on the wall of this card (in the card layer).

If you have the complete HyperCard package, you can easily add some professionally drawn **clip art.**

- ☐ **Press Command-H to go Home.**

☐ **Click on the Art Bits icon.**

If a dialog box appears, locate the Art Bits stack.

☐ **Read the Stack Overview and return to the Categories index.**

☐ **Click on Nature and Science and flip forward to the fourth of the five cards in this category by clicking on the arrows on the floating palette.**

☐ **Lasso (or Option-select with the Selection rectangle) the sun carving.**

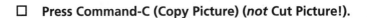

☐ **Press Command-C (Copy Picture) (*not* Cut Picture!).**

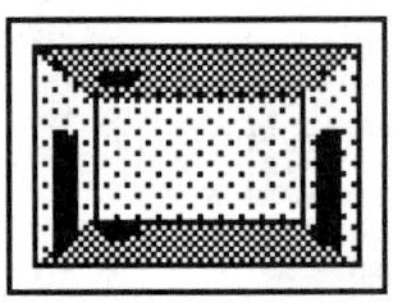

☐ **Press Command-R (Recent) and click on the miniature version of the unfinished dungeon room.**

☐ **Press Command-V (Paste Picture).**

☐ **Position the carving in the center of the wall.**

Here's the decorated room:

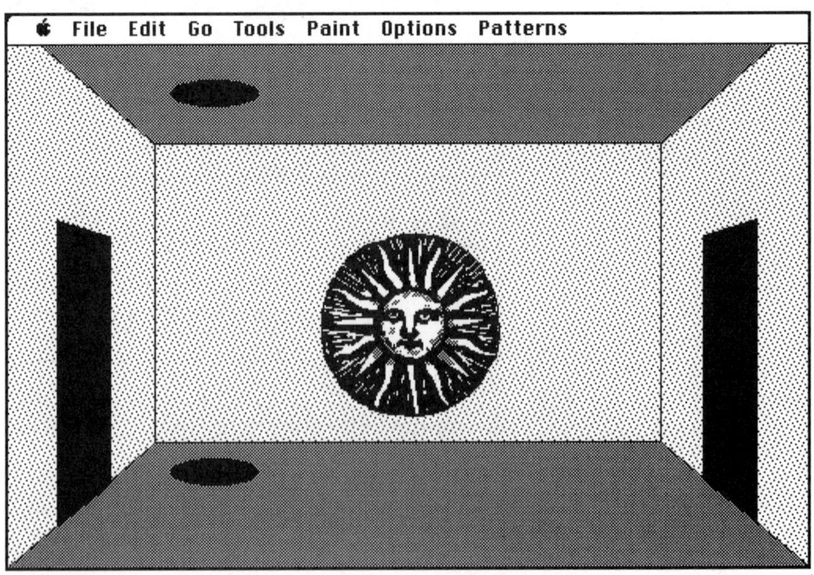

Using Clip Art

Clip art is available in a variety of formats. The HyperCard package includes the Art Bits and Background Art stacks, but there's a much wider variety of HyperCard-appropriate clip art stored in **MacPaint** files. The **Import Paint...** command allows you to import MacPaint pictures directly into HyperCard, but this command gives you no control over what part of the 8 × 10 inch MacPaint image you'll use.

It's often more effective to open the clip art document with MacPaint, SuperPaint, or some other paint application, copy to the Clipboard the portion of the picture you want, return to your HyperCard stack, and paste. (If you have several images to import, you can paste them all into the **Scrapbook** to minimize trips between your paint program and HyperCard.)

Appendix A describes paint applications, clip art sources, digital cameras, and **scanners** that allow you to turn drawings and photographs into HyperCard art.

Borrowing an Old Background

It's traditional in this kind of adventure game to display a message of condolences if the player blunders into an untimely death. We need to display just such a message if our unsuspecting player clicks on the pit. We should display the message on the scroll background that we used for our opening cards. How can we do that, though? If we create a new card here, the card will have the room background. If we go back to card 1 and create a new card, the background will be correct but the card will be in the wrong place. The solution is simple: Go to card 1, create a new card, and move that card to the end of the stack where it belongs.

☐ **Press Command-1 (First).**

☐ **Select New Card from the Edit menu.**

You're looking at a new card with a scroll background. It's located right after the first card in the stack.

☐ **Select Cut Card from the Edit menu.**

The new card is now in the Clipboard.

☐ **Press Command-4 (Last).**

☐ **Press Command-V (Paste Card).**

The card is now at the end of the stack.

☐ **Press Command-2 to go to the previous card in the stack.**

☐ **Select the Button tool.**

☐ **Select New Button from the Objects menu.**

☐ **Drag and stretch the new button so it covers the hole in the floor.**

☐ **Double-click on the button to open the Button Info dialog box.**

☐ **Choose Oval style.**

☐ **Click on Show Name to turn off that option.**

☐ **Type "pit" (optional).**

☐ **Click on Tasks... and select Visual Effect.**

☐ **Click on shrink to top.**

☐ **Select Go to Destination.**

☐ **Press Command-4 (Go Last).**

You're looking at your empty scroll card, right?

☐ **Click on Current Card and Assign Tasks.**

☐ **Use the Browse tool to test the button.**

You've now linked the pit to the scroll card. It's time to fill in the scroll.

☐ **Double-click on the Paint Text tool, select your traditional font and size, and click OK.**

☐ **Type a message on your scroll like this:**

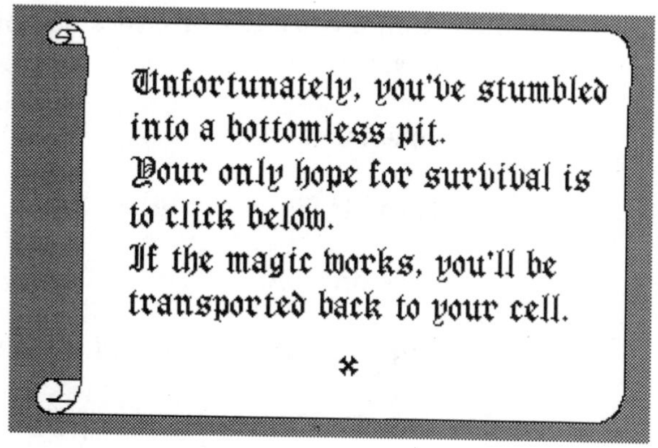

Unfortunately, you've stumbled into a bottomless pit.
Your only hope for survival is to click below.
If the magic works, you'll be transported back to your cell.

There's only one problem. To find out what it is,

☐ **Press Command-Tab (Browse) and click on the button.**

This button, installed in the background, always goes to the next card, which in this case means wrapping around to Card 1. We want a different kind of button on this particular card. If we change the background button's link, that will change the link for all cards with this background. We can get around this problem by taking advantage of basic layering principles.

> **Buttons on Buttons**
>
> Buttons in the card layer can cover background buttons in the same way that card layer graphics cover background graphics. If a card layer button covers a background button, the card layer button takes precedence. It's also possible to cover one button with another button in the same layer. In general, the button on top takes precedence. **Bring Closer** and **Send Farther** commands (objects menu) can be used to rearrange objects so the one on top is the one you want to be on top.

☐ **Press Command-4 (Last).**

☐ **Select the Button tool.**

☐ **Select New Button.**

☐ **Position and shape the new button so it covers the background button.**

☐ **Double-click on the new button to open the Button Info dialog box.**

☐ **Select Opaque.**

☐ **Turn off Show Name.**

☐ **Click on Icon....**

☐ **Select a magical icon and double-click.**

☐ **Double-click on the icon to bring back the Button Info box.**

☐ **Click on Tasks....**

☐ **Select Visual Effect. Click on stretch from center and slow.**

☐ **Choose Go to Destination.**

☐ **Press Command-3 repeatedly until you see the first room card.**

☐ **Click on Current Card.**

☐ **Use the Browse tool (Command-Tab) to try the new button.**

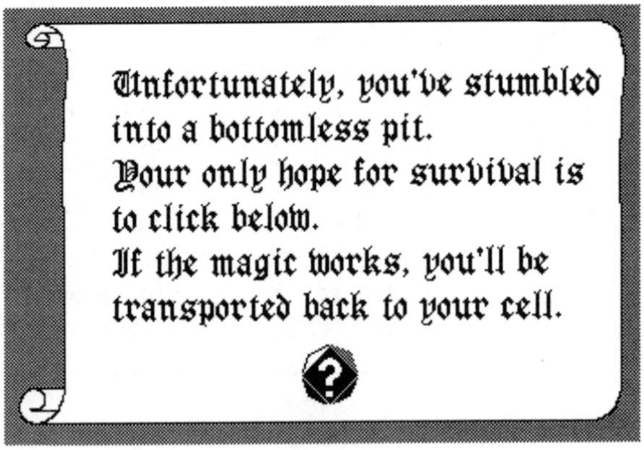

As your maze expands, you'll probably have lots of dead ends. Each time you need one, you can copy this card, complete with text, buttons, and background. When you paste the copy where it goes, all you need to change is the message. (In the interest of user friendliness, it might be a good idea to add a Home button to this card before you copy it.)

Loose Ends

Changing Links

Let's finish by illustrating another important design principle:

> Don't just tell the user; *show* the user.

Just for fun, let's add a graphic representation of the bottomless pit before the closing message. That means we'll have to insert a card between the pit room card and the final scroll, reconnecting the links as we do. The process is simple, provided you pay careful attention to what you're doing so you don't forget to tie everything up properly.

☐ **Press Command-4 (Last) and Command-2 (Previous).**

You should be looking at the room with the entrance to the pit.

☐ **Select the Button tool and double-click on the Pit button.**

☐ **Click on Tasks.... Select Go to Destination.**

☐ **Select New Background from the Objects menu.**

☐ **Click on Current Card, and press Return to assign tasks.**

☐ **Type Command-B to leave the background.**

☐ **Press Command-3 to go to the new white card.**

☐ **Double-click on the Regular Polygon tool to choose a shape.**

☐ **Click on the circle.**

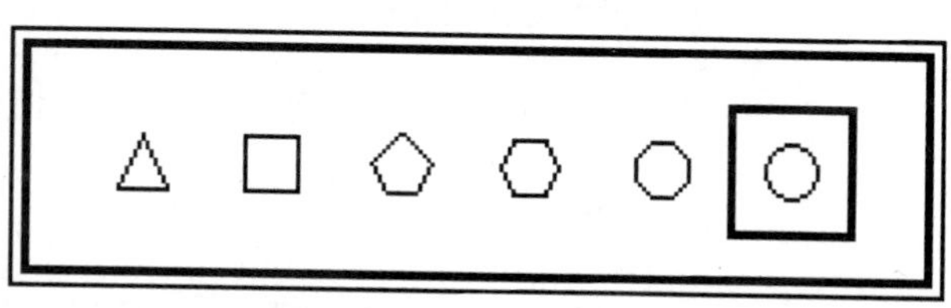

☐ **Select Draw Centered and Draw Multiple from the Options menu. (If there's a check mark in front of Draw Filled in the menu, select Draw Filled to turn it off.)**

☐ **Drag from the center of the screen outward with an even motion, creating a series of concentric circles. Without lifting your finger from the mouse button, drag back toward the center if you need to fill gaps.**

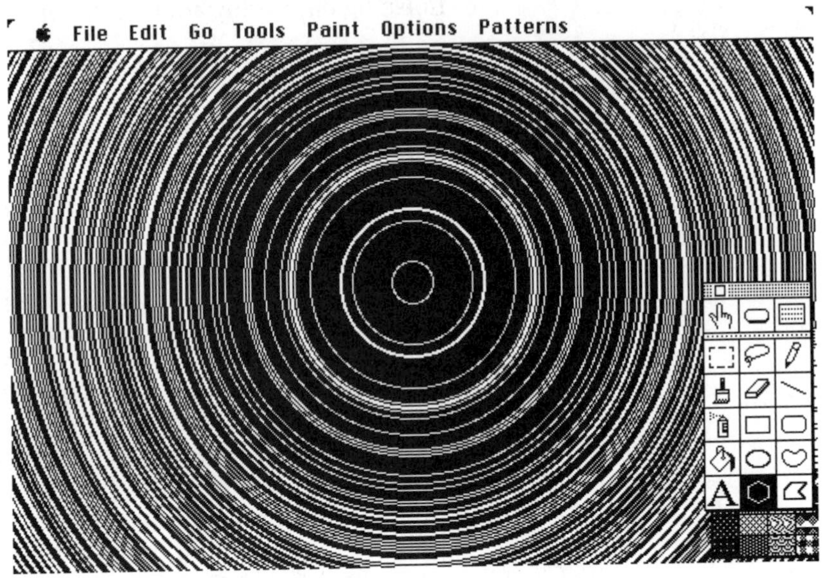

If necessary, double-click on the Eraser and repeat until you get the endless tunnel effect you like. (If you prefer, try one of the other shapes.)

We need a button to make this into a click-anywhere-to-continue screen.

☐ **Select the Button tool.**

☐ **Create a screen-sized new button.**

☐ **Double-click on the button to open the Button Info dialog box.**

☐ **Make it transparent.**

☐ **Turn on Auto Hilite and turn off Show Name.**

☐ **Click on Tasks....**

☐ **Select Visual Effect. Click on checkerboard and slow.**

☐ **Select Go to Destination.**

☐ **Press Command-3 (Next).**

You should be looking at the "sorry" scroll.

☐ **Click on Current Card and press Return to assign tasks.**

☐ **Use the Browse tool to test the new button.**

Finishing the Game

There's still much to do before this game is finished, but you have the tools and techniques you need to carry it through on your own. If you want to continue, add buttons to the two doors and the sun picture in the last room, and link those buttons to new rooms. (You already have one button installed on the right-hand door, but it links to the wrong card. Why?) Don't be afraid to be creative, but keep in mind a few tips as you create:

Keeping Your Stack Orderly

- As you add cards, try to keep the overall stack in some kind of logical order.
- Remember that whenever you create a new card, that card is inserted immediately after the current card. If that's not where you want it, use Cut Card and Paste Card to move it.
- A nonlinear structure has to have some buttons that jump to other parts of the stack, but it's best to keep cards in logical groups as much as possible.
- Flip through all the cards in your stack with Command-3. It's easy to leave unfinished, unwanted cards embedded in a stack, and this is a good way to find them.
- If you find several cards that look alike, use temporary marks to flag them so you can tell them apart while you're troubleshooting; you can remove the extra cards and the marks when the job is done.
- Use Option-Command to reveal hidden buttons on each card; try each of these buttons. When you copy cards, you often end up with buttons that you didn't want linked to places you don't want to go.

As you expand this stack, practice borrowing cards, art, and buttons from other stacks until you're comfortable with the process. Try the paint tools and menu options that we haven't covered here, referring to the HyperCard Help stack, if available, for information and inspiration. Have fun!

Summary

In the process of building a game, you've learned a number of HyperCard concepts that you can apply directly to all kinds of serious and not-so-serious projects. You've used new paint tools and techniques to create complex graphic scenes. You've put buttons and graphics in backgrounds shared by several cards. You've seen the possible interaction between card and background objects, and you've learned how to take advantage of HyperCard layers to minimize your work and maximize your stack's efficiency and effectiveness. You've also discovered some pitfalls of designing and building a complex stack, and you've learned principles that can help you avoid those pitfalls.

Next session you'll begin a journey underneath HyperCard's slick user interface into the fascinating world of HyperTalk. You'll see how this simple but powerful language can be used to add animation and sound effects to your presentations. You'll be amazed at the doors that a few well-chosen HyperTalk words can open for you!

Key Words

adventure game
Background command (Command-B)
background layer
Bring Closer command
bug
card layer
clip art
Curve tool
Distort command
Draw Centered command
Draw Multiple command
Edit Pattern... command
FatBits
Hand tool (Option-FatBits)
Import Paint... command
interactive fiction
MacPaint
network
New Background command
Opaque command
Oval tool
Perspective command
Regular Polygon tool
Rotate command
Rotate Left command
Rotate Right command
scanner
Scrapbook (desk accessory)
Send Farther command
simulation
Slant command
stretching/shrinking graphics (Command-drag)
stripes (on menu bar)
Transparent command

Exercises

1. List four reasons that it's a good idea to include common elements of cards in a shared background.
2. Can you have a background button in a two-card, one-background stack, that takes you back and forth between the two cards? Explain.

3. What do each of these HyperCard paint tool symbols represent?

   a.  b.  c.  d. 

4. Describe three different ways you can select an irregularly shaped object in the current layer of a card.
5. How can you switch to FatBits without using the menu? How can you get back to "skinny bits"?
6. Describe the difference between the Rotate and Rotate Right commands. Under what circumstances is each appropriate?
7. What is the difference between the Lasso and the Selection rectangle?

Projects

1. Design a map of a finished dungeon game based on the game you developed in this session. Add several more rooms and include several dead ends and a single escape path; link some rooms with secret passages. Use your imagination. Using your design, complete the game by adding rooms, decorating them, and linking them. Test your game thoroughly; then have others test it for you.
2. Create a map of your city with a list of points of interest along the side or at the bottom. Make each one of those points of interest into a button that, when clicked, highlights the named point on the map. Put the map in the background and create one highlighted card for each item. Should the buttons be in the card layer or the background layer? Why? Variations: Do the same thing for your house, your state, the world, or whatever you can think of.
3. Make a line drawing of a familiar object on a HyperCard card. Select that object with the Selection rectangle and capture the screen image as a MacPaint file with the Command-Shift-3 keystroke combination. Import that captured screen back into HyperCard and use it to create a demonstration of these effects in HyperCard's Paint menu: Fill, Invert, Darken, Lighten, Trace Edges, Rotate Left, Rotate Right, Flip Vertical, and Flip Horizontal. Your screen should list these commands down the left side in Chicago font. Clicking on any of the command names should change the screen so that (a) the command name is highlighted (inverted); (b) the selected part of the picture is transformed just as the command would transform it; and (c) an Undo button appears to take the user back to the previous card. Think carefully about what parts of the picture should be in the background before constructing this stack.

Session 5

By the end of this session you should be able to

- Create a slide-show presentation with visual transition effects between slides
- Create presentations with different kinds of on-screen animation
- Create, edit, and install custom icons
- Add simple sound and musical effects to HyperCard stacks
- Understand the relationships among HyperCard objects, messages, and scripts
- Locate and understand common HyperTalk scripts in a HyperCard stack
- Write and edit simple HyperTalk scripts

Behind the Buttons

Introducing HyperTalk

The Problem

Your planet is in trouble. The climate of the Earth is changing dramatically as a result of short-sighted human activity. You've been asked to give a presentation at a local school assembly, and you'd like to share your knowledge and concerns about this vital issue. You want to back up your words with visual aids that will capture the attention and the imagination of your audience. The school has a device for projecting Macintosh screens so the audience can see them. Perhaps HyperCard can help.

Introduction

Like an acquaintance from another culture, HyperCard won't reveal its most interesting secrets until you learn a little bit of its language. The native language of HyperCard is **HyperTalk**, a programming language that's about as close to English as any you'll find. This session will introduce you to HyperTalk: First you'll observe scripts written by others, and then you'll create your own. There's lots of new material here, so don't hesitate to break this session into shorter, more manageable sessions if you feel so inclined.

HyperTalk Revealed

Sending HyperTalk Messages

You may not be aware of it, but you've been using HyperTalk already. The **message box** that appears when you issue a Find command is designed for sending messages to HyperCard (and sometimes receiving messages from HyperCard). Those messages must be written in HyperTalk for HyperCard to understand them. So let's start the session by sending a HyperTalk message.

☐ **Start your computer and open HyperCard by double-clicking on your Home icon.**

☐ **Select Message from the Go menu (or press Command-M) to bring up the message box.**

☐ **Type the following, pressing Return at the end:**

```
Set UserLevel to 5
```

You're speaking HyperTalk now. When you pressed Return, you sent a message to HyperCard to reset the user level to level 5, scripting. If you don't believe it, go to the last card in the Home stack and see for yourself.

Let's try another HyperTalk message.

☐ **Type:**

```
the time
```

As soon as you press Return, HyperCard checks its watch and answers through the message box:

```
1:30 PM
```

> **`time`** is a HyperTalk **function**—a named value that is calculated when the statement (message) it is in executes. One way to call a HyperTalk function is to put the word `the` before it. Another is to follow the function name with parentheses like this: `time()`. When HyperCard sees either type of function call, it replaces the function with the current time according to the System clock.

The message box can be used as a calculator, too.

☐ **Type:**

```
510*340
```

HyperCard's answer:

```
173400
```

HyperTalk Calculations

Here's a list of the basic HyperTalk arithmetic operators, including examples with results:

+	add	`7 + 3.3` = 10.3
–	subtract	`7 - 3.3` = 3.7
*	multiply	`5 * 3.1` = 15.5
/	divide	`5 / 2` = 2.5
div	divide and truncate (chop off remainder)	`5 div 2` = 2
mod	modulo (remainder after integer division)	`5 mod 2` = 1
^	exponent	`5 ^ 2` = 25

When evaluating complex expressions with multiple operators, HyperTalk follows strict rules for ordering the operations:

1. **Operator precedence**. In a complex arithmetic expression, exponentiation is evaluated first, then multiplication and division (including `div` and `mod`), and finally addition and subtraction.
2. Left to right. Operators of equal precedence are evaluated in order from left to right.
3. Grouping. Parentheses may be used to override the first two rules by grouping operations; expressions inside parentheses are evaluated first.

Examples: `5 * 2 + 9 - 3 div 2 ^ 2` = 19,
but `5 * (2 + 9) - (3 div 2) ^ 2` = 54.

Eavesdropping with the Message Watcher

Even while you're typing these messages, HyperCard is sending messages of its own. A continuous stream of **system messages** provide a running commentary on the state of your computer as seen by HyperCard. You can monitor these messages with a tool called the **Message Watcher**. This window is part of the HyperTalk **debugging environment** that's provided to make it easier for you to find bugs (errors) in your stack scripts. We'll use the HyperTalk debugger later, but for now we just want to use the Message Watcher to monitor system communications. We'll invoke the Message Watcher with HyperTalk's show command.

show and **hide** commands are used to make the message box, the menu bar, the Tools palette, windows, and other objects visible and invisible. (`show` can also be used to display a sequence of cards in rapid succession, as in `show all cards` or `show 22 cards`.)

☐ **Type:**

```
show window "message watcher"
```

The Message Watcher window appears; you can move it around on the screen like any other window. It's empty because there are no HyperTalk messages currently being *used* for anything. Nonetheless, there are plenty of messages being sent.

☐ **Click on the "Hide unused messages" check box to turn it off.**

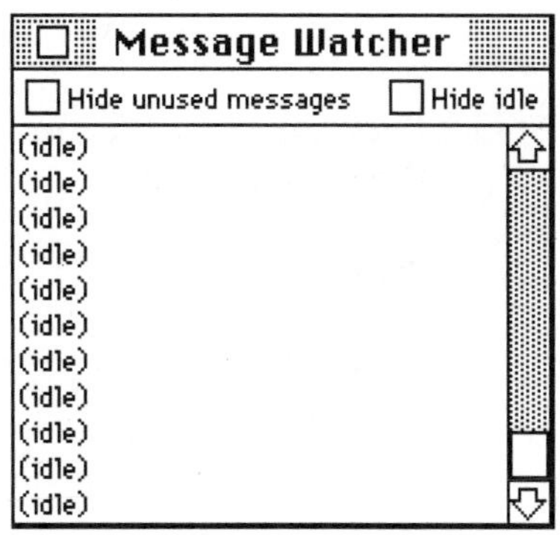

The Message Watcher should immediately start displaying a stream of **idle** messages. HyperCard is continually reminding itself that nothing's happening. We can turn off this idle chatter.

☐ **Click on the "Hide idle" check box to turn it on.**

☐ **Move the pointer over a button on the screen without clicking it; then move it off the button.**

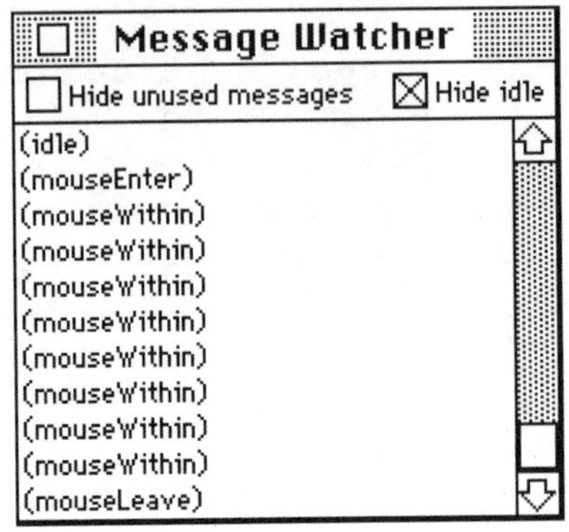

A series of system messages says that you moved the mouse pointer over a button (**mouseEnter**), then held it there for a while (**mouseWithin**), then moved it off the button (**mouseLeave**). (You might see a slightly different stream of messages, depending on whether you move the mouse over multiple buttons or fields.) As you'll soon see, HyperCard objects such as buttons can be programmed to use (respond to) messages like these. But the parenthesized messages you're seeing aren't used by any object in the stack; they're like radio broadcasts with no listeners. Let's send some messages that make things happen. But first, let's turn off the noise.

☐ **Click on the Hide unused messages check box in the Message Watcher window.**

☐ **Type:**

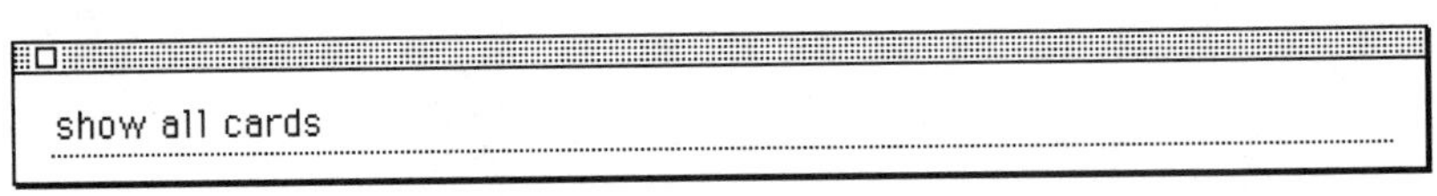

As you type, HyperCard responds to each keystroke by sending a **keyDown** system message. Each keyDown message also includes the letter typed, but that information isn't visible in the Message Watcher window. The keyDown messages are being used to construct a command in the message box, so they aren't in parentheses. Pressing the Return key sends two messages: keyDown and **returnKey**. When the Return key is pressed, the typed message—show—is sent by the System. To make strings of messages easier to interpret, the Message Watcher window indents messages that result from previous messages.

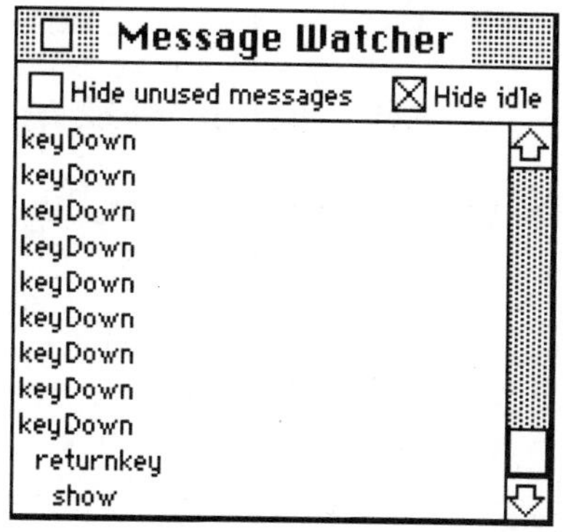

HyperCard responds to the message by flipping quickly through the entire stack of cards.

☐ **Next, type:**

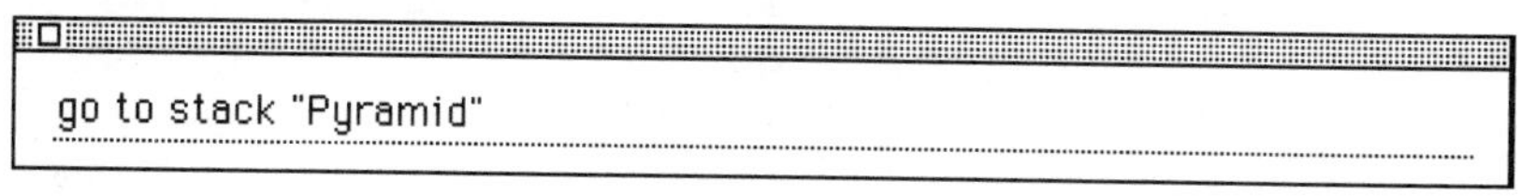

When you press Return, you may see the now familiar dialog box asking "Where is Pyramid?" Locate the stack you created in Session 3. (If you don't have that stack, just read along until we return Home.) The Message Watcher is flooded with new messages. You can scroll backward through the list of messages if you like, but don't expect to understand all of them. There are things going on behind the scenes that won't make sense to you at this point; that's why we're here.

Looking under a Button

Things don't happen accidentally in HyperCard; they happen because someone—or something—sends messages telling HyperCard to make them happen. In these examples, we told HyperCard what to do via the message box. When you click on a button, HyperCard responds by doing something, too. Let's peek under a button to see why HyperCard responds the way it does.

☐ **Select the Button tool from the Tools palette.**

The ever-vigilant Message Watcher tells you that a `choose` message has been sent.

- ☐ **Click on the Home button.**
- ☐ **Select Button Info... from the Objects menu.**
- ☐ **Click on the Script... button.**

When you click on that button, you're invoking HyperCard's script editor. The **script editor** is like a miniature word processor with special features to make working with scripts easier. The script editor responds to your click by opening a **script window** containing the HyperTalk script for this button.

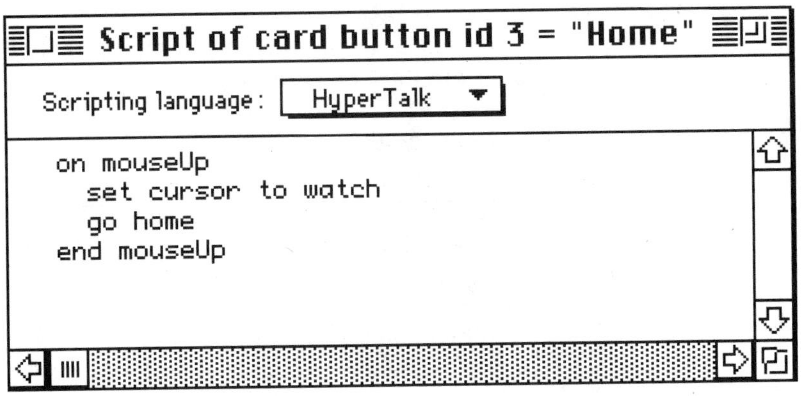

An English translation of the first line, **`on mouseUp`**, might be, "When the mouse button is pressed and released on this button, follow the instructions in order from the beginning to the end of this list." The list contains two instructions: one to temporarily change the pointer's symbol (**`cursor`**) so that it looks like a wristwatch and one to tell HyperCard to go to the Home card.

Notice that the `go home` command in this script has the same effect as the Home command in the Go menu. Scripts can be used to order HyperCard to do just about anything that can be done via HyperCard menus. However, `set cursor to watch` tells HyperCard to do something that has no menu equivalent: Change a **property** of the HyperCard environment.

If you've programmed in a computer language such as BASIC or Pascal, you're probably thinking, "This looks a little like the programming language I've seen before, but there's something strange here. Where's the rest of the program?" If you've never seen a computer program before, you're probably just thinking that the whole thing is strange. Either way, a word of explanation is in order.

Objects and Messages

A program is a set of instructions that tells the computer what to do in the same way that a recipe tells a chef what to do. A program written in a **procedural language** such as BASIC or Pascal is structured like a recipe; the computer works through it, one step at a time, in the order specified by the program.

HyperTalk has many similarities to procedural Pascal and BASIC, but it also has many characteristics of an **object-oriented language**. A HyperCard stack is made up of **objects**—cards, fields, buttons, backgrounds, and the stack itself. Each object has a program—a **script**—that gives HyperCard instructions if the object receives a message. A script is made up of one or more **message handlers**. Each message handler tells HyperCard what to do if a particular message is received. A message handler takes the form

```
on message
  command(s)
end message
```

Translation: If the message *message* arrives at this object, obey the *command(s)* in this list.

To help clarify this, let's take a second look at the `on mouseUp` handler used in the Home button's script.

The **`on mouseUp`** handler tells HyperCard what to do when the system message `mouseUp` is received by the button. `mouseUp` is the most common message for HyperCard buttons, although it can be received by fields, cards, and backgrounds, too. `on mouseUp` is HyperTalk for "if the user presses and lets go of the mouse button while the pointer is on this button (or field, or card, or background), do everything listed between this statement and **`end mouseUp`**." (Although it might seem strange to specify that the action take place when the user lets go of the button, rather than when he or she presses the button, it makes sense. A mouse click consists of two actions—pressing and letting go—and it's not complete until both actions are done.)

In this example, the button receives the message and says, in effect, "I know what to do with this; my script tells me to go to the Home card, turning the pointer into a wristwatch until I'm there." HyperCard responds by turning on the watch and going Home; upon arrival at the Home card, the interaction is over.

Stacks, fields, and backgrounds can receive and respond to messages, too. How do all these objects keep their messages straight?

The HyperCard Object Hierarchy

As you point and click your way through a HyperCard stack, you're generating a flurry of messages that are passed upward through the HyperCard bureaucracy. For example, when you click anywhere on a card, the System sends a `mouseUp` message to the topmost button or field at the current mouse pointer location. This means, for example, that a button in the card layer will receive the message rather than a background button in the same location. If the script of the topmost button or field has a message handler telling it what to do `on mouseUp`, then the object accepts the message and performs the action. If there's no `on mouseUp` message handler in the script, the button or field passes the message on to the next button or field, whether in the card or the background layer. If the message passes through all buttons and fields in both layers without matching a handler in any script, it is sent to the card and compared with the card's script. If that script contains no appropriate handlers, the message is passed to the background, and then to the stack, and then in some cases to other stacks, and then to the Home stack, and finally, to HyperCard.

☐ **Close the script window by clicking on the close box in the upper left corner.**

☐ **Select the Browse tool and click on the Home button. Observe how each message in the script translates into an on-screen action. Notice also the messages scrolling through the Message Watcher window. Scroll backward through the messages until you see the `mouseUp` system message.**

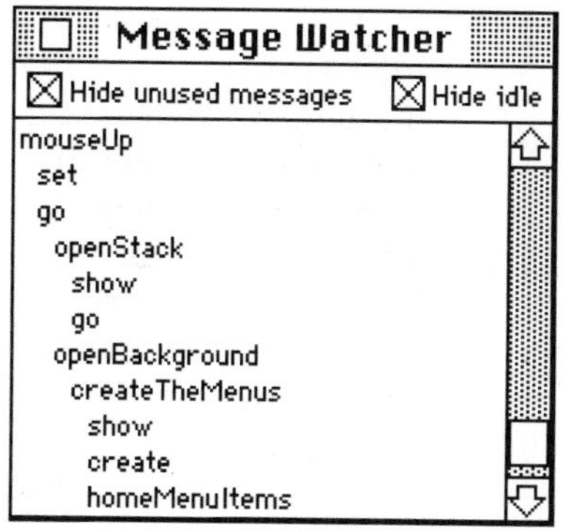

The next two messages, `set` and `go`, were sent by the `on mouseUp` handler when it executed. The `openStack` message was sent by the System when the Home stack opened; the rest of the messages were sent as a result of scripts built into the Home stack. You'll learn more about these messages in due time.

☐ **Press the Tilde (~) key (or select Back from the Go menu) to return to the Pyramid stack.**

Examining the Script of a Linked Button

☐ **Select the Button tool and click on the button labeled "Click here to see inside."**

☐ **Hold down the Shift key while selecting Button Info....**

This is a shortcut to the script window.

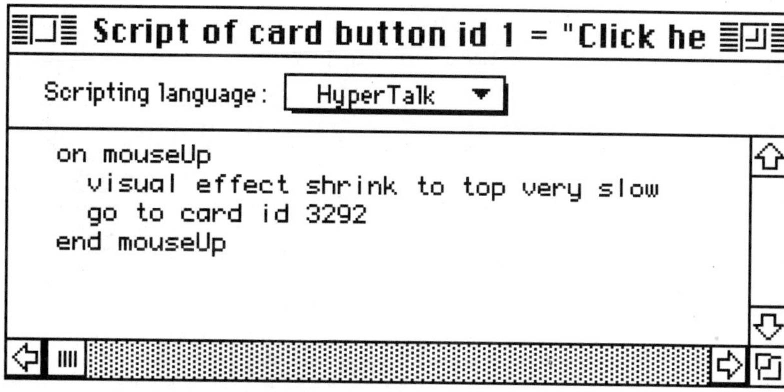

This button, like most buttons, has a single on mouseUp handler telling HyperCard what to do if the button is clicked. The handler says to implement a visual effect and go to the card assigned ID number 3292. (The number in the script probably won't be the same on your screen, but whatever it is, it's the ID number of the next card in the stack. You can check that by going to that card and selecting **Card Info...** from the Objects menu.) What does this number mean? Nothing; it's just a random ID number used for this kind of thing. HyperCard numbers every object you create; it's up to you to name those objects. By itself, the ID number 3292 tells you nothing about where that card is or what it does; that's why it's smart to give names to the things you create. If a card has a name, you can write scripts that say `go to card "Inside Pyramid"` instead of letting HyperCard say `go to card id 3292.`

☐ **Click on the script window's close box.**

If you're unclear about how the Button Info... button works, click it with the Browse tool while you watch the Message Watcher.

Checking the Script of a Relative Link

Let's check a button with a different kind of script.

☐ **Press Command-H (Home) and Command-4 (Last).**

You're transported to the last card of the Home stack.

☐ **Reselect the Button tool; then hold down the Shift key and double-click on the right-arrow button.**

You'll bypass the Button Info dialog box that way, and go straight to the script window.

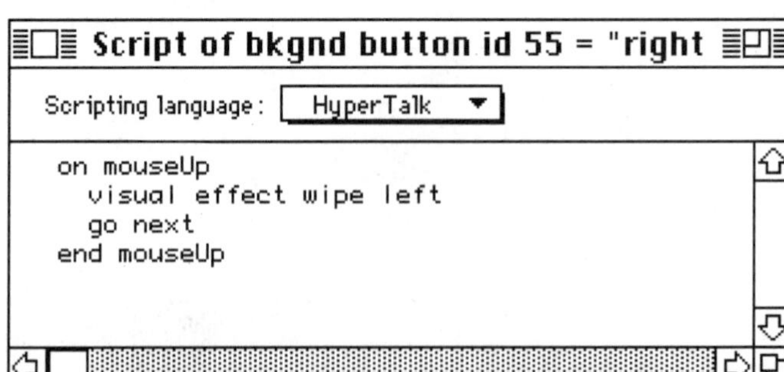

When the mouse is clicked and released on this button, it sends a message to HyperCard to use a wipe left visual effect as a transition while going to the next card in the stack. There's no mention of a card ID, just a reference to *next card*. This button script uses a logical reference, so it will always go to the next card, no matter what that might be. Compare it with the absolute link in the button labeled "Click here to see inside" in the Pyramid stack. While you're at it, compare it with this script from the left-arrow button of the Home stack in an earlier version of HyperCard.

Script of bkgnd button id 56 = "left arrow"

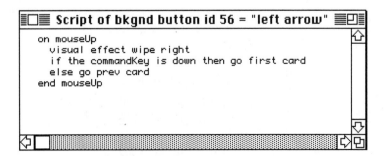

```
on mouseUp
  visual effect wipe right
  if the commandKey is down then go first card
  else go prev card
end mouseUp
```

This handler responds in different ways depending on whether the Command key is held down when the button receives the mouseUp message.

> The **`if` structure** sends no messages. Instead, it tests for a specific condition and, if the condition is true, executes the command statement that follows. Alternate forms of the `if` structure allow multiple statements to be executed if the condition is true, or allow for a different set of statements to be executed if the statement is false. `if` structures allow programmers to build "intelligent" scripts that can respond to changes in their software and hardware environment.

☐ **Close the Message Watcher window.**

We won't need it for a while, but you can open it whenever you want to monitor the messages sent by your stack. Later in this session you'll learn how to use the Message Watcher with other debugging tools.

Break Point

Building a Dynamic Presentation

Let's build a stack to make a presentation and use some simple scripts to give our stack some visual pizzazz.

Outlining the Problem

We know our audience won't learn much if we barrage them with facts and figures, so we have to carefully plan a few main points that we want them to remember. Here's one way to slice up the problem:

I. Global warming is a problem.
II. We're causing it.
III. It has serious consequences.
IV. We can do something about it.

We need to back up each of these points with some subpoints. We might flesh out our outline like this:

Global Warming: What Are We Doing to Our Planet?

I. What is global warming?
   A. We're changing the Earth's climate.
   B. The rate of change is greater than that of the glacial periods.
   C. We're changing the environment faster than we can predict the consequences.

II. How are we causing global warming?
   A. Burning fossil fuels produces carbon dioxide.
   B. Deforestation for fuel and grazing land eliminates carbon dioxide filters.
   C. Human activities produce other greenhouse gases (CFCs, methane, and so on).

III. What are the likely consequences?
   A. Heat waves, drought, and forest fires.
   B. Agricultural losses and famine.
   C. Rising sea level and flooding.
   D. Extinction of many trees and other species.

IV. What can we do?
   A. Reduce energy consumption.
   B. Recycle paper, metal, glass, and plastic.

C. Stop using plastic foam and CFC aerosols.
D. Eat less meat.
E. Plant more trees.
F. Work for public policies that encourage energy efficiency and discourage pollution.

This outline can be easily transformed into a **bullet chart**, one of the most frequently used forms of **presentation graphics**. Popular software packages such as Persuasion, PowerPoint, and Astound! are designed to instantly create bullet charts from outlines like this one. While HyperCard demands more effort, it also allows more flexibility, provided you're willing to speak a little HyperTalk.

Creating a Starry Background

☐ **Create a new stack called Earth (remember to turn off the Copy current background check box).**

We're going to add an animated introduction later, and that introduction will have a different background than that of the rest of the stack. So let's save a place for the introduction with a single card. (This will save us considerable effort later because there's no automatic way to insert a new card *before* the current card.)

Start with a background of stars.

☐ **Press Command-B (Background).**

☐ **Use the Paint Bucket to paint the background black.**

☐ **Select All of the background (using the command in the Paint menu or Command-A) and use the Lighten command in the Paint menu to produce a random star pattern.**

We'll use this starry pattern in two different backgrounds: one as a backdrop for animated sequences that will precede and follow our presentation, the other to frame our bullet charts. We can save a couple of steps later if we make a copy of the background now.

☐ **Press Command-C to copy the starry graphic to the Clipboard.**

Creating a Bullet Chart Background

☐ **Switch to the Browse tool and select New Background (*not* New Card) from the Objects menu.**

☐ **Press Command-V to paste the star-studded picture into the background.**

You're now looking at the new background of the second card. We want to put a field in this background because that's the easiest way to have text in exactly the same location on every card.

☐ **Select the Field tool.**

☐ **Select New Field from the Objects menu.**

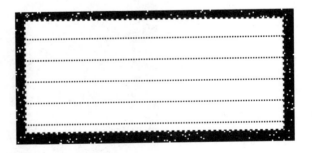

☐ **Drag and stretch the field so it covers most of the window, leaving a one-quarter-inch starry frame around all four sides. (If you're working on a small-screen Mac, the menu bar will hide part of the frame.)**

☐ **Double-click on the field to reveal the Field Info dialog box.**

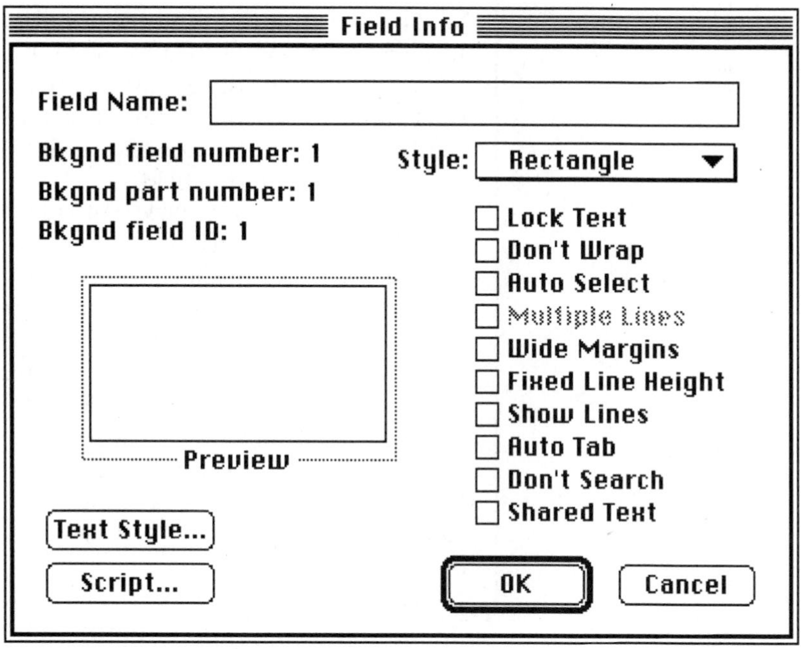

There are several options here, most of which we can ignore for now.

☐ **Type "bullet chart" to name the field.**

This step is optional, but it's a good habit to establish.

☐ **Click on Wide Margins, then click on Text Style... to open the Font dialog box.**

☐ **Select a font that's available in 18-point size in your system. (Helvetica, Geneva, New York, Palatino, and Times are likely candidates.) Click OK.**

Fonts in the Field: A Cautionary Note

Your choice of fonts for field text should be based on more than just aesthetics. While paint text blends into the pixel pattern on the card or background after you create it, field text remains text forevermore. Field text is displayed on the screen using fonts stored in the computer's current System, which may or may not be the same fonts in the System that was used to create the stack. If the fonts that were used to create the text are not available on the user's System, the System substitutes another font. The results may be aesthetically unsatisfactory or worse. In some cases, substitute fonts may cause text to disappear from the screen because it won't fit in the field.

If you're building a stack that is to be displayed on different computers, you can avoid these potential problems by sticking to standard fonts installed in all Macintosh Systems. The only fonts required in every Mac System are Geneva 9 and 12, Monaco 9 and 12, and Chicago 12. But it's usually safe to assume that several other sizes of Geneva are installed. Other commonly used fonts are Times, Helvetica, New York, and Palatino.

If you must include something in an unusual font and you can't predict which computers will run your stack, (1) use paint text to do the typing, or (2) supply the user with the font (provided it's in the public domain) and instructions for installing it in the System.

☐ **Press Command-B to leave the background.**

☐ **Select the Browse tool, click in the field, and type this title page, using the Return key and the space bar to center the text:**

Global Warming:
What Are We Doing to Our Planet?

Since HyperCard doesn't allow you to apply unique justification to individual lines or paragraphs in a field as your word processor does, you have to use the space bar to center the titles in a field where most of the text is left-justified.

Creating a Dynamic Bullet Chart

We're going to create four bullet charts—one for each main point in the outline. We'd like to have the bulleted points appear on the chart one at a time as we talk about them. So we'll start with a card containing only the first main heading.

☐ **Create a new card (Command-N) and type a title for the top of the card.**

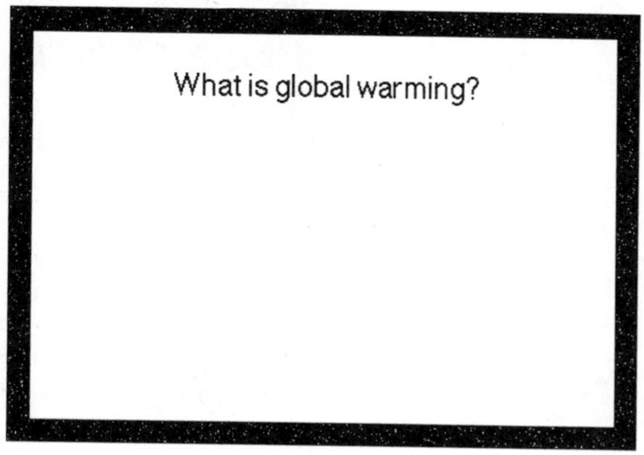
What is global warming?

☐ **Copy this card and paste it.**

☐ **Add another line of text. To type a bullet (•), press Option-8.**

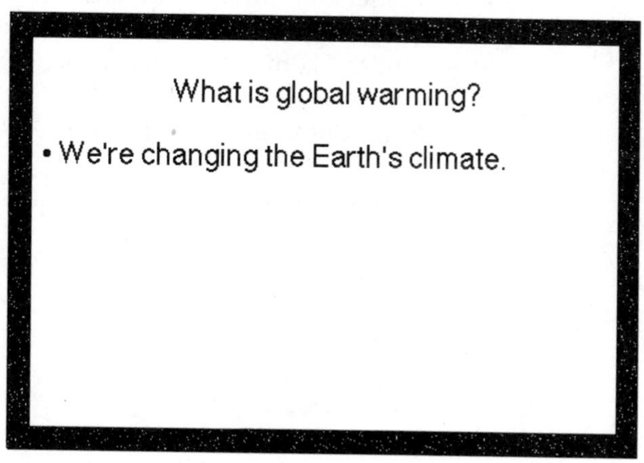
What is global warming?
• We're changing the Earth's climate.

- [ ] **Repeat the process (Copy Card, Paste Card, type text) for each of these cards:**

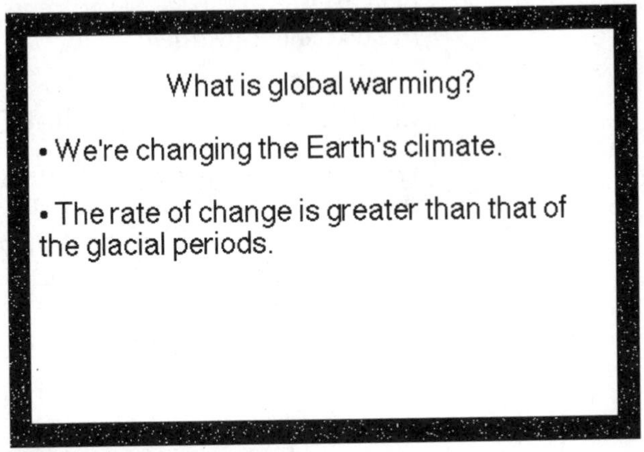

What is global warming?
• We're changing the Earth's climate.
• The rate of change is greater than that of the glacial periods.

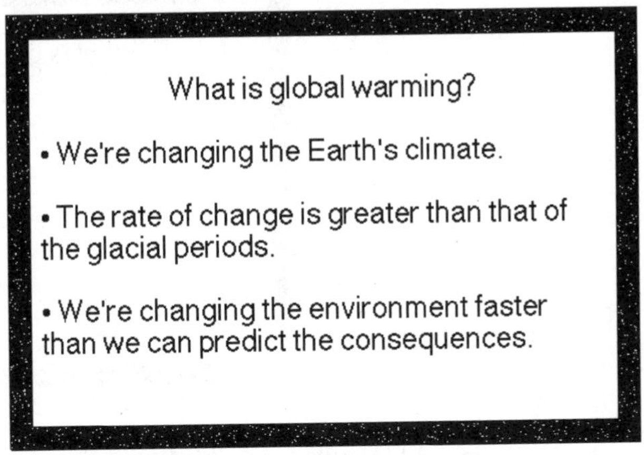

What is global warming?
• We're changing the Earth's climate.
• The rate of change is greater than that of the glacial periods.
• We're changing the environment faster than we can predict the consequences.

Building a Background Button

Rather than link these cards one at a time, let's create one big background button that will allow us to advance through all of our "slides," complete with a visual effect.

- [ ] **Press Command-B to go to the background.**

- [ ] **Create a new button. Drag and stretch it to fill the entire screen.**

- [ ] **Make it transparent and hide the name.**

- [ ] **Click on Script....**

As you can see, the script doesn't tell HyperCard what to do when the mouse is clicked. It's up to us to insert instructions between `on mouseUp` and `end mouseUp`.

☐ **Type the middle two lines of this script:**

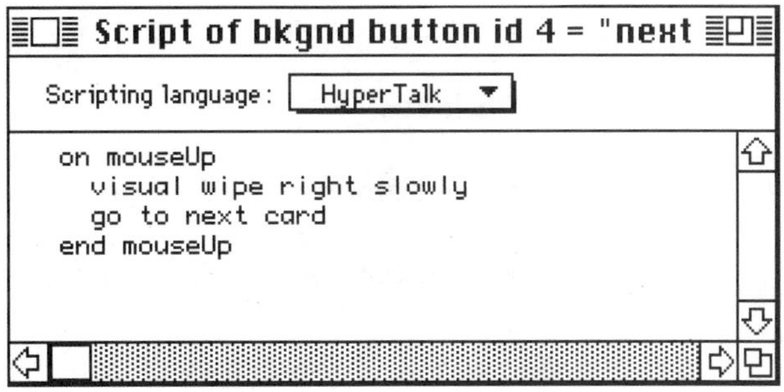

The Syntax of Scripts

You can type scripts in any combination of uppercase and lowercase letters; it's all the same in HyperTalk. You don't need to worry about indentation either, because the HyperTalk script editor takes care of that automatically. But HyperTalk, like most programming languages, is picky about spelling, spaces between words, order of words, ends of lines, and other matters of **syntax**.

In general, each line of a script represents a single command or statement. If a command is too long to be visible on a single line, you can insert a **soft return** (typed Option-Return, appearing in the script as ¬) to tell HyperCard that the command is continued on the next line.

HyperTalk allows enough flexibility that it's possible to write ambiguous statements. Since ambiguity breeds unpredictability, it's important to avoid it whenever possible. Quotation marks (" ") are often used to group words and symbols together to eliminate ambiguity.

Some HyperTalk statements and scripts are clear and unambiguous to HyperCard, but not to people. These statements should be followed by **comments**—clarifying notes for human script readers. A double dash (– –) in a script is a **comment marker**: Everything that follows this symbol on the line is ignored by HyperCard. Think of it as a stick-on note.

If you take liberties with syntax or mistype something, you're likely to see a dialog box with an error message when you try the button. If that happens, click on the Script... button in the dialog box and compare the script, line by line, with the original, editing the script as needed. Most of the traditional Macintosh editing techniques, including use of the Clipboard, work in the script editor.

☐ **Close the script window.**

A dialog box will ask you if you want to save changes to the script.

☐ **Click Yes.**

☐ **Press Command-B (Background).**

☐ **Press Command-1 (First) and Command-3 (Next).**

You're now looking at the first card of the presentation (not counting the unfinished introduction).

☐ **Select the Browse tool and click anywhere on the screen repeatedly to advance through the slides to the end.**

Notice the visual effect on card transitions. This time you typed the effect in the script rather than creating it in a dialog box, but it's there just the same.

Visual Effects in HyperTalk

Session 3 includes a list of HyperCard visual effects. Any of these effects can be incorporated into a HyperTalk script with the **`visual effect` command**. The basic syntax of the `visual effect` command is:

visual [effect] *effectName*

The word *effect* is optional (that's what the brackets mean). To use the command, substitute an effect name for the italicized placeholder *effectName.*

Examples:

```
visual effect iris open
```

```
visual dissolve
```

You can add an optional speed specification after the effect name, provided you arrange the command in this order:

visual [effect] *effectName* [*speed*]

Example:

```
visual effect barn door close very slowly
```

Speed choices:

`slow[ly]`	`very slow[ly]`
`fast`	`very fast`

You can also specify the screen image HyperCard will use during the transition:

```
visual [effect] effectName [speed] [to image]
```

Example:

```
visual effect checkerboard slowly to black
```

Image choices:

`black`	
`white`	
`gray`	
`card`	—the image of the destination card
`inverse`	—reverses the card image

Finally, you can include several visual effects in a row; they'll all happen in a sequence at the next `go` command. Experiment!

Rearranging Layers in the Background

Now it's time to add another card. You should currently be looking at the last card of the bullet chart sequence you just created. If not, type Command-4 to get there.

☐ **Press Command-N (New Card) and move the pointer over the background field.**

Something is wrong; the pointer doesn't turn into an I-beam. Why? Because the full-screen button we created is standing between our pointer and the field, blocking our attempts at typing. But we can move the field in front of the button with another useful command.

☐ **Select the Field tool, click on the background field, select Bring Closer from the Objects menu, and reselect the Browse tool.**

The pointer should turn into an I-beam when you move it over a field.

Creating More Bullet Charts

We need to type three more complete slides of information.

☐ **Create the following cards.**

If you're in a hurry, just create one of these cards. If you want to build a complete presentation, break each of these into several cards so the complete bullet chart builds one point at a time, like the first one.

How are we causing global warming?

- Burning fossil fuels produces carbon dioxide.

- Deforestation for fuel and grazing land eliminates carbon dioxide filters.

- Human activities produce other greenhouse gases (CFCs, methane, and so on).

What are the likely consequences?

- Heat waves, drought, and forest fires.

- Agricultural losses and famine.

- Rising sea level and flooding.

- Extinction of many trees and other species.

What can we do?

- Reduce energy consumption.
- Recycle paper, metal, glass, and plastic.
- Stop using plastic foam and CFC aerosols.
- Eat less meat.
- Plant more trees.
- Work for public policies that encourage energy efficiency and discourage pollution.

Adding a Card Layer Illusion

☐ **Go to the title card (the second card).**

☐ **Using the Button tool, select and copy the background button. (You don't need to go to the background to copy this button because there are no buttons in front of it.)**

☐ **Paste it onto the card layer of this title card.**

The background button is still there, but on this card it's completely covered by the new card button. When the mouse is clicked on this card, the card button will intercept a `mouseUp` command before the background button can receive it. We can now change the script of the card button so that it has a different visual effect.

☐ **Hold down the Shift key and double-click on the button.**

☐ **Change the visual effect in the script from `wipe right` to `scroll down`.**

☐ **Press the Enter key.**

This single keystroke closes the script window and saves changes to the script.

☐ **Try the button (using the Browse tool).**

The scroll is effective for creating the illusion that we're moving the current card out of the way so we can see the next one, just as the wipe creates the illusion that we're writing text on the card.

☐ **If you decide to complete the bullet chart presentation, copy this button onto each *completed* bullet chart card (showing every point), excluding the final "What can you do?" card.**

Once the text is typed and checked on each card, there's one more step:

☐ **Using the Field tool, select the background field; select Send Farther from the Objects menu to return it to its original layer.**

Hiding the field behind the button will provide some security against accidental deletion of the text. We don't need to lock the text in the field because there's no way to type in a buried field.

Shortcuts to Scripts

To see a button's script	Shift-double-click with Button tool selected, *or* Press Command-Option and click on the button, *or* Press Shift-Command-Option and click on the button
To see a field's script	Press Shift-Command-Option and click on the field
To see a card's script	Press Command-Option-C
To see a background's script	Press Command-Option-B
To see a stack's script	Press Command-Option-S
To see any script after an error message	Click on the Script... button in the dialog box
To close script window and save changes	Press Enter key
To close script window without saving changes	Click on the close box and then click No

Break Point

Moving Pictures

Now it's time to add some **animation** at the beginning to capture the attention of the audience. The simplest kind of animation in HyperCard is familiar to every child: flipping through a stack of cards with slightly different pictures on them—**card-flipping animation**. Let's create a series of cards to make the Earth gradually appear and then dramatically go up in smoke. But before we can destroy the Earth we have to create it.

Creating an Earth Icon

We'll add the Earth to the picture by creating a button with a custom icon. HyperCard 2 includes an **icon editor** that allows you to draw your own icons and install them in your stack. Unfortunately, the icon editor lacks many of HyperCard's sophisticated paint tools, including the Oval tool we use to draw circles. To make up for its drawing deficiencies, the icon editor includes a **Pickup command** that allows you to grab any 32 × 32 pixel area from any card or background and turn it into an icon. So we can create our 32-pixel-wide circle with the Oval tool. But how can we control the size of the circle to that degree of precision? We'll start by creating a dummy icon to frame the area; the rest will be easy.

- [ ] **Press Command-1 (First).**

- [ ] **Use the Paint Bucket to temporarily paint the card layer white.**

- [ ] **Select Icon... from the Edit menu.**

The icon editor is similar to the FatBits view of a painted scene; it allows you to edit every pixel of a 32 × 32 icon with a Pencil tool, a Selection rectangle, and several special menu items.

- [ ] **Name the icon "frame".**

The ID number has been arbitrarily assigned by HyperCard. You could change it, but why bother?

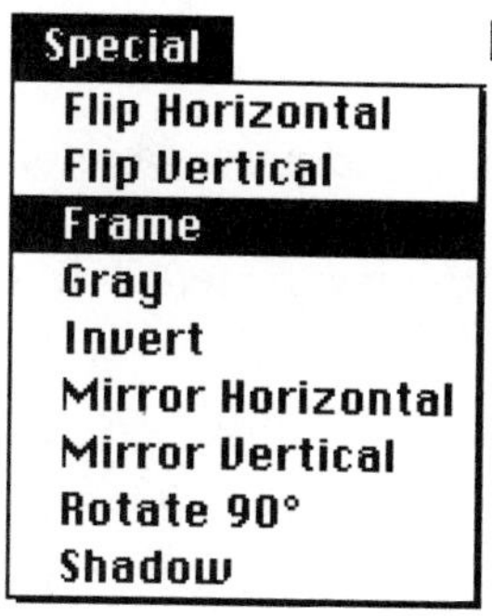

- [ ] **Select Frame from the Special menu.**

You've just drawn a 32-pixel square icon.

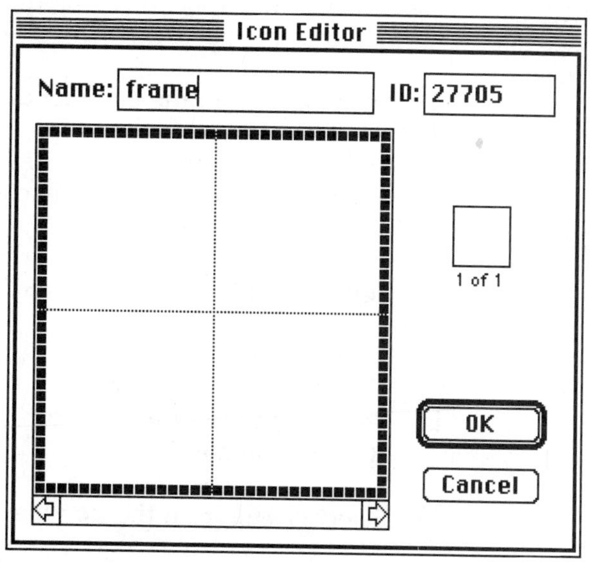

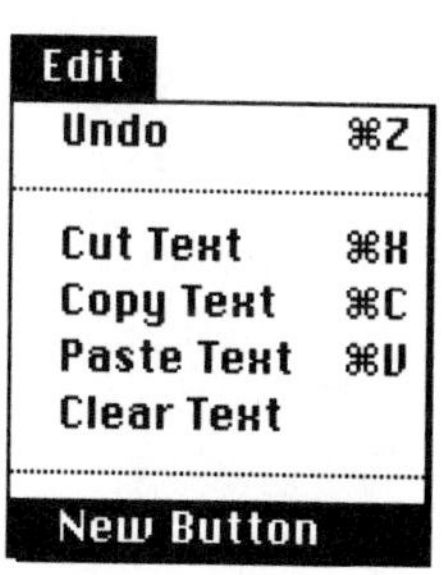

- [ ] **Select New Button from the Edit menu.**

We're out of the editor, looking at a new square button on the white card. We'll use it as a size guide for creating the circular icon we *really* want.

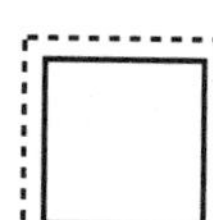

☐ **Drag the button close to the left edge of the window.**

☐ **Select from the Patterns palette one that looks like a cloud pattern on a distant planet.**

☐ **Double-click on the Oval tool to switch on the Draw Filled option, and click it again to select it.**

☐ **Position the cross hairs *exactly* on the upper left corner of the square icon and drag to the *exact* lower right corner. (Parts of the cross hairs will be white when they're in exactly the right position on each corner.)**

If you have trouble exactly positioning the cross hairs, you might want to do it with FatBits selected. Either way, you won't see what you're drawing because it's hidden by the button.

☐ **Select the Button tool, select the square button, and press Delete.**

The button is gone, revealing the circle. This is the raw material we'll use to create the Earth.

☐ **Select Icon from the Edit menu.**

The only icon currently attached to this stack is the Frame icon. (The other icons you've used are attached to your Home stack and therefore are available in every stack.)

☐ **Select Erase from the Icon menu.**

We'll start fresh.

☐ **Rename the now empty icon "earth1" (do not type a space between *earth* and *1*).**

☐ **Select Pickup from the Icon menu.**

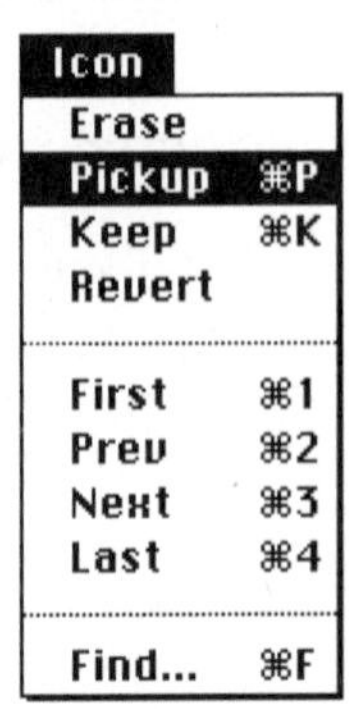

The pointer becomes an icon-sized frame.

☐ **Position the frame so it exactly surrounds the patterned circle and click.**

You've captured your painted circle as an icon.

☐ **Use the icon editor's Pencil to change the patterns so they look more like random clouds; include a white crescent in the upper right part of the circle to simulate sunshine on the sphere.**

The window includes an actual-size representation to give you a better idea of what you're creating. Don't copy every pixel shown here; clouds aren't that exact. You may use Keep and Revert to save your work and double back as you make changes.

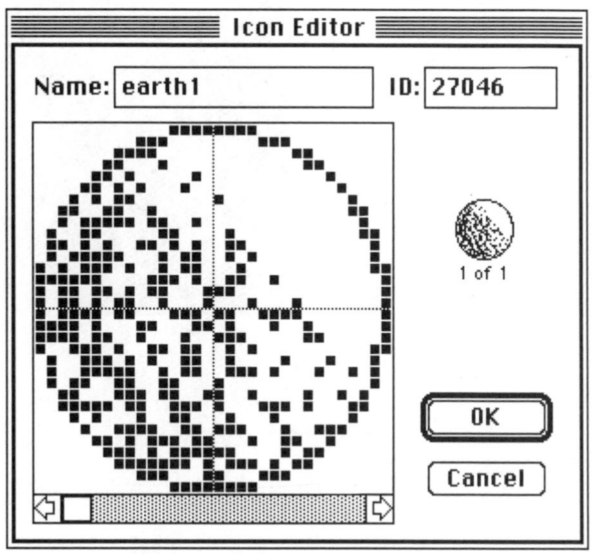

☐ **When you're happy with your icon, click OK.**

☐ **Double-click on the Eraser tool to erase anything left in this layer; then paint the whole layer black with the Paint Bucket.**

We'll start with this black card and fade into a view of the Earth from space. We'll put the Earth icon in the background.

☐ **Go to the background (Command-B).**

The stars are visible again.

☐ **Select the Button tool and select New Button.**

☐ **Double-click on the new button.**

☐ **Name the new button "earth", make it transparent, hide the name, and click on Icon....**

☐ **Select the earth1 icon and click OK.**

☐ **Reposition and reshape your button so it's in approximately the position shown here:**

Spraying Away Life as We Know It

Now you get to destroy the Earth with (what else?) an aerosol can.

☐ **Return to the card layer.**

Back to black.

☐ **Create a new card with the same background (Command-N).**

This card isn't painted black, so the Earth and the stars are visible again.

☐ **Copy the current card, paste it, select the Spray Can and white paint, and spray in small circles around the Earth until it looks like a cloud. (While you're at it, experiment with the Paintbrush with different brush shapes and sparse patterns.)**

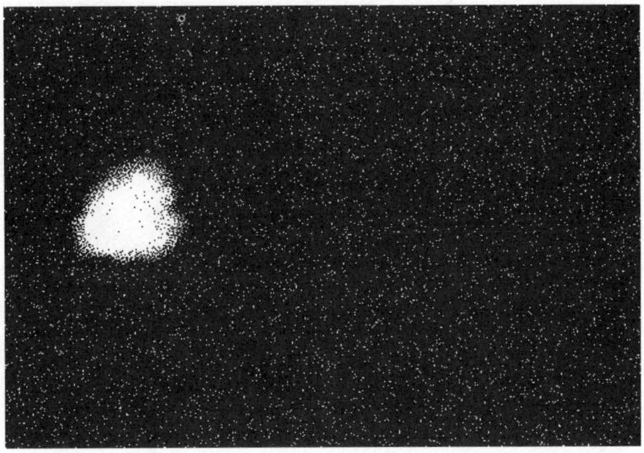

☐ **Copy the current card, paste it, and enlarge the cloud.**

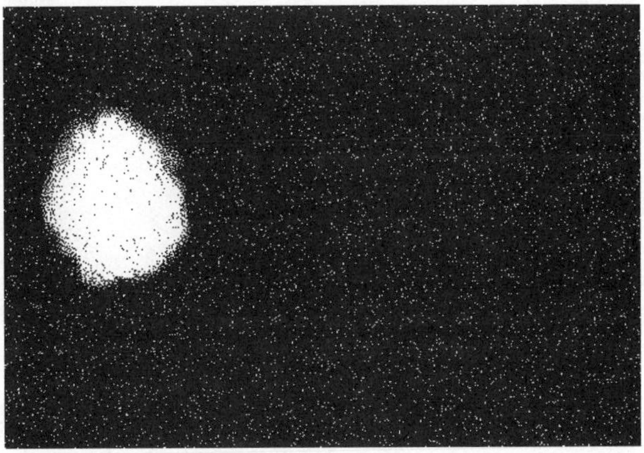

☐ **Repeat the process several times until the cloud fills the screen. Remember to paint behind the menu bar on the larger clouds; we're going to turn it off later so our presentation fills the whole screen. (Press Command-Space to hide the menu bar and to bring it back later.)**

> Create as many cards as you want. The more images, the more convincing the animation.

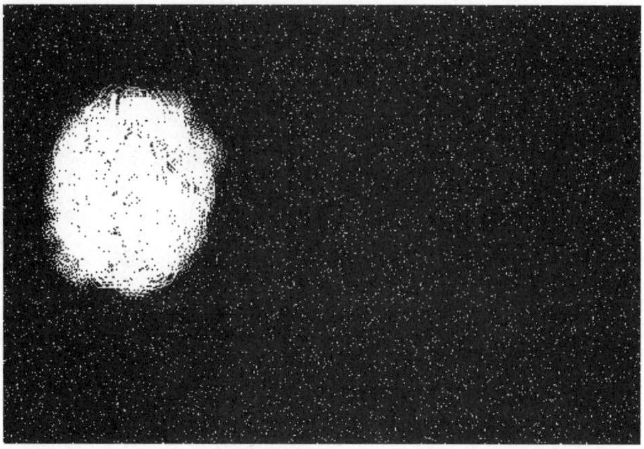

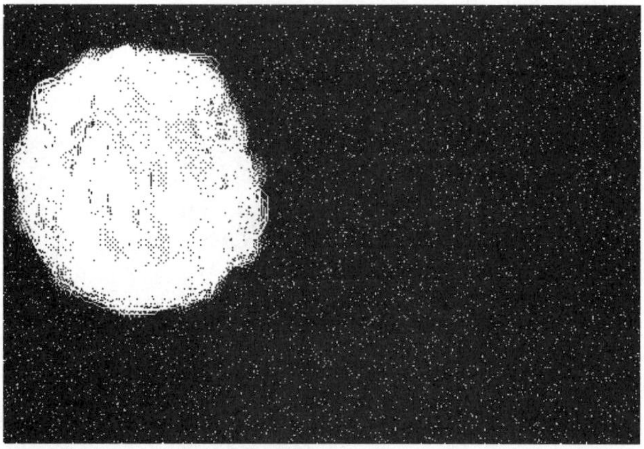

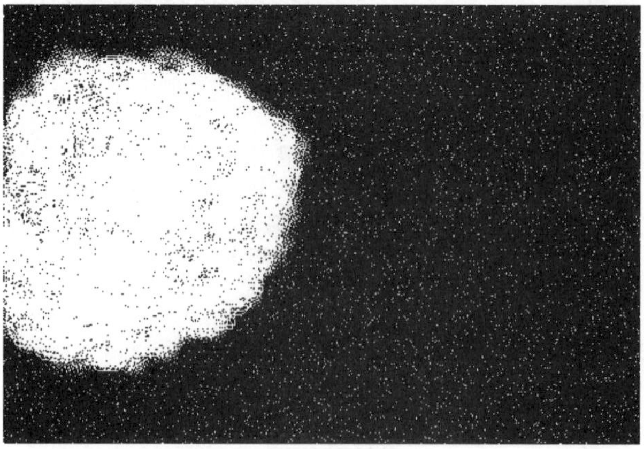

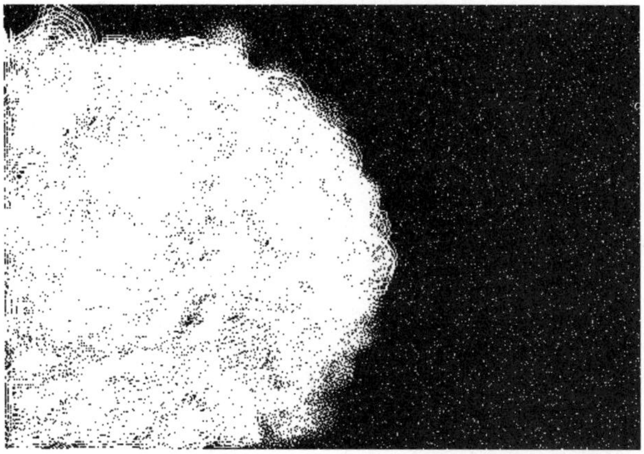

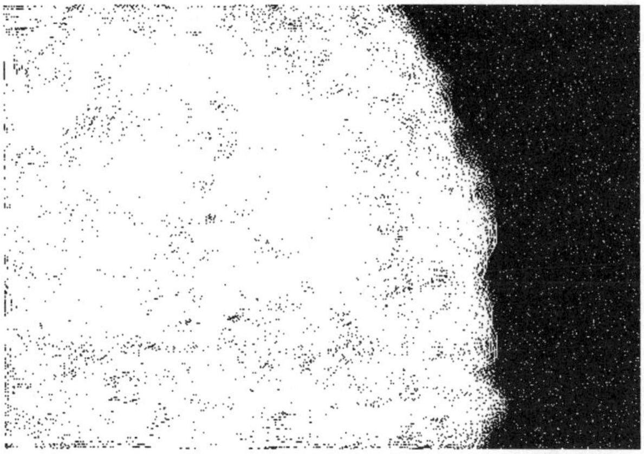

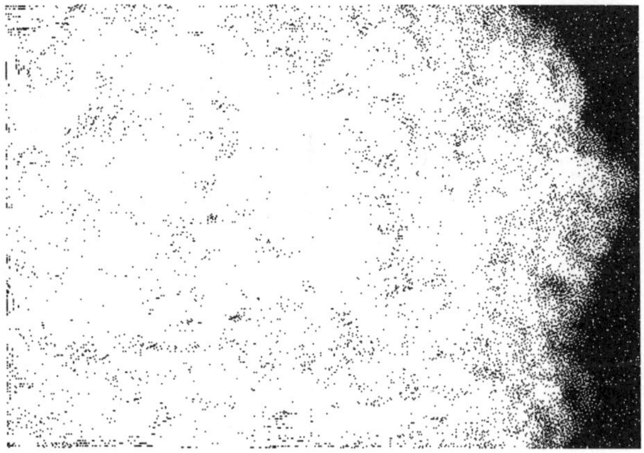

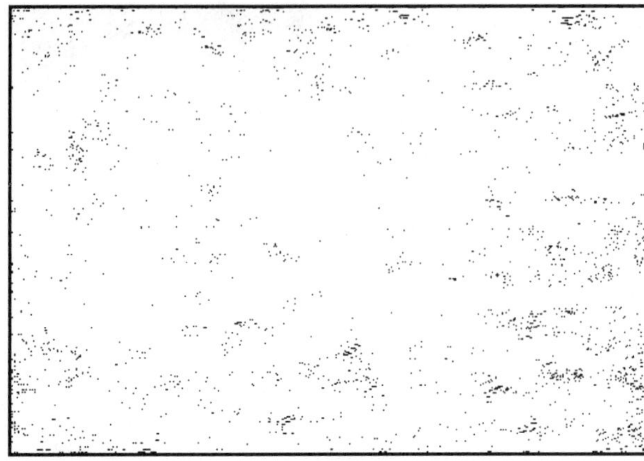

☐ **Copy the full-screen card and paste it; use the Spray Can to write:**

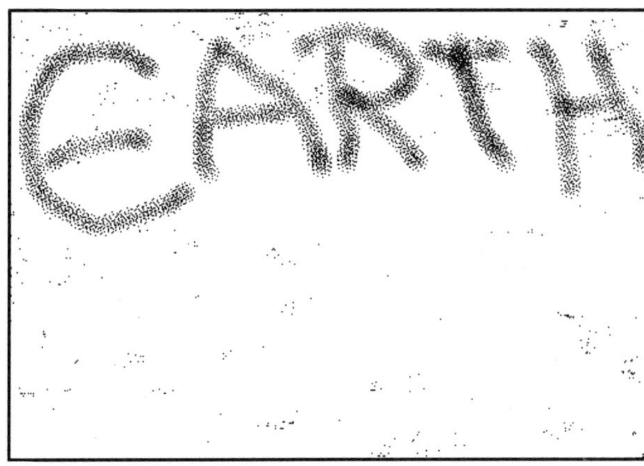

Remember that you can use the Revert command to erase the entire word if you aren't happy with it.

☐ **Copy and paste the card and add another word:**

☐ **One more time:**

Scripting an Animated Sequence

☐ **Try using the arrow keys to flip through these cards.**

The animation is a little jerky. We could link these cards, one at a time, and add scripts to dissolve from one card to another to smooth the transitions. But there's an easier, more effective way. We can put one button on the first card to start the show and add a script to that button that causes *all* of these cards to be displayed in order, with dissolve effects before each one. Here's how:

☐ **Go to the first card in the stack (Command-1).**

☐ **Create a new button, stretch and drag it to fill the screen, and double-click on it to bring up the Button Info dialog box.**

☐ **Name the button "blow up"; then select Transparent Style, click on Show Name (to turn it off), and click on Script....**

☐ **Type the missing lines of this script:**

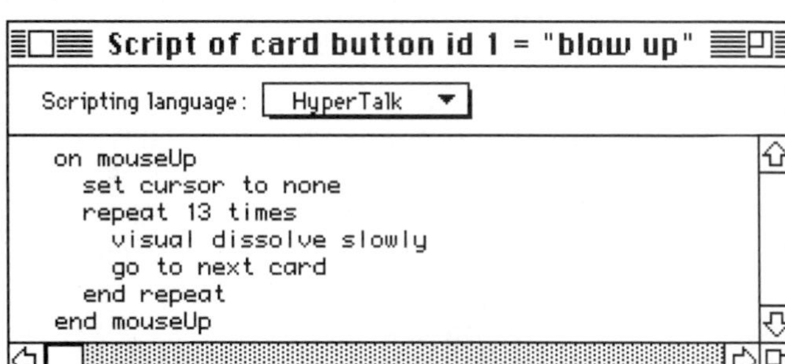

Depending on how many cards you have in your sequence, you might need to adjust the number in the `repeat` statement. Here's a rough translation of the script: "When the mouse is clicked, hide the cursor and repeat 'dissolve to next card' 13 times."

> **`set`** is a HyperTalk command for setting the properties of objects, windows, menus, and other HyperCard elements.
>
> `set [the]` *`property`* `[of` *`element`*`] to` *`value`*
>
> Every HyperCard object has properties: ID number, name, location, visibility, and so on. Some properties are unique to particular classes of objects. Buttons, for example, are the only objects that can have icons. Some properties, such as `cursor`, are **global**; they apply to the HyperTalk environment rather than to particular elements. Properties are often set by typing and clicking in dialog boxes. The `set` command allows you to automate the process of assigning a property to an object or the HyperTalk environment.

- [ ] **Select the Browse tool and click on the button to try the script.**

If the button works properly, the resulting sequence should be dramatic: The Earth gradually appears, then turns to a smoke cloud that overtakes the whole screen, revealing the title of the presentation one word at a time. If it doesn't end on the right card, you'll need to change the number in the repeat line. When it is working properly, you'll find yourself staring at the Earth Under Fire card when the sequence ends.

> The **`repeat`** `command` tells HyperCard to repeat everything between `repeat` and `end repeat`. This form of the `repeat` statement repeats the enclosed statements a specified number of times.
>
> `repeat [for] n [times]`
>
> Another form repeats a set of commands until some condition is true:
>
> `repeat until` *`condition`*
>
> Still another repeats while a condition is true.
>
> `repeat while` *`condition`*
>
> `repeat` and `if` are examples of what computer scientists call **control structures**. They determine the flow of control in a script: which statements will be executed in what order. `repeat` is a **loop structure**; it causes program control to loop through a sequence of repeated steps. `if` is a **conditional structure**; it causes control to branch to different statements depending on present conditions.

Linking the Introduction to the Presentation

We need a button on this card to dissolve into the framed title card.

☐ **Create a full-screen, invisible button on the Earth Under Fire card, name the button "fade", and insert this script in the `on mouseUp` handler:**

```
visual dissolve slowly to black
visual dissolve slowly to card
go to next card
```

☐ **Go to the first card in the stack and test the presentation so far.**

Break Point

Animating with Icons

This section contains more complex scripts than any you've seen so far. If you have no further interest in scripting in general and animation in particular, you may safely skip this section.

Creating a Spinning Planet

Once you start playing with HyperCard animation, it's hard to stop tinkering—there's always something that can be improved. In this presentation, for example, it could be argued that the Earth doesn't stay on the screen long enough for the audience to recognize it. Furthermore, the sequence might have more impact if the Earth rotated as a living, breathing planet should. Because we made the Earth a button with an icon, we can easily bring it to life by creating a few more icons showing different Earth views and writing a script telling the button to swap icons in rapid succession. This is called **icon animation**.

☐ **Go to the second card in the stack (the one with the visible Earth).**

☐ **Select Icon from the Edit menu.**

We're looking at the earth1 icon. Let's clone it.

☐ **Select Duplicate Icon from the File menu.**

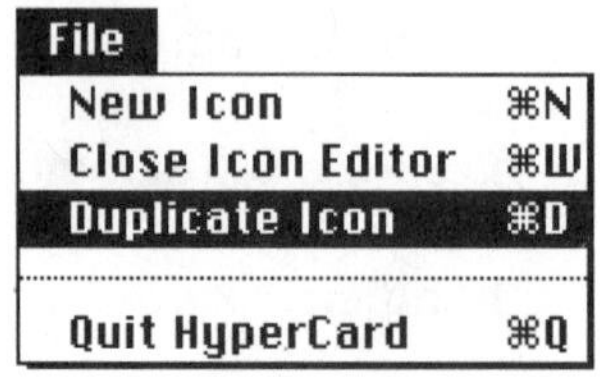

It has a new ID number, but everything else is the same as our original.

☐ **Change the name of the new icon to "earth2".**

We want earth2 to look like earth1 rotated a little bit.

☐ **Hold down the Command key and drag a rectangle through the area in the center and to the left of the icon, roughly like this:**

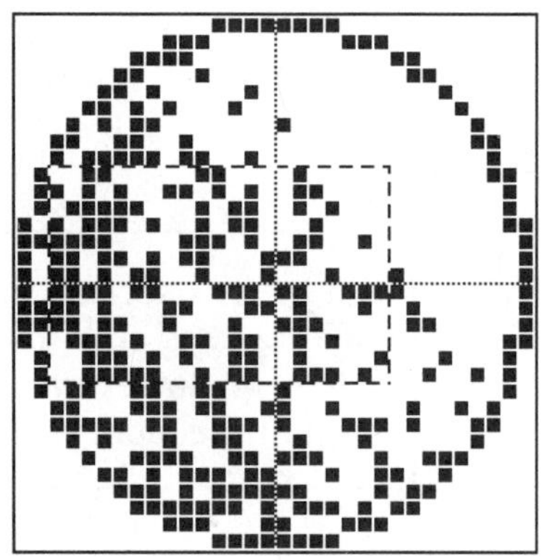

You've selected an area of the picture. You can move that selection to the right rather than trying to duplicate it with the Pencil.

☐ **Drag the selected area to the right about five pixels.**

☐ **Using a combination of selecting, dragging, and drawing, change some of the pixels in the remaining part of the icon, leaving the circular perimeter and the white crescent intact.**

Don't try to shift all the patterns in unison to the right; as long as some parts of the pattern shift rightward and others change randomly, you'll create the illusion of rotation with swirling clouds.

☐ **Select Duplicate Icon again.**

You'll be asked whether you want to save the changes to the earth2 icon.

- ☐ **Click Yes.**

- ☐ **Name the new icon "earth3" and change the cloud patterns in the same way.**

- ☐ **Repeat this process of duplicating and changing the icon one more time, creating an icon called "earth4". When you're finished, click OK to leave the icon editor.**

You have four Earth icons and one button; the next step is to add a script to the button telling it to rotate quickly through the icons, creating the illusion of movement.

- ☐ **Press Command-Option-C to open the script window for the card.**

- ☐ **Shrink the window so it's just large enough to display a few lines of text. (Use the size box in the lower right corner.)**

- ☐ **Type the following script:**

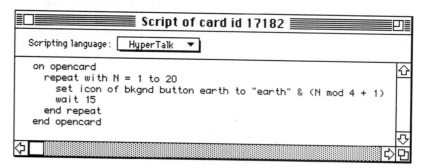

Script of card id 17182

Scripting language: HyperTalk

```
on opencard
  repeat with N = 1 to 20
    set icon of bkgnd button earth to "earth" & (N mod 4 + 1)
    wait 15
  end repeat
end opencard
```

This script contains several new HyperTalk words. Let's start by defining those words and then step through the script.

> **on OpenCard** is a handler that sends a message when the current card is opened. Whenever the user goes to this card, the script in this handler will be executed.
>
> This form of the `repeat` command tells HyperCard to repeat everything between `repeat` and `end repeat` using a variable as a counter. A **variable**, as its name suggests, can change in value. In this statement, the variable's value starts at a value (1) and is incremented (by 1) until it reaches the final value (20). With each increment the statements inside the `repeat` structure are repeated.
>
> **&** is an operator for combining character strings by attaching them end to end. The result is another string. Examples: `"earth" & "quake"` yields `"earthquake"`; `"earth" & 1`

yields `"earth1"`. Notice how the number is combined with the quoted string. In HyperTalk, a number is treated just like any other string of characters unless it's being used in an arithmetic operation.

The **`wait`** command tells HyperCard to wait a specified amount of time before proceeding. If no unit of time is specified, the default unit is the **tick**—one-sixtieth of a second.

So what is this script telling HyperCard to do when the card is opened? To execute the `set` statement 20 times, each time with a different value for the variable N, waiting one-fourth of a second after each execution. What, exactly, is the `set` statement doing? Telling HyperCard to attach an icon to the background button earth. Which icon? In order to determine that, HyperCard evaluates the numeric expression inside the parentheses and attaches the resulting number to the end of the character string "earth". The first time through, N has a value of 1, so (N mod 4 + 1) = (1 mod 4 + 1) = (1 + 1) = 2. The result of this calculation can be combined with the `"earth"` string, yielding `"earth2"`. This is the name of the icon the `set` statement attaches to the button called earth. The next time through the loop, N has a value of 2, so the set statement looks for the icon called `"earth3"` and attaches it to the button; then `"earth4"`; then `"earth1"` again. If this is confusing, never mind. HyperCard can do the calculations flawlessly, so you don't have to.

☐ **Test the script by saving the script, leaving the card, and returning.**

If all is well, you'll see the Earth's face change repeatedly for a few seconds. If it doesn't work, check the script and the icon names to make sure everything exactly matches what you've seen in this section.

☐ **Go to the beginning of the stack and click the button to start the card-flipping animation.**

Notice how the card flipping pauses when it reaches the Earth card. The `on openCard` handler temporarily takes control of HyperCard; when it's finished, control is passed back to the unfinished flipping script.

Creating Cards for a Finale

Let's use another kind of **button animation** to punctuate our conclusion.

☐ **Go to the second card (the Earth card) and select Copy Card. (You'll have to wait for the Earth to stop spinning.)**

☐ **Press Command-4 (Last) and Command-V (Paste Card) *twice*.**

☐ **On the last card (the one you're looking at after the last Paste command), use paint text and a large display font to type the sentence shown here. To get the white-on-black effect, use the Selection rectangle to select the white area around the text and select Invert from the Paint menu. (If the text still doesn't show, press Command-S to select all card-layer painted objects; then select Opaque from the Paint menu.)**

Finding the Mouse

☐ **Position the pointer so that it's fingering the Earth button.**

☐ **Press Command-M (Message), and type:**

```
the mouseloc
```

You just used the **`mouseLoc` function** to ask HyperCard where the mouse pointer is on the screen. When you press Return, HyperCard responds in the message box with a pair of numbers:

```
104,153
```

The card is made up of a 512 × 342 grid of pixels; each pixel has a unique address defined by two numbers: distance in pixels from the left, and distance in pixels from the top. The two numbers in the message box are the coordinates of the current mouse position. Those numbers represent the approximate location of the Earth button; the exact coordinates of that button can be retrieved, too.

☐ **Type:**

```
the loc of bg button earth
```

> **loc** (or **location**) is a property that applies to buttons, fields, and windows. It is made up of a pair of numbers, separated by commas, representing the horizontal and vertical offsets of the object from the upper left corner of the card window.
>
> **bg**, like **bkgnd**, is an abbreviation for background.

The numbers that appear represent the offset coordinates of the center of the button. Now we'll see how HyperTalk can change that location automatically.

Scripting a Moving Button

☐ **Press Command-2 twice to go back to the last bullet chart card.**

☐ **Create a full-screen invisible button named "finale", type the script shown here, and shrink the script window so it just frames the script.**

Script of card button id 1 = "finale"

Scripting language: HyperTalk

```
on mouseUp
  visual shrink to top
  go to next card
  put loc of bkgnd button earth into StartLoc
  put item 2 of StartLoc into NewLoc
  repeat until NewLoc > 299
    put NewLoc + 2 into NewLoc
    set loc of bkgnd button earth to item 1 of StartLoc,NewLoc
  end repeat
  repeat until NewLoc = Item 2 of StartLoc
    put NewLoc - 2 into NewLoc
    set loc of bkgnd button earth to item 1 of StartLoc,NewLoc
  end repeat
  visual wipe right slowly
  go to next card
end mouseUp
```

put evaluates an expression and puts the result in a **container**—a variable, a field, the message box, or the current selection.

An **item** is a group of characters (including punctuation, if any) separated by commas from other items. For example, item 1 of 144,153 is 144.

This script is telling HyperCard to perform these actions in order:

1. Use a visual effect to go to the next card (the first of the two new cards).
2. Copy the starting location of the Earth button into a variable called StartLoc. After this operation, StartLoc contains two numbers separated by a comma.
3. Copy the second number stored in StartLoc into another variable called NewLoc.
4. Repeat the following sequence, checking before each repetition to see whether NewLoc is greater than 299:
   a. Add 2 to the value of NewLoc; put the result back in the variable NewLoc, replacing the previous value. (Why 2? Because moving one pixel at a time takes too long on slower Macs.)
   b. Set the location property of the Earth button to the pair of numbers that includes the first item in StartLoc (which never changes from its starting value) and NewLoc (which has just been incremented by 2). The result of this substitution is that the horizontal position of the button remains unchanged, but the button moves two pixels down from its previous position.

   These two steps are repeated until NewLoc is greater than 299; that means that the button is now 300 pixels away from the top of the card. At this point, the next statement is executed.
5. Repeat the following sequence, checking before each repetition to see whether NewLoc is equal to the first of the two numbers stored in StartLoc:
   a. Subtract 2 from the value of NewLoc; put the result back in the variable NewLoc.
   b. Set the location property of the Earth button to the pair of numbers that includes the first item in StartLoc (still unchanged) and NewLoc (which has just been decreased by 2). The result of this substitution is that the horizontal position of the button remains unchanged, but the button moves two pixels up from its previous position.

   This loop terminates when NewLoc equals its original value, and the Earth is back where it belongs.

6. Wipe right into the next card—the one with the white-on-black concluding message.

If you find this confusing, don't feel alone. There's a lot happening here, and it's happening in a language that you've never seen before. Fortunately, HyperTalk comes with a tool that can help clarify this complex set of events: the HyperTalk debugger.

Using the HyperTalk Debugger

> If you're not interested in the technical details of the debugger, you can skip this section for now. Just remember it's here in case you need it later.

When you start writing longer scripts, bugs are inevitable. The HyperTalk debugger is designed to make it easy to track down and eradicate bugs. But even if your stack is completely bug-free, the debugger is a wonderful tool for learning how scripts work. You can use the debugger to slow down the action and observe messages and changes in variables while each script executes. Let's try it on the scripts we just created.

☐ **With the Finale button script window still open, click in front of the first line of the script and select Set Checkpoint from the Script menu.**

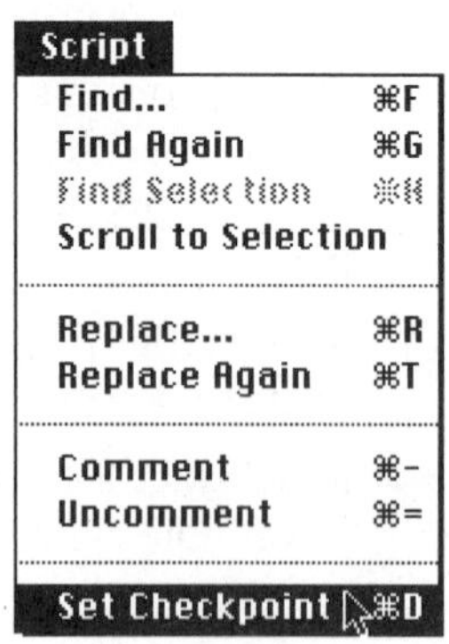

In the language of debugging, a **break point** is a spot in a program (script) where the execution of the program can be intentionally stopped so the programmer can see exactly what's going on at that instant, in the same way sports broadcasters use freeze-frame videos to analyze key plays in sporting events. In HyperTalk vernacular, break

```
✓ on mouseUp
```

points are called **checkpoints**. When you selected the Set Checkpoint command, you told HyperCard to make the current line of the script into a checkpoint. (That's what the check mark means.)

☐ **Close the script window, saving the changes.**

☐ **Click on the card to execute the script.**

```
✓ on mouseUp
    visual shrink to top
    go to next card
```

Since the first line of the script is a checkpoint, execution stops before it can get started, and the HyperTalk debugger takes over. The script reappears with a box around the checkpoint line.

The action is frozen until you tell the debugger what to do. That's what the bug in the menu bar is for.

HyperTalk Debugger Menu Commands

The HyperTalk debugging environment is opened when HyperCard encounters a checkpoint, or when you click the debug window in a dialog box specifying a script error, or when you press Option-Command-Period while a script is executing. The **Debugger menu** (under the bug) offers several options, including one you've already tried.

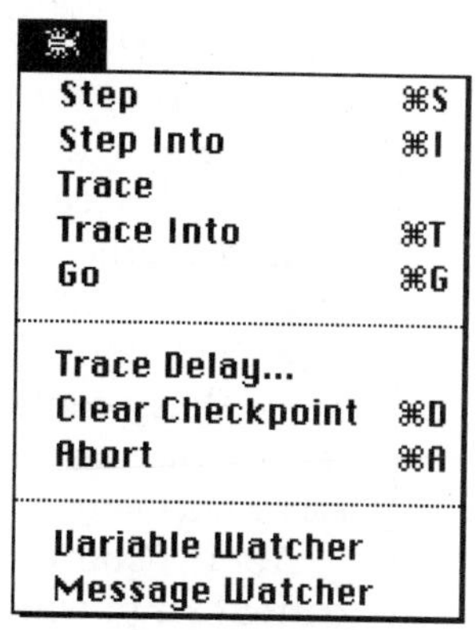

Message Watcher shows (or hides) the Message Watcher window, which allows you to monitor messages as scripts execute. Check boxes allow you to hide idle messages and unused messages. (You can also invoke the Message Watcher by typing "`mw`" or "`open window "message watcher"`" in the message box, whether or not the debugger is operational.)

Variable Watcher shows (or hides) the Variable Watcher window, which allows you to monitor the contents of variables as the script executes. In essence, the Variable Watcher is a window into the computer's memory where variable values are stored.

The Variable Watcher window also allows you to *change* the values for particular variables. (Like the Message Watcher, the Variable Watcher window can be viewed even if the debugger is turned off. But when it's used without the debugger, it displays only global variables, so you can't see the values of any variables defined and used inside particular handlers. Global variables are discussed in the next session.)

Set/Clear Checkpoint (Command-D) adds (or clears) a checkpoint marker at the current line of the script. Each checkpoint stops the execution of the script and turns on the HyperTalk debugger.

Step (Command-S) allows you to walk through a script one statement at a time. By typing Command-S repeatedly, you can examine the results of each statement as long as you like rather than trying to analyze things on the fly. If, in the course of stepping through a script, you cause another script to be executed (for example, the rotating Earth script is invoked when you go to the next card in the finale script), the second script is executed at normal speed before control is returned to the current script.

Step Into (Command-I) is like Step, except that it allows you to step into other scripts as they're invoked rather than having them execute behind the scenes. For example, if you repeatedly Step through the finale script, the rotating Earth script window opens when you go to the card that contains that script, so you can continue stepping through that script until it is completed, at which time the finale script window reappears.

Trace and **Trace Into (Command-T)** are similar to Step and Step Into, except that they continue through the script(s) automatically rather than waiting after each statement for input from you. Traces generally go too quickly to be of much use unless you slow the action by specifying a delay after each statement with the **Trace Delay** command. The Trace Delay dialog box allows you to specify the number of ticks (sixtieths of a second) to wait after each statement. Pressing **Command-Period** terminates any trace.

Abort (Command-A) turns off the debugger but leaves the current script window open.

Go (Command-G) turns off the debugger and closes the script window, allowing execution to continue from the point at which you entered the debugger.

Stepping through a Script

Let's use these menu commands to follow our scripts.

☐ **Select Message Watcher and Variable Watcher from the menu. Move the windows so you can still see the script and part of the card.**

- ☐ **Select Step Into.**

```
✓ on mouseUp
    visual shrink to top
    go to next card
```

The box moves to the second line of the script, the `visual` command. The keyboard shortcut is especially handy for this command.

- ☐ **Press Command-I (Step Into).**

```
✓ on mouseUp
    visual shrink to top
    go to next card
```

The box advances to the `go to next card` command.

- ☐ **Press Command-I again.**

When the `go to next card` command is executed, a `closeCard` message is sent through the message hierarchy followed by an `openCard` message. Depending on how your Home card is scripted, it may pass those messages to the Audio Help stack, which will intercept them and temporarily take over control of HyperCard while it executes the handlers that correspond to those messages. The Audio Help stack script doesn't do anything that would be visible to a normal user; it just does some behind-the-scenes checking that we don't need to be concerned with here.

- ☐ **If the Audio Help Stack script window appears on your screen, move it down so you can see part of the card behind it and press Command-I several more times, observing what happens while you do.**

You'll see the control box move through the script, one line at a time. When the `closeCard` handler completes its work, the next card appears with a visual effect. Audio Help executes its own `openCard` handler and passes control back to your stack, where the card that was opened takes over long enough to execute its own `openCard` handler.

```
on openCard
  repeat with N = 1 to 20
```

- ☐ **Step past the `repeat` statement (using Command-I).**

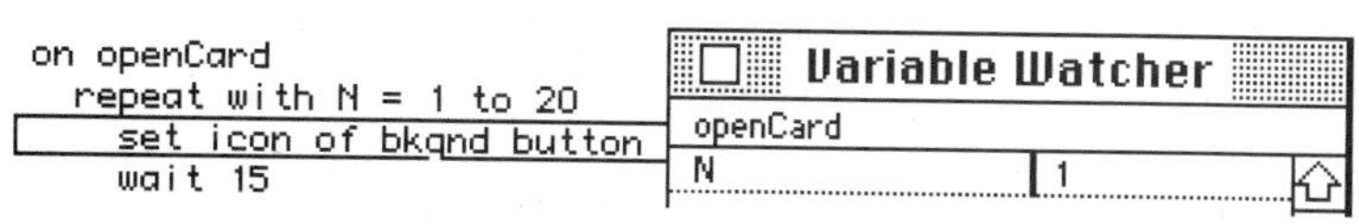

When we step past the `repeat` statement, the variable N appears in the Variable Watcher window, along with its initial value of 1. This value will be updated each time we go through the `repeat` loop until N reaches a value of 20. Every variable change is recorded in this way in the Variable Watcher while the debugger is operating.

Tracing a Script's Actions

We could continue stepping through the scripts, but let's automate the process by turning on a trace.

☐ **Set Trace Delay to 60 ticks (one second).**

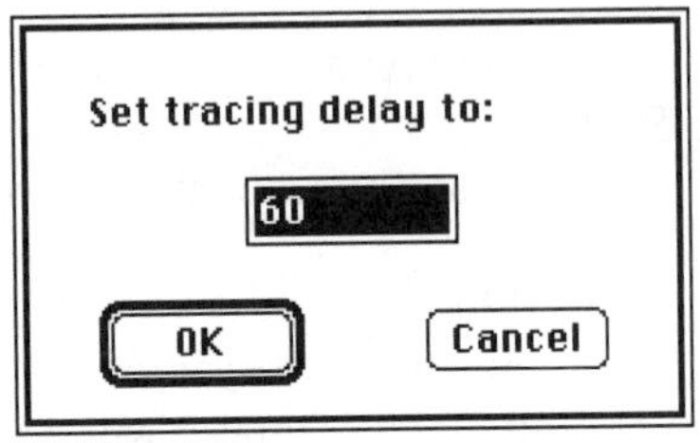

☐ **Select Trace or press Command-T.**

HyperCard will execute one statement each second until all invoked scripts have been completed. As the execution continues, you can monitor the current statement in the script, the messages being sent, changes in variables, and the resulting changes in appearance of the stack. (Of course, you may need to rearrange windows to see all these things.) If the action is too fast (or too slow) for you, or if it fails to terminate, you can press Command-Period to stop execution at any time.

☐ **When your trace is completed, return to the last bullet chart and press the Finale button again. Experiment with the debugger by tracing and/or stepping through the script again until you're satisfied that you understand what's happening behind the scenes while the scripts execute. When you're finished, remove the checkpoint by selecting that script line and pressing Command-D.**

Debugging with the Debugger: Examples

The debugger is a wonderful tool for illuminating the inner workings of stacks. Use it to display script execution in slow motion. Add checkpoints to stop action in tricky places. Monitor variables and messages as they change. There are all kinds of possibilities. But the debugger is most useful for figuring out—and fixing—scripts that don't work.

If your scripts don't do what they're supposed to, use the debugger to look for problems and clues. What kind of clues? Here are two examples from the current stack.

Example 1: Suppose you accidentally mistype the name of the variable NewLoc at one point in the finale script, so that the statement inside the repeat loop says `Put NewLock + 2 into NewLoc`. When you click the button, the script stops executing before the last card appears. Instead of a moving Earth, HyperCard displays this dialog box:

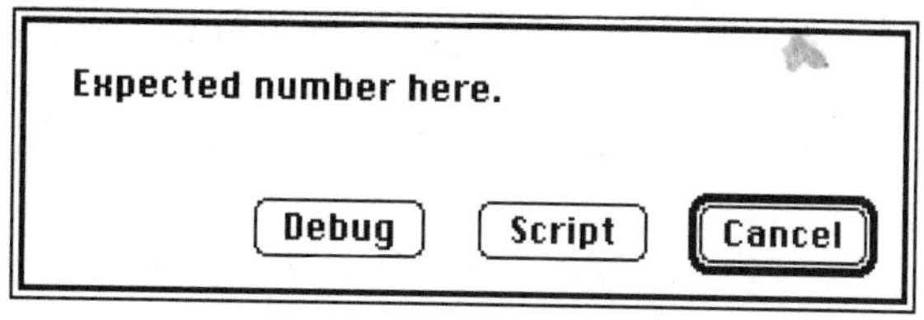

Clicking on the Debug button takes us into the debugger with the suspicious statement outlined:

```
repeat until NewLoc > 299
  put NewLock + 2 into NewLoc
  set loc of bkgnd button earth to item 1 of StartLoc,NewLoc
```

In this case, HyperCard has zeroed in on the problem statement; all we need to do is press Command-A to abort the debugger and correct the misspelling. (HyperCard isn't always so accurate, but it does its best.)

Example 2: Suppose you mistype the same statement so it says `Put NewLoc + 2 into NewLock`. When you try to execute the script, the Earth icon fails to move and the script fails to stop. This is an example of an **endless loop**—a loop with no way of terminating. It's important to remember that you can terminate any script, any time, by typing Command-. (Command-Period). **Command-Option-Period** terminates the script and transports you immediately into the debugger at the current script line, so you can set a checkpoint at a suspicious location and start a trace with the two watcher windows open. In this case, a trace isn't necessary because we can see the smoking gun through the Variable Watcher window.

```
repeat until NewLoc > 299
  put NewLoc + 2 into NewLock
  set loc of bkgnd button earth
end repeat
repeat until NewLoc = item 2 of
  put NewLoc - 2 into NewLoc
  set loc of bkgnd button earth
```

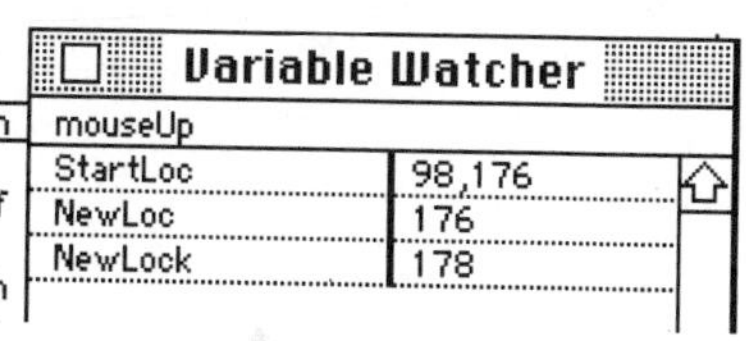

Instead of two variables, the window displays three. Why not? That's what the script says. Since we're incrementing NewLock and not NewLoc, it's safe to say that NewLoc will never reach 299, and the loop will never terminate on its own. Another case solved.

Use the debugger to trace any scripts you don't understand in the rest of this book. If you can't get a script to work after you type it in, use the debugger to help you locate the problem.

Singing Stacks

We've created an impressive finale for our presentation, but something is missing: sound. We'll use HyperTalk to add music to the finale, but first let's try something simpler.

Making a Noisy Button

HyperCard 2.3 makes it easy to add sound to a stack by simply assigning a task to a button. Try it:

- ☐ **Go to the last card of the stack (Command-4).**
- ☐ **Select the Button tool and create a New Button.**
- ☐ **Double-click on the button and choose Tasks... in the Button Info dialog box.**
- ☐ **Click on the Sound icon.**

Sound

- ☐ **Select Boing from the list of sounds and press Return to assign the task.**

Boing is one of the sounds that comes built into HyperCard. You'll learn later how to record or import other sounds into your stacks.

- ☐ **Select the Browse tool and click on your new button.**

The button should make a distinct sound. (If it doesn't, you may need to adjust the volume in the Sound Control Panel.) The script of this button is straightforward enough:

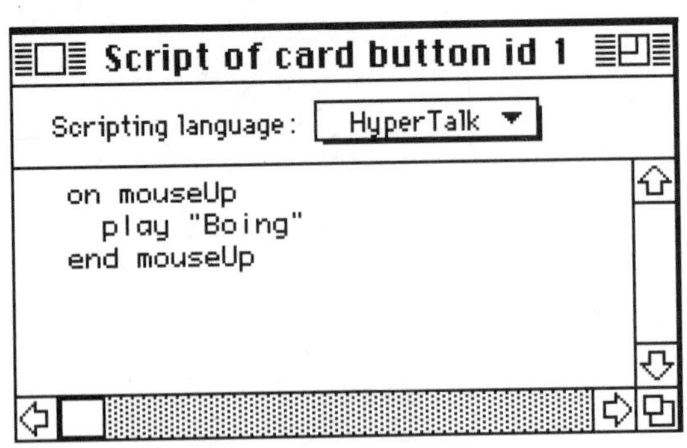

The **Play command**, as you've probably figured out, plays a sound. But with a little additional scripting, it can play music. Before we start the music, though, let's delete the boing button from our stack; it doesn't add anything of value to the presentation.

☐ **Select the Button tool, click on the button, and press the Delete key.**

Making a Musical Card

Most musical scripts are attached to buttons, but we're going to set up a script to play a borrowed bit of Bach automatically when the final animation sequence begins.

☐ **Go to the second-to-last card (the one with the Earth alone) and select Card Info... with the Shift key held down.**

This card, a copy of an earlier card, has a copy of that card's script. We'll replace it with something different.

☐ **Select all but the first and last lines of the script and replace them with the middle three lines of the script shown here:**

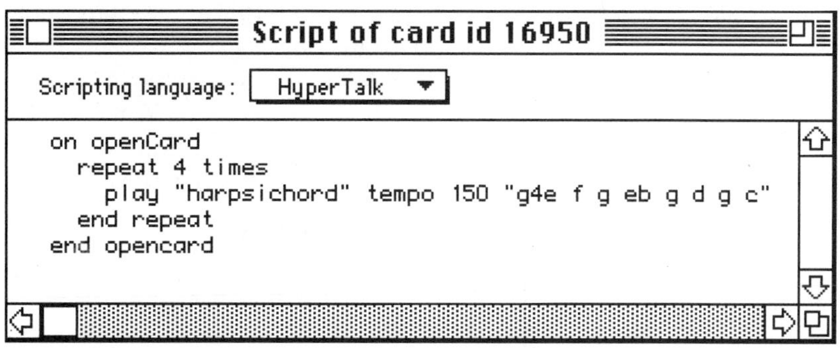

When the `openCard` message is received, this message handler tells HyperCard to repeat the Play command four times.

☐ **Save the script; then leave the card and return to try it out.**

The key to this script is the Play command. If you can read standard musical notation, this command is fairly easy to interpret once you understand how it works. If you're not a musician, the command is, at best, cryptic. Either way, this brief description of the command should make its function clearer.

The Play Command

The Play command takes the following form:

```
play "voice" [tempo tempoValue] "notes"
```

Here's a brief explanation of each element of the command:

`voice` tells HyperCard what kind of sound to play. `flute`, `harpsichord`, and `boing` are built into HyperCard. Session 7 will show you how to add other sounds.

`tempo` tells HyperCard how fast to play the sequence of notes. 100 is normal; larger numbers represent faster tempos.

`notes` that make up the melody to be played may be represented by their letter names (*a* through *g*), separated by spaces and followed by four optional characters: (1) accidentals (*b* for flat or # for sharp); (2) octave number, with 4 representing the octave for middle c; (3) the duration of the note (*w* for whole, *h* for half, *q* for quarter, *e* for eighth, *s* for 16th, *t* for 32nd, and *x* for 64th); and (4) . for dotted note or 3 for triplet.

Everything except accidentals stays in effect until changed, so you don't need to repeatedly specify note length or octave. In the example,

```
play "harpsichord" tempo 150 "g4e f g eb g d g c"
```

all the notes are eighth notes (*e*) in the fourth octave.

HyperCard doesn't stop working while a sound is playing, so it's possible to combine audio and video effects to create simple multimedia presentations. You can also get sounds to play almost simultaneously by changing the `soundChannel` property with the set command, like this:

```
set soundchannel to 1
play "harpsichord" c
set soundchannel to 1
play "harpsichord" e
set soundchannel to 1
play "harpsichord" g
```

(Sounds may be distorted if you're not running your stack from a hard disk; slower devices like floppy disk drives may not be able to access information fast enough for distortion-free sound.)

Those are the basics of the Play command, but if you're serious about sound, there's much more to learn. Consult Chapter 7 and Appendix A for more sound information, including how to put your own real-world sounds into stacks.

Hiding and Showing the Menu Bar

Finally, as promised, we'll make sure the menu bar doesn't get in the way when we're viewing the presentation. We'll put handlers for this in the stack script because we want the menu bar (and the title bar if we're using a Macintosh with a larger screen) to disappear as soon as the stack is opened and reappear when the stack is closed.

> The **on openStack** handler tells HyperCard what to do when the message `openStack` is received by the stack. `openStack` is a standard message sent by the System to each stack when it is opened. **closeStack** is sent when the stack is closed.

☐ **Press Command-Option-S to show the script for the stack, and type this script:**

```
on openStack
  hide menuBar
  hide titleBar
end openStack

on closeStack
  show menuBar
  show titleBar
end closeStack
```

> Always put things back the way you found them. If you hide the menu bar when the stack is opened, then show the menu bar when you close it. If you change the user level on openStack, then change it back on closeStack. And so on.

Bringing It Home

We have one more tiny script to write.

☐ **Put an invisible full-screen button on the last card and give it the following script:**

```
on mouseUp
  go Home
end mouseUp
```

☐ **Start at the beginning and test the whole stack.**

Enjoy the show!

Summary

In this session you went behind HyperCard's friendly front and learned a few words of HyperTalk, the scripting language of HyperCard. You learned how to send simple messages to HyperCard in the message box. You saw how the objects of HyperCard—buttons, fields, cards, backgrounds, and stacks—are controlled by scripts that interpret messages and execute commands. You used HyperTalk to add visual effects, animation, icon animation, button animation, and music to a stack. In the process, you learned enough about HyperTalk to easily learn more by examining other scripts, the HyperCard Help stacks, and other HyperTalk resources.

In the next session you'll learn more about HyperTalk by creating a nonlinear document using the powerful hypertext commands built into HyperCard. Session 7 will show you how to add color, custom sounds, and video to your Earth presentation without scripting. If you've had enough HyperTalk for now, you can safely skip to that session.

Key Words

&
Abort command (Command-A, debugger)
animation
`bg, bkgnd`
break point
bullet chart
button animation
Card Info... command
card-flipping animation
checkpoint (break point)
`closeStack` message
Command-Option-Period
Command-Period
comment (in script)
comment marker (`--`)
conditional structure
container
control structure
`cursor` (property)
Debugger menu
debugging environment
`div` (arithmetic operator)
`end mouseUp` statement
endless loop
Field Info dialog box
Field tool
Frame command (icon editor)
function
global property
Go command (Command-G, debugger)
`hide` command
HyperTalk
icon animation
Icon command
icon editor
`idle` message
`if` structure
`item`
`keyDown` message
Lighten command
`location` (`loc`) property
loop structure
Message command (Command-M)
message box
message handler
Message Watcher
`mod` (arithmetic operator)
`mouseEnter` message
`mouseLeave` message

mouseLoc function
mouseUp message
mouseWithin message
New Field command
object-oriented language
objects
on mouseUp (handler)
on openCard (handler)
on openStack (handler)
operator precedence
Pickup command (icon editor)
Play command
presentation graphics
procedural language
property
put command
repeat command
returnKey message
script
script editor
Script menu
script window
set command
Set/Clear Checkpoint commands (Command-D, debugger)
show command
soft return (Option-Return, ¬)
Spray Can
Step command (Command-S, debugger)
Step Into command (Command-I, debugger)
syntax
system messages
tick
time function
Trace command (debugger)
Trace Delay command (debugger)
Trace Into command (Command-T, debugger)
variable
Variable Watcher
visual effect command
wait command

Exercises

1. Explain what these script commands do:

   a. `visual wipe left slowly`

   b. `wait 30`

   c. `set cursor to watch`

   d. `play "boing"`

   e. `hide menuBar`

   f. `put Count + 1 into Count`

   g. `go to first card`

   h. `put 35 / 7 into Number`

2. Write a script to do each of the following:

   a. Have the computer make a "boing" sound 10 times when a button is clicked.

   b. Cause the screen (or card window) to slowly turn black when clicked.

c. Calculate the sum of the first 20 integers when a button is clicked and display the result in the message box. (*Hint:* The last statement might read `put sum in msg`.)

3. Where might you use button scripts? Field scripts? Card scripts? Stack scripts? Describe the reasons for your decisions.

4. What happens when you press Command-M?

5. What is the difference between an object and a message?

6. Why does a button script generally contain the phrase `on mouseUp`?

7. What is syntax and how is it important in HyperTalk?

8. What does `the mouseLoc` mean?

9. Describe three methods of HyperCard animation. Give an example of an application for each type.

10. Describe how the HyperTalk debugger can be used to track down errors. What's another way to use the debugger?

11. What is the difference between Step and Trace in the debugger?

Projects

1. In the background of the bullet chart portion of the Earth stack, create a thermometer shape along the left edge of the screen. If you like, put an Earth icon in the bulb at the bottom of the thermometer. On the card layer, draw a line representing the temperature on the thermometer. Have it rise a little on each successive card, until you get to the "What can we do?" cards. Have the temperature drop for each new point on these cards.

2. Create buttons on your Home card that will automatically open each of the stacks you've created.

3. Modify the Dungeon stack (from Session 4) so that the bed's button causes the bed to move slowly, revealing the secret passageway underneath as it moves. Use card-flipping animation techniques. Copy the first card showing the bed and paste it. Remove the two buttons from this new card. Use the Lasso to select the bed and move it a small amount. Copy the new card and move the bed again. After you've created cards showing the complete bed-moving sequence, work *backward* through these cards, adding the pit in successively smaller segments to each card. Create a button on the first bed card to flip through the cards. (You will need to know how many cards are in the series when you script the button.) For a final touch, have the Bed button make a boing sound when you click it.

4. Add sound effects and animation to the Pyramid stack and the Dungeon stack. Be creative!

5. Create a card containing musical buttons. Make each play a different note. Use paint tools to create a keyboard and put the buttons on each note. Play a tune.

Session 6

By the end of this session you should be able to

- Create a hypertext document with dynamic links between text fields
- Create, modify, and write scripts to work with different kinds of HyperCard text fields
- Modify the HyperCard user interface by creating custom dialog boxes and pull-down menus
- Design a complex document with a linear structure, a tree structure, and a network structure
- Understand how different document structures can be used by different kinds of hypertext readers
- Apply the principles of software design and stepwise refinement to the process of building a HyperCard stack

Creating Hypertext

Nonlinear Writing

The Problem

Your CS 101 instructor has asked you to produce a paper on basic computer anatomy. She wants you to write it in such a way that readers can either read it as a tutorial or use it as a reference to look up particular terms. She expects you to produce a document that presents an overview of the material but that allows the student to dig deeper into any concept to learn more. She also wants the paper to work as a reference guide for quickly looking up computer hardware terminology. This kind of flexibility isn't possible in a traditional term paper. Perhaps HyperCard can help.

Introduction

HyperCard is often described as Apple's brand of hypertext. But as you've seen, HyperCard is, at its core, a kind of hypergraphics tool. Nonetheless, text manipulation is an integral part of HyperCard, and that's what we'll focus on during this session. In order to create a hypertext document that gives the user maximum flexibility, we'll design our document from the top down, filling in details as we go.

Designing Hypertext

> This session is the most technical in the book. If you're more interested in multimedia presentations than in scripting, you may safely skip this session. But even if you're not a serious scripter, you'll find useful design ideas in the hands-off discussions at the beginning and end of the session.

Defining the Problem

When all is said and done, a computer is a tool for solving human problems. If we keep that in mind when we're working with HyperCard, it's easy to remember and apply one of the most important rules of thumb in programming:

> *Start by defining the problem clearly.* A program (or stack) with stunning graphics, elaborate special effects, impressive content, and mind-boggling structure is worth less than a simple stack that addresses and solves the problem at hand.

Our problem, described at the beginning of this session, is to create a document that can give CS 101 students an understanding of how the basic parts of a computer function. Our readers, after a brief introduction, should be able to read the material sequentially, like a book, or explore particular topics in detail while ignoring others, or look up words for quick definitions and illustrations. We need a hypertext document.

(A note about vocabulary: **Hypertext**, as it was defined by its original champions, dealt mainly with text documents. Today, many hypertext systems include graphics as well as text. The creators of HyperCard insist that it is not a hyper*text* system but a **hyper*media*** system because it allows the linking of cards containing text, graphics, and sound. The emerging consensus suggests that hypertext systems are limited to text, whereas hypermedia can include any form of information.)

The implicit assumption in the statement of our problem is that we are to use appropriate resources—in this case, HyperCard. (This may seem obvious, but it's still important. A HyperCard document would be of little use if no HyperCard-compatible computers were available to our potential audience. As standards develop across platforms, this restriction is likely to become less significant.)

Breaking the Problem into Pieces

The problem definition may seem clear, but it is vague in its generality. Computers don't tolerate vagueness, so we need to break the problem into more specific pieces.

> After you've defined the problem (what you're trying to do), break it down into subproblems (how you're going to do it).

What, then, are the subproblems? If we were writing a traditional term paper, we might divide it into (1) introduction, (2) body, and (3) conclusion. We've agreed to throw out the traditional model, but before we do, let's examine each traditional component critically to see if it has a place in our hypertext document.

The introduction usually prepares the reader by (a) stating the goal(s) of the paper and (b) providing the necessary orientation for understanding the material in the paper. A hypertext reader needs to be prepared, too. A potential reader is not likely to browse through your stack if it's impossible to figure out what he or she is going to get out of it. Furthermore, because a hypertext document can be read in a variety of ways, it's especially important to make sure the reader is primed with whatever basic information is needed to make use of the stack: underlying assumptions, layout of the stack, and so on. So our introduction might contain a title card, how-to-navigate-this-stack information, and a brief introduction to the concepts that will apply throughout the stack.

The body of a traditional term paper presents arguments, ideas, facts, quotations, and sources, tied together in prose that makes sense when read from beginning to end. In this case we'll be presenting facts and ideas, but we can't assume that our reader will be plowing through the material sequentially. For some readers, the "body" of our hypertext document might be more like an encyclopedia than a term paper. So we need to make sure that each section makes sense whether the reader approaches it from point A or point B. If the structure is complex, it's safest to make each section self-contained, assuming only that the reader has read the introduction.

The conclusion of a traditional term paper generally presents a summary of the main idea(s) so that the reader can see the forest as a whole after examining all the trees in the body. In many hypertext documents, there's no real conclusion because there's no way to make sure the self-guiding reader ends the journey on a particular card. If our stack is strictly a reference stack (like a dictionary), we probably don't need to worry about a conclusion. But if the stack is to work as an introductory tutorial, too, we *may* want to guide readers through a closing card or two on their way home. We can defer that decision until we have a clearer idea of our structure.

Let's use these ideas to break the problem or project into pieces:

1. Introduction (title screen, overview, navigation instructions)
2. Body (details of computer components upon request)
3. Conclusion (if necessary and appropriate)

The components of this structure are still too vague for a computer to deal with, so we need to practice what's known as **stepwise refinement**. Stepwise refinement, like building the outline for a term paper, involves repeatedly breaking down each component into smaller and smaller pieces until each piece is small enough to deal with easily.

Fleshing Out the Pieces

Let's start by considering the body, since that's the most important part of the stack and it will determine what the reader needs to be told in the introduction. The reader or user should be able to look at some kind of menu screen that shows the basic components of a computer and to click on each component to get more information about it. For example, the user might click on Output Devices to see a general description of output devices and a menu of buttons to click for more information about specific output devices: screen, printer, speaker, and so on.

Here's a map of what this part of the hypertext document might look like:

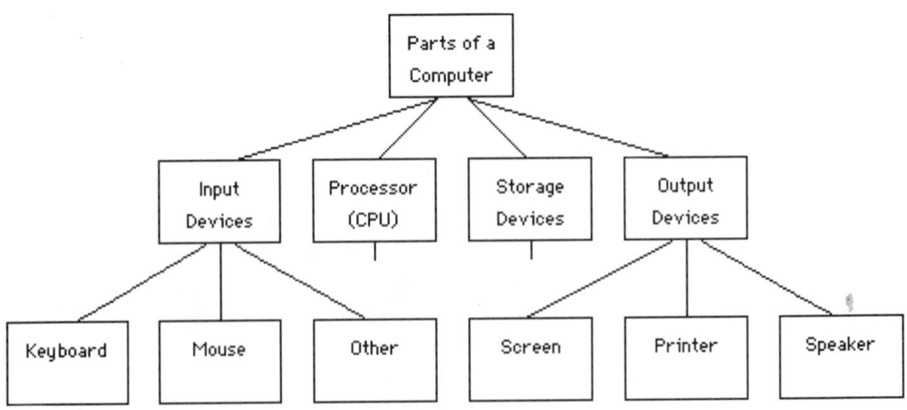

This is called a **tree structure**. (In computer science, trees are generally drawn with **roots** at the top and **branches** that grow downward.) Unlike the network structure we used to create the dungeon stack, a tree structure has well-defined characteristics that make it predictable and easy to navigate. One advantage of a tree is that we can add more leaves to allow for more detailed descriptions or delineations. The user simply has to click on buttons to go deeper and deeper into the hierarchy and expose more details. Of course, we should provide a button on every card for returning to higher levels of the hierarchy, another button for returning to the main menu card, another button for returning to the Home card or quitting HyperCard, and (possibly) a fourth button for taking the user to a map that shows an overview of the stack.

We aren't going to enforce a rigid tree structure, though, because different readers have different needs. First-time readers should be able to read everything in sequential order so they don't miss anything; that means putting left- and right-arrow buttons on each card. Users who are really in a hurry might want to use the Find command to jump directly to a particular subject; that means including a Find button on each card. Because all of these buttons should appear on every card, we should consider putting them in the background.

What Goes in the Background?

- Which elements repeat themselves in your outline or map?
- Which elements could appear on most or all cards without causing unnecessary confusion or complication?

Any element that appears in the answer to either of these questions should be considered as a candidate for the background.

The introduction in our three-step outline should start with a title page that allows the user to quickly choose a path through the information. New users, in addition to needing some kind of how-to-use-this-stack information, may need an introduction to provide the background they need to understand the material in the document. In the interest of brevity, we'll bypass this introduction for now and assume that all readers have a basic understanding of computers. We can easily add an introduction later if the need arises. Our opening screen can be thought of as a title page with several options: Introduction (if we add one later), Main Menu (the tree-structured body), Find (quick search), Help (stack instructions), and Exit.

We might want to include a conclusion at some later time, but for now we just need to provide a way for the user to exit the stack gracefully. We'll include an Exit button in the background of every card.

Designing the User Interface

There's always a risk that too many buttons can overwhelm the user unless they're arranged in a clear, understandable way. Because we're using several buttons on every card, we can arrange the screen so that the universal buttons are all together in a row and so that they all look and act the same way. For example, in this stack we'll arrange the buttons across the top of the background, and we'll make them all shadow-style buttons that auto-hilite when clicked. These kinds of details may seem unimportant, but they can make a tremendous difference to the people who will be using your creation.

> Design your card so that the buttons have a consistent look and feel, so the user knows what to expect when clicking them.

One way to determine what kinds of user interfaces work best is to look at stacks that work well and study their user interfaces. It's sometimes helpful to borrow directly from these stacks.

At this point in the planning process, we probably should study (and perhaps borrow from) the user interfaces of similar stacks that work well and, at the same time, notice what kinds of user interfaces don't work well. We may want to draw several prototype screens to experiment with different user interfaces and designs. We might find that some of our ideas don't work well when actually applied to paper or pixels, and have to come up with alternative approaches.

> Never be afraid to backtrack when designing a stack. It's almost never worthwhile to continue building on a flawed plan.

There are many more design decisions to be made, but let's use our fast-forward button to jump to the moment when we've completed the design and we're ready to actually build the stack. From that perspective, we can look back on those decisions that we bypassed.

Building a Background

Painting the Background

☐ **Open your Home stack.**

☐ **Select New Stack... from the File menu.**

☐ **Name the stack "Computer Anatomy", locate the appropriate disk and folder in the dialog box, and click New.**

☐ **Go to the background layer and use the paint tools to draw an approximation of this background:**

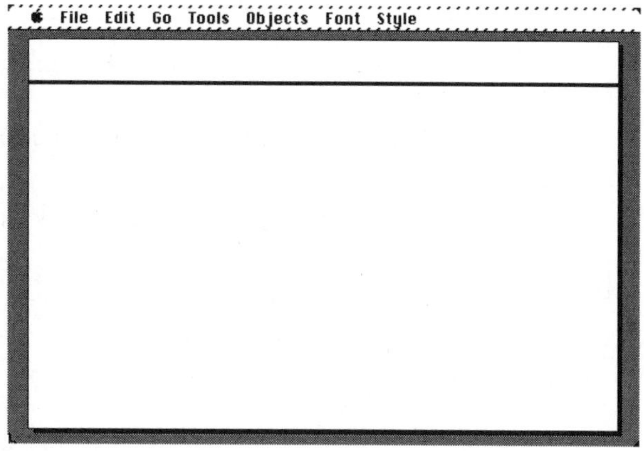

Building a Button Bar

The next step is to put a row of navigation buttons in the background.

☐ **Select the Button tool and create a row of background buttons with the following names, properties, appearances, and visual effects. (Remember, it's easier to produce identically shaped buttons if you create one and clone it with Option-Drag.)**

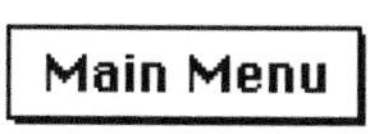

- **Main Menu, Shadow style, Show Name, Auto Hilite, Enabled, stretch from center Visual Effect.**

- **Find, Shadow style, Show Name, Auto Hilite, Enabled, stretch from center Visual Effect.**

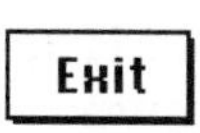

- **Exit, Shadow style, Show Name, Auto Hilite, Enabled, iris close Visual Effect.**

- **Go Back, Shadow style, Auto Hilite, Enabled, small return arrow icon, shrink to center Visual Effect.**

- **Go First, Shadow style, Auto Hilite, Enabled, small first card arrow icon, shrink to center Visual Effect.**

- **Go Prev, Shadow style, Auto Hilite, Enabled, small prev arrow icon, wipe right Visual Effect.**

- **Go Next, Shadow style, Auto Hilite, Enabled, small next arrow icon, wipe left Visual Effect.**

☐ **Align the buttons in the white strip near the top of the background like this:**

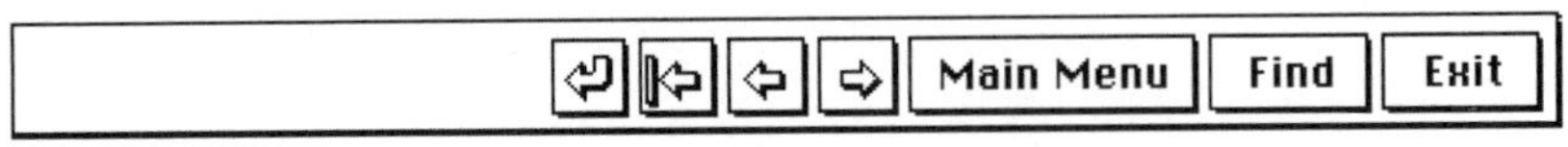

For now, the buttons don't need to do anything; we'll add scripts later.

Adding Fields to the Background

☐ **Still in the background, select the Field tool and create these two fields (one in the button strip at the top and the other covering the rest of the card):**

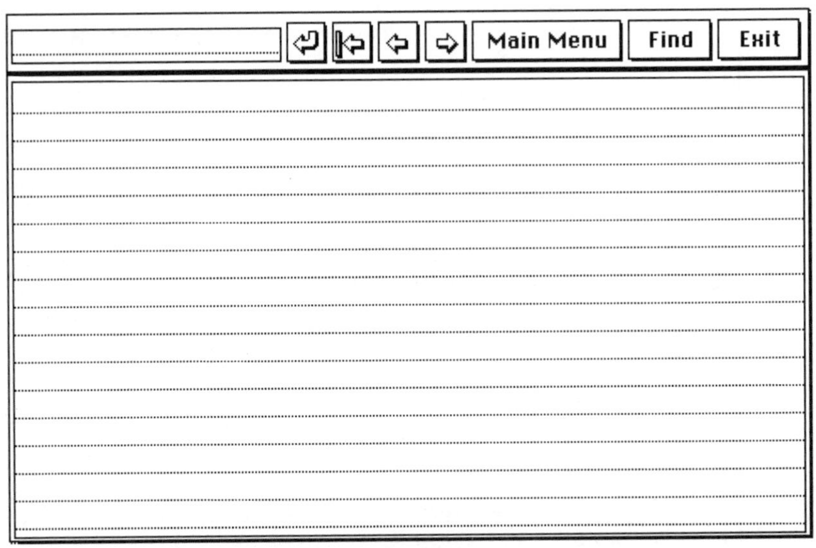

☐ **Double-click on the upper field to bring up the Field Info dialog box. Name the field "Title" (the name is *not* optional; we'll refer to it in a script later), make it transparent, give it wide margins, and assign it a default Text Style of 12-point Chicago.**

☐ **Name the larger field "Details", make it transparent, give it wide margins, and assign it a default Text Style of 12-point Geneva.**

The background is complete.

☐ **Return to the card layer.**

Headlines and Footnotes

The first card in the stack will be a title page, complete with simple start-up instructions, a title headline, and a pop-up footnote.

Filling in the Blank

We'll use the smaller Title field to display the only instructions a novice user might need.

☐ **Select the Browse tool and type this in the Title field:**

Click on a button >->

We aren't going to use the large Details field on the first card because we want a title in a large display font.

Painting a Title

☐ **Use the Paint Text tool to create a title and byline with an asterisk after your name. Use centered 18- or 24-point text in your choice of fonts (24-point Palatino is shown here).**

Bear in mind that paint text can't be edited once you click elsewhere or select another tool.

Creating a Pop-Up Field

Now it's time to add a dynamic footnote. We want a message to appear when the user clicks on the asterisk. That message will be in a **pop-up field.**

☐ **Create a field and position it in the white space below the painted text. Name the field "Thanks" (required) and give it a Shadow style.**

☐ **Using the Browse tool, type something like this in the field:**

> * with special thanks to my CS 101 instructor, without whom I never would have tackled this important and illuminating project.

If you decide to add a longer list of acknowledgments later, you can change the field style from shadow to scrolling. **Scrolling fields** have standard Macintosh scroll bars.

We don't want the user to be able to change this, so let's lock the text.

☐ **Select the Field tool again and lock the text via the Field Info... command.**

If we're going to have a button to make the field appear, we should also have a way to make the field disappear.

☐ **Open the field's script window and type this script:**

```
on mouseUp
  hide me
end mouseUp
```

> **me** in a script represents the object containing the currently executing handler.

The field should appear when the user clicks on the asterisk, so we'll put an invisible button there.

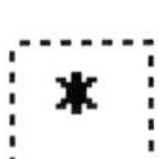

☐ **Use the Button tool to put a transparent button named "asterisk" on the asterisk.**

☐ **Script the button like this:**

```
on mouseUp
  set visible of card field "Thanks" to ¬
  not the visible of card field "Thanks"
end mouseUp
```

(Remember, the ¬ character is a soft return, created by typing Option-Return; its only purpose is to allow a single statement to stretch across multiple lines.)

In essence, this script says: If the Thanks card field is not visible, make it visible; if it's visible, make it not visible. A more accurate translation of the actual script might be "make the visibility property (called `visible`) of the Thanks card field the opposite of what that property is now."

If all is well, clicking on the asterisk should make the pop-up field appear. The field should disappear when the user clicks on the field or the asterisk.

☐ **Test the button and the field.**

Hiding Buttons with Buttons

Many of the buttons we created in the background are either irrelevant or inappropriate for the title page. All those choices are likely to overwhelm a first-time user of the stack. All we need on this card are a few simple choices: Go to the main menu, find a particular topic, and exit. (It's a good idea to have a Stack Overview or Help button, too, but we'll save that for a later project.) We can hide the other choices with an opaque do-nothing button on the card layer.

☐ **Create a button, make it opaque, name it "mask", hide the name, and drag/stretch it so that it covers all of the background icon buttons:**

Stacking the Deck

Card 1 is done. Now we need to provide the Main Menu button with someplace to go. This is a background button that will appear on every card. No matter where we are in the stack, we want a click on this button to take us to the Main Menu card: the root of our hypertext tree. That means that the button should be hard-linked to that card with an absolute reference.

Making the Main Menu Card

☐ **Select the Button tool, double-click on the Main Menu button, click on Tasks..., and select Go to Destination.**

☐ **Press Command-N (New Card), click on the Current Card radio button, and press Return to assign the task.**

As usual, the new card shares a background with the previous card—buttons, fields, and all. You can't see the fields, but your browsing pointer should turn into an I-beam whenever it passes over them.

☐ **Locate each of those fields and fill them with the text shown here (with field text, using the Browse tool, *not* the Paint Text tool). Press Option-8 to type a bullet (•).**

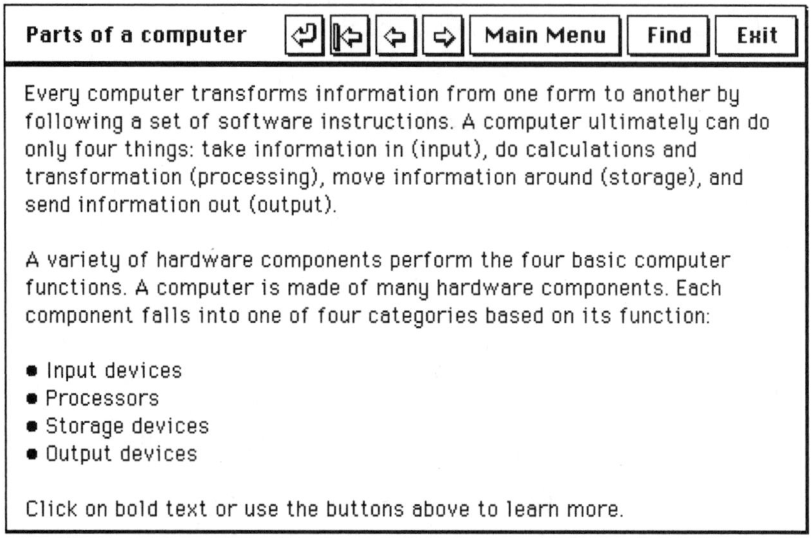

Parts of a computer
Main Menu
Find
Exit
Every computer transforms information from one form to another by following a set of software instructions. A computer ultimately can do only four things: take information in (input), do calculations and transformation (processing), move information around (storage), and send information out (output).
A variety of hardware components perform the four basic computer functions. A computer is made of many hardware components. Each component falls into one of four categories based on its function:
• Input devices
• Processors
• Storage devices
• Output devices
Click on bold text or use the buttons above to learn more.

What bold text? The bold text you're about to add.

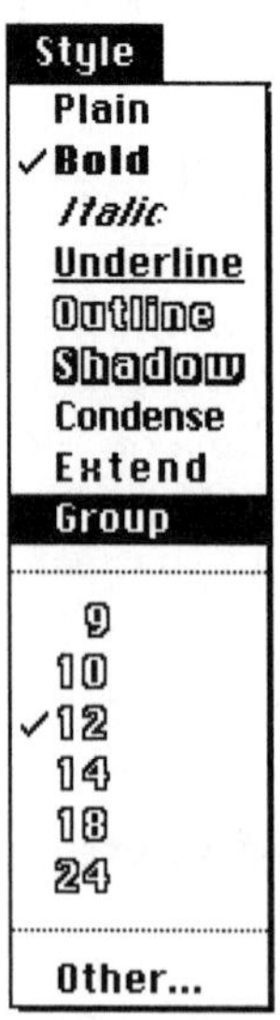

☐ **Double-click-drag to select the phrase *Input devices*. Then select Bold from the Style menu. Finally, with the phrase still selected, select Group from the Style menu.**

When you selected Bold, you saw the selected text change to boldface. Selecting Group caused no such cosmetic change. In truth, neither of these style changes is for cosmetic reasons. Later we're going to write a script for this field that will check to see whether the mouse is clicking on boldface text. We'll use bold as the cue for **hot text**: text that triggers a jump to another card in the stack.

> The Group style simply specifies that multiple words should be treated as a group when they're clicked, rather than as individual words.

☐ **Repeat the process of selecting, making bold, and grouping each of the remaining bulleted hardware categories: *Processors, Storage devices,* and *Output devices.* (There's no need to group *Processors* because it's a single word.)**

- **Input devices**
- Processors
- **Storage devices**
- **Output devices**

This card indicates that there are four possible branches from this point, just as the map indicated. To save time and typing, we'll skip the first two branches and create cards for just the last two categories. We can always come back to this point and insert additional cards.

Before we finish with the Main Menu card, we should take care of one more detail. There's no point in having a button that links the Main Menu card to the Main Menu card; it's likely to just confuse the user. We can hide that button behind a do-nothing button, just as we did with the arrow buttons on card 1. But instead of making the button completely invisible, let's give it the name Main Menu and let it provide a "you are here" reference for the card; that way, the button can serve to orient, rather than disorient, the user.

☐ **Create an opaque button with a visible name "Main Menu"; place it directly on top of the Main Menu background button.**

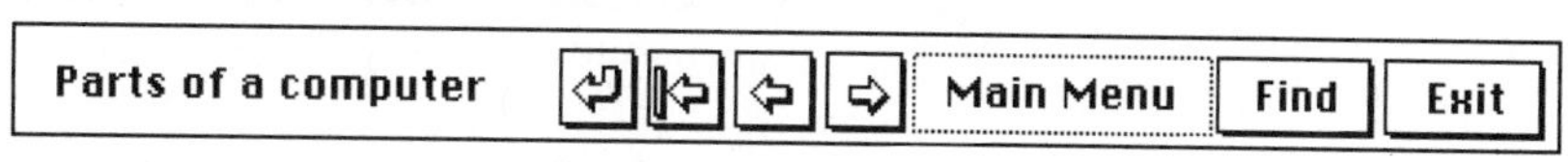

This button doesn't do anything when clicked. It just serves as a visual reminder that the user is looking at the Main Menu card.

Creating Reference Cards

The main body of our hypertext document is to be tree structured, with buttons that allow the user to branch in several directions from a root menu. At the root level, we offer the reader four choices, corresponding to the four component types we've introduced.

Remember that some of our readers may want to read every card of the stack in order, from first to last. If we don't plan the order of the cards, sequential readers might find themselves being jerked from storage to output to processors to input devices. Such unplanned structure is confusing and disorienting, especially for beginners. We should plan a logical order and add cards in such a way that they end up in the order we planned.

Let's plan the stack so the sequential reader sees the branches in this order: Input, Processors, Storage, Output. The New Card command always inserts the new card after the current card, so we should create our cards in the order they're to be sequenced. If we decide to go back and add more cards later to provide additional branches, we should insert those cards, not at the end, but in the logical place for sequential readers.

The process of creating each of the remaining cards is the same as for the Main Menu card:

1. Create a new card for the next topic in the sequence.
2. Type the appropriate text into each of the two fields (remembering to use the Browse tool).
3. Apply Bold and (if necessary) Group styles to words and phrases that are to be hot text.

There's no need to explicitly link any of these cards. Readers will travel between cards with the arrow buttons, hot text, and Find button, none of which depends on absolute links.

☐ **Following the steps outlined above, create each of these cards.**

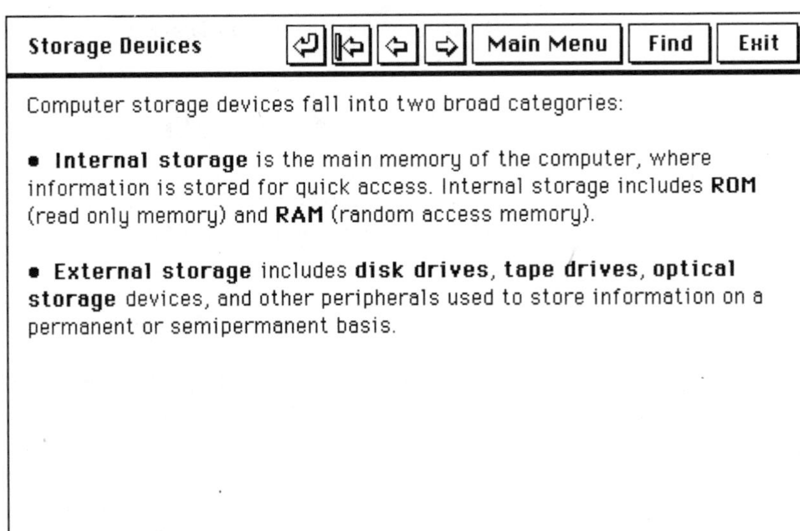

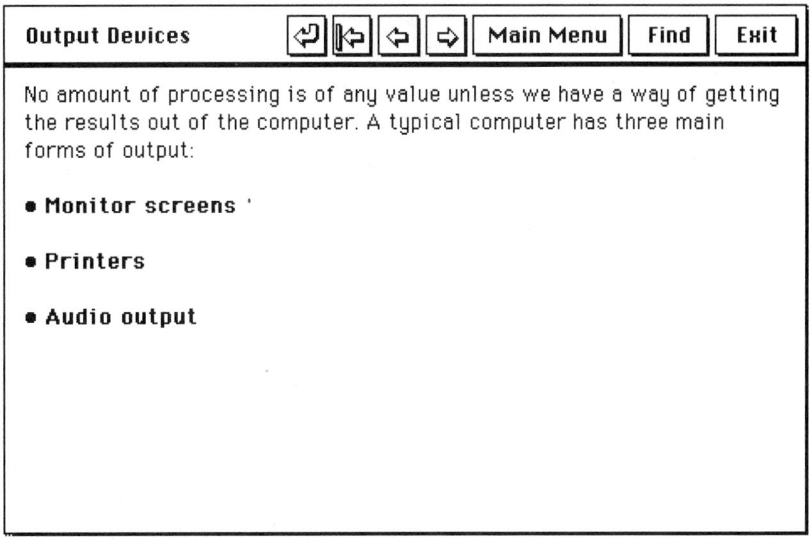

Output Devices
Main Menu
Find
Exit
No amount of processing is of any value unless we have a way of getting the results out of the computer. A typical computer has three main forms of output:
• Monitor screens
• Printers
• Audio output

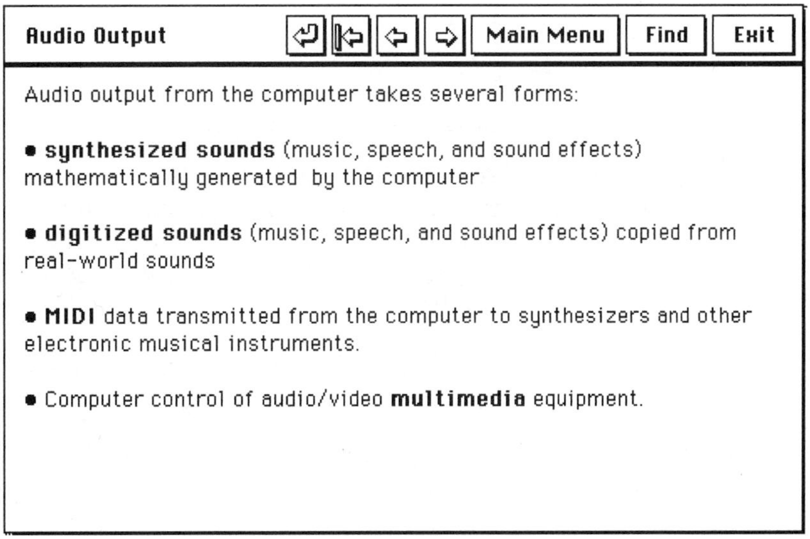

Audio Output
Main Menu
Find
Exit
Audio output from the computer takes several forms:
• synthesized sounds (music, speech, and sound effects) mathematically generated by the computer
• digitized sounds (music, speech, and sound effects) copied from real-world sounds
• MIDI data transmitted from the computer to synthesizers and other electronic musical instruments.
• Computer control of audio/video multimedia equipment.

Scripting the Sequence Buttons

Let's activate the arrow buttons so a sequential reader can navigate the stack with them. These are all background buttons, but you can script them without leaving the card layer.

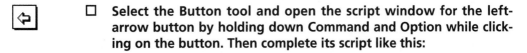

☐ **Select the Button tool and open the script window for the left-arrow button by holding down Command and Option while clicking on the button. Then complete its script like this:**

```
on mouseUp
  visual effect wipe right
  go to previous card
end mouseUp
```

☐ **Complete the script for the right-arrow button:**

```
on mouseUp
  visual effect wipe left
  go to next card
end mouseUp
```

☐ **Complete the script for the Go First button:**

```
on mouseUp
  visual shrink to center
  go first
end mouseUp
```

☐ **Try the arrow buttons.**

Creating a Dead End

You should see a potential problem here: When you reach the last card of the stack, the right arrow abruptly transports you to the title card. There's no reason to introduce the potentially confusing concept of a wrap-around stack. It makes more sense to have a concluding card that has no visible right-arrow or Go Next button.

☐ **Create a final card at the end of the stack. Mask the right-arrow button with an opaque Do Nothing button.**

This card might contain a concluding summary, a picture of a complete computer system, or a list of references. For simplicity's sake, let's just add a simple message.

☐ **Type "You've reached the end of the stack." in the Details field.**

Break Point

Planting a Hypertext Tree

Automatic Backtracking

This short stack now works for readers who want to traverse it from beginning to end. It's time to add hypertext scripts to allow for non-sequential navigation. One of the most important parts of creating a hypertext stack is providing the user with a simple, reliable way of backtracking. A document that allows readers to jump from one section or level to another must provide a way to jump back.

For example, if the reader of our stack has worked through the tree to the branch on MIDI, he or she should be able to go back up to the next highest level of the tree—Audio Output—without going all the way back to the root. That's what the Go Back button is for in this stack. Ideally, this button should be smart enough to know where you want to go when you press it, rather than mindlessly backtracking through every card you've visited. If you click it twice in a row, it should take you from MIDI to Audio Output to Output Devices, even if you've examined several branches of audio output in the meantime.

The problem becomes even more complex when we open up the possibility of jumping *between* branches of the tree. Suppose, for example, we decide to add a hot link from one of the audio input cards to the MIDI card because MIDI is used for both input and output. The Go Back button can't be hard-linked to the Audio Output card; it needs to be flexible enough to return to your exact point of departure, *wherever that may be*. We can't create a telepathic return-arrow button, but we *can* create a button that takes the user back to a point in the stack that has been previously marked as the point of return. In this example, the script that dropped you down to the MIDI level should mark the Audio Output card (or the Audio Input card) before transporting you to MIDI.

Hot text and the Go Back button will work as a team. For example, you click on hot text—the word *MIDI* on the Audio Output card. This click effectively does two things: It makes a note of the current card (in the same way you might write down your page number before temporarily flipping to another reference in a book) and it jumps to the appropriate card—MIDI. You might, while you're at that level, decide to use the arrow buttons to explore some other audio output devices. When you're through, you click on the Go Back button. The Go Back button checks the note that was left when you last clicked on hot text (just as you might check your page number before returning to your original page) and returns to the marked spot. HyperTalk makes this possible with two commands.

Push and Pop Card

Each time HyperCard encounters a **`push` command**, it pushes a reminder onto its stack of reminders in memory. This reminder will tell HyperCard where to return when it's later told to pop a card off the stack. Here's the syntax:

push *card*

The **`pop card` command**, in its most commonly used form, takes you back to that point and deletes the note from the reminder stack. If the `push` command has been issued more than once, `pop card` returns to the last card for which a reminder was pushed onto the stack, and that reminder is removed from (popped off) the stack. This is the syntax of the basic `pop card` command:

```
pop card
```

This kind of reminder **stack** is not the same as a HyperCard stack; it's a special kind of **data structure** that allows information to be recovered in the opposite order that it was stored, so that the last item added to the stack is the first one removed. The conventional metaphor for a stack data structure is a spring-loaded stack of cafeteria trays, but a more appropriate metaphor might be an old-fashioned spindle for holding small paper notes.

The keyboard shortcuts for `push` and `pop card` are useful for navigating back and forth through such stacks during the stack development process. **Command-↓** (Command-down-arrow) pushes a reminder for the current card onto the memory stack; **Command-↑** (Command-up-arrow) pops the top reminder off the stack, returning you to that card.

That's the theory; here's how to make it happen.

Providing Many Happy Returns

Let's start by scripting the Go Back button.

☐ **Complete this script on the Go Back button.**

```
on mouseUp
  visual shrink to center
  pop card
end mouseUp
```

The pop card command will return to the card that was visible when the push card command was last issued. In order for this button to work properly, we need to modify the stack so a push card command is issued whenever the user clicks on hot text. We'll make the text hot by adding a script to the Details field.

Creating Hot Text

☐ **Type this script for the large Details field.**

```
on mouseUp
  get the clickText
  if the textStyle of the clickChunk contains bold ¬
  then
    lock screen
    push card
    find whole it in bg field "title"
    if the result is not empty then ¬
    answer "Missing card:" && It
    unlock screen with stretch from center
  end if
end mouseUp
```

In order to explain this script, we need to define several new HyperTalk terms:

get *expression*

The **get command** puts the value of any expression into the variable **It**. (The variable **It** also serves as a destination for the ask, answer, and read commands.)

clickText is a function that returns the word in a field last clicked on by the user. (If the word has been specified to be part of a group, clickText returns the whole group.) **clickChunk** is a function that returns a chunk expression *describing* the word or group of words clicked in the field. A **chunk** is a piece of a character string represented as a chunk expression. For example, if the user clicks on the first word of the Main Text field on the Main Menu card, clickText returns the value "Every", and clickChunk returns the chunk expression "char 1 to 5 of bkgnd field 2". That is, clickText returns the content; clickChunk returns the description.

textStyle is a function that returns a list of the text styles (italics, bold, underline, outline, shadow, extend, condense, and/or group) of a text string; in this script, the textStyle returns the styles of the text string contained in the clickChunk.

```
lock screen
unlock screen [with effectName]
```

The **lock screen command** sets the **lockScreen** global property to true, preventing HyperCard from updating the screen until the **unlock screen command** is issued, setting the lockScreen property back to false. Everything that happens between these two commands is hidden from the user.

```
find text [in field]
find chars text [in field]
find word text [in field]
find whole text [in field]
find string text [in field]
```

The **find command** comes in many variations, but they all do basically the same thing: search through all card and background fields in the stack for the specified text strings. This is the command that appears in the message box when you select the Find menu command. The find form finds the match only at the beginning of words. **find chars** finds matches anywhere within words. **find whole** searches for a specific word or phrase, including spaces. **find string** searches for strings, including spaces and punctuation, that don't necessarily start at the beginning of words. If the search is unsuccessful (the string is not found), the **result** function returns the explanatory message "Not found"; otherwise result returns an empty string. (result returns explanatory messages for unsuccessful completion of many HyperTalk commands.)

bg, like bkgnd, is an abbreviation for background.

The simplest form of the **answer command** is used to create a dialog box containing a message with an OK button. (The answer command is discussed in more detail in a later example.)

&& concatenates (combines) two strings with a space between.

Let's walk through the script. Suppose the user clicks on the first word in the Details field on the Main Menu card. The clickText function returns "Every", so the get command puts "Every" in the local variable It. The clickChunk function returns the chunk expression "char 1 to 5 of bkgnd field 2", making the next statement begin

```
if the textStyle of char 1 to 5 of bkgnd field 2 ¬
contains bold then ...
```

It doesn't, so execution jumps to end if and end mouseUp. Nothing else happens.

Now suppose the user clicks on **Output Devices.** Because these two words are grouped, "Output Devices" is put in It by the get statement. `clickChunk` returns "char 553 to 566 of bkgnd field 2", making the `if` statement

```
if the textStyle of char 533 to 566 of bkgnd ¬
field 2 contains bold then ...
```

Since it does contain bold, the statements between `if` and `end if` are executed. The screen is locked, the location of the current card is pushed onto the reminder stack, and the `find whole` command searches the background Title field on every card for text matching `It`; the search stops when it finds the Output Devices card. Because the search was successful, `result` returns an empty string, so the `answer` command is skipped. The screen is unlocked with a visual effect, revealing the Output Devices card with a box around the title.

Finally, suppose the user clicks somewhere on `Input Devices` on the Main Menu card. Because these two words are grouped, `clickText` returns "Input Devices", which is placed in `It`, and the `if` statement checks characters 506 to 518 of the field, which contain boldface text. The screen is locked, the location of the current card is pushed onto the reminder stack, and the `find whole` command searches the background Title field on every card for text matching `It`—that is, "Input Devices". Since "Input Devices" isn't in that field on any existing card (because we haven't created an Input Devices card yet), `result` returns the message "Not found". The next statement checks to see whether `result` is empty; since it's not, the `answer` command puts together "Missing card:" and the contents of `It` (with a space between, as specified by the `&&` operator), and displays this dialog box:

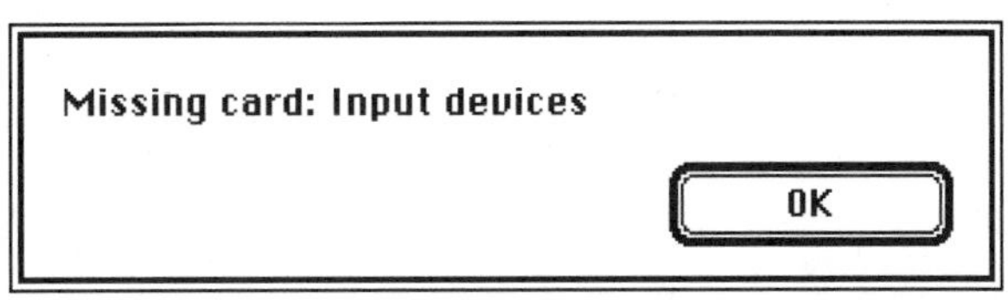

When the user clicks OK, the screen is unlocked with a visual effect and the `end if` and `end mouseUp` statements are processed.

The visual effect seems out of place here because we're still on the same card. But this particular branch of the program isn't really designed for the user to see, anyway. When the stack is completed, there should be a card corresponding to every boldface word or phrase on every card. We've included this `if` statement more for the stack developer than for the user. As we're developing and testing the stack, the dialog box message can provide a helpful reminder that a card hasn't been created yet. The dialog box will also appear if the stack contains a spelling error that prevents a successful search. Even after the stack is theoretically completed and tested, it's probably a good idea to leave the `if` statement in the stack, just in case we've overlooked something.

The script won't work until we lock the text in the field, because the pointer turns into an I-beam whenever we place it over an unlocked field. It's important to lock both fields, anyway, to protect the information in those fields.

☐ **Lock the text in the two fields.**

☐ **Test the hot-text script. Try different combinations of hot-text clicks and Go Back button clicks to make sure they work as expected.**

You can use the debugger to slow the action so you can see exactly what happens as the script unfolds.

☐ **Put a checkpoint in the first line of the script. Turn on the Message Watcher and the Variable Watcher. Trace or Step through the script several times, reproducing the examples described in the last few paragraphs.**

Obviously, there are plenty of potential hot links on each of the cards we've created. For small items, we might want to include buttons that reveal pop-up footnotes rather than jump to another card. But other items lend themselves to cross-referencing with other cards. It's possible to turn this stack into a complex structure that's more like a network than a simple tree. But before you decide to build a labyrinthine stack, take a minute to consider a few issues.

The Hazards of Hypertext

Where am I? When links can take a reader to anywhere from anywhere, it's easy for the reader to become disoriented, wondering, "Where am I?" "How did I get here?" "How do I get back where I was?" "How do I get out of here?" Too much freedom can cause anxiety.

What's left? When you finish reading a book, you know you've read every page. Many hypertext documents leave the reader with the uneasy feeling that something important has gone unnoticed. Some HyperCard documents keep track of the reader's progress automatically, marking each completed session. Until you can build this kind of intelligence into your stacks, it's important to give your stack a structure that makes it easy for the reader to know what he or she has seen so far and what's left to see.

Which text is hot? It's easy to create hidden buttons on chunks of text—you did it on the title card of this stack. But buttons that aren't obvious to the user generally aren't a good idea. (They also cause problems when you edit the text or use scrolling fields, because they don't stay with the text when it moves.) In this document, we've marked hot text with boldface. This makes it easier to write the hypertext scripts, but it also makes it easier for the reader to know where to click.

Try all the buttons from several different locations in your stack. As you can see, we don't have a true tree structure, because you can get almost anywhere from almost anywhere else. But the casual user who's uncomfortable with all those choices can *use it* like a tree. Readers uncomfortable with the hypertext concept can continue flipping through the stack with the right-arrow button.

Break Point

Buttons That Talk Back

Scripting the Find Button

We still have to write a script for the Find button. Since there's a Find command in the menu, we could simply ask HyperCard to execute that command when the button is clicked with this script:

```
on mouseUp
  doMenu Find...
end mouseUp
```

`doMenu` *`itemName`* `[`*`menuName`*`] [without dialog]`

doMenu tells HyperCard to execute a menu command. It can be used to automate just about any menu action, provided the command is spelled correctly, including punctuation. (`without dialog` suppresses dialog boxes.)

When a button with this script is clicked, the message box pops up with the `find` command already typed, just as it would if you selected Find from the menu. But with a slightly more complex script, we can create a Find option that will be less intimidating to HyperCard novices:

Find

☐ **Complete the following script for the Find button.**

```
on mouseUp
  global StringToFind
  ask "What are you looking for?" with
StringToFind
  if It is not empty then
    push card
    put It into StringToFind
    find StringToFind
  end if
end mouseUp
```

To understand this script we need another vocabulary lesson.

`global` *`variableList`*

Most variables are **local variables**—they are valid only within a single handler. As soon as the handler is executed, the local variables used in the handler cease to exist. A **global variable** is valid for all handlers in which it is declared with the **`global` command**. Global variables retain their values until they are changed or until the HyperCard session is terminated. Normally variables are declared global so they can be used in two or more handlers; in some cases (like this one) a variable is declared global so that its value can be retained until the same handler is executed later in the session.

```
ask question [with defaultAnswer]
ask password [clear] question [with defaultAnswer]
ask file [prompText] [with [default] filename]
```

The **`ask` command** displays a dialog box containing a question with a text box for receiving the user's typed answer. If a *`defaultAnswer`* string is included in the command, that string is highlighted in the text box when it appears. When the user clicks OK or presses Return, the text in the text box is put into the local variable `It`. (Other forms of the `ask` command are used for requesting passwords and creating standard file dialog boxes.)

Here's what happens now when a user clicks the Find button: HyperCard notes that StringToFind is to be a global variable and sets aside a space to keep track of that variable's value from this moment on. (Its current value is empty; it contains nothing.) The `ask` command displays this dialog box:

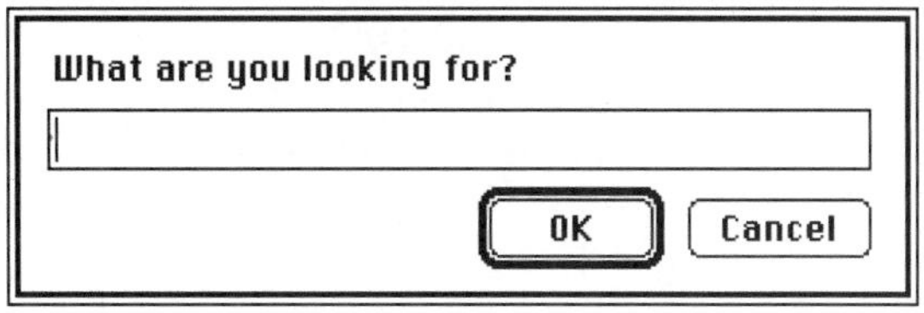

(If we had not declared StringToFind as a global variable, the text box would have contained "StringToFind" highlighted rather than just a flashing cursor, because HyperCard would have no way of knowing that StringToFind was a variable rather than just a text string.)

Suppose the user types "MIDI" and presses Return. The string "MIDI" is put into the local variable `It`. The `If` statement checks the value of `It` and determines that it is not empty. The current card is noted with the `push card` command so the user can use the Go Back button to return to that point. "MIDI" is copied from `It` into StringToFind by the `put` command. The `find` command then searches every field on every card until it finds a match for "MIDI".

When execution of the handler is done, the global variable StringToFind keeps its value so that the next time the user clicks the Find button, the dialog box looks like this:

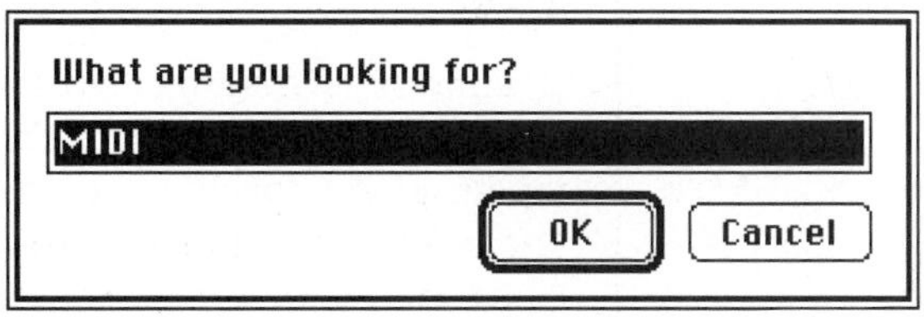

If the user types nothing, `It` is assigned "MIDI" once again and the script plays out the same as before. This provides a convenient way to search repeatedly for the same string.

☐ **Test the Find button at least twice. Use the debugger to trace the script if its operation isn't clear to you.**

Adding an Interactive Exit

The only button yet to be scripted is the Exit button. We can use the `answer` command to create a dialog box that provides exit choices.

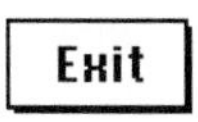

☐ **Complete the following script for the Exit button.**

```
on mouseUp
  answer "Are you sure you want to quit?" ¬
  with "Go Home" or "To the Finder" or "Cancel"
  if It is "Cancel" then
    exit mouseUp
  else
    if It is "Go Home" then
      go home
    else
      doMenu Quit HyperCard
    end if
  end if
end mouseUp
```

You've seen most of these statements before, but they're put together in a slightly different way. Before we walk through the script, let's fill in some details about the `answer` command and define the `exit` statement.

```
answer question [with reply [or reply2 ¬
[or reply3]]]
answer file [promptText][of type fileType]
```

`answer` is used to create a dialog box containing a message or question and one, two, or three buttons for the user's replies. If replies aren't specified, a single OK button appears in the box. The user's reply choice is stored in the variable `It`. (The `answer file` form shown here is used for displaying a standard file dialog box allowing the user to select a file.)

```
exit messageName
```

When HyperCard encounters the **`exit` command**, it terminates execution of the specified handler.

When the Exit button is clicked, the `answer` command displays this dialog box:

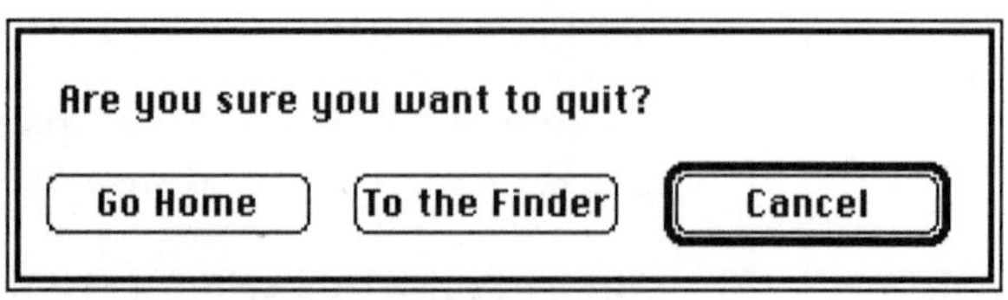

The option chosen by the user is stored in the local variable `It`. A **nested if structure** is used to compare the user's response with possible options and perform the appropriate action. If the user clicks

Cancel, the handler is terminated by the `exit` statement; the dialog box disappears, and the user returns to the card where the Exit button was clicked.

If the user clicks Go Home, the first `if` statement is false, so the statements following `else` are executed. The first of those statements is another `if` statement, which checks to see whether `It` contains "Go Home". Since it does, the user is transported to the Home stack by the `go home` statement.

If the user clicks on the To the Finder button, both `if` statements test false, so the statement after the innermost `else` is executed: `doMenu` tells HyperCard to execute the menu command Quit HyperCard.

☐ **Test the Exit button.**

Break Point

Modifying the Menu Bar

This section is optional; if you have no interest in modifying the menu bar or in advanced scripting techniques, pass it by.

Although it's far from complete, our stack now has a complete set of working buttons and fields. We've built a working user interface; we just need to add content cards. But before we dash off dozens of computer component cards, let's add one more wrinkle to the user interface: custom menus. HyperCard 2 makes it easy to modify the menu bar by adding new menus and menu items, deleting standard menus and menu items, and disabling existing menu items. This kind of power shouldn't be taken lightly, though.

The single greatest strength of the Macintosh menu bar is consistency. In well-designed Macintosh applications, menus are consistent with Macintosh standards, making it possible for new users of an application to feel immediately at home. Think carefully about the implications of your actions before you modify the menu bar. Don't confuse the user with unnecessary changes.

Designing the Stack Script

The Home stack, the Help stack, and the Addresses stack all have something that's missing in your stack: a custom stack menu. A well-designed stack menu can provide Macintosh veterans with a comfortable and consistent tool for navigating the stack. Let's build one.

Our stack has plenty of navigation options in the button bar. The most sensible approach is to duplicate those options in a Navigate menu so that users have a choice of navigation tools: menu or buttons. Suppose we want to create a menu that looks like the one shown here.

At the same time, we want to temporarily delete the Edit and File menus to avoid problems that might result when a naive user selects unfamiliar menu items. (Once again, this is not a decision that should be made lightly.) Using the same reasoning, we decide to disable some of the items in the Go menu that could put the first-time user in unfamiliar territory. Of course, if we cause the menu bar to change when the stack is opened, we should put everything back the way we found it when the stack is closed.

(It's possible to open another stack without closing this one; if we've changed the menu bar, we should think about what happens when our stack is temporarily **suspended** and another stack is opened. But since we're eliminating the File menu, we'll naively assume this isn't a problem and ignore the complications of coding for this situation. A more realistic approach was taken by the creators of Home, Help, Addresses, and the other standard stacks. Study those stack scripts for ideas on how to handle suspended stacks.)

Even with the Home command disabled in the Go menu, it's possible for the user to inadvertently go to the Home stack by clicking the Go Back button one time too many. Each click pops a card off the reminder stack; when all the cards are popped, Go Back takes the user Home. To minimize the chances of this happening, we should push the title card onto the stack so that the Go Back button will take the user there before going Home.

While we're thinking about protecting the naive user, we might want to consider protecting our stack from the naive user. We can easily set the user level to browsing when the stack is opened, provided we make a commitment to return it to its former level upon exit.

We've discussed several things that should happen when the stack is opened. To keep everything straight, let's make a list of the things we'd like to have the stack do when it opens. We'll use **pseudocode**—a cross between a computer language (in this case, HyperTalk) and English:

```
on openStack
  lock screen
  lower user level
  add navigate menu
  delete other menus
  disable Go menu items
  push card
  unlock screen
end openStack
```

(If we lock the screen before we do everything else and unlock it when we're through, all the cosmetic changes happen at once.)

Some of the statements (such as `lock screen`) are pure HyperTalk; others can be made into messages for soon-to-be-written handlers. Here's a refinement of the preceding handler in syntactically correct HyperTalk:

```
on openStack
  lock screen
  lowerUserLevel
  addNavigateMenu
  deleteOtherMenus
  disableGoMenuItems
  push card
  unlock screen
end openStack
```

We now need to write handlers that can intercept and make sense out of the following messages: `lowerUserLevel`, `addNavigateMenu`, `deleteOtherMenus`, and `disableGoMenuItems`.

Here's a handler for `lowerUserLevel`:

```
on lowerUserLevel
  global oldUserLevel
  get userLevel
  put It into oldUserLevel
  set userLevel to 1
end lowerUserLevel
```

This script, executed when the `lowerUserLevel` message is sent from the `on openStack` script, gets the current user level and puts it into the global variable `oldUserLevel`, where it remains until the stack is closed. (We'll write a script later to restore the original user level using this variable.) The last command in this handler sets the user level to browsing level 1. At the `end lowerUserLevel` statement, execution returns to the `on openStack` script, ready for the next statement in that script.

Writing Menu Manipulation Scripts

Before we can write the menu handlers, we need to learn a little more HyperTalk.

Menu Manipulation Commands and Properties

```
create menu menuName
delete menu
reset menuBar
```

The **`create menu` command** creates a menu with the specified name. The menu continues to exist until it is deleted with the **`delete menu` command**, or until the default HyperCard menus are reinstated with the **`reset menuBar` command**, or until the HyperCard session is ended. (The `delete menu` command can be used to delete standard HyperCard menus, too.) Menu creation and deletion commands are generally included in the stack script so the menus will exist while the stack is open.

```
put itemName preposition [menuItem of] menu ¬
[with menuMsg message]
```

This special form of the `put` command is used for putting new menu items in existing menus. The optional `with` clause specifies that a particular message is to be sent when the menu item is chosen; it's the easiest way to make the menu item functional. Here's an example for adding a new item (with a keyboard shortcut) to the Go menu:

```
put "Second" after menuItem "First" of menu "Go" ¬
with menuMsg "Go second card"
set the cmdChar of menuItem "Second" ¬
of menu "Go" to 5
```

The **`cmdChar`** property can be used to specify a command-key shortcut for any existing menu item.

```
disable menu
disable menuItem of menu
```

The **`disable` command** turns a menu or menu item gray and makes it inactive. Here's an example:

```
disable menuItem "Recent" of menu "Go"
```

For now, let's skip the message `addNavigateMenu` and work on `deleteOtherMenus` and `disableGoMenuItems`. The scripts are self-explanatory:

```
on deleteOtherMenus
  delete menu "Edit"
  delete menu "File"
end deleteOtherMenus

on disableGoMenuItems
  disable menuItem "Recent" of menu "Go"
  disable menuItem "Help" of menu "Go"
end disableGoMenuItems
```

Writing Custom Functions and Handlers

The `addNavigateMenu` handler is slightly more complex:

```
on addNavigateMenu
  show menuBar
  create menu "Navigate"
  put NavigateItems() into menu "Navigate" ¬
  with menuMessages NavigateMessages()
  set cmdChar of menuItem "Exit" ¬
  of menu "Navigate" to "E"
end addNavigateMenu
```

First the script ensures that the menu bar is visible with the `show menuBar` command. Next it creates a new menu called Navigate. The `put` statement puts the appropriate menu items in that menu and assigns messages to each of those items. But instead of listing all five items after `put`, we included a call to a **custom (programmer defined) function** called `NavigateItems`. This function, after we write it, will return the list of menu item names that belong here: `Title Card,Main Menu,-,Find,Exit`. Similarly, we've included a call to function `NavigateMessages`. This function will return the list of messages associated with the five menu items: `doMenu First, goMain, empty, doFind, DoExit`. When the `put` statement is executed, each of the function names is replaced by the value returned by the function. In effect, the statement says

```
put "Title Card,Main Menu,-,Find,Exit" into ¬
menu "Navigate" with menuMessages ¬
"doMenu First,goMain,empty,doFind,DoExit"
```

In fact, we could have written the statement exactly like this from the beginning. But most seasoned programmers prefer to break large programs and statements into smaller modules by creating separate functions and message handlers. We've chosen to write a shorter, more readable `put` statement by including calls to two functions. Here's what the functions look like:

```
function NavigateItems
  return "Title Card,Main Menu,-,Find,Exit"
end NavigateItems

function NavigateMessages
  return "doMenu First,goMain,empty,doFind,DoExit"
end NavigateMessages
```

This second function includes three more messages that have no corresponding handlers so far. Here are the missing handlers:

```
on goMain
  send mouseUp to bg button "Main Menu"
end goMain

on doFind
  send mouseUp to bg button "Find"
end doFind

on doExit
  send mouseUp to bg button "Exit"
end doExit
```

Notice that all three handlers do the same thing: send a `mouseUp` message to a background button. If the user selects Main Menu from the Navigate menu, the message `mouseUp` is sent to the background button Main Menu. This has exactly the same effect as a mouse click on that button; it's as if the computer clicked the button because you told it to via the menu. The button responds to the `mouseUp` message by pushing a card onto the stack and jumping to the Main Menu card with a visual effect transition.

> `send "`*`messageName [parameterList]`*`" [to `*`object`*`]`
>
> The **send command** sends a message to any specified object in the current stack or to another stack (but not to an object in another stack). If no object is specified, HyperCard is the object.

Covering Our Tracks

We've practiced stepwise refinement on the list of things to do when the stack is opened, and the result is a complete set of handlers and functions to set up the stack properly and modify the menu bar. All that remains is to create a set of scripts to handle the necessary housekeeping when the stack is closed.

Here's what we want to happen when we close the stack:

```
on closeStack
  set user level to old user level
  hide card field "thanks" on card 1
  reset menu bar
end closeStack
```

(We want to hide the card field credits so that it doesn't appear the next time the stack is opened. That way, every user who opens the stack has the same startup screen.) Converting pseudocode to HyperTalk, we have:

```
on closeStack
  global oldUserLevel
  set userLevel to oldUserLevel
  hide card field "thanks" on card 1
  reset menuBar
end closeStack
```

When the stack is closed, this script tells HyperCard to set the user level to the value stored in the global variable oldUserLevel; then to hide the credits field on the Title card; and finally to reset the menu bar so it contains default HyperCard menus and nothing more.

Putting the Stack Script Together

Here, then, is the complete stack script:

```
on openStack
  lock screen
  lowerUserLevel
  addNavigateMenu
  deleteOtherMenus
  disableGoMenuItems
  push card
  unlock screen
end openStack

on closeStack
  global OldUserLevel
  set userLevel to OldUserLevel
  hide card field "thanks" of card 1
  reset menuBar
end closeStack
```

```
on lowerUserLevel
  global OldUserLevel
  get userLevel
  put it into OldUserLevel
  set userLevel to 1
end lowerUserLevel

--  MENU-HANDLING SCRIPTS  --
on addNavigateMenu
  show menuBar
  create menu "Navigate"
  put NavigateItems() into menu "Navigate"¬
  with menuMessages NavigateMessages()
  set cmdChar of menuItem "Exit" of ¬
  menu "Navigate" to "E"
end addNavigateMenu

on deleteOtherMenus
  delete menu "Edit"
  delete menu "File"
end deleteOtherMenus

on disableGoMenuItems
  disable menuItem "Recent" of menu "Go"
  disable menuItem "Help" of menu "Go"
end disableGoMenuItems

function NavigateItems
  return "Title Card,Main Menu,-,Find,Exit"
end NavigateItems

function NavigateMessages
  return "doMenu First,goMain,empty,doFind,doExit"
end NavigateMessages

on goMain
  send mouseUp to bg button "Main Menu"
end goMain

on doFind
  send mouseUp to bg button "Find"
end doFind

on doExit
  send mouseUp to bg button "Exit"
end doExit
```

☐ **Type the script into the stack's script window. As you type, make sure the automatic indentation matches the indentation shown here. If it doesn't, you probably made a typing error. Check your typing and save the script.**

Adding a Temporary Script

Before you test the script, you should be aware of one potential problem: When you open the stack, almost all navigation commands will be disabled. This is fine for novice users, but it can be terribly inconvenient for you when you're debugging and refining the stack. How do you move around the stack if something is wrong with the script of the buttons you created? How do you modify the scripts when the user level has been set to browsing? To protect yourself from such potential problems, you can create a temporary button that allows you to undo some of the disabling commands.

☐ **Create a button somewhere near the bottom of the background. Name it "Emergency Override" and give it the following script:**

```
on mouseUp
  reset menuBar
  addNavigateMenu
  set userLevel to 5
end mouseUp
```

☐ **Test the openStack script by going to the Home stack and returning to the stack. Try out the modified menus. Test the closeStack script by using the Navigate menu to return Home. If you encounter any problems that require damage control, click on the Emergency Override button (or use the message box to reset the user level and the menu bar), fix the script errors, and retest. (The debugger might help you locate the errors.) If you don't understand how the scripts work, put a checkpoint at the beginning of the stack script and step/trace through the script, watching how variables, messages, and commands translate into actions.**

☐ **When the stack is thoroughly tested and debugged, delete the Emergency Override button.**

Missing Links

Keeping Track of Loose Ends

There is much to do before this stack is truly finished. In truth, a stack like this is never finished, because you can always think of some way to improve it.

It's important to maintain an Unfinished Business List as you create large projects. The human brain can create loose ends much more efficiently than it can keep track of them.

Here's a To Do list that covers the most important missing features. We need to:

- Add a full-fledged introduction between the Title card and the Main Menu card, providing computer novices with the background they need to make sense of the rest of the stack.
- Complete the remainder of the Output branch (screens and printers). When we reach the leaves on each branch (leaves are cards that don't have branches, such as Dot Matrix Printer and Color Monitor), we might include pictures of the components being described. (You'll need to unlock the text in both fields to type information on the new cards, and lock them when you're through.)
- Complete the other three branches (Storage, Processors, Input).
- Add a conclusion for sequential readers of the stack. Most other users probably aren't interested in a conclusion, so we can just add information and/or pictures to the final card we've already created.
- Add graphics. Some cards, such as the root of the tree, could benefit from a little creative painting.
- Add a Help card and a Stack Map card, and add buttons to get to and from those cards.
- Add digitized sound effects. For example, you might include spoken comments, samples of sound output, or audio cues corresponding to page turning, jumping around, and other common actions.

Finally, the most important step of all:

Test every button and feature of your stack carefully. Test the stack yourself; then ask members of your target audience to test it while you watch.

Critiquing Our Stack

By now, you may be thinking, "This stack has problems; I could design a better one myself." You're likely to have those kinds of thoughts even while you're turning your own design into reality.

HyperCard invites experimentation, so stacks tend to evolve as they're being created. Halfway through a project you might come up with a better way to implement a particular feature. Whether you choose to modify your original design or stick with it, it's a good idea to take some time to critique your stack to see if it really achieves your original goals.

If we look at our stack critically after testing it ourselves and with novice users, we might start a list of suggested improvements. For example:

1. The user interface is busy. Because we provided the user many ways of navigating the stack, it's possible for the user to lose track of what's been seen and what remains to be seen. We should consider ways for the user to mark his or her progress through the stack.
2. `closeStack` removes the menu we created, but what if we don't close the stack, but simply open another stack in a new window, instead? Our menu is still there, ready to send an error message if the user issues a menu command with it. We need a more sophisticated approach using the **`suspendStack`** and **`resumeStack`** system messages. (For a good example of how this might be implemented, examine the stack script for the HyperCard Help stack.)

This kind of criticism isn't always easy; when you've invested considerable time and energy in a project, it's hard to admit that it has structural flaws. But easy or not, critical analysis is important. Many serious stack designers take the process even beyond critiquing and fine tuning. Here's what those experts advise:

> When you've completed your rough draft of your stack, take an inventory of the ways that it might be improved. Then start over, building it a second time, applying what you learned the first time to your second stack. Repeat as needed.

HyperTalk Housekeeping

HyperTalk is a rich and powerful language with capabilities that go far beyond what we've covered here. You've had enough of a taste of HyperTalk to be well equipped to explore the language further. HyperTalk is the kind of computer language that encourages experimentation, and experimentation is a wonderful way to learn. But as you're exploring, remember that HyperTalk, like any powerful tool, can lead to problems as well as solutions.

Avoiding HyperTalk Hazards

- Use the Save a Copy... command regularly when you're working on an important stack. The more often you back up your work, the less work you'll lose if something goes wrong.
- Use the **Compact Stack command** after you've been working on a stack for a while. This command gets rid of pockets of **free space** that develop whenever you delete anything; the free space makes the stack slower and larger. (You can check the amount of free space in the Stack Info dialog box.)
- Plan ahead, and don't be afraid to backtrack or start over.
- Name everything with meaningful names, and write scripts that `Go to` *`name`* rather than `Go to` *`number`*. It's much easier to debug a script full of names than it is to debug a script full of numbers.
- Avoid duplicate names; HyperCard does not prevent two things from having the same name, so it's up to you.
- Use quotation marks to keep things together that belong together.
- Make your scripts as readable as possible, and add comments anywhere that the meaning or purpose of a statement isn't obvious.
- Use temporary scripts to help you debug your stacks. For example: When you're creating a stack with many links going in different directions (such as Dungeon or Computer Anatomy), it's easy to lose track of the card sequences. Add a field to each background, check its Field Info dialog box to see what number has been assigned to it, and create a background script like this:

  ```
  on openCard
    put "Card" && number of this card into field 1
  end openCard
  ```

  Translation: When the card is opened, put a character string that's made up of "Card" and the number of the current card, separated by a space, into field 1. In some stacks, such as Pyramid, this field might be useful as a permanent fixture. In other stacks, such as Dungeon, where you don't want the card number displayed, the script should be removed when the stack is finished.
- Use the **Comment** and **Uncomment commands** in the Script menu. Because you may need to resurrect temporary scripts during future debugging sessions, it's sometimes wise to deactivate them rather than delete them. Comment may be used to insert a comment marker at the insertion point; Uncomment deletes the preceding comment mark. If you se-

lect several lines of a script and use the Comment (or Uncomment) command, comment markers appear (or disappear) at the beginning of every selected line.

- Put scripts, buttons, and fields where they are most appropriate. If a button or field affects only one card, put it on that card. If something affects many cards with the same background, put it in the background. If it affects many cards with different backgrounds, put it in the stack. If it affects many different stacks, put it in a separate stack and reference that stack with the `startUsing` command (explained in the Help stack and in the *HyperCard Script Language Guide*). Use a consistent method for deciding where to put scripts so you can easily find them later.
- Don't reinvent the wheel unless you have to. HyperCard comes with stacks full of buttons, cards, backgrounds, and clip art that can be used in your stacks. Many commercial, shareware, and public domain programs include buttons, cards, and art designed for borrowing. If somebody has created a script that does what you want and has given the world permission to copy it, feel free to do so. (However, it's important to respect copyright laws and the ethical underpinnings of intellectual property rights; don't borrow from copyrighted material without the author's permission.)
- Take advantage of the HyperCard Power Tools. One especially useful tool for debugging allows you to export all the scripts of your stack into a single text file so you can print it out and examine every detail.
- Learn from the masters. Study the best stacks that you can find; apply the programming techniques of those stacks to your own work. (A sampler of first-rate stacks is included in Appendix A.)

Summary

You've seen how to create nonlinear hypertext documents using HyperCard. Specifically, you combined several different structures—a sequence, a tree, and a complex network—into a document that can be read in several different ways. You learned many new HyperTalk commands, including several for building hypertext documents and others for customizing the HyperCard user interface. More important, you learned how to apply basic design principles to your work so the stacks you create can accomplish the goals you've set for them.

Next session, you'll see how to add color, sound, and video to your stacks by taking advantage of scripts written by others. You'll also learn how to save stacks as stand-alone applications.

Key Words

`&&`
`answer` command
`ask` command
`bg`
branch
chunk
`clickChunk` (function)
`clickText` (function)
`cmdChar` (property)
Comment command
Compact Stack command
concatenate
`create menu` command
custom (programmer defined) function
data structure
`delete menu` command
`disable` command
`doMenu` command
`exit` command
`find` (command)
`find chars` (command)
`find string` (command)
`find whole` command
free space
`get` command
`global` command
global variable
Group style
hot text
hypermedia
hypertext
`It`
local variable
`lock screen` command
`lockScreen` (property)
`me`
nested if structure
`pop card` command (Command-↑)
pop-up field
pseudocode
`push` command (Command-↓)
`reset menuBar` command
`result` function
`resumeStack` message
root
scrolling field
`send` command
stack (data structure)
stepwise refinement
Style menu
`suspendStack` message
suspended (stack)
`textStyle` (function)
tree structure
Uncomment command
`unlock screen` command

Exercises

1. What kind of structure (linear, tree, or network) is most appropriate for a stack that

   a. provides users with a list of legislators, with options for seeing the voting record of each one?

b. guides users through a walking tour of your town, highlighting main scenic attractions along the way?

2. What happens when a button in the card layer covers a button in the background layer?

3. What happens when a field in the card layer covers a field in the background layer?

4. What happens when a button in the card layer covers a field in the background layer?

5. What happens when a field in the card layer covers a button in the background layer?

6. What is hot text?

7. What is the variable `It` used for?

8. What is the difference between a local variable and a global variable? When is it appropriate to declare a variable as global?

9. What is the relationship between the `push` and `pop card` commands? Give examples of how they can be used in stack scripts. What are their keyboard shortcuts, and how might the shortcuts be useful?

10. What is the difference between the `ask` command and the `answer` command? Give examples of how each might be used.

11. Why would you lock text? How?

12. What is a function? Give examples of built-in functions and user-defined functions.

13. The following HyperTalk commands contain words you haven't seen before. What do you think each statement does?

    a. `set textFont of field "bullet chart" to Times`

    b. `set textSize of word 1 of field "bullet chart" to 18`

    c. `set textAlign of field "bullet chart" to center`

    d. `set textFont of button 1 to Helvetica`

    e. `set textStyle of button 1 to italic, extend`

    f. `set autoHilite of button 2 to true`

    g. `set style of button 1 to radioButton`

    h. `put the number of cards into msg`

    i. `put the number of windows into msg`

14. What do the following handlers do? (If you have trouble figuring something out, type it in and try it out.)

a.
```
on getName
  ask "What is your name"
  put it into yourName
  if yourName is empty then exit getName
  put "Hello Welcome to HyperCard, " & ¬
  yourName into the message box
end getName
```

b.
```
on nonsense
  ask "Give a starting number for Bozo"
  put it into Bozo
  repeat 10 times
    add 1 to Bozo
  end repeat
  put "The answer is " & Bozo into ¬
  message box
end nonsense
```

c.
```
on mouseUp
  ask "Enter a temperature in Fahrenheit"
  put Fahrenheit(it) into temp
  put "The Centigrade temperature is: " & ¬
  temp into msg
end mouseUp
function Fahrenheit temperature
  return (temperature - 32) * 5/9 ¬
  -- Fahrenheit to Centigrade
end Fahrenheit
```

d.
```
on mouseUp
  get the clickText
  if the textStyle of the clickChunk ¬
  contains bold then
    put char 1 of word 1 of field "my name" ¬
    & char 1 of word 2 of field "my name" ¬
    into msg
  end if
end mouseUp
```

e. (*Hint:* This handler contains some unfamiliar words, but it's not hard to figure out. Assume there's a picture of a car in the card layer at location (100, 320) and that the background layer contains the rest of the picture of a city street. This technique is sometimes called *paint animation.*)

```
on mouseUp
  choose select tool
```

```
        type "s" with commandkey
        doMenu opaque
        set dragspeed to 70
        drag from 100, 320 to 400, 320
        choose browse tool
    end mouseUp
```

15. Write a script for a button that, when clicked, causes HyperCard to do the same thing that it does when you select the following menu items:

    a. New Card

    b. Recent

    c. Message

    d. Quit HyperCard

16. Write a handler to create a menu named Other Stuff when the stack is opened. Include the following items in the menu:

    a. Userlevel to Scripting

    b. Play a Song

    c. Get Card Info

17. Write handlers for each of the menu items in question 16.

Projects

1. Complete as many of the items on the To Do list at the end of this session as you can.
2. Add page numbers to your stack using the trick described in the box called "Avoiding HyperTalk Hazards."
3. Add and implement a Help button on the first card: (a) with a pop-up field, (b) by going to the last card in the stack (remember to provide a way to get back).
4. Add a glossary to the Computer Anatomy stack. Underline words and phrases in the main text that appear in the glossary, and write a script for the field that links those words and phrases to the glossary entries.
5. As an alternative to a glossary, add pop-up definitions to underlined words in the text.
6. Modify the Pyramid stack from Session 3 so that it displays informative pop-up fields when buttons are clicked.

7. Modify the Map stack (Project 6, Session 3) so that it displays fields describing particular areas when those areas are clicked.

8. Write an interactive story that allows users to click on buttons to choose different paths through the story.

9. Create a stack to catalog your collection of tapes, records, or CDs. Include fields for artist, title, music category, favorite tracks, and comments. Borrow and/or create buttons to find and sort cards in your stack. After entering data for several recordings, test both of these buttons.

10. Create a glossary of terms for a specific field of study (computers, hypermedia, biology, anthropology, or whatever) with each term defined and/or illustrated on a single card. Create cross-links that connect related terms so that readers can jump from definition to definition instantly. For example, if the card for *disk drive* includes the term *peripheral*, that term should have a button that links to a card for *peripheral*.

11. Make a genealogy stack that includes at least three generations. Develop a plan before you actually start to create the stack. Include in the background five text fields: name, birthdate, birthplace, interesting information, and date of death. Think about the field attributes carefully in terms of their function. (Should any of these fields scroll?) Design a good-looking background; allow space for several card buttons. In the card layer create the following buttons where appropriate: Mother, Father, Spouse(s), and Child(ren). (Why should these buttons be in the card layer?) Link each button to the appropriate card. If the button has nowhere to go, display a message to that effect using a pop-up field. Finally, when you have completed the stack, critique it as if someone else had created it and you were the user.

Session 7

At the end of this session you should be able to

- Colorize the buttons, fields, and graphical elements in a HyperCard stack
- Import color graphic images from other applications into your stacks
- Record, edit, and import digitized sounds so that they can be played in your HyperCard stacks
- Add QuickTime video clips to your stacks
- Understand how you can use HyperCard to control external devices like videodisc players, CD-ROM drives, and electronic musical instruments
- Create multimedia documents that use color graphics, video, and audio to help you communicate your message
- Save a finished stack as a stand-alone application

Multimedia in Minutes

Beyond Black and White

The Problem

Your HyperCard creations don't electrify audiences the way you'd like them to. You face stiff competition in the battle for people's attention. Big-budget Hollywood productions, high-tech commercials, and rapid-fire music videos stimulate our senses in ways that nobody fully understands. Even many classic black-and-white films have been colorized to suit the sensibilities of modern viewers. How can you make your presentations more colorful, more contemporary, and more lively? Perhaps HyperCard can help.

Introduction

On the same August day in 1987, Apple introduced two revolutionary products: HyperCard and the first color Macintosh. Today the original monochrome Mac has been superseded by a plethora of color models used for applications like desktop publishing, graphic art, animation, image processing, video production, and interactive multimedia. In the world of multimedia where color is commonplace, HyperCard's black-and-white interface seems underpowered and old-fashioned.

Fortunately, HyperCard was designed to be flexible so that new features can be—and have been—added as user needs change. By using a handful of HyperCard accessories you can colorize your stacks. Other add-ons allow you to include CD-quality music and video in your stacks. Beneath its aging interface, HyperCard is still one of the most powerful and flexible multimedia authoring tools available on any computer.

In earlier sessions you worked with HyperCard basics—standard tools and commands that give you control over HyperCard and your computer. In this session you'll see how a handful of accessories can enhance HyperCard's power as a multimedia authoring tool. We'll focus on the accessories that come bundled with HyperCard, but we won't ignore commercial products from other vendors. Each section begins with an introduction that provides an overview of the technology so you can read about the basic principles without actually performing the step-by-step instructions that follow. Because these sections are independent, you can choose to do any or all of the sections in any order. Many of the examples use the Earth stack created in Session 5. For obvious reasons, much of the material in this session requires more than a minimal Macintosh. If HyperCard doesn't respond appropriately when you're working with color, sound, or video, it may need more memory. Detailed requirements for Color Tools, QuickTime Tools, and the Audio Palette are described in those stacks.

Resources and Externals: Extending Your Stacks

As any dictionary editor will tell you, languages evolve to meet the changing needs of people. The HyperCard team designed HyperTalk so that its vocabulary could change with its users' needs. Specifically, they made HyperCard **extensible** so that new words could be added to the HyperTalk vocabulary. These new words are called **XCMDs**, for external commands, and **XFCNs**, for external functions; they're sometimes referred to collectively as **externals**. Hundreds of XCMDs and XFCNs have been written to allow HyperTalk to display color pictures, play audio CDs, show video clips, communicate with modems, and perform other tasks that it couldn't do without them.

Some externals don't give HyperCard new capabilities; they simply allow it to perform routine tasks faster and more efficiently. HyperTalk is an interpreted language, which means that the HyperTalk **interpreter** translates it on the fly, like an interpreter at the United Nations. Programs written in compiled languages like Pascal or C++ are translated all at once into machine language by **compilers**, the way this book might be translated from English to Spanish. The tradeoff is between immediacy and speed; because it's an interpreter, HyperTalk produces relatively slow-running programs. (Technically, HyperTalk scripts are partially compiled, but they're still no match in speed for fully compiled programs in other languages.) Because externals can be compiled, they can speed up a stack's response time.

Writing externals requires considerable programming skill, but borrowing externals is easy. Many externals are available in commercial and public domain packages. Some are even included in Apple's HyperCard package.

XCMDs and XFCNs are stored in the **resource fork** of your stack—the part of the file that also contains icons, sounds, and other types of data that make your stacks work properly. Because **resources** are stored in the resource fork rather than as part of the stack's instructions, you can use specialized software tools to change them without rewriting scripts. For example, when you created and edited icons in Session 5, the Icon Editor was creating and modifying icon resources.

Resources play a critical role in multimedia because much multimedia data is stored as resources. In this session you'll be working with a variety of resources, including XCMDs, XFCNs, color graphics, and sounds. You'll use several stacks that make resource manipulation easy, starting with those included in Apple's Color Tools.

Colorizing a Stack

"Everything looks worse in black and white," according to Paul Simon's classic song "Kodachrome." It's probably more accurate, if less poetic, to say that many things look better in color, including most computer screens. The latest version of HyperCard is still, at its heart, a black-and-white program. But by popular demand, Apple has included several tools for adding color to stacks. The **Color Tools** stack allows you to colorize buttons, fields, and rectangular areas on cards and backgrounds. It also allows you to display color pictures created elsewhere. The newest version even includes color paint tools for creating and editing color pictures. In this section you'll use the Color Tools XCMDs to colorize the Earth stack created in Session 5. You'll also see how you can use HyperCard's Picture XCMD to display color pictures without using the Color Tools stack.

> When you're working with color, you'll get best results if you have a color Macintosh with *at least* 4 megabytes of memory and System 7. You should set the Monitor's control panel to 256 colors and set HyperCard's memory partition to at least 2200K on a 68000-based Macintosh or 5120 on a Power Mac (higher if you can) by following the procedures described at the beginning of Session 1. If HyperCard doesn't respond appropriately when you're working with color, it may need more memory. If your machine doesn't meet the minimal requirements, you may want to skip this section. If you have the hardware but don't have the Color Tools stack, skip to Using the Picture Command.

Exploring and Installing Color Tools

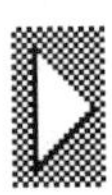

☐ **Open HyperCard and click on the right-arrow button to go to the second card of the Home stack.**

This card contains several icons linked to other stacks.

☐ **Click on the Color Tools icon to open the Color Tools stack.**

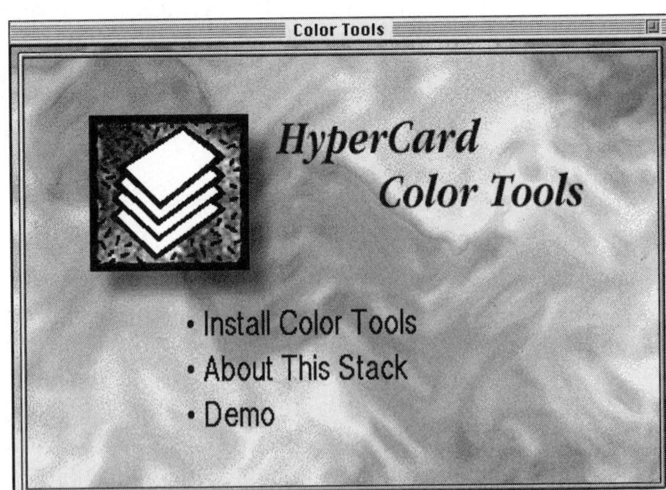

If you see a black-and-white (or an empty) window, you probably forgot to set the Monitors control panel to 256 colors. Quit HyperCard, reset the control panel, and return to this point.

- ☐ **Click on Demo. When the demo card appears, click on the Demo button at the bottom of the card. Watch the short demo to get an idea of how Color Tools work.**

- ☐ **When the demo is done, click on the right-arrow button to go to the "About This Stack" card.**

- ☐ **After you've skimmed the text on this card, click on the Main Menu button.**

- ☐ **Click on Install Color Tools to go to the installation card. If this card contains a button that says "Remove," then Color Tools have already been installed in your Home stack. If it says "Install," click on it to install Color Tools in your Home stack.**

Using Color Tools

- ☐ **Go Home. Your Home card should contain an icon labeled "Color Tools are ON" or "Color Tools are OFF." If it says "Color Tools are OFF," click on it to turn them on.**

> The Color Tools button on the Home Card toggles between ON and OFF. When the button is toggled on, a Color menu provides access to tools for adding color to stacks.

You'll use this menu to modify your Earth stack.

- ☐ **Use the Open Stack command to open your Earth stack from Session 5.**

The menu bar should disappear because of your stack script.

- ☐ **Type Command-Space to show the menu bar.**

- ☐ **Choose Save a Copy.... to save a copy named "Earth 1".**

> Color isn't free. When you install the color externals in your stack, the stack takes up more space on your disk, and some of its actions may have a slower response time. What's more, black-and-white visual effects will no longer work. Finally, your colorized stack probably won't work properly if you ever need to run it on a black-and-white Mac. Saving a copy allows you to go back to black-and-white if you prefer. It's *always* a good idea to make an extra copy of a stack when you're about to make major modifications.

- [ ] **Choose Open Color Tools from Color menu.**

You'll see a warning dialog box.

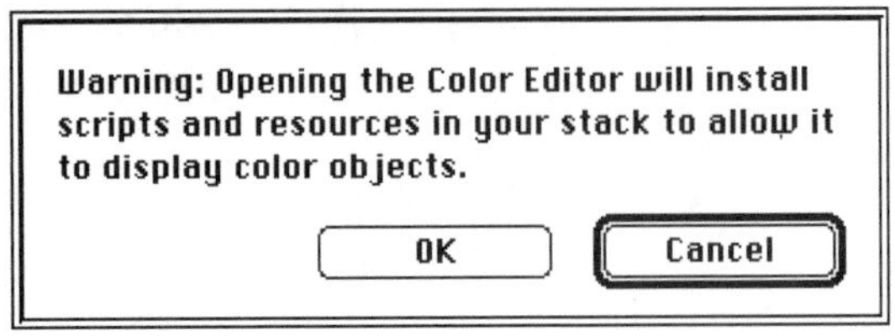

Warning: Opening the Color Editor will install scripts and resources in your stack to allow it to display color objects.
OK
Cancel

No problem; you have another copy of your stack.

- [ ] **Click OK.**

The Color Editor appears and several color-related menus replace the standard HyperCard menus.

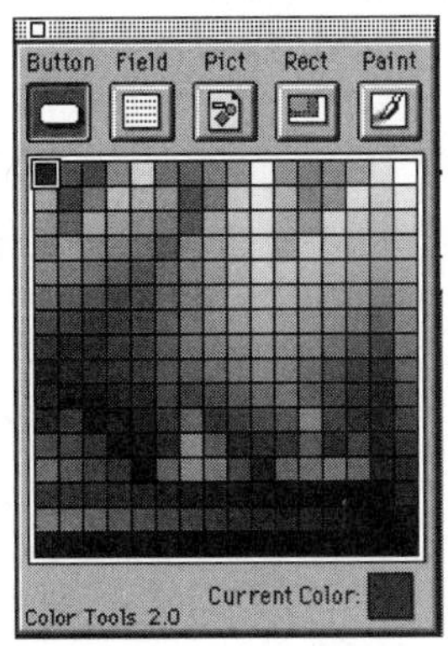

Adding Color Transitions

If you were to try your stack now, you'd see that the visual effects are inoperative. (If you want to see this for yourself, you'll need to close the Color Editor palette to use the Browse tool and reopen it to continue with these instructions.) Fortunately, you can add substitute visual effects.

> Color effects aren't attached to button scripts the way black-and-white ones are; they're attached to cards, backgrounds, or entire stacks. When an effect is attached to a card, it happens every time that card appears. An effect attached to a background works whenever any card with that background appears. An effect attached to a stack works with every card in the stack.

The Earth stack contains three backgrounds—one starry sky with an Earth button, one without Earth, and the bullet chart field. We want to add transition effects to two of these backgrounds so that we see transitions when we enter those cards. We'll start with the Earthless starry background.

☐ **Press the right-arrow key twice to go to the third card in the stack—the first one showing a cloud of smoke against a starry background.**

Go Next (Command-3) won't work because the Go menu isn't available while the Color Tools are open.

☐ **Choose Background Transition from Effects menu.**

You'll see a dialog box with two pop-up menus—one for effect and one for speed. Stamp is the default effect; it's the same as no transition effect at all.

☐ **Choose Dissolve from the pop-up effects menu in the dialog box and click OK.**

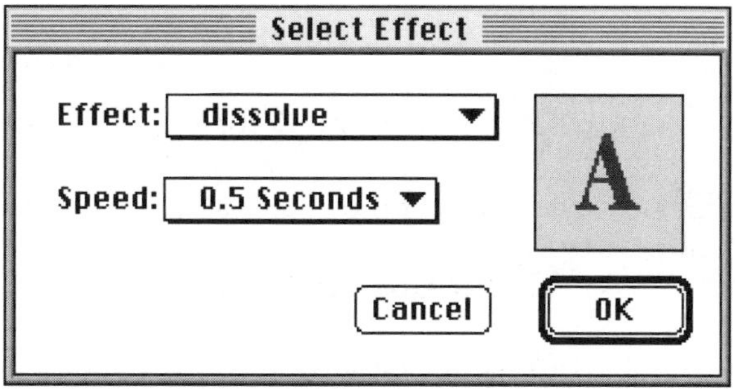

☐ **Go to one of your bullet chart cards.**

For these cards you'll want something like the wipe right effect you used in Session 5.

☐ **Choose Background Transitions again. Choose Effect FromLeft, Speed 1.5 Seconds, and OK.**

☐ **Choose Close Color Tools from the Color menu.**

The Browse tool will return.

☐ **Go through the stack, testing the new visual effects.**

The color transitions are rougher, but they'll do the job.

Colorizing a Button

The Earth stack uses a transparent button on a black card to start the presentation. Let's paint the card white and turn the transparent button into a colorful, three-dimensional button that says "Show time!"

☐ **Go to the first card of the Earth stack.**

☐ **Select the Paint Bucket tool and the white paint pattern; click anywhere on the card to turn it from black to white.**

☐ **Choose the Button tool and double-click on the large transparent button to open the Button Info dialog box.**

☐ **Change the button name to "Show time!", change the button style to Rectangle, turn on Show Name and Auto Hilite, change the Text Style to 18-point Times, and click OK.**

☐ **Resize the button so it looks something like this:**

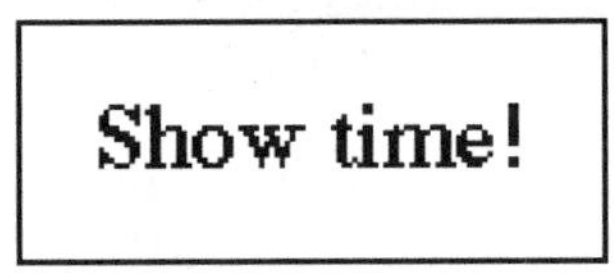

☐ **Select Open Color Tools from the Color menu.**

☐ **Click on the button icon in the Color Editor.**

☐ **Click on the Show time! button.**

☐ **Click on a color in the palette.**

The button should be colorized. If you don't like the results, choose another color by clicking in the Color Editor.

☐ **Double-click on the button.**

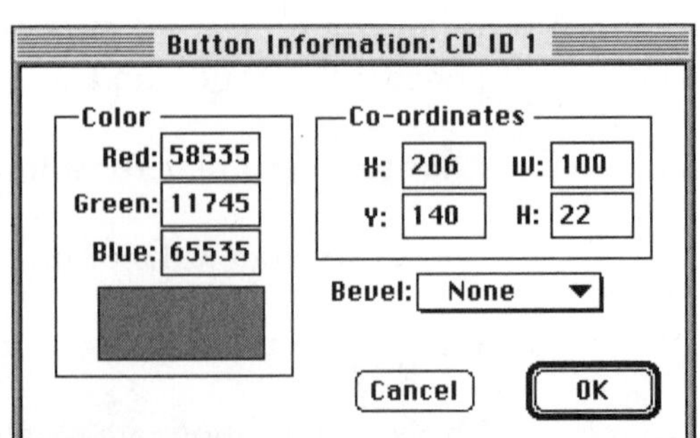

Because the Color Tools are open, you'll see a dialog box showing color information about the button. You can adjust the color by changing the numbers in the three boxes on the left. You can adjust the position and dimensions of the button by changing the numbers on the right. But we came here to add a **bevel**—a three-dimensional trim around the edge.

☐ **There's a pop-up menu in the dialog box for controlling the bevel; it's currently set to None. Click and hold down the mouse button on None to reveal the menu; change the bevel to 4 Pixels. Then click OK.**

You can colorize buttons with icons, too, but the color covers the entire button—not just the icon. We'll colorize the Earth button in the background of the second card. Because the icon is surrounded by a mostly black background, the colored rectangle around the icon won't be visible except through stars close to the icon. If you choose a light color, these colorized stars won't stand out.

☐ **Use the right-arrow button to go to the second card, select the Earth icon, and select a light blue shade from the Color Editor.**

On this card, the colorized Earth looks fine. But when the Earth button moves at the end of the presentation, sharp-eyed observers may notice a problem. See for yourself.

☐ **Turn off Color Tools and use the Browse tool to click your way through the presentation. Notice how the patch of blue stays behind when the Earth slides down the screen.**

When the Earth bounces back, the blue patch once again surrounds it. The blue patch is even visible on the first card because it shares the background that contains this button.

> Colors aren't really part of objects in HyperCard 2.3. When an object moves, its color doesn't immediately go with it. The color is reunited with its object the next time HyperCard redraws the card—for example, when you return to the current card after visiting another card. Even if you don't move objects, you'll probably notice occasional glitches where colors don't appear where they should. That's what the **Redraw Screen** menu item is for. When you select it, HyperCard stops to check once again where all the colors are supposed to be and draws the screen accordingly.

Colorizing a Field

Colorizing a field involves the same steps as colorizing a button.

- ☐ **Go to any of the bullet chart cards in your Earth stack.**

- ☐ **Open Color Tools.**

- ☐ **Click on the field button at the top of the Color Tools menu.**

- ☐ **Click on the large bullet chart field.**

- ☐ **Select a pale yellow from the Color Editor to colorize the field.**

Since this background field is shared by several cards, the yellow color will be visible on all those cards.

Colorizing a Rectangle

You can add rectangular patches of color to cards and backgrounds even if there are no buttons or fields there.

- ☐ **Go to the last card in the stack—the one that says "Let's turn things around."**

- ☐ **Click on the Rect button in the Color Editor.**

- ☐ **Select Place Rectangle from the Items menu.**

A small square appears in the center of the window.

- ☐ **Move and reshape the square until it just covers the words "Let's turn things around."**

- ☐ **Select a shade of green from the Color Editor.**

The letters should change to the selected color. You can choose other colors until you find one you like. Then you're ready to color one more rectangle.

- ☐ **Go to the first card in the stack.**

- ☐ **Double-click on the Rect button in the Color Editor.**

That's a shortcut for making a new color rectangle appear in the center of the screen.

- ☐ **Drag the rectangle so that it fills the entire card.**

☐ **Select sky blue from the palette; try the sixth square down in the second column from the right.**

Your color rectangle obscures the color of the button you created earlier. You can fix this by moving the rectangle backward through the layers of color so that the button's color layer is on top.

☐ **While the rectangle is still selected, select Send to Back from the Items menu.**

The button should regain its original color.

You can add colors to the card and background layers. You can go back and change colors of buttons, fields, and rectangles any time by selecting them with Color Tools open. You can rearrange the way they're layered using the commands in the Objects menu. Experiment!

Importing and Creating Art

You can't draw color pictures with HyperCard's paint tools, but you can make your stacks display pictures created with other applications, as long as those pictures are stored in the right format.

Graphics Background

Color graphics are stored in different formats for different purposes. Color Tools allow you to display pictures stored in the **PICT** format—the standard Macintosh format for screen images. Most graphics applications allow you to save files in a variety of formats, including PICT. If you want to use a graphic image in your stack that isn't in PICT format, you'll need to convert it to PICT using one of those applications.

HyperCard can be scripted to display color pictures stored as PICT files. But a stack that uses separate graphics files won't work properly if those files are deleted or moved. A more reliable way to use color images in your stack is to include those images as resources stored in the stack. Resources make the stack bigger, but they make the desktop cleaner and they reduce the risk that critical pieces can't be found. The Color Editor allows you to add color picture resources without scripting.

Importing a Picture Resource Using Color Tools

☐ **If it's not already open, open Color Tools.**

☐ **Double-click the picture icon in the Color Tools palette.**

A dialog box appears asking you to "Select a Picture to Place." There's a "PICT file..." button for importing a picture stored as a PICT file, but in this case you want to import a color picture stored as a resource in another stack.

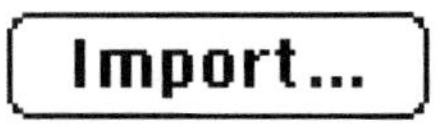

☐ **Click on the Import button.**

☐ **Locate the Power Tools stack by navigating in the dialog box. It's probably in a folder called "More Stacks." When you find it, double-click on it to open it.**

A new dialog box appears. The Import Picture dialog box shows a list of pictures stored as resources in the Power Tools stack.

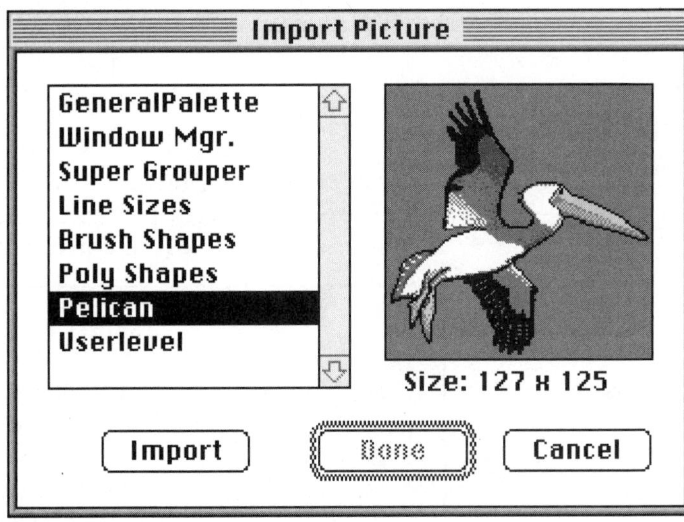

☐ **Select Pelican.**

☐ **Click Import and Done.**

You're returned to the "Select a Picture to Place" dialog box.

☐ **Click on Place.**

The picture appears floating above the card.

☐ **Drag the picture so that it is centered below the button.**

Now the picture will appear in that position whenever you open that card, creating the illusion that the picture is part of the card.

☐ **Turn off Color Tools and try navigating through your colorized stack.**

Using Color Paint Tools

What if you can't find the image you're looking for? You can always create your own or modify an existing image. You don't need to leave HyperCard to create or edit color pictures; HyperCard 2.3 includes built-in color paint tools. In this section you'll have a chance to experiment and be creative with those tools.

☐ **Turn on Color Tools and double-click on the paintbrush button.**

You're telling HyperCard you want to create a new color painting to include in the resource fork of this stack. A dialog box will ask you to name the painting.

☐ **Type "My Picture" (or whatever you want to call your picture). The name won't be visible to the user if the picture is stored as a resource in your stack.**

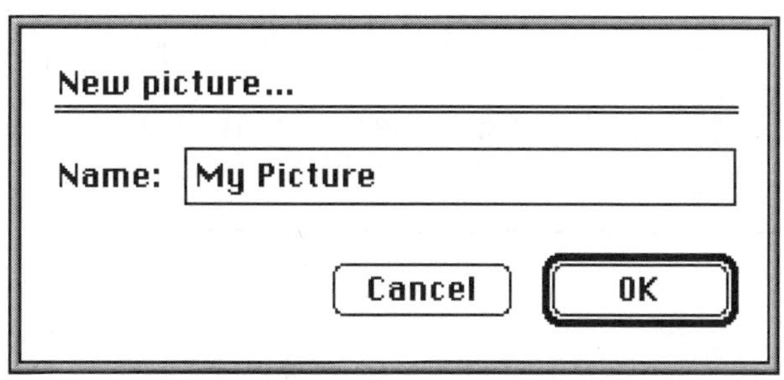

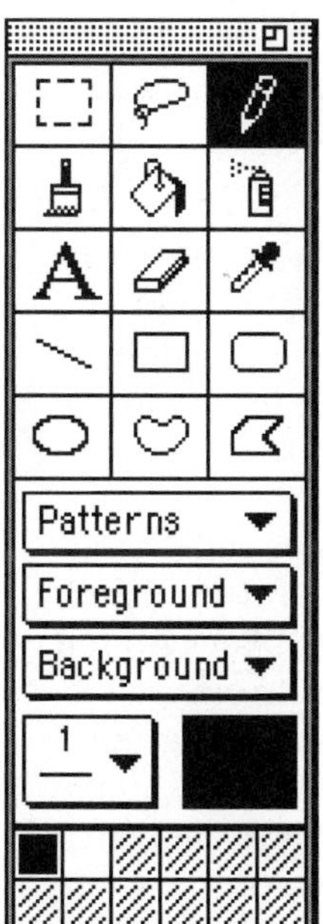

You'll see a new set of menus, a new color Paint Tools palette, and a small window titled the name you typed. This is your canvas for creating or editing a color painting.

☐ **Click on the expand box in the upper right corner of the Tools palette.**

The palette expands to reveal several more icons, as shown on the next page; these icons correspond to commands in the Effect menu.

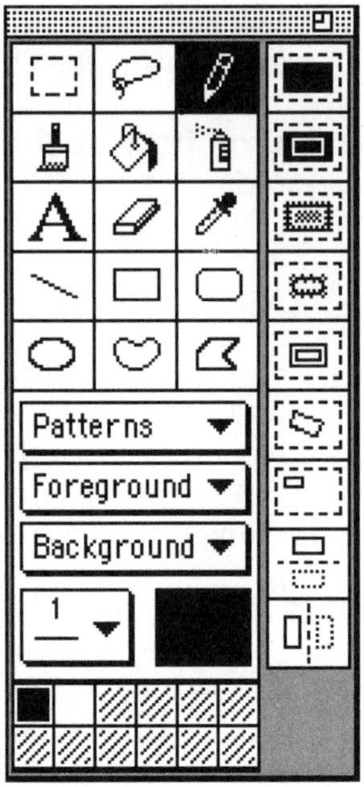

☐ **Stretch the lower right corner of the untitled window until the window is a comfortable size for painting but smaller than your stack's card size.**

You have everything you need to create a small work of art.

☐ **Experiment with the tools in the palette, using your knowledge of other painting programs and this box to guide you:**

Color Paint Tools in a Hurry

If you're familiar with HyperCard's built-in black-and-white paint tools and commands, you'll recognize most of the color tools and commands. In fact, most of the tools perform the same functions as their monochrome counterparts as listed in the table on the inside back cover of this book. Here are the major differences:

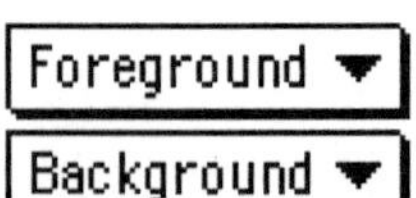

Foreground and background colors. The big difference in color painting is that you can change the **foreground color** and the **background color** at any time using the Foreground and Background pop-ups. (When you're using HyperCard's monochrome tools, black is always the foreground color and white is the background color.) The Pencil, Spray Can, Text tool, Line tool, and shape boundaries are made with the foreground color (unless the pencil line starts on a pixel colored with the foreground color, in which case the line is colored with the background color). The Paint

Bucket, Paintbrush, and filled shape interiors use the selected pattern made up of the foreground and background colors. The Eraser erases to white, and the Lasso selects any nonwhite shape, regardless of the foreground and background colors.

Other tool differences. The Spray Can works more like an airbrush than a spray can; double-click on it to change the settings. The line width is controlled by a separate pop-up, not by double-clicking on the Line tool. Double-clicking on the Text menu allows you to control only the font; the Text menu contains commands for controlling text size and style.

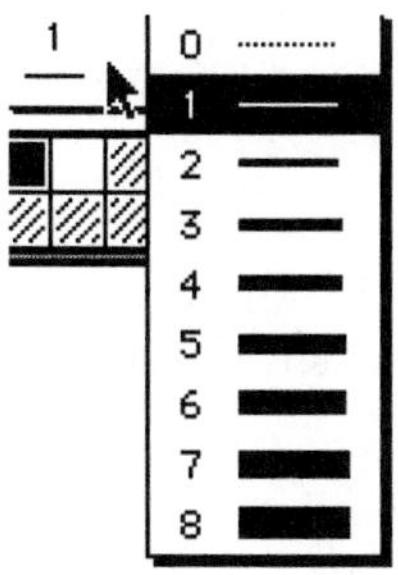

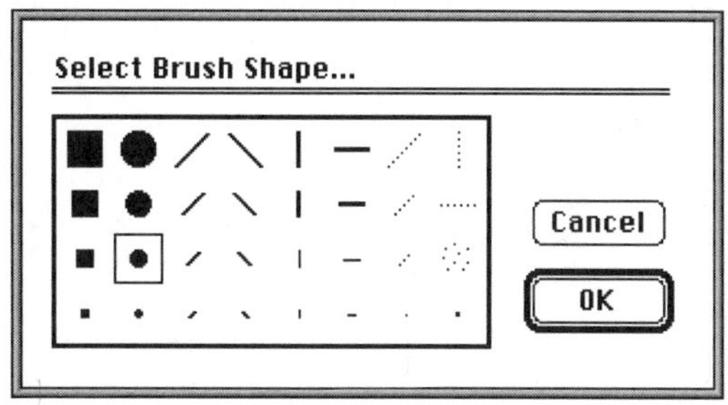

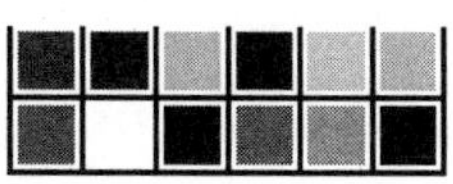

Picking up colors. The Color Pickup tool (the eye dropper) allows you to select any color from part of your image and make it the foreground color. The selected color appears in the Recent Colors palette at the bottom of the palette. This palette keeps the 12 most recently used colors handy so you can grab one quickly. The Color Pickup tool can also be used to color parts of your image. If you hold down the Option key while clicking on part of your picture, the currently selected color replaces all parts of the picture that are the same color as the one you clicked. Holding down the Option and Command keys while clicking on your picture replaces the clicked-on color with the current gradient (discussed shortly).

File menu commands. These commands allow you to open, save, import, and export graphic images.

New... allows you to open and name a new window for image editing. It's possible to have more than one image window open at a time.

Open... allows you to open and edit any graphic image stored as a resource in the current stack.

Import Graphics allows you to bring a color image created or captured by another application so you can edit it using HyperCard's color paint tools.

Export Graphics. This command allows you to save your color picture as a separate file.

New Effect menu commands. Most of the commands in the Effect menu can be accessed via icons on the expanded Paint Tools palette:

Fill Picture fills the selected area with the foreground color.

Invert Picture replaces each color in the selected region with its complement.

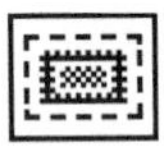

Tint Picture nudges the selected region toward the foreground color or the background color, depending on which option you select.

Anti-alias Picture causes sharp, jagged edges in a selected image to be slightly blurred. **Anti-aliasing** is particularly useful for improving the appearance of large text.

Trace Picture Edges is similar to its monochrome counterpart.

Rotate Picture is similar to the monochrome Rotate commands.

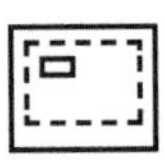

Scale Picture gives you precise control over the amount by which a selected image is reduced or enlarged.

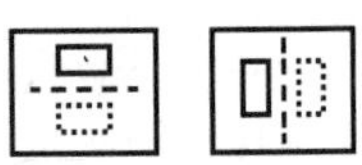

Flip Picture Vertical and Horizontal work like their monochrome counterparts.

New Options menu commands. Most of the Options commands are similar to standard HyperCard painting commands, but a few differences are worth noting:

Zoom In is a multicolor, multilevel FatBits; it allows you to magnify the picture to 2:1, 4:1, or 8:1. Double-clicking the Pencil cycles through all four magnifications.

Zoom Out demagnifies in the same increments.

Edit Gradient produces a dialog box showing the current **gradient**—a gradual transition from one color to another. Use the two pop-ups at the bottom of the dialog box to determine the two end colors. Click on any or all of the intersecting lines to the left to control the shape and direction of the gradient. To place the gradient in your picture, Command-Option-click in your picture with the Color Pickup tool (the eye dropper) selected; the color you click on will be replaced by the gradient wherever it appears in your picture.

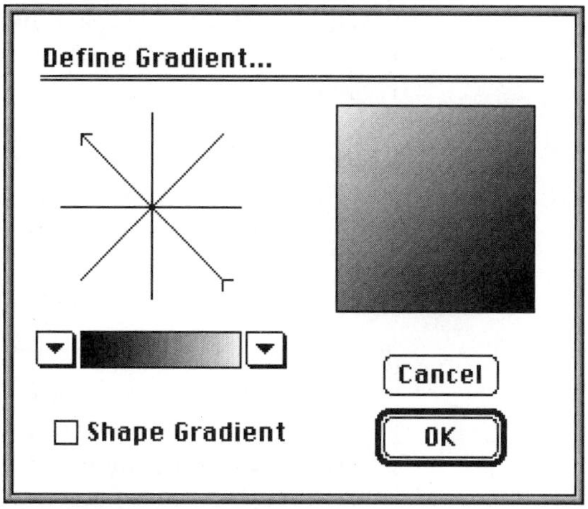

Taken together, these color tools and commands are amazingly powerful—and fun. Experiment!

☐ **When you're through playing, chose Close Color Paint Tools from the File menu.**

☐ **When a dialog box asks whether you want to save the changes to your picture, click Yes.**

Your picture disappears, but it's still stored as a resource in the current stack.

☐ **Choose Place Picture from the Items menu (or double-click on the Pict button).**

You'll see the same dialog box you saw when you imported the pelican picture earlier.

☐ **Select your new picture from the list, click on Place, and position the picture where you want it.**

Of course, you may *not* want it. Because your color image is stored as a resource, you can't just delete it from the stack by selecting it and pressing Delete; you need to delete it from the resource fork of your stack.

- [ ] **If you want to delete your picture, double-click on the Pict button (or choose Place Picture), select your picture from the list, click on Delete, and click on Cancel to close the dialog box.**

In this case, Cancel *doesn't* undelete the picture, so click with care when you delete images. When the dialog box closes, your color picture may still be visible on the card, but it will disappear the next time HyperCard redraws the screen.

- [ ] **When you're done experimenting, choose Close Paint Tools from the File menu, choose Close Color Tools from the Color menu, and try navigating through your colorized stack.**

Using Color with Style

Color can add a new dimension to a HyperCard stack. It also adds new responsibilities for HyperCard authors accustomed to working in black and white. Here are a few tips for using color effectively in your stacks:

- Use color sparingly and consistently. Too many colors, like too many fonts, can make a stack look tacky. Choose a palette of a few coordinated colors, and use these colors consistently throughout your stack. To be safe, err on the side of subtle.
- Try to make your stack "color optional." Keep in mind that some people have trouble distinguishing colors, and remember that millions of Macintoshes have monochrome monitors. What's more, color creates some inconsistencies in the HyperCard user interface; for example, color pictures don't show up in the Recent dialog box. If color conveys a message in your stacks, use position, icons, or text to convey the same message.
- Don't waste disk space and memory on unnecessary pixels and colors. Color pictures can quickly turn a small stack into a disk and memory hog. The amount of space taken by each picture depends on its size, **pixel density** (the number of pixels of data per inch of picture) and **bit depth** (the number of bits of memory reserved for each pixel's color information). Standard Macintosh screen **resolution** (pixel density) is about 72 dots per inch. If your picture has higher pixel density, the extra dots won't be displayed; they'll just take up space on disk and in memory. A number of paint and image processing

programs allow you to change a file's pixel density. Those same programs allow you to eliminate unnecessary bit depth, another potential waste of memory. HyperCard black-and-white pictures use one bit per pixel; realistic photographs commonly use a 32-bit color code for each pixel. For most HyperCard applications, 8-bit color depth is sufficient. Although it's possible to limit bit depth with a HyperCard script, it usually makes more sense to use a graphics editing program to change the picture's bit depth before using it in your stack.

Using the Picture Command

The Color Tools stack is easy to use, but it can make a stack sluggish on slower Macintoshes. If speed is important and you're willing to write a few scripts, the **Picture** command can display color pictures more quickly. The Picture command offers many options—far more than most of us need. The examples in this section illustrate a few common uses. If your needs are unusual—for example, you're writing a script that displays on multiple monitors, or you need to change the scale of an imported image at the time you import it—you should consult a HyperCard reference that covers this command in detail.

Assume that you have a color picture saved as a PICT file named "MyPicture" in the same folder as your stack. A button in the stack has this script:

```
on mouseUp
  picture "MyPicture"
end mouseUp
```

Clicking this button makes a picture appear in a standard (separate) window centered on the screen. The MyPicture window remains visible until you quit HyperCard, close the window, or activate another script that closes it. If this isn't exactly what you want, you can change many of the details by adding parameters or changing properties of the window. For example, if the MyPicture window is stored as a stack resource rather than a file, you can add a parameter to the command like this:

```
on mouseUp
  picture "MyPicture", resource
end mouseUp
```

```
picture [name[,type[,windowstyle[,visible[,¬
  bitdepth[,floating]]]]]]
```

The Picture command has a number of parameters for customizing picture displays:

`name`: the name of the picture file or resource. If this isn't included, a dialog box prompts the user for the picture to be displayed.

`type`: `file`, `resource`, or `clipboard` are the three possibilities. If the picture is a file, it should be stored where HyperCard can find it—preferably in the folder with the stack. If the picture is a resource, it can be added to the stack with a graphics program capable of installing resources. The Power Tools Resource Mover, described later in the session, makes it easy to move resources between stacks.

`windowstyle`: choices include

`Plain`	a no-frills window with a title bar and close box
`Document`	like plain with scroll bars added
`Zoom`	like document with a zoom box
`Windoid`	with a palette-like title bar
`RoundRect`	like the calculator
`Rect`	just a box; useful for making a picture appear to be part of the card
`Dialog`	framed like a dialog box
`Shadow`	a shadow box

The last three windowstyles don't include close boxes and therefore must be closed with scripts or commands.

`visible`: true if the picture window is visible; false otherwise. To avoid startling changes, you can have your script change this property to true after all other parameters and properties are set.

`bitdepth`: only necessary if you want HyperCard to change the bit depth of the picture; it usually makes more sense to use a picture that already has the appropriate bit depth.

`floating`: set to `true` if the picture is to float above the card in the palette layer, `false` if the picture is to be part of the card layer. Although it may seem strange, floating is the best choice for creating the illusion that the picture is part of the card. If the picture is *not* floating, a mouse click in the picture can make it disappear behind the card rather than remain in the foreground.

Here's an easy way to use the Picture command to make any card appear to be a color card:

1. Create buttons on the card. Don't worry about the artwork.
2. Use any color painting or drawing application to create a color card image, including "fake" color buttons in the same positions as the real buttons on the card. Save the color image as a PICT file in the folder with the stack. You can call it anything you like; in this example, we'll call it FakeCard.
3. Give the card this script:

```
on openCard
  picture "FakeCard", file, rect, false, ,true
  set loc of window "FakeCard" to "0,0"
  set visible of window "FakeCard" to true
end openCard
on closeCard
  close window "FakeCard"
end closeCard
```

If you install the color picture as a resource in the stack, it won't be visible to the user as an icon. To make this script work, change the word "file" to "resource".

Art Alternatives

Whether you use the Picture command, Color Tools, or some other mechanism for displaying color images in your stacks, those images will have to come from somewhere. You have several options: You can create them using HyperCard's color paint tools or one or more other color graphics programs; you can use clip art created by others; or you can use a scanner, digitizer, or digital camera to convert photographs, drawings, or real-world scenes to digital images. See Appendix A for details about these options.

Break Point

Audio Options

Sound is a critical part of multimedia. To understand the importance of sound, watch the emotional impact of a movie or television program go down when you mute the sound track. In Session 5 you learned how to harness HyperCard's built-in sounds with the Sound button task and with the Play command. HyperCard allows several additional sound options: You can record sounds using the Sound button task or the Audio Palette; copy sounds from other stacks, applications, or files; or use HyperCard to play CDs, synthesizers, or other sound-generating devices. In this section we'll explore these options, starting with another look at the Sound button task.

Recording a Sound as a Button Task

For this section you'll need a microphone or other sound input device attached to your Macintosh. Newer Macintoshes include sound input hardware and software, although the microphone isn't always included in the package. For older Macs designed with only sound output in mind, an add-on sound input device like Macromedia's MacRecorder is necessary for creating custom sounds. If you don't have sound recording hardware, skip to Importing Sound Resources.

☐ **Open the Earth stack if it's not already open.**

You're going to add more sound to that stack, starting with a simple test sound.

☐ **Select the Button tool and choose New Button. Position the button in the lower left corner of the window.**

☐ **Double-click on the new button to open the Button Info dialog box. Name the button "Attention".**

☐ **Click on Tasks... and choose the Sound task icon.**

☐ **Click on Record....**

A new recording window opens.

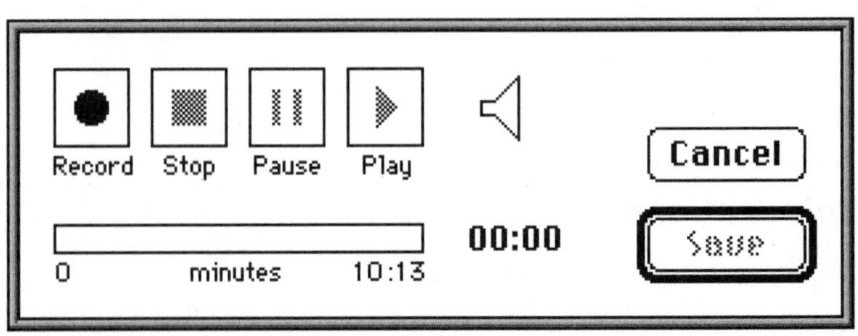

☐ **Speaking into the microphone in a normal tone of voice, try saying something and watch the small speaker icon.**

If your microphone is connected and the Sound Control Panel is set for microphone input, you'll see blips emanating from the speaker icon as you speak. If it doesn't respond, your Sound Control Panel may be set to receive sound from a CD-ROM drive or other source. On most newer Macintoshes, you can change the settings if you open the Sound Control Panel, select Sound Input from the pop-up menu at the top, click on the Options button, select External Audio, click on OK, and close the Control Panel window. When the speaker icon responds to your speaking, you're ready to record.

☐ **Click on the Rec button and, after the wristwatch pointer disappears, say something like "May I have your attention, please?" When you're done recording, click on the Stop button.**

If you make a mistake, simply click Stop and click Record again. (If you click Pause and click Record, the new recording is attached to the end of the old one.)

☐ **Click on the Play button to hear your recording. If you can't hear your recording, use the Sound Control Panel to turn up your computer's sound input volume.**

☐ **When you're happy with your recording, click Save.**

A dialog box asks you to name the sound.

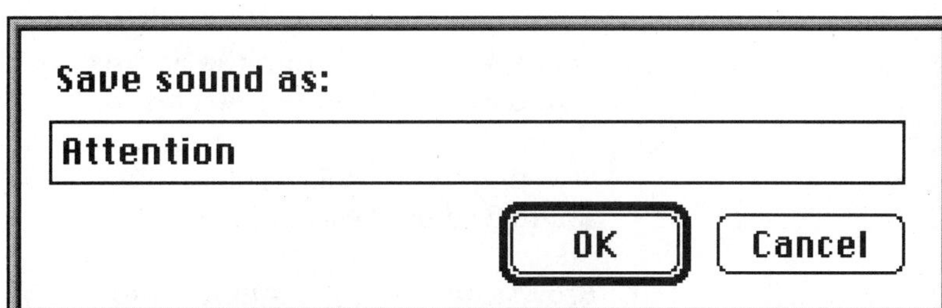

☐ **Type "Attention" and Click OK.**

The sound isn't saved as a file; it's saved as a resource in the stack so that it can be played by any script in the stack. Now you need to assign the task of playing the sound to the button.

☐ **Click Assign Task.**

HyperCard adds the command "`Play "Attention"`" to the button's script.

☐ **Use the Browse tool to try your button.**

If you want more buttons in your stack to play this sound, you can copy this button and paste the copy wherever you want it. To combine the sound with other actions, you can add "`Play "Attention"`" to any script in the stack.

The Sounds task makes it easy to record simple sounds, install them in stacks, and attach them to buttons. If you want to make higher fidelity recordings (and you have the extra disk space and memory to allow it), you can choose Better or Best recording options. But the sound button task doesn't give you the flexibility to edit or delete sounds. That's where the Audio Palette comes in handy.

Exploring the Audio Palette

For this section you'll need the Audio Help stack and a microphone or other sound input device. If you don't have sound recording hardware, skip to Importing Sound Resources.

☐ **If your computer is silent, use the Sound Control Panel to turn the volume up.**

☐ **Select Audio Help from the Edit menu. If it's not there, click on the Audio Help icon on the second card of the Home stack.**

Selecting Audio Help opens a small stack that describes the basics of sound recording with the Audio Palette.

☐ **Browse through the Audio Help stack to get an overview of the HyperCard Audio Palette—a tool for recording, editing, and saving sounds in HyperCard stacks.**

Recording a Sound with the Audio Palette

- ☐ **Open the Earth stack if it's not already open.**

- ☐ **Select Audio... from the Edit menu.**

The Audio Palette appears. Recording a sound with this palette is similar to recording a sound with the Sound button task tools.

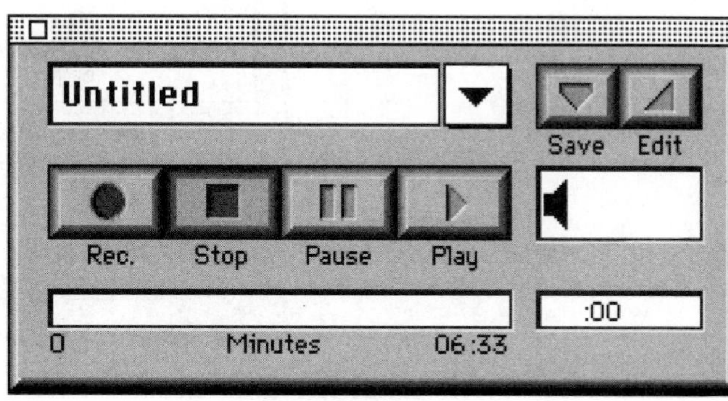

- ☐ **Speaking into the microphone in a normal tone of voice, watch the small speaker icon for activity.**

If it doesn't respond, check the Sound control panel as described in the previous section.

☐ **Click on the Rec button and, after the wristwatch pointer disappears, say something like "Somewhere on the edge of the Milky Way, a small blue planet. . . ." When you're done recording, click on the Stop button.**

If you make a mistake, you can simply record again. When the Audio Palette looks like the screen shown on page 271, rerecording replaces the currently recorded sound.

☐ **Click on the Play button to hear your recording. If you can't hear your recording, use the Sound control panel to turn up your computer's sound input volume.**

Actually, you can fix some mistakes without rerecording. Let's experiment.

Editing a Sound

☐ **Click on the Edit button to expand the Audio Palette.**

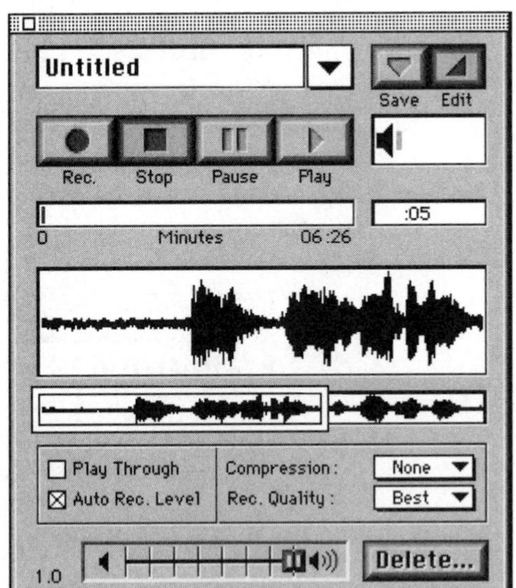

The palette expands to show two **waveforms**—visual representations of the sound waves that make up your recording. In each of these boxes, the recording is represented from left to right, with the beginning of the recording on the left. The lower bar shows the waveform for the entire recording with a view box around the first (leftmost) part; the upper bar shows a close-up view of that part—sort of an audio version of FatBits. You can move, stretch, or contract the view box to change what you see in the upper box. You can also select parts of this image for editing just as you would select characters in a text field. Louder sounds are represented by thicker waves; silence is a thin line.

- ☐ **Select any part of the sound by dragging horizontally from one point to another.**

The selected part of the wave is highlighted in black.

- ☐ **Press Play to hear the selected segment.**

With a little practice, you should be able to select particular words or phrases for editing. Let's start with something easy. Your recording probably has some blank space at the beginning, indicated by a thin line.

> A second of silence takes just as much disk space as a second of sound. To save disk space, delete silent segments at the beginning and end of recordings.

- ☐ **Select the flat part of the wave at the beginning and play it.**

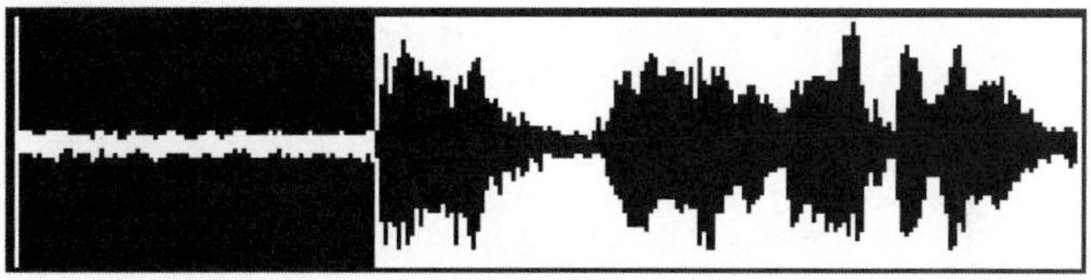

- ☐ **If it is, in fact, silent, press the Delete key to delete it.**

There's probably some silence at the end of your recording, too. You can eliminate it after you display it in the upper box.

- ☐ **Drag the view box in the lower box to the right so that it includes the end of the sound wave.**

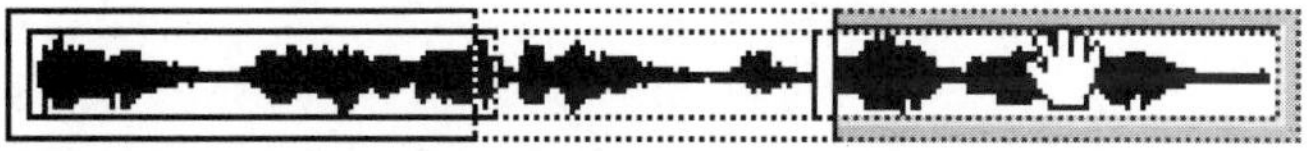

- ☐ **Select the flat line at the end and choose Cut from the Edit menu.**

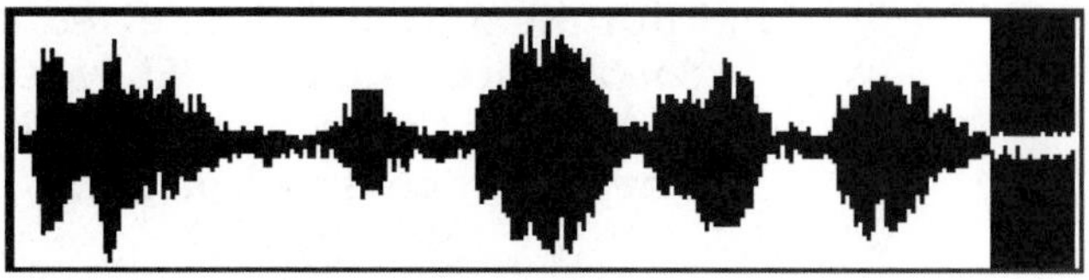

When the Audio Palette is expanded so that the waveform boxes are visible, you can insert new sounds in the current sound by positioning the insertion point and recording. You can replace part of a sound by selecting that part and recording something new to replace it. What's more, the standard Edit commands work on sound segments. Using Cut, Copy, and Paste you can eliminate unwanted words and sounds, repeat musical passages and sound effects, turn spoken phrases into percussive rap-style sounds, turn famous speeches into gibberish, and completely undermine the credibility of sound recordings as evidence.

Saving a Sound in a Stack

☐ **When you're done editing, click the Save button.**

☐ **Type "Somewhere" to name the sound.**

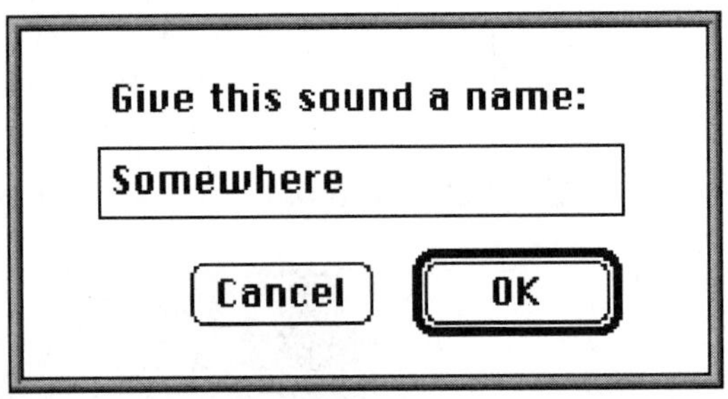

The sound is saved as a resource in the stack so that it can be played by any script in the stack. Once you've saved the sound, the Audio Palette automatically creates a button that's scripted to play the sound when clicked. At the same time, the message box displays the message, "To move your button, hold down the Option key and drag."

☐ **Position the new button and try it. If you're curious about the script, examine it. When you're through, select the button with the Button tool and delete it.**

The script in this button is unnecessarily complicated for our purposes. The only thing that's really necessary in a script is the same Play command you used in Session 5. We'll add a line to the button that's already on this card to play the script.

☐ **With the Button tool selected, hold down the Shift key while double-clicking on the "Show time!" button to open the script window for that button. (If you skipped the section on color, note that the button is transparent.)**

☐ **Add this line to the script after "`On mouseUp`":**

```
Play "Somewhere"
```

☐ **Close the window, save the changes, and try the rescripted button.**

It should play the sound while transporting you to the next card.

Deleting Sound Resources

Now that you have this fancy introduction, you don't really need the "Attention" button you created earlier in this session. But deleting the button won't delete the sound; you need to delete the sound resource from the stack. The easiest way to do that is with the Delete button at the bottom of the Audio Palette.

☐ **Open the Audio Palette (if it's not already open) and expand it by clicking on the Edit button.**

☐ **Click on the Delete button.**

A dialog box shows a list of sounds stored in this stack, the Audio Help stack, and the System file. It's possible to delete something you might want later, so proceed with care.

☐ **Locate the sound named "Attention", click on it, and click on Delete.**

Now that the sound is gone, the "Attention" button is worthless.

☐ **Go to the first card of the Earth stack and delete the "Attention" button.**

Importing Sound Resources

Even if you don't have hardware that supports sound recording, you can import sounds from other sources. As you explore HyperCard stacks, you're likely to run across buttons that play other sounds, ranging from symphonic strings to the theme song of *The Simpsons*. You can copy one of those buttons and paste it into your stack, but the new button won't play sounds unless the corresponding sound resource is copied into the resource fork of your stack.

Resources can't be copied like buttons; they have to be moved with special tools. The most widely available program for moving resources is **ResEdit**, a tool used by Macintosh software developers for creating and modifying resources. But ResEdit can be a dangerous tool in the hands of the uninitiated because it provides the power to destroy a stack or a System with a click of the mouse. A safer, friendlier tool for copying stack resources is **Resource Mover**, included in the Power Tools stack in the HyperCard package. Resource Mover allows you to copy resources, including sounds, from other stacks into your stack. Once you've done that, you can play those sounds in a variety of ways with the Play command.

> HyperCard 2.3's Sound button task allows you to import a sound and attach it to a button script without using the Resource Mover. The Import Sound button in the Sound Task dialog box allows you to locate a file containing sounds and select the sound to be imported from the file. Importing a sound with the Resource Mover stack isn't quite as simple, but it's more versatile—it can be used to import or delete sounds, icons, pictures, and other types of resources.

Power Tools

- ☐ **Go to the second card of the Home stack and click on Power Tools to open the Power Tools stack. (It's probably in the More Stacks folder.) Click on Resource Mover to go to the Resource Mover card.**

> Resource Mover, a card in the Power Tools stack, allows you to open and work with two stacks at a time. (In this context, the word "open" doesn't mean to make a stack visible on the screen; it has a meaning closer to opening the hood of a car to examine the inner workings.) Each side of the card displays a list of resources for one of the stacks. Once the two stacks are open, you can examine each list, delete resources from either stack, and move resources from one stack to the other.

- ☐ **Click on the light bulb icon to see an overview of the Resource Mover. When you're done reading, click to return to the Resource Mover.**

- ☐ **Click on the Open... button on the left. When an Open dialog box appears, locate and open the Earth stack you've been working with throughout this session.**

The scrolling list shows you the resources in the Earth stack, including pictures, sounds, icons, XCMDs, and miscellaneous other under-the-hood items. You can view icons and pictures and listen to sounds by clicking on them. You can also rename or remove any items in the list. But this time we want to add another sound resource to the list—one from the System file.

> To open a non-HyperCard file with Resource Mover, hold down the Option key while clicking on the Open... button. The file is opened as **read-only**; you can copy resources into your stack but can't change the original file.

- ☐ **Hold down the Option key and click the Open... button on the right side of the card. Locate the System file and click Open. (If you don't want to use the System file, open HyperCard Tour, Audio Help, or any other stack with built-in sounds.)**

As you can see, the System file has many resources.

- ☐ **Scroll through the list until you locate sound resources; they have "snd" ID codes.**

- ☐ **Click on one of these sounds—Quack, Indigo, or whatever is available. Whichever sound you choose, remember *exactly* how its name is spelled. You'll need to refer to it by name in a few minutes.**

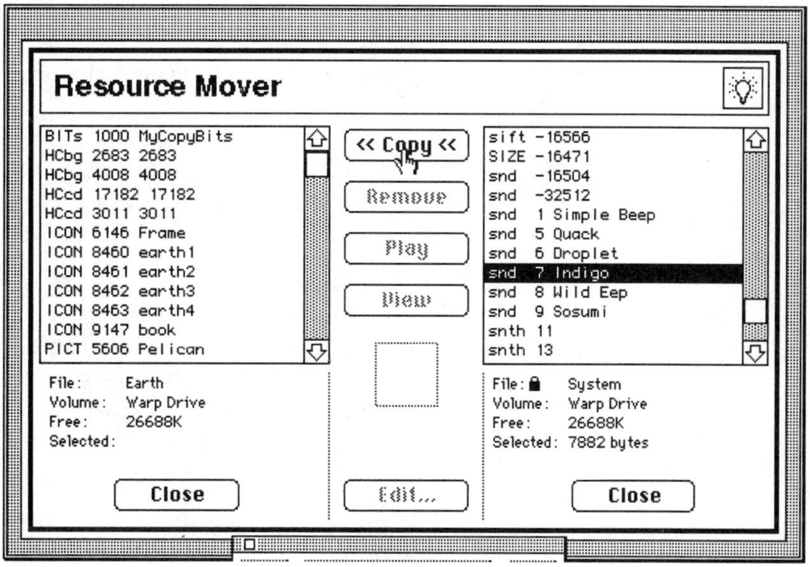

- ☐ **Click on the Copy button in the middle of the window to copy the selected sound resource into the Earth stack.**

After a short wait, the Earth stack's list should include the sound.

- ☐ **Use the Open Stack command to open the Earth stack, and locate the card whose script plays the Bach snippet. (It's the first card after the last bullet chart.)**

- ☐ **Hold down the Shift key while selecting Card Info... to open the card's script.**

- ☐ **In the script, replace "harpsichord" with the *exact* name of the new sound.**

- ☐ **Close the script and save the changes.**

- ☐ **Press the left-arrow key and the right-arrow key to leave the card and return.**

If your sound surgery was successful and you spelled the sound's name correctly, HyperCard will locate the resource and play the Bach passage with that sound. You can do this kind of tinkering with any sound, recorded or borrowed, and any melody. Imagine the possibilities...

Sound Advice

With a little creativity you can add a powerful audio dimension to your stacks. Here are some tips for making sound work for you:

- If disk space is at a premium, choose and use sounds sparingly. An otherwise tiny stack can expand to fill a floppy disk with the addition of just a few digitized sounds.
- If memory and disk space are scarce, sacrifice fidelity to save space. The Audio Palette allows you to record sounds at lower **sampling rates** to save memory and disk space. It also has **compression** options for squeezing information out of sounds so that they take up less disk space. In both cases, the price for the saved space is fidelity. If you're recording speech rather than music, the lower-quality recordings probably won't matter.
- For maximum fidelity, record directly from the source. If you're recording from a radio, stereo, or video source, try using a patch cord to connect the sound source directly to the computer's audio input rather than using a microphone. If your computer has an internal CD-ROM drive, you can adjust the Sound Control Panel's Sound Input controls so that you can record directly from an audio CD into HyperCard. (Under Options, select Internal CD and check Playthrough.)

- Look beyond HyperCard for editing possibilities. The Audio Palette's editing capabilities are limited to basic cut-and-paste functions, but other programs offer more interesting possibilities. See Appendix A for details.
- Don't forget copyright laws. If you're using recordings from television, radio, or other outside sources, make sure you have permission from the owners.

Synthetic Speech

HyperCard's audio tools make it easy to add **digitized** (digitally recorded) **speech** to your stacks. But the resource-hungry nature of digitized sound makes it less than ideal when disk space is at a premium. And with digitized speech, every syllable must be recorded before it can be spoken—a requirement that can greatly limit the flexibility of an interactive stack.

These limitations make digitized speech impractical for some speech-intensive applications like talking dictionaries, interactive storybooks, and talking text processors for visually impaired users. For those applications, **synthesized speech** may make more sense. Because the computer generates synthetic pronunciation from raw text, there's no need to store recordings in advance; the sounds are mathematically generated on the fly by PlainTalk text-to-speech extensions to the operating system. Of course, synthetic speech has a downside: It *sounds* synthetic. Still, if you can tolerate a mechanical accent, synthetic speech is a potential solution to many practical problems.

> To use HyperCard's text-to-speech capabilities you'll need a Macintosh with a 68040 processor or a Power Mac. The required PlainTalk software is included with HyperCard 2.3.

We'll illustrate with a simple example, once again using the modified Earth stack.

☐ **With the Button tool selected, create a button on the last card of the modified Earth stack.**

☐ **Double-click on the new button to open the Button Info dialog box.**

☐ **Click on Tasks.**

Speak Text

☐ **Select the Speak Text icon.**

☐ **Click on Speak String.**

You're telling the button to pronounce the string of characters you're about to type in the box.

☐ **Type "Let's turn things around."**

☐ **Choose a voice gender and style.**

☐ **Click on Assign Tasks.**

☐ **Customize and test the button.**

As you may have noticed, you can also have HyperCard speak text directly from a selected field. (To select the field, you need to switch to the Field tool and click on the field before you can complete the task assignment.) This opens up all kinds of possibilities for having your stacks read aloud to users. By examining the script of the button you just created, you'll be able to see how speech commands can be incorporated in other scripts.

CD and MIDI: Other Audio Options

Synthesized speech isn't the only alternative when you don't have the storage space to record all the sounds you need. If disk space is limited or fidelity is critical, built-in sounds might not be the best alternative. Instead of storing sounds in your stacks, you can store messages that can be sent to other devices capable of playing sounds. With some added XCMDs, your Macintosh can play high-fidelity sound through a CD-ROM drive or electronic musical instruments. These XCMDs aren't included with HyperCard, but they're worth the additional investment for many multimedia applications.

The growing popularity of CD-ROM opens up all kinds of multimedia possibilities. Because a CD-ROM disc can hold hundreds of floppy disks' worth of information, sound and graphics no longer need to be limited by the comparatively small capacities of typical magnetic disks. This larger capacity isn't free; CD-ROM access is slower than that of a magnetic hard disk, and CD-ROMs aren't erasable. But for applications that require access to massive amounts of information, CD-ROM has no equal in today's market. Because CD-ROM drives can also play audio compact discs, you can use HyperCard to control access to audio CDs by computer. Because audio CDs are digital storage media, the data from those discs can be manipulated just like any other data. With some added XCMDs, your stacks can rapidly access and play any passage from any track on a CD at the click of a button. See Appendix A for information about stacks containing those XCMDs and a number of tools for integrating electronic music into HyperCard.

Synthesizers, samplers, and other digital instruments today are all capable of communicating with each other—and with computers—because of a standard interface called **MIDI** (musical instrument digital interface). By connecting a MIDI interface to one of the Macintosh serial ports, you give the Macintosh the capability of talking to just about any modern electronic musical instrument. This means that you can use your Macintosh as a sequencer—a sort of multitrack digital tape recorder for composing and arranging electronic music. Sequencers accept input from the Mac's standard input devices or from a MIDI-equipped music keyboard and play back the edited output files via any MIDI-compatible synthesizer or sound source. Most sequencers are capable of working with standard MIDI files, so they can produce files that can be read by other MIDI software. If you don't have the time, talent, or keyboard for creating a sequenced MIDI file, you can buy professionally arranged MIDI files for hundreds of popular and classical pieces; many are even available for free through public domain sources. MIDI files from any source may require some tweaking with a sequencer before they'll work with your particular synthesizer unless you have a sound source that supports the General MIDI standard for assigning codes to musical instrument sounds. Apple's QuickTime 2.0 system software extension opens up the possibility of playing standard MIDI files without additional hardware. Many MIDI sounds are stored in a QuickTime-accessible software file so MIDI notes can be played by the Mac, not by an external sound source. In the next section you'll learn how to use QuickTime to add video *and* audio clips to your stacks.

Break Point

Video Options

Video is, by any measure, an important component of modern multimedia. Many experts predict that the line that separates computer and television will blur as a new interactive video technology takes over. Today it's possible to experiment with interactive video using HyperCard with some additional software and hardware.

Using QuickTime with HyperCard

Apple's **QuickTime** is a software standard for recording, compressing, and presenting time-based data like video and audio footage. QuickTime technology makes it easy to embed video clips in all kinds of documents so that they can be played with the click of a mouse. With the **QuickTime Tools** stack that's included with HyperCard, you can easily add video segments to your stacks, provided you have the hardware and software.

> To work with QuickTime you'll need the QuickTime extension in your System folder with a "color capable" Mac—anything except a Plus, SE, or Classic. A color monitor set to at least 256 colors is recommended but not required. If you're using System 7, you need at least 4 megabytes of RAM with the HyperCard Get Info preferences set to at least 2 MB. If your computer doesn't meet these requirements, or if you don't have the QuickTime Tools stack, you'll have to skip this section.

☐ **Go Home and click on the QuickTime Tools icon to open the QuickTime Tools stack.**

The title card of the stack presents a menu of options.

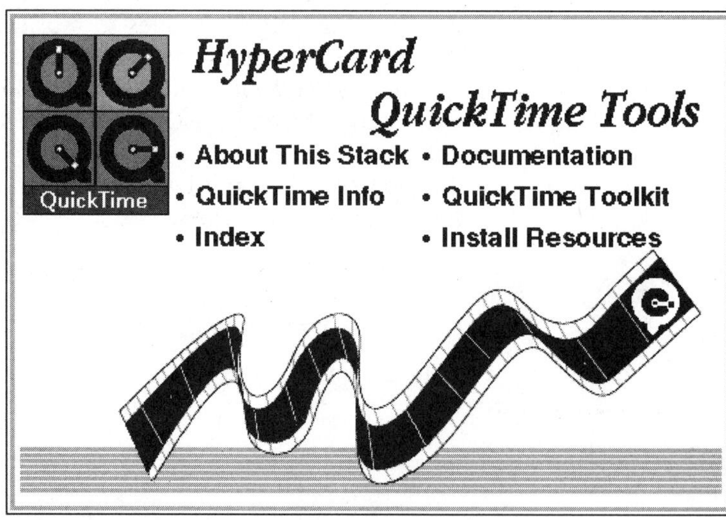

☐ **Click on QuickTime Info and read the introductory page.**

☐ **Return to the main menu.**

QuickTime is a complex technology with myriad possibilities, and the QuickTime Tools stack provides detailed documentation for writing scripts to take advantage of that technology. But for using QuickTime in the simplest way—displaying a simple video clip in a stack—it's not necessary to write scripts at all. Assuming you already have the movie stored on disk so that your stack can find it, you can use the

QuickTime Tools stack to (1) install the necessary QuickTime resources in your stack and (2) install a button that's scripted to display the movie. But with HyperCard 2.3 there's an easier way: the Movie button task option. The button task option combines both steps in a single dialog box that doesn't even mention resources.

Creating a Button to Play a Movie

We'll install a short movie at the beginning of the colorized Earth stack. If you have a QuickTime movie with an environmental theme, use that. If not, simply use the QuickTime Logo movie that comes with HyperCard.

- ☐ **With the Button tool selected, create a button on the first card of your modified Earth stack.**
- ☐ **Double-click on the button to open the Button Info dialog box; then click on Tasks.**

- ☐ **Click on the Movie task icon.**
- ☐ **Click on Play movie. A dialog box will prompt you to locate and choose a movie. If you don't have a more appropriate movie, use the QuickTime Logo Movie.**

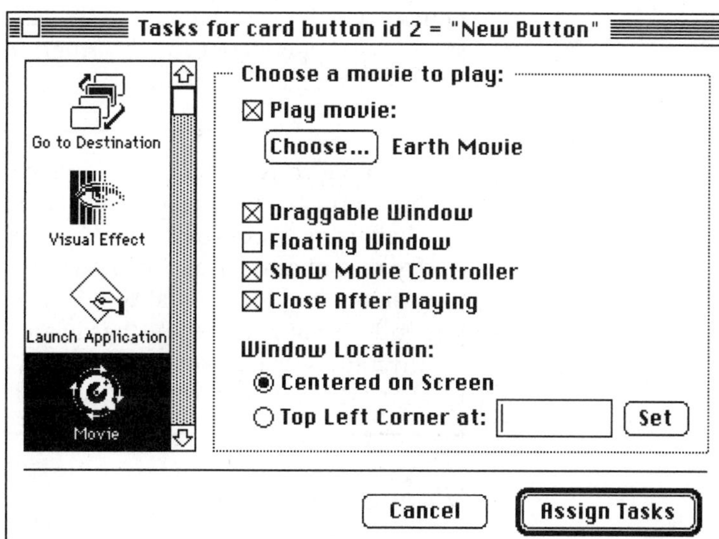

The rest of the check boxes should be set the way we want them. A "draggable" movie has a title bar so you can move it around like a tiny window. A floating window "floats" above the card layer. The movie controller's VCR-like controls allow you to control the movie's playback.

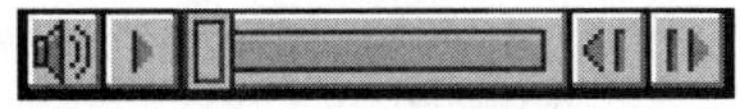

And "Close After Playing" makes the movie disappear when it's finished playing.

You can also specify whether the movie should be centered on the screen or positioned in a particular location. (If you choose the latter option, the pointer turns to a crosshair so you can click exactly where the top left corner of the movie should appear.)

You may need to locate the movie the first time you click the button unless it's stored in the same folder.

☐ **Click on Assign Tasks, customize the button to suit your taste, and try it.**

As you can see, it's easy to include movies in your stacks. You might want to try using the Install Resources card and the QuickTime Toolkit in the QuickTime Tools stack to install a movie in another stack. This two-step process offers a few more options but still allows you to create a movie-playing button without scripting.

What if you want to trigger a movie with something besides a button click—maybe the opening of a stack? If you examine the script of the button you just created, you'll find a series of commands that are easy to modify for use in other scripts. There are plenty of other QuickTime HyperTalk commands described in the QuickTime Tools stack. See Appendix A for information on QuickTime-related hardware, software, and references.

> Digital video is even more resource-intensive than sound, so it's important to understand the techniques for saving disk space when using QuickTime. QuickTime is a rapidly evolving technology that involves tradeoffs between movie size, frame rate, compression, and image quality. The compromises you make will depend on your needs and hardware resources. Experiment with different settings when capturing and saving video footage. That's the only way to really find out what works best for you.

Videodisc Options

QuickTime videos can gobble up massive amounts of disk space and still not measure up to the kind of broadcast-quality video we're used to. For some purposes it makes more sense to use HyperCard with XCMDs to control a **videodisc** player connected to an external TV monitor. Not all videodisc players can be computer controlled, and the ones that can require special hardware interfaces. But if you can overcome the hurdles, you can use HyperCard to produce truly interactive video. See Appendix A for more information on video hardware and software.

The Final Touch

You've learned how to create HyperCard stacks that can be put to work in a variety of ways. In this last section you'll see how to turn those stacks into stand-alone, double-clickable applications.

Creating a Stand-Alone Application

Before HyperCard 2.2, there was no easy way to share your HyperCard creations with friends who didn't have HyperCard. But an option now allows you to save your stacks as **stand-alone applications** that can be run on any Macintosh, with or without HyperCard. It won't work with every stack, and it's not perfect, but the stack-to-application option opens up all kinds of interesting possibilities for distributing your work.

> To save a stack as an application, you'll need the StackToApp extension in your System Folder's Extensions folder. (This extension is needed only for conversion, not for running a stack that's been converted to an application.) If you don't have this extension installed, you'll need to install it and restart, or skip this section.

It's easy to save a stack as an application. Here's how:

☐ **If it's not already open, open your Earth stack (either the color or black-and-white version will do).**

You'll want a new icon for your application; you can borrow it from the stack.

☐ **Select Icon... from the Edit menu.**

You should see one of your Earth icons.

☐ **Select Copy Icon from the Edit menu.**

The icon is on the Clipboard. You'll use it later.

☐ **Choose Save A Copy... from the File menu.**

☐ **Change the name to Earth Presentation.**

☐ **Drag the File Type pop-up menu to select Application.**

A "Version String" Dialog box asks you what version number should appear in the application's Get Info box.

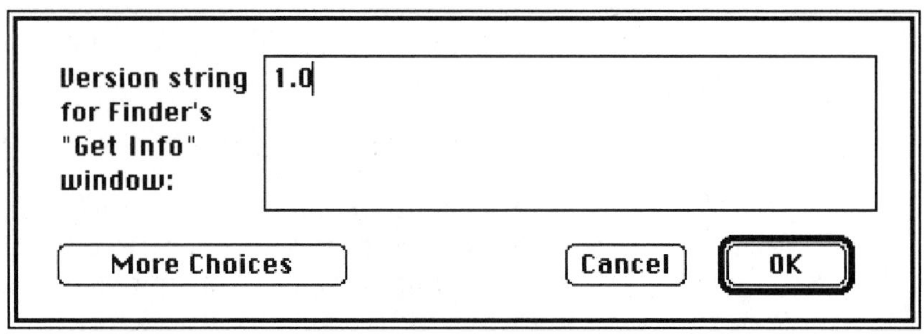

☐ **Type "1.0" and click OK.**

Eventually an icon for the application appears in the folder containing the original stack. Your stack is now an application, but you're not quite finished.

☐ **Locate the new Earth Presentation icon in the folder that contains your original stack. Press Command-I to open the stack's Get Info dialog box.**

☐ **If you're using System 7, click on the icon in the Get Info dialog box and press Command-V (paste).**

Your Earth Presentation now has an Earth icon (unless you're using System 6, which doesn't allow pasting icons). If your presentation is based on the color Earth stack, you'll need more memory than the amount suggested in this window. You can set the preferred size high so that your computer will reserve a large chunk of memory for your application while it's running. For this example, there's no harm in asking for far more than you need.

☐ **Change the Preferred Size to 5000.**

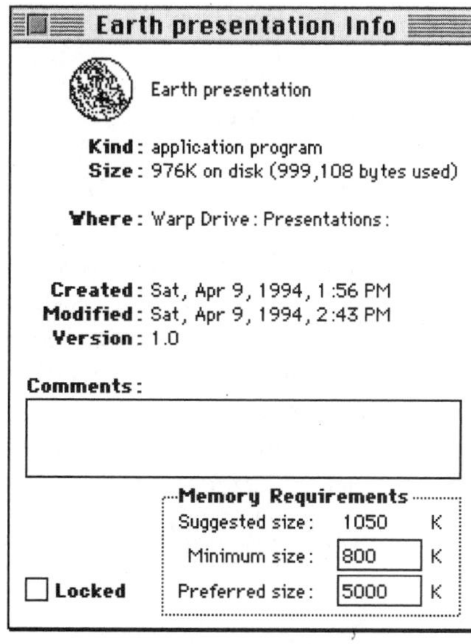

☐ **Close the Get Info box.**

You can drag the Earth Presentation icon onto a floppy disk, copy it onto another Macintosh that doesn't have HyperCard installed, and run it as an application.

☐ **Double-click your new application to try it out.**

> The possibility of creating stand-alone applications is exciting, but there are some important reasons to consider *not* converting your stacks to applications. First, the conversion process doesn't work perfectly with all stacks; you should carefully test each application you create to make sure it works properly. What's more, when you convert a stack to an application, HyperCard essentially builds a copy of the HyperCard player into the stack copy, adding more than 750K to the size of the stack. If you save 10 stacks as applications, you may use 10 megabytes or more of disk real estate. The larger size can add to the cost and time needed for uploading and downloading files via modem. Since almost all Macintosh owners have either HyperCard or the HyperCard player, this added space, time, and cost may be unnecessary for most uses. If you decide it's worth it, make sure your stack is completed before you convert it. You can always add new features to your stacks as long as they remain stacks, but a stand-alone application can't be changed. So when you save a stack as an application, make sure you keep a copy of the unconverted stack—you just might change your mind later.

The Endless Stack

The stacks you've built in this book should give you a feel for the basic mechanics of HyperCard and HyperTalk. You'll be surprised how much more you can learn by snooping in scripts of other people's stacks, consulting the Help stacks to look up commands that are unfamiliar. The set of Help stacks, like its printed counterpart, *The HyperCard Script Language Guide*, is designed to be a reference tool, not a tutorial. You may want a more systematic introduction to advanced HyperTalk scripting. See Appendix A for several such sources, as well as software tools specifically designed to facilitate the stack-building process.

Even if you never learn another word of HyperTalk, you'll be able to apply what you've learned in this book to build impressive and useful stacks. You now have the tools to make things happen. Go for it!

Summary

HyperCard is one of the most widely used tools for creating multimedia applications. In this session you learned how to take advantage of external commands that add multimedia power to HyperCard. You learned how to install externals in the resource fork of your stack along with sounds, pictures, and other multimedia tidbits. You saw how you can add color to a stack, record and edit a sound, display QuickTime video clips, and even save your stack as a stand-alone application, all without writing a script.

Multimedia is a rapidly changing field, so tomorrow's multimedia applications may go far beyond what we've included in this session. But because of its extensible nature, HyperCard has the potential to support all kinds of new multimedia technologies as they emerge.

Key Words

anti-aliasing
Anti-alias Picture
Audio Palette
background color
bevel
bit depth
Color Tools
compiler
compression
digitized speech
Edit Gradient
Export Graphics
extensible
external
Fill Picture
Flip Picture
foreground color
gradient
Import Graphics
interpreter

Invert Picture
MIDI
New...
Open...
PICT
Picture command
pixel density
QuickTime
QuickTime Tools
read-only
Redraw Screen
ResEdit
resolution
resource
resource fork
Resource Mover
Rotate Picture
sampling rate
Scale Picture
stand-alone application
synthesized speech
Tint Picture
Trace Picture Edges
videodisc
waveform
XCMD
XFCN
Zoom In
Zoom Out

Exercises

1. What is a resource? How are resources used in HyperCard?
2. In what way is HyperCard extensible? How does this property make HyperCard more useful?
3. What are the advantages and disadvantages of using Color Tools to add color to your stacks? What are the advantages and disadvantages of the Picture command?
4. Under what circumstances is color necessary in a stack? Under what circumstances is it desirable?
5. What are the advantages of storing a color picture as a resource instead of a file? What are the disadvantages?
6. Why is it important to edit unnecessary silence out of recorded sounds in a stack?
7. What is compression and why is it important when you work with sound and video?
8. HyperCard can play sounds stored as resources, sounds played by MIDI-compatible instruments, digitized speech, or CD audio sounds. What are the advantages and disadvantages of each?
9. What are the tradeoffs involved in QuickTime video display?
10. What are the advantages and disadvantages of videodiscs when compared to digitized QuickTime video?
11. Under what circumstances would it be a good idea to save your HyperCard stack as an application? What are the advantages and disadvantages?

Projects

1. Use Color Tools to colorize the buttons in the Pyramid stack.
2. Use Color Tools to colorize the buttons and fields in the Computer Anatomy stack.
3. Use Color Tools to add color to the rear walls and doors in the Dungeon stack.
4. Record sound effects and add them in appropriate places in the Pyramid, Dungeon, Earth, and Computer Anatomy stacks. If your Macintosh doesn't have a microphone and sound-recording capability, use prerecorded sounds from clip-sound collections, on-line services, or other sources.
5. Add a sound track to the Dungeon stack using your own compositions or recordings from another source. One possibility is to record conventional instruments using the Audio Palette or another sound recording program. Or if you have the necessary hardware and software, you can add a digital sound track using MIDI-compatible equipment or CD audio.
6. Modify the Computer Anatomy stack so each text field is read aloud with digitized speech.
7. Add a QuickTime movie to the Dungeon stack. Make the movie play when the user enters a room. You might want to make the movie represent a scene viewed through a window or some kind of action taking place within the room.
8. Add entries to your Computer Anatomy stack describing CD audio, MIDI, and digitized video. If you have the hardware and software, add buttons to these cards that allow users to "play a sample."
9. Use HyperCard to create a music video. Use digitized sound and/or a MIDI file for the music. Use some combination of QuickTime movies, color graphics, and animation to display a rapidly changing collage of images that complements the musical sound track.
10. Use HyperCard to create a multimedia TV documentary about some community activity or issue. Include an audio sound track with a musical theme, narration, and sound effects. If you have access to a Macintosh with standard TV video-out capability, copy your finished documentary onto videotape. If your community has a public access cable TV channel, see whether you can have your documentary broadcast to the community.

11. The Power Tools stack contains the Resource Mover and several other important stack construction software tools. Browse through the stack and consider how you might use each of these tools. Try constructing a stack using several of the power tools. You may want to use one of the templates in the Stack Templates stack as a starting point for your stack.

Appendix A

HyperCard Sources and Resources

HyperCard 2.3 in a Hurry is designed to give you a quick but thorough introduction to HyperCard. If you decide to work seriously in software development with HyperCard, you'll want to learn more about HyperCard and other tools that extend your powers as a stack builder. This appendix surveys software and hardware tools for adding graphics, animation, sound, scripts, and other enhancements to your stacks. In addition, it describes an assortment of exemplary stacks available through commercial and public domain channels so that you can see how professionals and serious amateurs are putting HyperCard to work. (Addresses and phone numbers for all software sources are listed at the end of this appendix.) Finally, this appendix lists several books that you can use to expand your knowledge of HyperCard, HyperTalk, and multimedia.

Graphics Software

HyperCard's monochrome paint tools are adequate for many applications, and the new color paint tools go a long way toward rounding out the basic graphics toolbox. But HyperCard's graphics capabilities are limited, so many stack builders turn to other tools for supplementing HyperCard's basic tools. If you can't easily accomplish your graphical goals within HyperCard, consider one or more of the color picture options described here.

Clip art. If your picture needs are mainstream, you may be able to find the pictures you want in collections of clip art and clip photography. High-quality images are available from a number of commercial and public domain sources. But if you use images created by others in your stacks, make sure you aren't violating any copyright laws.

Painting and image editing programs. If you aren't happy with HyperCard's paint tools, you have no shortage of alternatives. Programs like Brush Strokes (Claris Corporation) and ColorIt! (MicroFrontier) are based on the same idea as HyperCard's paint tools: They turn the mouse into a paint brush and a variety of other tools for painting pixels. Both programs include color palettes, tools, and menu options that go far beyond HyperCard's graphics capabilities. Both are extensible; plug-in modules (designed for Photoshop, described below) allow you to add new commands and effects to the menus.

Painter (Fractal Design) is a professional tool that takes the paint metaphor to its natural conclusion—and beyond. Painter is called a natural media paint program because it includes dozens of tools for simulating watercolors, charcoal, crayons, oil paints, and other natural art media. But Painter allows you to perform distortions and transformations that aren't possible outside a computer, and its power can be extended even further with Photoshop plug-ins. Painter allows you to layer painted "objects" in the same way you can layer buttons and fields in HyperCard. Because these objects exist in separate layers, they can be moved and edited independently. Painter is one of the most powerful and flexible tools available to digital artists. For those who don't need (or can't afford) all of Painter's high-end features, the same company offers a low-cost program, called Dabbler, especially for beginners.

Any paint program can be used to edit digitized photographs and drawings, but some programs are designed specifically for that purpose. Adobe Photoshop (Adobe) is the de facto standard for image manipulation. This powerful, versatile program lacks HyperCard staples like the rectangle and oval tools, but it's packed with features for adjusting colors, textures, lighting effects, and other image details. It can be extended with plug-ins like Kai's Power Tools (HSC Software) that add all kinds of mind-boggling features and options to the program. If you want more customization than even Kai's Power Tools provide, consider HSC's KPT Convolver. This industrial-strength program allows you to, in effect, design custom filters and effects for Photoshop, Painter, ColorIt!, and other compatible image-editing programs.

For users who think Painter and Photoshop take themselves too seriously, there's always Kid Pix (Brøderbund), the premier color graphics toy for preschoolers. As a productivity tool for serious artists, it's no match for the other programs listed here. Nonetheless, Kid Pix is arguably the most original paint program since MacPaint—and the most fun. Recommended for kids of all ages.

Drawing programs. Programs like ClarisDraw (Claris Corporation) and Canvas (Deneba Software) are often called object-oriented graphics programs because they're designed for manipulating on-screen objects rather than tweaking pixels. With a drawing program you can always rearrange shapes and edit text, but you can't easily manipulate individual dots on the screen.

Spreadsheets and charting programs. The easiest way to create quantitative charts and graphs is generally to supply the numbers and let the computer produce the graphics. Just about any spreadsheet program can turn an array of numbers into a pie chart, a line chart, a bar chart, a stack chart, or a scatter chart. If your spreadsheet program's graphics capabilities are too limited, there's a good chance you'll find what you're looking for in DeltaGraph Pro (Delta Point, Inc.), a specialized graphing program with a wealth of charting options.

Integrated software. If you want maximum flexibility for minimum price, an integrated software package is a good choice. The most popular and powerful Macintosh integrated package is ClarisWorks (Claris Corporation), which seamlessly integrates drawing, painting, charting, desktop publishing, and several other applications in an easy-to-use, compact, inexpensive package. Many Macintosh users find that ClarisWorks is the only application program they need.

3D graphics tools. Most painting, drawing, and charting programs are designed to produce two-dimensional images to display on screen or print to paper. But many graphical applications can be used to produce images and scenes with depth, as if they extended into a virtual three-dimensional space inside the computer's monitor. Objects created with most of these applications can be rotated so they can be viewed, displayed, and edited from any angle.

Strata Corporation produces some of the most powerful 3D modeling tools for the Macintosh. Studio Pro is widely used by professionals for creating photo-realistic scenes, objects, and animated sequences. The stunning scenery in the popular HyperCard-based game Myst was created with this powerful tool. For artists who can't afford Studio Pro's high price or don't need all its extensive features, Strata produces a more accessible program called Vision.

Both of these programs, and most other professional 3D modeling programs, require a significant time investment to master. A number of specialized tools are designed to produce 3D images more easily by doing some of the work for you. addDepth (Ray Dream) is an easy-to-use program that specializes in adding depth to type and other flat images. KPT Bryce (HSC Software), named for the spectacular rocky park in southern Utah, is an unusual program that designs and renders natural and supernatural landscapes almost automatically. Fractal Design's Poser simplifies one of the most difficult 3D tasks: creating realistic human figures. All three of these programs are relatively inexpensive and capable of producing impressive results for a minimal labor investment.

Graphics utilities. If you're creating how-to-use-the-computer stacks, or if you just need to convert an image on your computer screen to a PICT file, a screen capture utility like Capture (Mainstay) or Exposure Pro

(Baseline Publishing) may be necessary. When the standard key combination Command-Shift-3 won't do the job, one of these will.

There are dozens of different formats for computer graphics files. Because HyperCard can display only color pictures stored in PICT format, you may need a tool for converting other images to that format. If your image-editing program can't convert your files, try the shareware classic GIFConverter, widely available on-line and in shareware collections. If GIFConverter can't handle the conversion, DeBabelizer (Equilibrium Technologies) almost certainly can. This translate-anything-to-anything program also includes a number of other graphics power tools for transforming and fine-tuning images. DeBabelizer is a standard fixture in publishing service bureaus. DeBabelizer Lite is a less expensive version that has everything most users need.

Graphics Hardware

Graphics tablets. It's an improvement over the keyboard, but the mouse is a less-than-ideal drawing tool. Many professional artists prefer to use a graphics tablet with a pressure-sensitive stylus. For example, the Wacom Art-Z (Wacom) is a low-priced, high-quality tablet that allows you to use a pen-shaped wireless stylus as a mouse substitute with any program. Many high-end graphics programs, including Painter and Photoshop, recognize pressure variations in the stylus, allowing you to draw lines of variable thickness and darkness. If you do a lot of drawing or painting, a graphics tablet is a good investment.

Scanners. With a good scanner it's possible to digitize hand-drawn pictures, photographs, and other images from noncomputer sources so that they can be edited and imported into HyperCard. (It's important, though, to be aware that copyright laws and intellectual property rights apply when you're scanning published materials.) Flatbed scanners typically read face-down pages like a photocopier, but instead of making physical copies, they make digital copies stored on computer disk. They're generally capable of scanning images at much higher resolution than you can see on the Macintosh screen. Gray-scale scanners are less expensive, but more versatile color scanners dominate the market today. A less expensive—and less accurate—alternative to the flatbed scanner is the hand-held scanner, which sucks up images like a tiny information vacuum cleaner while you roll it across a page. If your scanning needs and your budget are minimal, a hand-held scanner might be worth considering. PaperPort (Visioneer) represents a third scanning alternative. The PaperPort is a small, inexpensive box that sits between the keyboard and monitor waiting for you to feed sheets of paper into its slot. It scans those sheets, converting them to grayscale images and text files automatically. Although it's designed more for traditional office tasks than for multimedia, it's a cost-effective choice when color isn't necessary.

Digital cameras. A digital camera works like a regular camera except that it stores pictures as digital images. Professional-quality digital cameras cost thousands of dollars, but inexpensive digital cameras like Apple's QuickTake are more than adequate for capturing images to be displayed on-screen.

Video digitizers. A video digitizer allows you to capture images from any video camera, laser disc player, VCR, or other standard video source. Some digitizers are designed for capturing still images from video sources; others can capture full-motion QuickTime video clips. Apple's AV Macintoshes have built-in hardware for capturing still images and video clips from standard video sources. If your Macintosh doesn't have AV capability built in, you'll need to add a video capture board to import your own videos. Although many professional video boards cost thousands of dollars, inexpensive boards are available for most Mac models.

Animation and Video Tools

Animation. In Session 5 you learned several ways to animate HyperCard stacks. (These animation effects are illustrated, along with others, in the freeware stack by Jeremy Ahouse called Animation Help, available through many user groups and other public domain sources.) Although HyperCard offers plenty of possibilities for making moving pictures, it places clear limitations on the artist or programmer interested in serious animation.

Fortunately, there's a HyperCard add-on designed for creating and displaying color animation within HyperCard. ADDmotion II (Motion Works), bundled with HyperCard 2.3, installs as a series of XCMDs directly into HyperCard. When you install ADDmotion II and activate it with a button on the Home card, new HyperCard menu options provide you with access to color animation tools. Color pictures created with ADDmotion II or imported from elsewhere become backgrounds and "actors" for animated sequences. ADDmotion's Media Controller palette makes it easy to put up to 100 actors into motion at a time. Animated sequences can be controlled by keyboard and mouse events, and they can be sequenced to include sound effects and control of external devices such as synthesizers and CD players.

Like most animation programs, ADDmotion II is a complex program that requires time and effort to learn. But if you're willing to make the investment, you can do amazing things to your stacks.

If HyperCard and ADDmotion won't do the job, there are other animation options available. The Multimedia Utilities package from Motion Works, bundled with HyperCard 2.3, includes a more powerful animation program called MotionPaint. Macromedia's Director has long been the premier two-dimensional animation tool for the Mac. Over the years Director has evolved into a full-featured multimedia authoring tool that happens to have built-in animation tools. Fractal Design's Painter now includes animation features that allow you to apply its natural media graphics approach across a series of frames. For producing three-dimensional animation, Strata's Studio Pro is one of the best all-in-one-box tools.

QuickTime tools. When compared to animation, video is usually less labor-intensive but more hardware-intensive. If you decide to go the QuickTime video route, your choices are the same as they are for still images: You can use video clips created by others or create and import your own footage. Video clips are available from public domain and commercial sources. Because of their massive disk requirements, videos are almost always stored and sold on CD-ROMs rather than floppy disks.

If you have an AV Mac or a video capture board and the right software, you can import video clips from video cameras, VCRs, and televisions. Of course, virtually everything that's broadcast on TV or available on rental videotapes is copyrighted, so you may need to record your own footage to avoid copyright complications.

Your homemade movies will be more impressive if you edit them. Many popular programs are available for sequencing video clips, adding special effects and transitions, and overlaying sound tracks. One such program, Quickedit, is part of the Multimedia Utilities package bundled with HyperCard 2.3. If you need an industrial strength QuickTime editor, your best choice is probably Adobe Premiere (Adobe), the most popular video capture and editing program. Premiere comes with dozens of impressive effects filters and an extensible architecture that allows plug-in filters to be added.

With the right software, your computer can create video clips that no video camera can capture in the real world. For example, QuickMorph (part of the Multimedia Utilities collection that's included with HyperCard 2.3) allows you to start with two still images and produce a sequence wherein one image gradually melts into the other, science-fiction style. The pioneering Mac morphing program, Morph (Gryphon), has a much more extensive set of features and capabilities. An unusual program called BlissPaint (Imaja) allows you to create animated "paintings" made up of flowing patterns of colors and shapes, reminiscent of the 1960s psychedelic light shows. You can save your dynamic paintings as QuickTime movies so they can be played from within HyperCard or other applications.

If you're creating how-to-do-it computer tutorials, screen shots are critical ("Your screen should look like this . . ."). But with QuickTime it's possible to display multiframe screen activities ("Watch how we do it and then try it on your screen . . ."). Two utilities designed to capture screen sequences are Instant Replay (Strata) and CameraMan (Motion Works). CameraMan is included in the Multimedia Utilities package bundled with HyperCard 2.3.

Videodisc tools. Because of QuickTime's small image and big storage requirements, some HyperCard stack developers choose to use video clips and images stored on videodisc. The HyperCard stack controls a commercial-quality videodisc player, which is connected to a separate TV monitor. (This won't work unless your videodisc player has a computer control interface, not commonly found on players marketed for home use.) Videodisc-controller XCMDs are available in several packages, including MediaMAX (Videodiscovery), a HyperCard stack designed specifically for creating educational videodisc presentations without scripting, and Clip Creator (AABACA), which also contains resources for controlling audio CDs and electronic musical instruments.

Sound Resources

Sound recording and editing. HyperCard's cut-and-paste sound editing capabilities are handy but limited. Fortunately, several software options, including the ADDmotion II graphics/animation package shipped with HyperCard 2.3, are available for more serious sound work. For example, ADDmotion II (included with Hypercard 2.3), SoundMate (part of the Multimedia Utilities shipped with HyperCard 2.3), AudioShop (OpCode Systems), and SoundEdit 16 (Macromedia) allow you to capture and edit sounds in a variety of ways. You can add echoes and other effects, control dynamics, and even turn them around so they play backward. As usual, the stand-alone commercial programs offer more features than the free-with-HyperCard programs. But none of these programs can take full advantage of the superb audio capabilities of an AV Mac. For CD-quality audio, Deck II (OSC) and DigiTrax (OpCode) can turn an AV Mac into a multitrack digital recording studio.

CD audio. If you prefer to use a CD as your sound source, you have several choices. If you need to include only a few short passages from a CD in your stack, you might want to turn those passages into digital sound files and install them as resources in your stack. Apple's Sound Manager allows you to choose an internal CD as the sound source when you're capturing sound with HyperCard or other applications. Optical Media International's Disc to Disk is a more flexible utility that can capture CD audio from a variety of CD-ROM drives and store them in a variety of formats. Of course, either approach involves making copies of the original sound files, which may violate copyright laws unless you acquire permission of the copyright owner.

A second approach doesn't involve copying the audio tracks into your stack; instead, the stack contains commands for playing specified parts of the CD using the CD-ROM drive. To use this approach you'll need to install CD audio XCMDs in your stack. These XCMDs add a handful of new HyperTalk commands that can control the playing of any audio CD in your CD-ROM drive. The CD Audio Stack (The Voyager Company) is the most popular and best-documented source for these XCMDs, but they're also included in several other stack authoring tools. A bargain-priced stack called Clip Creator (AABACA), designed to help build music education stacks, includes the CD audio XCMDs, videodisc controller XCMDs, and XCMDs for controlling electronic musical instruments as described in the next section. (For examples of how CD audio is being used in professionally produced stacks, see the section "Prime Examples" in this appendix.)

MIDI hardware and software. Another multimedia track open to HyperCard stack builders is electronic music. With a MIDI interface and a MIDI-compatible instrument or sound source, your HyperCard stack can actually *play* music rather than playing a *recording* of music. If your instrument supports general MIDI (the new standard that allows MIDI files created on one instrument to be played on another), you can take advantage of a wealth of classical and popular MIDI clips available commercially and in the public domain. (Even if your instrument doesn't support general MIDI, you can use a sequencer to remap the sound codes of general MIDI files so that they match your machine.) With QuickTime 2.0, your Macintosh can play many general MIDI files with no additional hardware, but the sound quality won't measure up to that of a MIDI synthesizer.

To create your own MIDI files or edit MIDI files, you'll need a sequencer. Because the Macintosh has long been a favorite tool of musicians, it's no surprise that professional sequencers like Vision (OpCode Systems) and Master Trax Pro (Passport) are packed with state-of-the-art features. For mere mortals, low-cost sequencers like MusicShop (OpCode Systems) and Music Time (Passport) have options aplenty for most users, but not so many as to overwhelm amateurs.

Whatever sequencer you use, you can "record" tracks one at a time, adding layers of sound and editing them to meet your needs. The process can be time-consuming, especially for nonmusicians. You can jump-start your sequences with Band in a Box (PG Music), a program that can turn any chord progression into a rhythm section playing your choice of musical styles; you can save the results as a MIDI file and edit it with any sequencer. (OpCode offers an attactive beginner's MIDI package that includes a hardware MIDI interface, the MusicShop sequencer, and Band in a Box at a special price.)

You'll need to add MIDI XCMDs to your HyperCard stack to play your MIDI file from HyperCard. The most widely used MIDI XCMD package is HyperMIDI 3 (EarLevel Engineering). HyperMIDI 3 is a powerful development package and a worthwhile investment for anyone serious about programming with MIDI from HyperCard.

Authoring Aids

Many software tools are available to assist you as you build stacks, so you don't need to do everything the hard way. Some are power tools to make the script-writing process easier and to improve the quality of finished stacks. Others are packages of prefabricated buttons, art, cards, and XCMDs that can easily be incorporated into stacks. Still others are basic utilities to make the stack construction process simpler. This section describes several examples.

AppleScript (Apple Computer) is Apple's universal scripting language. The language looks a lot like HyperTalk, but it's not limited to functioning within one application. Using AppleScript, you can design custom solutions to complex problems that involve several applications. For example, you might create a HyperCard stack that automatically sends data to a spreadsheet program on another computer at the click of a button. Right now HyperCard is one of the few applications that understands AppleScript, but as more application programs become AppleScript-savvy, interapplication communication possibilities will explode.

HyperGASP (Caliban Mindwear) is a collection of utilities and resources designed to automate many of the messiest aspects of multimedia stack construction. HyperGASP allows you to add color, PICT files, QuickTime video, sound, hot text, and interactive quizzes to stacks without scripting. The package also makes it easy to import and export formatted text, and it includes libraries of ready-made cards, buttons, and sounds to help streamline stack construction. HyperGASP is widely used in schools to make multimedia authoring with HyperCard easier for beginners.

The Expanded Book Toolkit (The Voyager Company) is the tool used by The Voyager Company to produce their popular Expanded Books. With this tool kit you can quickly turn your written works into interactive documents without scripting.

WindowScript (Heizer Software) is a user interface design kit that's packed with extensions to HyperCard's interface tools. WindowScript doesn't automatically create interfaces like some of the other tools listed here; most of its tools require scripting. But WindowScript makes it possible to create color icons, scrolling pictures, fields with mixed fonts, complex dialog boxes, and other interface features that go beyond anything HyperCard can do by itself.

CompileIt! (Heizer Software) is a compiler to convert HyperTalk scripts into XCMDs or XFCNs (external functions). CompileIt! speeds up overall stack performance, protects scripts so that they can't be bootlegged, saves time on character manipulations and integer calculations, and is useful for for accessing the Macintosh ToolBox ROM routines. Mastering CompileIt! requires considerable technical know-how, but the package includes a debugger that eases the troublesome process of finding errors. (Heizer Software publishes several other useful HyperCard utilities. Anyone serious about HyperCard should study their catalog.)

Thunder 7 (Baseline) is an interactive spelling checker that works with any Macintosh application, including HyperCard. The interactive checker beeps immediately whenever you type a word that's not found in the dictionary. Many people find the instant feedback makes the program an effective spelling tutor. Thunder 7 includes an extensive dictionary, a thesaurus, and a "Ghostwriter" feature that records every keystroke just in case your system crashes before you save your work.

QuicKeys (CE Software) isn't designed specifically for HyperCard, but it's the kind of tool every HyperCard stack builder should know about. With QuicKeys, you can automate all those repetitive tasks that take so much time and mental real estate. Need to copy a string of cards from one stack to another? Perform the operation on a single card while QuicKeys is recording, and the rest of the job is reduced to a few keystrokes. Once you've tried QuicKeys, you'll wonder how you got along without it.

Finally, hundreds of public domain and shareware tools, buttons, cards, and art collections are available via electronic bulletin boards and user groups. Many are almost worthless, but others are nearly priceless. For example, the Rinaldi XCMD collection provides free solutions to hundreds of common HyperTalk scripting problems; no serious scripter leaves Home without it.

Prime Examples

Imitation may be the sincerest form of flattery, but it's also a great way to learn. Thousands of stacks have been created since HyperCard was introduced in 1987. Many of these stacks have modest price tags; others are available free through public domain software channels. By snooping through some of these stacks, studying their design, and analyzing their scripts, you can learn tricks and techniques that you aren't likely to find in books. Here's a highly subjective survey of stacks that are particularly noteworthy.

Exploratory fiction. The award here goes to Cyan, the company that pioneered the genre and defines the state of the art today. The

Manhole: CD-ROM Masterpiece Edition (Cyan) is the latest incarnation of the classic children's stack that created a surrealistic world packed with surprises for point-and-click explorers. The new color CD-ROM version, like the original, has an Alice-in-Wonderland kind of magic that should appeal to just about anybody with a playful spirit. But the photo-realistic graphics and stereo sound in this edition make it an entirely new experience.

Cosmic Osmo and the Worlds Beyond the Mackerel (Cyan) is a science-fiction cartoon universe with a sense of humor. The CD-ROM version has more to explore than the original, but it hasn't been redone in color, so its HyperCard roots are more obvious. It's amazing what can be done with HyperCard's basic black-and-white graphics.

Spelunx and the Caves of Mr. Seudo (Brøderbund) is Cyan's third outing. Spelunx has the same exploratory quality as their earlier efforts, but it includes several educational games designed to make science fun. The latest version has been colorized and doesn't require a CD-ROM drive.

Myst (Brøderbund), the latest from Cyan, is a masterpiece of an interactive story/game for older audiences. Myst combines dazzling photo-realistic 3D graphics, dreamlike music and sound, and an engrossing story line to create an experience somewhere between a mystery movie and a mythological dream. Myst is as close as HyperCard has gotten to virtual reality. It's little wonder that Myst is one of the best-selling CD-ROMs ever.

Video visions. A Hard Day's Night (The Voyager Company) is a shining example of how QuickTime and HyperCard can turn an old film into a new experience. The CD-ROM includes the complete Beatles movie, the songs, the script, extensive commentary with hypertext links, and several related tidbits in an intelligently designed interactive package. The tiny QuickTime window is no substitute for the big screen, but where else can you watch the movie while the script scrolls by on the screen?

Comic Book Confidential (The Voyager Company) is a multimedia documentary that explores comics from their earliest days to the present. Videos, color reproductions, and text are cleverly combined in an interactive package that's fun and informative.

Interactive education. There are literally thousands of educational HyperCard stacks, including many prime examples of quality interactive media.

One of the best examples of an interactive educational stack is Bird Anatomy (public domain, available from many user groups and online sources). This comprehensive study of bird anatomy, complete with sound effects, is a great model for educational stacks.

The Freedom Trail (public domain, Boston Computer Society) is an award-winning interactive educational stack created by volunteers of one of the largest and most active Macintosh user groups in the world. If you're interested in American history, Boston, or educational hypermedia, study this stack.

EarthTreks (Magic Quest) is an ambitious stack designed to provide students with an interactive tool for exploring ecology, biology, geography, astronomy, and a number of other interrelated topics. This highly interactive and entertaining stack links everything with almost everything else.

KanjiMaster (HyperGlot) is an award-winning interactive tutorial designed to help students learn to recognize, understand, write, and pronounce basic kanji, the characters that make up the Japanese writing system. KanjiMaster takes advantage of HyperCard's flexibility by offering a variety of teaching tools and techniques. (HyperGlot has an extensive library of high-quality programs for learning Spanish, French, English, and other languages; many of these programs are HyperCard-based.)

Educator Home Card (Intellimation) is a set of productivity tools for teachers. Grade books, seating charts, and a variety of other tools are linked together in this stack designed by Apple's education experts.

If Monks Had Macs (The Voyager Company) is a massive hypertext tour de force that started out as a public domain stack occupying several floppy disks. A new, enhanced, and expanded version has just been released. This amazing stack is eccentric, eclectic, inspiring, and mind-boggling. A medieval virtual environment serves as a hypertext home for a feast of ideas ranging from philosophy to psychology, from conspiracy to contemplation.

Some of the best education takes place when the students are creating rather than consuming. Links to the Past I and II ($25 donation to SMILE) were created by junior high American Indians during two-week math camps at Oregon State University in the early days of HyperCard. Each stack graphically illustrates several native American legends. The results, although far from professional, show the kinds of amazing creations that motivated kids can produce with just a few hours of Macintosh/HyperCard training.

Musical offerings. The marriage of audio CD and HyperCard has produced some beautiful children: the CD Companion Series, including Beethoven's Symphony No. 9, Stravinsky's "The Rite of Spring," Mozart's "Dissonant" Quartet, and Dvorak's Symphony No. 9 (The Voyager Company); and the Warner Audio Notes Series, including Beethoven's String Quartet and The Orchestra (Time Warner Interactive). Using any of these stacks in a CD-ROM-equipped computer system, you can take an interactive tour of some of the world's great music, watching text, graphics, and background information unfold on your computer screen while high-quality digital audio pours from your stereo speakers, all controlled by your mouse.

XPLORA1, Peter Gabriel's Secret World (Interplay Productions), is one of the first CDs to apply interactive multimedia technology to the popular music video genre. XPLORA1 is far more than a music video with buttons; it's an interactive work of art that includes exploratory excursions to other musical cultures, adventure-style puzzles, a mixer for customizing recorded tracks, myriad paths to explore, and lots of surprises.

Beyond books. Expanded Books—including *The Complete Annotated Alice* by Lewis Carroll, *The Complete Hitchhiker's Guide to the Galaxy* by Douglas Adams, and dozens of other best-sellers and classics (The Voyager Company)—are designed to turn PowerBooks and other Macs into power-books. Using HyperCard's hypertext and search capabilities, Expanded Books allow readers to explore text sequentially or nonsequentially. An Expanded Book Toolkit, also available from The Voyager Company, makes it easy to turn your own written works into Expanded Books.

Beyond HyperCard

When HyperCard was introduced in 1987, it was a breakthrough product unlike anything that had come before. Since then, HyperCard has inspired several other multimedia and hypermedia authoring tools. The most successful challengers offer something that's not readily available in HyperCard. In some cases that something is ease of use; in other cases it's power. This list is divided into two groups: education-oriented programs that simplify processes that are complicated in HyperCard, and powerful authoring environments that are available for both Macintosh and IBM-compatible computers.

Educational media tools. Because it puts so much communication power into the hands of students and teachers, HyperCard has become a favorite software tool in schools. But some students and teachers want a HyperCard-like authoring environment that doesn't depend on scripting and extra steps for animation and color. HyperStudio (Roger Wagner Publishing) and Digital Chisel (Pierian Springs Software) are two easy-to-use, HyperCard-inspired authoring tools designed for those students and teachers. Because it's built on top of SuperCard (see below), Digital Chisel isn't as fast or flexible as HyperStudio. HyperStudio also has the advantage of being available in both Mac and Windows versions, so it's possible to port stacks between platforms. But both programs automate some tasks that are unnecessarily complicated in HyperCard so students can produce impressive multimedia documents with minimal training. The other side of the coin, though, is that both of these programs currently lack the flexibility and extensibility that HyperTalk provides HyperCard users. HyperGASP (Caliban Mindwear) is a shell—a new user interface—for HyperCard that provides many education-oriented features without sacrificing HyperCard's versatility.

Cross-platform professional multimedia tools. HyperCard may be the most popular multimedia authoring tool on the Macintosh, but there are millions of non-Macintosh computers in the world that can't run HyperCard stacks. In a world dominated by IBM-compatible computers, the lack of cross-platform capability may be HyperCard's biggest limitation.

Apple's HyperCard team is committed to overcoming that limitation. Until they do, HyperCard stack developers might want to look into ConvertIt! (Heizer Software), a utility that allows you to convert your HyperCard stacks into ToolBook "books" for use on a Windows-equipped PC. The process of translating a stack with ConvertIt! is slow, and it's not completely effective; there are simply too many differences between the two environments for everything to cross over intact. Still, ConvertIt! provides stack builders with an opportunity to add several million people to their potential audience.

If developing cross-platform multimedia is your goal, you may be better served by an authoring tool that can create multimedia documents for both Macintosh and Windows machines. HyperStudio is a good choice for simple cross-platform stacks, but it's not designed for industrial-strength multimedia development. Several professional cross-platform authoring environments have emerged recently. These tools are all far more expensive than HyperCard, and none except SuperCard and Oracle Media Objects shares HyperCard's intuitive stack-of-cards interface. But for serious multimedia work, they're worth considering.

SuperCard (Allegiant Technologies) is one of HyperCard's most direct competitors. Its interface is like a color version of HyperCard's stack of cards, and its scripting language is similar to HyperTalk. Recent releases incorporate many multimedia and hypertext capabilities. When the promised Windows version is released, SuperCard may be the closest thing we have to a cross-platform HyperCard.

Another recent contender for that honor is called Oracle Media Objects (Oracle). This program, whose roots lie in an older program named Plus, shares many of HyperCard's strengths, including its friendly stack-of-cards user interface and a HyperTalk-like scripting language. Cross-platform capability and ties to database giant Oracle make Oracle Media Objects very enticing. Its main shortcoming is that it lacks a Find command.

Astound! (Gold Disk) is a presentation program whose user interface is based on familiar outline and slide show metaphors. But unlike typical presentation programs, Astound! includes a rich complement of interactive multimedia tools, including QuickTime movies, animation, sound recording and editing, and interactive buttons. The Mac version currently lacks several key authoring features found in the Windows version.

Apple Media Tool (Apple Computer) is a professional authoring program designed for integrating media. Media Tool comes in two parts: an intuitive, icon-based authoring environment and a programming environment for writing custom code. Programming in Apple Media Tool isn't as easy as HyperTalk scripting; it's generally done by professional programmers.

Director (Macromedia) has evolved from an animation tool into a multimedia authoring tool regarded by many as the standard against which other animation and multimedia programs should be measured. Director's user interface, based on a film metaphor, is complicated and requires time and effort to master. Like HyperCard, Director includes a scripting language, Lingo, that can be extended with XCMDs. HyperCard programmers appreciate Lingo's similarity to HyperTalk and the fact that many HyperCard XCMDs work unchanged with Director.

Authorware (Macromedia) is one of the most expensive programs listed here, but many satisfied customers swear it's worth the four-digit price. The Authorware interface allows you to construct interactive applications by connecting icons on a flowchart. Authorware is weak on text manipulation but well suited for computer-based training, computer-assisted instruction, and other applications where it's important to keep track of user responses as they proceed through the document. The latest version of Authorware is designed to work well with Director, so Authorware users can take advantage of Director's animation capabilities.

User Groups and Bulletin Boards

Many of the best HyperCard stacks, clip art collections, and other useful software tools are available for free or with a pay-if-you-like-it understanding. User group libraries and electronic bulletin boards (BBS) are good sources for public domain software and shareware.

User groups have different policies on public access to their libraries. The Berkeley Macintosh User Group (BMUG), one of the largest in the world, maintains a large, well-organized collection of public domain and shareware programs on disks and CDs that may be purchased by members and nonmembers for a nominal fee. Their occasional catalogs are excellent tools for sorting through the mountains of free and almost-free software for the Macintosh. The Boston Computer Society (BCS) Macintosh User Group is BMUG's East Coast counterpart. Their library is well organized, and their impressive CD-ROMs include HyperCard-based navigation tools that make it easy to quickly find what you're looking for.

Macintosh user groups offer far more than software libraries. They can be a valuable source of answers, ideas, and other kinds of support that are difficult to package on a disk. In addition, many user groups publish newsletters with folksy tips and tidbits that are often overlooked by *Macworld, MacUser, MacWeek, New Media,* and *Wired.* To locate the user group nearest you, call Apple's User Group Hotline: 800/538-9696, ext. 900.

Electronic bulletin boards are also a good source of stacks, software tools, and HyperCard information. But because many of these services charge by the hour for connect time, they may not be the cheapest stack source. Three of the most popular nationwide public information utilities with Macintosh bulletin boards are CompuServe (800/848-8199 or 614/457-0802), America Online (800/227-6364 or 703/893-6288), and GEnie (800/638-9696). Apple's eWorld service (800/775-4556) is likely to be another good source for HyperCard-related discussions and software. Internet users have access to a HyperCard-specific Usenet discussion group (comp.sys.mac.hypercard) and several multimedia-related news groups and World Wide Web home pages.

If you can't regularly make the pilgrimage through cyberspace to bulletin boards or on-line services for current information and software, you might be able to have the postal service deliver the goods to your door. A monthly CD-ROM magazine called *Nautilus* packs hundreds of megabytes of shareware, public domain software, photography, clip art, MIDI files, software demos, and features on each disk. *Nautilus* isn't as up-to-the-minute as the typical on-line service, but it's an inexpensive way to stay up-to-the-month.

Other Books

No single book can tell you everything you need to know to take full advantage of HyperCard. Each book listed here has something to offer for anyone serious about HyperCard stack development in particular and multimedia authoring in general.

HyperCard Script Language Guide: The HyperTalk Language (Cupertino, CA: Apple, 1993). This is the official Apple guide to HyperTalk. It's the definitive reference book for serious HyperTalk programmers. It comes with HyperCard.

HyperCard Reference Manual (Cupertino, CA: Apple, 1993). This is the other book that comes with HyperCard. It's well written, but it's really more of an introductory tutorial than a reference manual.

HyperCard Stack Design Guidelines (Reading, MA: Addison-Wesley, 1987). This official Apple publication explores the human side of stack development. It doesn't deal with all the latest features of HyperCard, but it still covers the psychology of stack design better than any other HyperCard book. Appropriately, the book has a style and user interface that make it fun and easy to read. If you're serious about stack design, read this book carefully.

The Complete HyperCard 2.2 Handbook, Fourth Edition, by Danny Goodman (New York: Bantam Books, 1994). The first edition of this book was released the day HyperCard was introduced to the world, and this book is still the most popular HyperCard book on the market. Much of the early material will be review for you, but later chapters are packed with detailed information on HyperTalk, complete with many sample scripts and suggestions. Goodman does a good job of filling in the pieces that are missing in Apple's manuals. Whether you're a beginner or a HyperTalk hacker, you're likely to find much valuable information in this massive volume.

HyperTalk 2.2: The Book, Second Edition, by Dan Winkler, Scot Kamins, and Jeanne DeVoto (New York: Random House, 1994). This isn't a beginner's guide; it's a tutorial, idea book, and reference for serious scripters. The authors know the subject matter better than anybody; Winkler designed HyperTalk, Kamins was a member of the original HyperCard development team, and DeVoto is a well-known contributer to several on-line scripting forums.

Macintosh Multimedia Machine, by David S. Mash (San Francisco: Sybex, 1994). This book/CD-ROM package is especially strong on music and sound as components of multimedia. The CD-ROM includes a HyperCard shell for creating multimedia documents.

Multimedia Demystified: A Guide to the World of Multimedia from Apple Computer, Inc. (New York: Random House, 1994). This book provides a broad overview of interactive multimedia design and production. Its colorful design uses a quasi-hypertext approach that cross-references different sections. There's a wealth of information in this book for anyone who's interested in breaking into the multimedia business.

Multimedia Power Tools, by Peter Jerram and Michael Gosney (with others) (New York: Random House, 1993). When it was released in 1993, this book/CD combination was probably the most complete overview of the field. Today its only problem is its age, but a new edition is in the works.

How Multimedia Works, by Eric Holsinger (Emeryville, CA: Ziff-Davis Press, 1994). This book uses lavish color illustrations and concise explanations to illustrate the basic concepts of multimedia.

Sources of Software and Hardware

AABACA
5750 Shady Oak Rd.
Minnetonka, MN 55343
612/933-7307

Adobe Systems, Inc.
1585 Charleston Rd.
P.O. Box 7900
Mountain View, CA 94039
415/961-4400

Allegiant Technologies, Inc.
6496 Weathers Place, Suite 100
San Diego, CA 92121
619/587-0500

Apple Computer
20525 Mariani Ave.
Cupertino, CA 95014
408/996-1010

Baseline Publishing Inc.
1770 Moriah Woods Blvd.,
Suite 14
Memphis, TN 38117-7118
901/682-9676

Berkeley Macintosh User Group
(BMUG)
1442A Walnut St. #62
Berkeley, CA 94709
510/549-2684

Boston Computer Society (BCS)
Macintosh User Group
1972 Massachusetts Ave.
Cambridge, MA 02140
617/864-1700

Brøderbund Software, Inc.
500 Redwood Blvd.
P.O. Box 6121
Novato, CA 94948-6121
415/382-4400

Caliban Mindwear
6590 Camino Carreta
Carpinteria, CA 93013
805/684-7765

CE Software
1801 Industrial Circle
West Des Moines, IA 50265
515/224-1995

Claris Corporation
5201 Patrick Henry Drive
Box 58168
Santa Clara, CA 95052-8168
408/727-8227

Cyan
P.O. Box 28096
Spokane, WA 99228
509/468-0807

Delta Point, Inc.
2 Harris Court, Suite B-1
Monterey, CA 93940
408/648-4000

Deneba Software
7855 N.W. 12th St., Suite 202
Miami, FL 33126
800/622-6827 or 305/594-6965

EarLevel Engineering
21213-B Hawthorne Blvd.,
Suite 5305
Torrance, CA 90509-2881
310/316-2939

Equilibrium Technologies
475 Gate Five Rd., Suite 225
Sausalito, CA 94965
415/332-4343

Fractal Design
335 Spreckels Drive, Suite F
Aptos, CA 95003
408/688-5300

Gold Disk
P.O. Box 789
Streetsville, Mississauga
Ontario L5M2C2
Canada
800/465-3375 or 800/982-9888

Gryphon Software
7220 Trade St., Suite 120
San Diego, CA 92121-2325
619/536-8815

Heizer Software
P.O. Box 232019
Pleasant Hill, CA 94523
800/888-7667 or 510/943-7667

HSC Software
1661 Lincoln Blvd., Suite 101
Santa Monica, CA 90404
310/392-8841

HyperGlot
P.O. Box 10746
Knoxville, TN 37939-0746
800/800-8270

Imaja
P.O. Box 6386
Albany, CA 94706
510/526-4621

InterPlay Productions, Inc.
17922 Fitch Ave.
Irvine, CA 92714
800/428-8200

Macromedia
410 Townsend, Suite 408
San Francisco, CA 94107
415/252-2000

Magic Quest
125 University
Palo Alto, CA 94301
415/321-5838

Mainstay
591-A Constitution Ave.
Camarillo, CA 93012
805/484-9400

MicroFrontier, Inc.
3401 101st St., Suite E
Des Moines, IA 50322
515/270-8109

Motion Works
130-1020 Mainland St.
Vancouver, B.C. V6B2T4
Canada
604/685-9975

Nautilus
7001 Discovery Blvd.
Dublin, OH 43017-3299
800/637-3472

OpCode Systems
3950 Fabian Way, Suite 100
Palo Alto, CA 94303
415/856-3333

Optical Media International
180 Knowles Drive
Los Gatos, CA 95030
800/347-2664 or 408/376-3511

Oracle Corporation
500 Oracle Parkway
Redwood Shores, CA 94065
800/672-3531

OSC
480 Potrero Ave.
San Francisco, CA 94110
415/252-0460

Passport
100 Stone Pine Rd.
Half Moon Bay, CA 94019
415/726-0280

PG Music
111-266 Elmwood Ave.
Buffalo, NY 14222
416/528-2368

Pierian Spring Software
5200 SW Macadam Ave.
Suite 250
Portland, OR 97201
503/222-2044

Ray Dream, Inc.
1804 N. Shoreline Blvd.
Mountain View, CA 94043
800/846-0111 or 415/960-0768

Roger Wagner Publishing
1050 Pioneer Way
El Cajon, CA 92020
800/421-6526

SMILE
c/o Sue Borden
Oregon State University
Corvallis, OR 97331

Strata
2 West St. George Blvd.
St. George, UT 84770
800/787-2823 or 801/628-5218

Time Warner Interactive
2210 W. Olive Ave.
Burbank, CA 91506
818/955-9999

Videodiscovery
1700 Westlake Ave. North,
Suite 600
Seattle, WA 98109-3012
800/548-3472

Visioneer
2860 West Bayshore Road
Palo Alto, CA 94303
800//787-7007 or 415/493-9599

The Voyager Company
One Bridge St.
Irvington, NY 10553
800/446-2001

Wacom Technology
501 SE Columbia Shores Blvd.,
#300
Vancouver, WA 98661
360/750-8882

Appendix B

Ask Doctor Hyper:
A Beginner's HyperCard Troubleshooting Guide

Home

HyperCard won't open, or it quits unexpectedly, or it doesn't allow me to perform necessary operations. What's wrong?

You probably don't have enough available memory. If you're sure that the machine you're using has *at least* 1 megabyte of memory (2 megabytes with System 7), make sure MultiFinder is not operating and the RAM cache is turned off.

When I double-click on HyperCard, it responds by asking me, "Where is Home?" Why?

HyperCard needs to have a Home stack to open. It looks for Home in the immediate neighborhood, and if it can't find it, it asks for help. Locate the Home stack using the dialog box (as explained in Session 1) and double-click on it.

I can't find a button for the ______ stack in my Home card. Where is it?

It's probably nowhere. The Home card is not a complete directory of all your stacks, like the Macintosh Finder. Home includes buttons to launch some stacks. If you want your Home card to include buttons to open other stacks, you have to install them yourself.

When I click on the ______ button on the Home card, HyperCard asks me, "Where is ______ ?" Why?

HyperCard looks for stacks in the folders where it has found them before. It keeps this information on one card of the Home stack. If the stack isn't in one of those folders, it will probably ask you to help find it. As long as you don't move that stack later, HyperCard will know next time where to look for it.

Menus

The menu bar is missing. How do I get it back?

To make the menu bar disappear or reappear, press Command-Space bar. (If this doesn't work, a Control Panel named SCSIProbe is probably interfering; you'll need to open that Control Panel and change the default keystroke option.)

I have only three (or four) menus. What's wrong?

Your user level is probably set to one of the first three levels. If you need to create stacks or modify buttons, fields, or scripts, set the user level to authoring or scripting.

I see seven menus, but the Objects menu is missing. Where is it?

A paint tool is selected, so the Objects menu has been replaced by the Paint menu, the Options menu, and the Patterns menu. To see the Objects menu, select one of the three tools at the top of the Tools menu or palette.

I can't find the Paint menu, the Options menu, or the Patterns menu. How can I get them back?

Click on any of the paint tools. See the previous answer.

Getting Around

When I select Recent from the Go menu, I see the cards in my stack, but they aren't in the right order. How can I rearrange them?

Your cards may, in fact, already be in the right order. Recent shows you the cards not in stack order but in the order in which you last visited them, duplicates excepted. Recent is like a roll of film you use to take a snapshot of each new card that you visit.

When I flip through my stack with the arrow keys, I find extra cards that I don't want anymore. What should I do?

Use the Delete Card command to remove the offending cards.

Typing

When I move the pointer over text that I want to edit, it doesn't turn into an I-beam. Why?

The text is probably paint text, which can't be edited like field text but must be repainted instead. Another possibility is that the text is in a locked field; check the Field Info dialog box for the field. A third possibility is that a button is sitting on top of the field; hold down the Option and Command keys to see if a button is outlined there.

I know that one of the cards has the phrase "XYZ" written on it; I've seen it. But when I issue a Find "XYZ" command, HyperCard just beeps at me. Why can't it find that phrase?

The Find command *will* find the card with "XYZ" on it, but only if (1) "XYZ" is on a card in the *current stack*; (2) "XYZ" is *field text*, not paint text; and (3) the field that contains "XYZ" has not been scripted to prevent searches. If HyperCard can't find a phrase, then you can be sure that one of these three conditions hasn't been satisfied.

Painting

When I try to erase my picture, part of it won't go away. Why?

The Eraser tool removes only painted material from the current layer. The part that you can't erase is probably either an icon, which can be removed only with the Button tool, or painting on the background, which can be erased only after you switch to the background (Command-B).

When I try to move an object that I've drawn, I have trouble separating it from its surroundings. Why won't it move easily like objects in Works or MacDraw?

HyperCard's graphics are bit-mapped rather than object-oriented. In plain English, that means that whatever you paint is stored in the computer as just a collection of dots on the screen. When you add a new graphic flourish to your card, the computer initially sees it as a separate flourish, so you can remove it with the Undo command or select and edit it with the Select command. But as soon as you do anything else, the flourish ceases to exist as a separate entity; it becomes just another part of the bit-mapped dot pattern that makes up the graphics of the card. From that point on, it can be edited only as part of the bigger picture.

I created a new card and redesigned its background to show something different from what's on the other cards in the stack. To my dismay, I found out too late that the new background is now on all the old cards. Where did I go wrong?

The New Card command assigns the background of the current card to the new card, so if you change the new card's background, you're also changing all other cards with that background. Instead of selecting New Card, you should have selected New Background. That command creates a new card, too, but it assigns it an all-new background that's completely unrelated to the background of the other cards in the stack.

Working with Buttons

I created a button and linked it to the wrong card. Do I need to get rid of it and start over?

No, just double-click on the button with the Button tool selected, click on Link To..., and link it to the right card. The old link will be replaced.

I have an extra button on my card that I don't want anymore. How do I get rid of it?

With the Button tool selected, click on the button to select it and press the Delete key. Gone.

Appendix C

HyperCard Menus

General Menus

File

New Stack...		Creates a new stack
Open Stack...	⌘O	Opens an existing stack
Close Stack	⌘W	Closes the current stack
Save a Copy...		Saves a copy of the current stack on disk (recommended before making major changes)
		The next two menu items are visible when any paint tool is selected
Import Paint...		Imports the top left corner of a selected paint document; pastes it as a card graphic
Export Paint...		Creates a MacPaint document from the current card and background picture
		Only one of the following two menu items is visible at any time
Compact Stack		Eliminates free space caused by deleting objects; makes the stack smaller and faster
Convert Stack...		Converts version 1.x stack to HyperCard version 2 format (necessary before stack can be changed)
Protect Stack...		Allows you to limit access, prevent changes, and control user level within the current stack
Delete Stack...		Deletes all cards in the current stack and takes you to the Home stack
Page Setup...		Controls printer features and layout of printouts on page
Print Field...		Prints field text on the current card with a variety of options
Print Card	⌘P	Prints the current card
Print Stack...		Provides several options for printing the current stack
Print Report...		Provides options for printing text-only reports from the current stack
Quit HyperCard	⌘Q	Returns to the Finder

Edit	The last five menu items are visible only at the painting, scripting, and authoring user levels
Undo ⌘Z	Undoes the last editing or painting action
Cut ⌘X	Removes currently selected text, picture, icon, button, or field and places it in Clipboard
Copy ⌘C	Places a copy of currently selected text, picture, icon, button, or field in Clipboard
Paste ⌘V	Places Clipboard contents (text, picture, icon, button, or field) in current position
Clear	Removes currently selected text, picture, icon, button, or field
New Card ⌘N	Inserts a new card with the current background after the current card
Delete Card	(Command-Delete) Deletes the current card, revealing the next card in the stack
Cut Card	Deletes the current card and places a copy (including background) in the Clipboard
Copy Card	Copies current card (including background) into the Clipboard
Text Style... ⌘T	Displays dialog box for controlling text style, font, size, justification, and spacing
Background ⌘B	Switches between card layer and background layer
Icon... ⌘I	Opens icon editor for adding, editing, or deleting icons in current stack

Go	
Back ⌘~	Takes you back one card (to the one most recently visited)
Home ⌘H	Takes you to the first card of the Home stack
Help ⌘?	Takes you to the first card of the Help stack, if available
Recent ⌘R	Presents the 42 most recent cards in the dialog box; click on one to go there
First ⌘1	Takes you to the first card of the current stack
Prev ⌘2	Takes you to the card before this card in the current stack
Next ⌘3	Takes you to the card after this card in the current stack
Last ⌘4	Takes you to the last card of the current stack
Find... ⌘F	Displays the message box containing Find command; type characters and press Return
Message ⌘M	Displays the message box; type command or message and press Return
Scroll ⌘E	Displays the scroll window, allowing you to scroll around partially visible cards
Next Window ⌘L	Moves to the next open stack

Tools	Visible only at painting, scripting, and authoring user levels; see Tools table inside back cover
Font	Visible only when Browse, Button, or Field tool is selected, except at browsing user level; changes font of field or button text
Style	Visible only when Browse, Button, or Field tool is selected, except at browsing user level; changes size and style of field or button text

Objects — Visible only at authoring and scripting user levels when Browse, Button, or Field tool is selected

Button Info...	(Double-click on button with Button tool selected) Displays Button Info dialog box
Field Info...	(Double-click on field with Field tool selected) Displays Field Info dialog box
Card Info...	Displays Card Info dialog box
Bkgnd Info...	Displays Background Info dialog box
Stack Info...	Displays Stack Info dialog box
Bring Closer ⌘+	Brings a selected button or field one level closer
Send Farther ⌘-	Sends the selected button or field one level farther
New Button	Creates a new button; double-click button to display Button Info dialog box
New Field	Creates a new field; double-click field to display Field Info dialog box
New Background	Creates a new card with a new, blank background

If you hold down Shift while selecting any of these five commands, you're taken directly to the script window

Home Menu (available only from the Home stack)

Home

New Link to Stack...	Allows you to add to the Home stack a button that opens another stack
New Link to Application...	Allows you to add to the Home stack a button that opens an application program
New Link to Document...	Allows you to add to the Home stack a button that opens a document and application
Rename This Card...	Renames a Home card and associated buttons for moving to the card
Reorder Cards...	Allows you to reorder Home cards and move buttons to reflect the new order
Home Cards	Takes you to the first Home card in the Home stack
Preferences	Takes you to the Preferences card for setting the user level and other options
Search Paths	Takes you to the first of three Search Path cards in the Home stack

Reports Menus (available only after selecting Print Reports... from the File menu)

Reports

New Report	⌘N	Displays a dialog box for creating and naming a new report template (Command-N)

Items

Available only after selecting Report Items... from the Edit menu

New Item	⌘N	Creates an item for a report (Command-N)
Item Info...	⌘I	Allows you to specify the contents and appearance of an item in a report (Command-I)

Edit — Report Version

Undo	⌘Z	
Cut	⌘X	Cuts the selected item in the Report Items dialog box
Copy	⌘C	Copies the selected item in the Report Items dialog box
Paste	⌘V	Pastes the selected item in the Report Items dialog box; pastes a report template copied or cut from another stack
Clear		Clears the selected item in the Report Items dialog box
Delete Report		Completely removes a report template
Cut Report		Moves a report template from one stack to another
Copy Report		Copies a report template to move to another stack
Report Items...	⌘E	Allows you to define the items for a report
Report Name...		Displays a dialog box to rename an existing report template

Icon Menus (visible only when the icon editor is active)

File

New Icon	⌘N	Creates a new icon
Close Icon Editor	⌘W	Closes the icon editor
Duplicate Icon	⌘D	Makes an exact copy of current icon
Quit HyperCard	⌘Q	Quits HyperCard and returns to the Finder

Edit

Command	Shortcut	Description
Undo	⌘Z	
Cut Icon	⌘X	Removes the current selected icon from the stack and copies it to the Clipboard
Copy Icon	⌘C	Puts a copy of the current selected icon in the Clipboard
Paste Icon	⌘V	Pastes icon from the Clipbard into the icon editor
Clear Icon		Permanently removes icon from the stack
New Button		Creates a new button with the new icon

Icon

Power Keys	Command	Shortcut	Description
E	Erase		Erases whole image of current selected icon
	Pickup	⌘P	Turns pointer into snapshot tool for capturing graphic image (with a click) as a new icon
	Keep	⌘K	Saves changes to icon without leaving icon editor
R	Revert		Reverts to last saved image of the icon, discarding any changes made since last save
	First	⌘1	Takes you to first icon in current stack
	Prev	⌘2	Takes you to the previous icon in the current stack
	Next	⌘3	Takes you to the next icon in the current stack
	Last	⌘4	Takes you to the last icon in the current stack
	Find...	⌘F	Lets you search for a specific icon by name or ID

Special

Power Keys	Command	Description
H	Flip Horizontal	Flips icon horizontally around an imaginary center axis
V	Flip Vertical	Flips icon vertically around an imaginary center axis
F	Frame	Draws a border around the icon
G	Gray	Dims the icon
I	Invert	Inverts icon: black pixels become white and white pixels become black
M	Mirror Horizontal	Makes the right half of the icon a mirror image of the left half
	Mirror Vertical	Makes the bottom half of the icon a mirror image of the top half
	Rotate 90°	Rotates the icon 90 degrees
S	Shadow	Draws a shadow to the right and bottom of the image

Script Menus (available only in the script editor)

File

Close Script	⌘W	Closes script and saves changes (Command-Option-click)
Save Script	⌘S	Saves the current script and stays in the editor
Revert to Saved		Reverts to the last saved version of the script
Print Script	⌘P	Prints selection or entire script
Quit HyperCard	⌘Q	Quits HyperCard and goes to Finder

Script

Find...	⌘F	Searches script for a specified word or phrase
Find Again	⌘G	Searches script for the next occurrence of specified text
Find Selection	⌘H	Searches script for the next occurrence of currently selected (highlighted) text
Scroll to Selection		Displays portion of script where the insertion point is or where text is selected
Replace...	⌘R	Changes a word or phrase in script to word or phrase that you specify
Replace Again	⌘T	Changes the next occurrence of the specified text
Comment	⌘-	Places a double hyphen before the selected text or lines
Uncomment	⌘=	Removes any double hyphens from the selected text or lines
Set Checkpoint	⌘D	Places a checkmark in the left margin before a statement in the script (Set Checkpoint changes to Clear Checkpoint when cursor is on line with a checkpoint)

Go Used to navigate between stack and script windows

Debugger Menu (available only when the debugger is active)

Menu item	Shortcut	Description
Step	⌘S	Steps to the next line in the current handler
Step Into	⌘I	Steps to next executed line in any handler
Trace		Traces through current handler without user interaction
Trace Into	⌘T	Traces execution through all handlers to completion (or next checkpoint)
Go	⌘G	Exits debugger and continues running the script from the current line
Trace Delay...		Sets delay time in ticks between steps of a trace
Clear Checkpoint	⌘D	Toggles between Set Checkpoint and Clear Checkpoint (see Script menu)
Abort	⌘A	Stops the handler and exits the debugger
Variable Watcher		Opens the Variable Watcher window
Message Watcher		Opens the Message Watcher window

Paint Menus (visible only when a paint tool is selected)

Power Keys	Options	Description
G	Grid	Constrains paint tools so they work along the lines of an invisible grid (toggles on and off)
	FatBits	Zooms in for detailed graphic work; Option key turns pointer to grabber hand
	Power Keys	Allows single keystrokes to activate paint tools and commands (shown to left of menus here)
1-8	Line Size...	Displays dialog box for selecting line size for lines, polygons, ovals, and rectangles
	Brush Shape...	Displays dialog box for selecting Paintbrush shape
	Edit Pattern...	Displays dialog box for editing selected pattern
	Polygon Sides...	Displays dialog box for selecting the number of sides of regular polygon
	Draw Filled	Causes shape tools to draw shapes filled with selected pattern (toggles on and off)
C	Draw Centered	Causes shape tools to draw shapes from center rather than from edge (toggles on and off)
M	Draw Multiple	Causes shape tools to draw repeated images automatically (toggles on and off)
	Rotate	Allows free rotation of selected graphic
	Slant	Allows controlled slanting of selected graphic
	Distort	Allows stretching and other distortion of selected graphic
	Perspective	Allows changing of 3D perspective of selected graphic

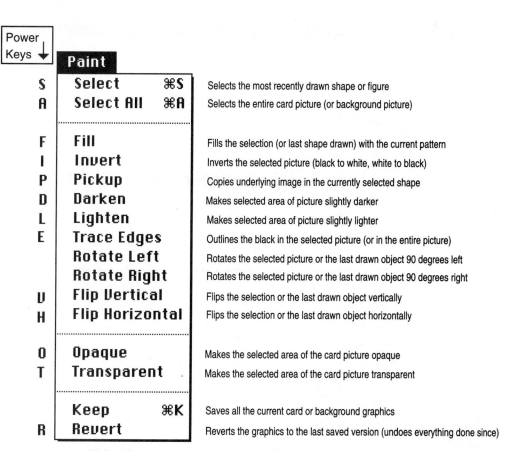

Power Keys ↓	Paint		
S	Select	⌘S	Selects the most recently drawn shape or figure
A	Select All	⌘A	Selects the entire card picture (or background picture)
F	Fill		Fills the selection (or last shape drawn) with the current pattern
I	Invert		Inverts the selected picture (black to white, white to black)
P	Pickup		Copies underlying image in the currently selected shape
D	Darken		Makes selected area of picture slightly darker
L	Lighten		Makes selected area of picture slightly lighter
E	Trace Edges		Outlines the black in the selected picture (or in the entire picture)
	Rotate Left		Rotates the selected picture or the last drawn object 90 degrees left
	Rotate Right		Rotates the selected picture or the last drawn object 90 degrees right
V	Flip Vertical		Flips the selection or the last drawn object vertically
H	Flip Horizontal		Flips the selection or the last drawn object horizontally
O	Opaque		Makes the selected area of the card picture opaque
T	Transparent		Makes the selected area of the card picture transparent
	Keep	⌘K	Saves all the current card or background graphics
R	Revert		Reverts the graphics to the last saved version (undoes everything done since)

	Patterns
W	(white pattern)
B	(black pattern)

Other patterns have no power key equivalents

Appendix D

HyperCard Keyboard Commands and Menu Equivalents

Action	*Keyboard Command*	*Menu Equivalent*
General		
Copy selection to Clipboard	⌘-C	Edit: Copy
Cut selection to Clipboard	⌘-X	Edit: Cut
Paste selection in Clipboard	⌘-V	Edit: Paste
Undo last action (with exceptions)	⌘-Z	Edit: Undo
Cancel current action (such as printing)	⌘-Period	
Access full File menu from user level below painting	⌘ when selecting menu	
Quit HyperCard, return to Finder	⌘-Q	File: Quit HyperCard
Navigation		
Go to the Home stack	⌘-H	Go: Home
Go to the Help stack (when available)	⌘-?	Go: Help
Go to the first card in this stack	⌘-1 or up-arrow	Go: First
Go to the last card in this stack	⌘-4 or down-arrow	Go: Last
Go to the previous card in this stack	⌘-2 or left-arrow	Go: Prev
Go to the next card in this stack	⌘-3 or right-arrow	Go: Next
Go back through the previously viewed cards	~, Esc, or down-arrow	
Go forward through retraced cards	up-arrow	
Open a new stack	⌘-O	File: Open Stack...
Open a new stack in a new window	⌘-Shift-O	
Close an open stack	⌘-W	File: Close Stack
Move between open stacks	⌘-L	Go: Next Window

Action	*Keyboard Command*	*Menu Equivalent*
Store current card's location for quick return (`push`)	⌘-down-arrow	
Return to stored location (`pop`)	⌘-up-arrow	
Show		
Show most recent 42 cards visited	⌘-R	Go: Recent
Show message box	⌘-M	Go: Message
Show message box with Find	⌘-F	Go: Find
Show or hide Tools palette	Option-Tab	
Show or hide Patterns palette (paint tool selected)	Tab	
Show or hide the menu bar	⌘-Space bar	
Show all buttons (Browse or Button tool selected)	⌘-Option	
Show all fields (Field tool selected)	⌘-Option	
Show all fields and buttons (Browse tool selected)	⌘-Shift-Option	
Show scroll window	⌘-E	Go: Scroll
Show Text Styles dialog box	⌘-T	Edit: Text Style...
Show size box in bottom right of window	⌘-Shift-E	
Tools		
Select Browse tool	⌘-Tab	Tools: Browse tool
Select Button tool	⌘-Tab-Tab	Tools: Button tool
Select Field tool	⌘-Tab-Tab-Tab	Tools: Field tool
Select Browse tool and leave background layer	⌘-Shift-Tab	
Objects		
Bring field or button all the way to the front	⌘-Shift-Plus	
Send field or button all the way to the back	⌘-Shift-Minus	
Move a button or field closer relative to another	⌘-Plus	Objects: Bring Closer
Send a button or field back relative to another	⌘-Minus	Objects: Send Farther
Go to/from the background layer	⌘-B	Edit: Background
Paste miniature picture of card from Clipboard	⌘-Shift-V	
Create a new card	⌘-N	Edit: New Card
Delete the current card	⌘-Delete (⌘-Backspace)	Edit: Delete Card
Print Card	⌘-P	File: Print Card
Fields		
Select all text in current field	⌘-A	
Paste field, text included with field	⌘-Shift-V	
Revert field to previous contents	⌘-Shift-Z	
Boldface all selected text in a field	⌘-Shift-B	
Condense all selected text in a field	⌘-Shift-C	
Change all selected field text to default format	⌘-Shift-D	

Action	*Keyboard Command*	*Menu Equivalent*
Make all selected text in a field into plain text	⌘-Shift-P	
Shadow all selected text in a field	⌘-Shift-S	
Extend all selected text in a field	⌘-Shift-X	
Change selected field text to next font (alphabetically)	⌘-Shift-F	
Group all selected text in a field (for hot text)	⌘-Shift-G	
Italicize all selected text in a field	⌘-Shift-I	
Outline all selected text in a field	⌘-Shift-O	
Underline all selected text in a field	⌘-Shift-U	
Make all selected text in a field a smaller font size	⌘-Shift-<	
Make all selected text in a field a larger font size	⌘-Shift->	
Decrease the height of the field's line	⌘-Shift-Minus	
Increase the height of the field's line	⌘-Shift-Plus	
Go to the next field on a card	Tab	
Go to a previous field on a card	Shift-Tab	
Reports		
Create a new report	⌘-N	Reports: New Report
Show Item Info dialog box	⌘-I	Items: Item Info...
Create item for a report	⌘-N	Items: New Item
Show Report Items dialog box	⌘-E	Edit: Report Items...
Paint		
Show opaque areas (paint tool selected)	Option-O	
Select the last graphic object created	⌘-S	Paint: Select
Select all of the graphics on this layer	⌘-A	Paint: Select All
Save current picture for next Revert	⌘-K	Paint: Keep
Revert to picture saved with last Keep	⌘-R	Paint: Revert
Enter or leave FatBits	⌘-F	Options: FatBits
View only the card picture	Option-D	
Undo most recent action (paint tool selected)	Tilde (~)	
Icons		
Open the icon editor	⌘-I	Edit: Icon...
Pick up an image to edit as icon	⌘-P	Icon: Pickup
Save changes without leaving icon editor	⌘-K	Icon: Keep
Go to first icon in current stack	⌘-1 or ⌘-left-arrow	Icon: First
Go to previous icon in current stack	⌘-2 or left-arrow	Icon: Prev
Go to next icon in current stack	⌘-3 or ⌘-right-arrow	Icon: Next
Go to last icon in current stack	⌘-4 or right-arrow	Icon: Last
Search for a specific icon by name or ID	⌘-F	Icon: Find...
Create a new icon	⌘-N	Icon: New Icon
Completely remove the selected icon	⌘-Delete	
Duplicate an icon	⌘-D	Icon: Duplicate Icon
Select part of an icon picture	⌘-Drag	

Action	*Keyboard Command*	*Menu Equivalent*
Peel off a copy of the selected icon	Option-Drag	
Paste *picture* of icon from Clipboard	⌘-Option-V	
Close the icon editor	⌘-W	Icon: Close Icon Editor
Scripts		
Edit current card script	⌘-Option-C	
Edit current background script	⌘-Option-B	
Edit current stack script	⌘-Option-S	
Open button or field script (Button or Field tool selected)	⌘-Option-click on object	
Select entire line	Triple-click	
Select entire script	⌘-A	Edit: Select All
Set (or remove) a checkpoint	⌘-D or Option-click	Script: Set (or Clear) Checkpoint
Clear all checkpoints that are set	Shift-Option-click on checkpoint	
Find text	⌘-F	Script: Find...
Find next occurrence of same text	⌘-G	Script: Find Again
Find current selection	⌘-H	Script: Find Selection
Find and replace text	⌘-R	Script: Replace...
Replace next occurrence of same text	⌘-T	Script: Replace Again
Comment current line or selected lines	⌘-Hyphen	Script: Comment
Uncomment current line or selected lines	⌘-Equals	Script: Uncomment
Print selection or entire script	⌘-P	File: Print Script
Save the current script	⌘-S	File: Save Script
Close script without saving changes	⌘-Period	
Close script and save changes	Enter, ⌘-W, ⌘-Option-click	File: Close Script
End of HyperTalk statement	Return	
Wrap line without return character (soft return)	Option-Return	
Format script	Tab	
Enter debugger while script is running	⌘-Option-Period	
Debug		
Step one line at a time through current handler	⌘-S	Debug: Step
Step one line at a time through current and called handlers	⌘-I	Debug: Step Into
Trace without delays through all handlers	⌘-T	Debug: Trace Into
Continue running script at next command	⌘-G	Debug: Go
Set (or remove) checkpoint	⌘-D	Debug: Set (or Clear) Checkpoint
Exit debugger, abort current handler	⌘-A	Debug: Abort

Appendix E

A HyperTalk Dictionary

This appendix lists and defines, in alphabetical order, all of the HyperTalk vocabulary words introduced in this book, plus many not included in the main text. Some entries include a number referring to the page of this book containing an example and/or more complete explanation. More than half of HyperTalk's native vocabulary is included here. The HyperTalk words omitted from this list are, for the most part, either special-purpose words of little interest to the typical HyperCard user or trivial words with obvious meanings (for example, `two`). A more complete list is published in the *HyperCard Script Language Guide* (Cupertino, CA: Apple, 1993).

Term	*Category*	*Meaning*	*Page*
`abs`	Function	Returns the absolute value of a number.	
`add`	Command	Adds the value of an expression to a value in a container.	
`after`	Preposition	Used with the `put` command, directing HyperCard to append a new value following any preexisting value in a container.	
`all`	Adjective	Specifies total number of cards in stack to `show cards` command.	
`answer`	Command	Displays a dialog box with question and reply buttons.	220, 226
`answer file`	Command	Presents the standard dialog box for locating a file; used for opening files of a specified type.	

Term	*Category*	*Meaning*	*Page*
`any`	Ordinal	Special ordinal used with object or chunk to specify a random element within its enclosing set.	
`arrowKey`	System message	Sent to current card when an arrow key is pressed.	
`ask`	Command	Displays a dialog box with a question and default answer.	224
`ask file`	Command	Presents the standard dialog box for locating where to save a file; used for saving files.	
`ask password`	Command	Displays a dialog box with a field for a password.	
`autoHilite`	Property	Determines whether or not the specified button's `hilite` property is affected by the message `mouseDown`.	
`average`	Function	Returns the average value of numbers in a list.	
`background`	Object	Generic name of background object; used with specific designation (`go to next background`). Also used to specify containing object for buttons and, optionally, fields (`background button 2`).	184, 220
`beep`	Command	Causes the Macintosh to make a beep sound.	
`before`	Preposition	Used with `put` command, directing HyperCard to place a new value at the beginning of any preexisting value in a container.	
`bg`	Object	Abbreviation for `background`.	184
`bkgnd`	Object	Abbreviation for `background`.	184
`blindTyping`	Property	Allows typing into the message box when it's hidden.	
`bottom`	Property	Determines or changes the value of item 4 of the `rectangle` property when applied to the specified object or window.	
`bottomRight`	Property	Determines or changes items 3 and 4 of the value of the `rectangle` property when applied to the specified object or window.	
`browse`	Tool	Name of tool from Tools palette; used with the `choose` command or returned by the `tool` function.	
`brush`	Property	Determines the current brush shape.	
`brush`	Tool	Name of tool from Tools palette; used with the `choose` command or returned by the `tool` function.	
`btn`	Object	Abbreviation for `button`.	
`bucket`	Tool	Name of tool from Tools palette; used with the `choose` command or returned by the `tool` function.	
`button`	Object	Generic name of button object; used with a specific designation (`hide button one`).	

Term	*Category*	*Meaning*	*Page*
`button`	Tool	Name of tool from Tools palette; used with `choose` command or returned by the `tool` function.	
`card`	Object	Generic name of a card object; used with a specific designation (`go to card "fred"`). Also used to specify containing object for fields and, optionally, buttons (`card field "date"`).	
`cd`	Object	Abbreviation for `card`.	
`center`	Adjective	Specifies center alignment of text in a field.	
`centered`	Property	Determines whether shapes are drawn from the center or from the corner.	
`char[acter]`	Chunk	A character of text in any container or expression.	
`choose`	Command	Changes the current tool.	149
`click`	Command	Causes same actions as clicking at a specified location.	
`clickChunk`	Function	Returns chunk information about text that is clicked.	219–220
`clickLine`	Function	Returns line information about text that is clicked.	
`clickLoc`	Function	Returns location of most recent click.	
`clickText`	Function	Returns text information about word or group phrase that is clicked.	219
`closeBackground`	System message	Sent to current card just before you leave the current background.	
`closeCard`	System message	Sent to current card just before you leave it.	189
`closeField`	System message	Sent to unlocked field when it closes.	
`closeStack`	System message	Sent to current card just before you leave the current stack.	195, 237
`close file`	Command	Closes a previously opened disk file.	
`commandKey`	Function	Sent to current card when a combination of the Command key and another key is pressed.	
`commandKeyDown`	System message	Returns the Command key.	
`commands`	Property	Returns a list of the commands associated with the buttons in a palette XCMD.	230
`compound`	Function	Computes present or future value of a compound interest-bearing account.	
`controlKey`	Command	Sends the `controlKey` system message.	
`controlKey`	System message	Sent to current card when a combination of the Control key and another key is pressed.	
`create menu`	Command	Creates a new menu with the specified name.	230
`create stack`	Command	Creates a new stack with the specified name and background.	

Term	*Category*	*Meaning*	*Page*
`cursor`	Property	Sets image appearing at pointer location on screen. You can only set `cursor`; you can't get it.	178
`curve`	Tool	Name of tool from Tools palette; used with the `choose` command or returned by the `tool` function.	
`date`	Function	Returns a string representing the current date.	
`debug checkpoint`	Command	Sets a checkpoint in a script to invoke the built-in debugger.	
`delete` (text)	Command	Removes a chunk of text from a container.	
`delete` (menu)	Command	Deletes a menu without a dialog box.	230
`delete` (menu items)	Command	Deletes a menu item without a dialog box.	
`dial`	Command	Generates touch-tone sounds through audio output or a modem attached to serial port.	
`disable`	Command	Disables the specified menu or menu item.	230
`diskSpace`	Function	Displays the amount of free space available on the disk containing the current stack.	
`div`	Command	Divides the value in a container by the value of an expression.	146
`do`	Command, Keyword	Sends the value of an expression as a message to the current card.	
`doMenu`	Command	Performs a specified menu command.	
`doMenu`	System message	Sent to the current card when any menu item is chosen.	223, 227
`dontSearch`	Property	Determines whether a card, background, or background field can be searched by the `find` command.	
`dontWrap`	Property	Determines whether the text in a field wraps onto the next line.	
`down`	Constant	Value returned by various functions to describe the state of a key or the mouse button.	
`drag`	Command	Performs same action as a manual drag.	
`dragSpeed`	Property	Sets pixels-per-second speed at which the pointer moves with the `drag` command.	
`else`	Keyword	Optionally follows `then` clause in an `if` structure to introduce an alternative action clause.	
`empty`	Constant	The null string; same as the literal `""`.	
`enable`	Command	Enables the specified menu or menu item.	
`enabled`	Command	Determines whether the specified menu or menu item is enabled.	
`end`	Keyword	Marks the end of a message handler, function handler, `repeat` loop, or multiple-statement `then` or `else` clause of an `if` structure.	151

Term	*Category*	*Meaning*	*Page*
`enterKey`	Command	Sends contents of the message box to the current card.	
`enterKey`	System message	Sent to the current card when the Enter key is pressed unless the text insertion point is in a field.	
`eraser`	Tool	Name of tool from Tools palette; used with `choose` command or returned by the `tool` function.	
`exit`	Keyword	Immediately ends execution of a message handler, function handler, or `repeat` loop.	226–227
`exp`	Function	Returns the mathematical exponential of its argument.	
`false`	Constant	Boolean value resulting from evaluation of a comparative expression and returned from some functions.	
`field`	Container	Generic name of field container; used with specific designation (`put the time into card field "time"`).	
`field`	Object	Generic name of field object; used with specific designation (`get name of first field`).	
`field`	Tool	Name of tool from Tools palette; used with the `choose` command or returned by the `tool` function.	
`filled`	Property	Determines the Draw Filled setting.	
`find`	Command	Searches card and background fields for text strings derived from an expression.	220
`first`	Ordinal	Designates object or chunk number one within its enclosing set.	
`fixedLineHeight`	Property	Determines whether or not a field has fixed line spacing.	
`foundChunk`	Function	Returns a chunk expression describing the text found with the `find` command.	
`foundField`	Function	Returns an expression describing the field the text was found in with the `find` command.	
`foundLine`	Function	Returns an expression describing the line the text was found in with the `find` command.	
`foundText`	Function	Returns the text found with the `find` command.	
`function`	Keyword	Marks the beginning of a function handler. Connects the handler with a particular function call.	
`get`	Command	Puts the value of an expression into the local variable `It`.	219
`global`	Keyword	Declares specified variables to be valid beyond current execution of current handler.	224
`go`	Command	Takes you to a specified card or stack.	150, 153

Term	*Category*	*Meaning*	*Page*
`grid`	Property	Determines the Grid setting.	
`help`	Command	Takes you to the first card in the stack named Help.	
`height`	Property	Determines or changes the vertical distance in pixels occupied by the rectangle of the specified button or field.	
`hide`	Command	Hides the specified window from view.	147
`hide groups`	Command	Hides the gray underline displayed beneath text by the `show groups` command.	
`hide menuBar`	Command	Hides the HyperCard menu bar.	
`hilite`	Property	Determines whether a specified button is highlighted.	
`icon`	Property	Determines the icon that is displayed with a specified button.	
`ID`	Property	Determines the permanent ID number of a specified background, card, field, or button.	
`idle`	System message	Sent to the current card repeatedly whenever nothing else is happening.	147
`if`	Keyword	Introduces a conditional structure containing statements to be executed only if a specified condition is true.	155, 178
`in`	Operator	Used with the comparison operators `is in` and `is not in`.	
`in`	Preposition	Used as a connective preposition in chunk expressions. For example, `card 12 in this stack`.	
`into`	Preposition	Used with the `put` command, directing HyperCard to replace any preexisting value in a container with a new value.	
`It`	Container	Local variable that is the default destination for the `get`, `ask`, `answer`, `read`, and `convert` commands.	219
`item`	Chunk	A piece of text delimited by commas in any container or expression.	185
`items`	Chunk type	Specifies items as type of chunk to the `number` function.	
`keyDown`	System message	Sent to the current card when a key is pressed.	148
`lasso`	Tool	Name of tool from Tools palette; used with the `choose` command or returned by the `tool` function.	
`last`	Ordinal	Special ordinal used with object or chunk to specify the element whose number is equal to the total number of elements in its enclosing set.	
`length`	Function	Returns the number of characters in the text string derived from an expression.	

Term	*Category*	*Meaning*	*Page*
`left`	Adjective	Specifies left-justified alignment of text in a field.	
`left`	Property	Determines or changes the value of item 1 of the `rectangle` property when applied to the specified object or window.	
`line`	Chunk	A piece of text delimited by return characters in any container.	
`line`	Tool	Name of tool from Tools palette; used with the `choose` command or returned by the `tool` function.	
`lineSize`	Property	Determines the thickness of lines drawn with line and shape tools.	
`loc[ation]`	Property	Determines the location at which a window, field, or button is displayed.	184
`lock screen`	Command	Prevents updating of the screen from card to card.	220
`lockScreen`	Property	Determines whether the screen is updated when moving from card to card.	220
`lockText`	Property	Determines whether text editing is allowed in a specified field.	
`mark`	Command	Marks cards.	
`marked`	Property	Determines whether or not a specified card is marked.	
`max`	Function	Returns the highest-value number from a list of numbers.	
`me`	Object	The object containing the executing handler.	210
`menuMsg`	Property	Determines the message to be sent by a specified menu item.	
`menu`	Function	Returns a list of the menu items in a specified menu.	
`message [box]`	Container	The message box.	151
`messageWatcher`	Property	Determines the message watcher to use.	187
`mid[dle]`	Ordinal	Special ordinal used with an object or chunk to specify the element whose number is equal to one more than half the total number of elements in its enclosing set.	
`min`	Function	Returns the lowest-value number from a list of numbers.	
`mouse`	Function	Returns state of the mouse button: `up` or `down`.	
`mouseClick`	Function	Returns whether the mouse button has been clicked.	
`mouseDown`	System message	Sent to a button, unlocked field, or the current card when the mouse button is pressed down.	
`mouseEnter`	System message	Sent to a button or field when the pointer is first moved inside its rectangle.	148

Term	*Category*	*Meaning*	*Page*
`mouseH`	Function	Returns the horizontal offset in pixels of the pointer from the left edge of the card window.	
`mouseLeave`	System message	Sent to a button or field when the pointer is first removed from its rectangle.	148
`mouseLoc`	Function	Returns the point on the screen where the pointer is currently located.	183
`mouseStillDown`	System message	Sent to a button, unlocked field, or the current card repeatedly when the mouse button is held down.	
`mouseUp`	System message	Sent to a button, unlocked field, or the current card when the mouse button is released after having been previously pressed down within the same object's rectangle.	150–153
`mouseV`	Function	Returns the vertical offset in pixels of the pointer from the top of the screen.	
`mouseWithin`	System message	Sent to a button or field repeatedly while the pointer remains inside its rectangle.	148
`msg [box]`	Container	The message box.	
`multiple`	Property	Determines whether multiple images are drawn with a shape tool.	
`multiply`	Command	Multiplies the value in a container by the value derived from an expression.	
`multiSpace`	Property	Determines the space between objects drawn when the `multiple` property is `true`.	
`name`	Property	Determines the name of a stack, background, card, field, button, menu, or menu item.	
`newBackground`	System message	Sent to the current card as soon as a background has been created.	
`newButton`	System message	Sent to a button as soon as it has been created.	
`newCard`	System message	Sent to a card as soon as it has been created.	
`newField`	System message	Sent to a field as soon as it has been created.	
`newStack`	System message	Sent to the current card as soon as a stack has been created.	
`next`	Keyword	Ends execution of current iteration of a `repeat` loop, beginning next iteration.	
`next`	Object modifier	Used with `card` or `background` to refer to the one following the current one.	
`number`	Function	Returns the number of buttons or fields on the current card or background, the number of marked cards, the number of HyperCard menus, the number of menu items in a menu, the number of windows in HyperCard, or the number of a specified type of chunk within a value.	
`number`	Property	Determines the number of a background, card, field, or button.	

Term	*Category*	*Meaning*	*Page*
`open`	Command	Launches the specified application.	
`openBackground`	System message	Sent to a card when you go to it and its background is different from the one you were formerly on.	
`openCard`	System message	Sent to a card when you go to it.	181, 182
`openField`	System message	Sent to an unlocked field when you place the insertion point in it for text editing.	
`open file`	Command	Opens the specified file for a `read` or `write` command operation.	
`openStack`	System message	Sent to a card when you go to it and it's in a stack different from the one containing the card you were formerly on.	153, 195
`optionKey`	Function	Returns the state of the Option key: `up` or `down`.	
`oval`	Tool	Name of tool from Tools palette; used with the `choose` command or returned by the `tool` function.	
`palette`	Command	Invokes the specified palette XCMD.	
`pass`	Keyword	Ends execution of a message handler or function handler and sends the invoking message or function call to the next object in the hierarchy.	
`pattern`	Property	Determines the Paint pattern.	
`pencil`	Tool	Name of tool from Tools palette; used with the `choose` command or returned by the `tool` function.	
`pi`	Constant	The mathematical value pi to 20 decimal places, equal to the number 3.14159265358979323846.	
`picture`	Command	Displays the specified picture file in an external window.	
`play`	Command	Starts the HyperCard sound-playing feature.	
`poly[gon]`	Tool	Name of tool from Tools palette; used with the `choose` command or returned by the `tool` function.	
`polySides`	Property	Determines the number of sides created by the Regular Polygon tool.	
`pop card`	Command	Returns you to last card saved with the `push card` command.	218, 219
`powerKeys`	Property	Provides keyboard shortcuts of commonly used painting actions.	
`prev[ious]`	Object modifier	Used with `card` or `background` to refer to the one preceding the current one.	
`print`	Command	Prints the specified file.	
`print card`	Command	Prints the current card or a specified number of cards beginning with the current card.	

Term	*Category*	*Meaning*	*Page*
`push`	Command	Saves the identification of a specified card in a LIFO memory stack for later retrieval.	218, 219
`put`	Command	Copies the value of an expression into a container.	185, 230
`quit`	System message	Sent to the current card when you choose Quit HyperCard from the File menu (or press Command-Q), just before HyperCard goes away.	
`random`	Function	Returns a random integer between 1 and the integer derived from a specified expression.	
`read`	Command	Reads a file previously opened with the `open file` command into the local variable `It`. See also `write`.	
`rect[angle]`	Property	Determines the rectangle occupied by a specified window, field, or button.	
`rect[angle]`	Tool	Name of tool from Tools palette; used with the `choose` command or returned by the `tool` function.	
`reg[ular] poly[gon]`	Tool	Name of tool from Tools palette; used with the `choose` command or returned by the `tool` function.	
`repeat`	Keyword	Introduces a `repeat` loop, an iterative structure containing a block of one or more statements executed multiple times.	178, 181
`reset menuBar`	Command	Reinstates the default values of all the HyperCard menus and removes any user-defined menus.	230
`reset paint`	Command	Reinstates the default values of all the painting properties.	
`reset printing`	Command	Reinstates the default values of all the printing properties.	
`result`	Function	Returns the status of commands previously executed in the current handler. See the `result` function.	220
`resume`	System message	Sent to the current card when HyperCard resumes running after having been suspended.	
`resumeStack`	System message	Sent to the current card when HyperCard returns to a stack.	237
`return`	Keyword	Returns a value from a function handler or message handler.	
`returnKey`	Command	Sends any statement in the message box to the current card.	
`returnKey`	System message	Sent to current card when the Return key is pressed.	148
`right`	Adjective	Specifies right-justified alignment of text in a field.	

Term	*Category*	*Meaning*	*Page*
`right`	Property	Determines or changes the value of item 3 of the `rectangle` property when applied to the specified object or window.	
`round`	Function	Returns the number derived from an expression, rounded off to the nearest integer.	
`round rect[angle]`	Tool	Name of tool from Tools palette; used with `choose` command or returned by the `tool` function.	
`save stack`	Command	Saves a copy of the specified stack with a specified name.	
`script`	Property	Retrieves or replaces the script of the specified stack, background, card, field, or button.	
`select`	Tool	Name of tool from Tools palette; used with `choose` command or returned by the `tool` function.	
`selectedChunk`	Function	Returns a chunk expression describing the selected text in a field.	
`selectedField`	Function	Returns an expression describing the field the selected text is in.	
`selectedLine`	Function	Returns an expression describing the line in a field where the selected text is.	
`selectedText`	Function	Returns the selected text in a field.	
`selection`	Container	Currently selected area of text in a field.	
`send`	Command	Sends a specified message directly to a specified object.	232
`set`	Command	Changes the state of a specified global, painting, window, or object property.	153, 158
`sharedHilite`	Property	Determines or sets whether a background button shares the same highlight state on each card.	
`sharedText`	Property	Determines if a background field shares the same text on each card. If set to `true` it also sets the `dontSearch` property of the field to `true`.	
`shiftKey`	Function	Returns the state of the Shift key: `up` or `down`.	
`show`	Command	Displays a specified window or object.	147
`show groups`	Command	Displays a gray line under all text with a `textStyle` property of `group`.	
`show cards`	Command	Displays a specified number of cards in the current stack.	
`showLines`	Property	Determines whether or not the text baselines are visible in a field.	
`show menuBar`	Command	Displays the menu bar if it was hidden.	
`showName`	Property	Determines whether or not the name of a specified button is displayed in its rectangle on the screen.	

Term	*Category*	*Meaning*	*Page*
`showPict`	Property	Determines whether or not a specified card or background picture is displayed.	
`show titleBar`	Command	Shows the title bar of the current card window if it was hidden.	
`sort`	Command	Puts all of the cards in a specified stack in a specified order.	
`sound`	Function	Returns the name of the sound that is currently playing.	
`space`	Constant	The space character (ASCII 32); same as the literal `" "`.	
`spray [can]`	Tool	Name of tool from Tools palette; used with the `choose` command or returned by the `tool` function.	
`sqrt`	Function	Returns the square root of a number.	
`stack`	Object	Generic name of stack object; used with specific name (`go to stack "help"`).	
`startUp`	System message	Sent to the current card (first card of the Home stack) when HyperCard first begins running.	
`startUsing`	Command	Specifies a stack to add to the message-passing hierarchy.	
`stopUsing`	Command	Specifies a stack to remove from the message-passing hierarchy.	
`style`	Property	Determines the style of a specified field or button.	
`subtract`	Command	Subtracts the value of an expression from the value in a container.	
`suspend`	System message	Sent to the current card when HyperCard is suspended by launching another application with the `open` command.	
`suspendStack`	System message	Sent to the current card when you leave an open stack to go to another.	237
`tabKey`	System message	Sent to the current card or a field when Tab key is pressed.	
`target`	Function	Indicates the object that initially received the message that initiated execution of the current handler.	
`text`	Tool	Name of tool from Tools palette; used with the `choose` command or returned by the `tool` function.	
`textAlign`	Property	Determines the alignment of characters created with the Paint Text tool, or those in a field, or those in the name of a button.	
`textArrows`	Property	Determines the functions of the arrow keys.	
`textFont`	Property	Determines the font of characters created with the Paint Text tool, or those in a field, or those in the name of a button.	

Term	*Category*	*Meaning*	*Page*
`textHeight`	Property	Determines the space between the baseline and characters created with the Paint Text tool or those in a field.	
`textSize`	Property	Determines the size of Paint text, or text in a field, or text in the name of a button.	
`textStyle`	Property	Determines the style of Paint text, text in a field, text in the name of a button, or text of a menu item.	219
`the`	Special	Precedes a function name to indicate a function call to one of the built-in functions of HyperCard. You can't call a user-defined function with `the`. Also allowed, but not I required, to precede special container names (`the message box`) and properties.	145
`then`	Keyword	Follows the conditional expression in an `if` structure to introduce the action clause.	
`this`	Modifier	Used with `card`, `background`, or `stack` to refer to the current one.	
`ticks`	Function	Determines the number of ticks since the Macintosh was turned on or restarted.	
`time`	Function	Returns the current time as a text string.	145
`to`	Preposition	Used to specify ranges (`3 to 5`), connect a message to its destination when used with `send`, specify a format for the `convert` command, assign a container for the `add` command, and connect values to object properties.	
`tool`	Function	Returns the name of the current tool.	
`top`	Property	Determines or changes the value of item 2 of the `rectangle` property when applied to the specified object or window.	
`topLeft`	Property	Determines or changes items 1 and 2 of the value of the `rectangle` property when applied to the specified object or window.	
`traceDelay`	Property	Determines or changes the delay between the execution of lines of HyperTalk during a debugger trace.	
`true`	Constant	Boolean value resulting from evaluation of a comparative expression and returned from some functions.	
`trunc`	Function	Determines the integer part of a number.	
`type`	Command	Inserts the specified text at the insertion point.	
`unlock screen`	Command	Allows updating of the screen.	220
`unmark`	Command	Unmarks the specified marked card.	
`up`	Constant	Value returned by various functions to describe the state of a key or the mouse button.	

Term	*Category*	*Meaning*	*Page*
`userLevel`	Property	Determines the user level from 1 to 5.	
`visible`	Property	Determines whether or not a window, field, or button appears on the screen.	211
`visual`	Command	Sets up a specified visual transition to the next card opened.	189
`wait`	Command	Causes HyperCard to pause before executing the rest of the current handler.	182
`wideMargins`	Property	Determines whether or not additional space is displayed in the margins of a specified field.	
`width`	Property	Determines or changes the horizontal distance in pixels occupied by the rectangle of the specified button or field.	
`within`	Operator	Tests whether or not a point lies inside a specified rectangle.	
`word`	Chunk	Piece of text delimited by spaces in any container or expression.	
`words`	Chunk type	Specifies words as type of chunk to the `number` function.	
`write`	Command	Copies specified text into a specified disk file starting at a specified point.	
`zero`	Constant	String representation of the numerical value 0.	

Glossary

actual parameters: See **parameters.**

algorithm: A step-by-step procedure for solving a problem or accomplishing a task. Writing HyperTalk handlers or programs in other languages often begins with figuring out a suitable algorithm for a task.

AppleScript Component: A scripting system integrated at the system level that utilizes the Component Manager. This technology, through the use of its scripting language, AppleScript, enables users to create scripts to control applications and the system.

background: A type of HyperCard object; a template shared by a number of cards. Each card with the same background has the same background picture, background fields, and background buttons in its background layer. Like other HyperCard objects, every background has a script. You can place handlers in a background script that you want to be accessible to all the cards with that background.

background button: A button that is common to all cards sharing a background. Compare with **card button.**

background field: A field that is common to all cards sharing a background; its size, position, and default text format remain constant on all cards associated with that background, but its text can change from card to card. Compare with **card field.**

background picture: The graphics in the background layer; the entire picture that is common to all cards sharing a background. You see the background picture by choosing Background from the Edit menu. Compare with **card picture.**

Browse tool: The tool you use to click buttons and to set the insertion point in fields.

button: A type of HyperCard object; a rectangular "hot spot" on a card or background that responds when you click it according to the instructions in its script. For example, clicking a right-arrow button with the Browse tool can take you to the next card. See also **background button, card button.**

Button tool: The tool you use to create, change, and select buttons.

card: A type of HyperCard object; a rectangular area that can hold buttons, fields, and graphics. All cards in a stack are the same size. Each layer can contain its own buttons, fields, and graphics.

card button: A button that belongs to a card; it appears on, and its actions apply to, a single card. Compare with **background button.**

card field: A field that belongs to a card; its size, position, text attributes, and contents are limited to the card on which the field is created. Compare with **background field.**

card picture: A picture that belongs to and applies only to a specific card. Compare with **background picture.**

chunk: A piece of a character string represented as a chunk expression. Chunks can be specified as any combination of characters, words, items, or lines in a container or other source of value.

chunk expression: A HyperTalk description of a unique chunk of the contents of any container or other source of value.

command: A response to a particular message; a command is a built-in message handler residing in HyperCard. See also **external command.**

Command key: The key at the lower-left side of the keyboard that has a propeller-shaped symbol. This key also has an Apple symbol and is sometimes called the *Apple key.*

comments: Descriptive lines of text in a script or program that are intended not as instructions for the computer, but as explanations for people to read. Comments are set off from instructions by symbols called delimiters, which vary from language to language. In HyperTalk, two hyphens (- -) indicate the beginning of a comment.

constant: A named value that never changes. For example, the constant `empty` stands for the null string, a value that can also be represented by the literal expression `" "`. Compare with **variable.**

container: A place where you can store a value (text or a number). Examples are fields, the message box, the selection, and variables.

control structure: A block of HyperTalk statements defined with keywords that enable a script to control the order or conditions under which specific statements execute.

current: (adj.) Applies to the card, background, or stack you're using now. For example, the current card is the one you can see on your screen.

debug: To locate and correct an error or the cause of a problem or malfunction in a computer program, such as a HyperTalk script.

delimiter: A character or characters used to mark the beginning or end of a sequence of characters; that is, to define limits. For example, in HyperTalk double quotation marks act as delimiters for literals, and comments are set off with two hyphens at the beginning of the comment and a return character at the end.

descriptor: The combination of an object's generic name, immediately followed by its particular name, number, or ID number.

dynamic path: A series of extra objects inserted into the path through which a message passes when its static path does not include the current card. The dynamic path comprises the current card, current background, and current stack. Compare with **static path.**

expression: A description of how to get a value; a source of value or complex expression built from sources of value and operators.

external command (XCMD): A command written in a computer language other than HyperTalk but made available to HyperCard to extend its built-in command set. External commands can be attached to a specific stack or to HyperCard itself. See also **external function.**

external function (XFCN): A function written in a computer language other than HyperTalk but made available to HyperCard to extend its built-in function set. External functions can be attached to a specific stack or to HyperCard itself. See also **external command.**

factor: A single element of value in an expression. See also **value.** Factoring is the separation of the interface links to the application and to core functionality. By factoring an application, all features are accessed through event handlers via *Apple events.*

field: A type of HyperCard object; a container in which you type field text (as opposed to Paint text). HyperCard has two kinds of fields—card fields and background fields.

Field tool: The tool you use to create, change, and select fields.

formal parameters: See **parameter variables.**

function: A named value that HyperCard calculates each time it is used. The way in which the value is calculated is defined internally for HyperTalk's built-in functions, and you can define your own functions with function handlers.

function call: The use of a function name in a HyperTalk statement or in the message box, invoking either a function handler or a built-in function.

function handler: A handler that executes in response to a function call matching its name.

global properties: The properties that determine aspects of the overall HyperCard environment. For example, `userLevel` is a global property that determines the current user level setting.

global variable: A variable that is valid for all handlers in which it is declared. You declare a global variable by preceding its name with the keyword `global`. Compare with **local variable.**

handler: A block of HyperTalk statements in the script of an object that executes in response to a message or a function call. The first line in a handler must begin with the word `on`, and the last line must end with the word `end`. Both `on` and `end` must be followed by the name of the message or function. HyperTalk has message handlers and function handlers.

hierarchy: See **message-passing hierarchy.**

Home cards: The first five cards in the standard Home stack, designed to hold buttons that take you to stacks, applications, and documents. Choose Home from the Go menu (or press Command-H) to get to the card in the standard Home stack that you've seen most recently. You can also type `go home` in the message box or include it as a statement in a handler.

HyperTalk: The HyperCard built-in script language for HyperCard users.

identifier: A character string of any length, beginning with an alphabetic character; it can contain any alphanumeric character and the underscore character. Identifiers are used for variable and handler names.

keyboard equivalent key: A key you press together with the Command key to issue a menu command.

keyword: Any one of the 14 words that have a predefined meaning in HyperTalk. Examples of keywords are `on`, `if`, `do`, and `repeat`.

layer: The order of a button or field relative to other buttons or fields on the same card or background. The object created most recently is ordinarily the topmost object (on the front layer).

literal: A string of characters intended to be taken literally. In HyperTalk, you use quotation marks (`" "`) as delimiters to set off a string of characters as a literal, such as the name of an object or a group of words you want to be treated as a text string.

local variable: A variable that is valid only within the handler in which it is used (local variables need not be declared). Compare with **global variable.**

loop: A section of a handler that is repeated until a limit or condition is met, such as in a repeat structure.

message: A string of characters sent to an object from a script or the message box, or that HyperCard sends in response to an event. Messages that come from the system—from events such as mouse clicks, keyboard actions, or menu commands—are called system messages. Examples of HyperTalk messages are `mouseUp`, `go`, and `push card`. See also **handler.**

message box: A container that you use to send messages to objects or to evaluate expressions.

message handler: A handler that executes in response to a message matching its name.

message-passing hierarchy: The ordering of HyperCard objects that determines the path through which messages pass.

number: A character string consisting of any combination of the numerals 0 through 9, optionally including one period (.) representing a decimal value. A number can be preceded by a hyphen or a minus sign to represent a negative value.

object: An element of the HyperCard environment that has a script associated with it and that can send and receive messages. There are five kinds of HyperCard objects: buttons, fields, cards, backgrounds, and stacks.

object class: An application defines specific objects as distinct classes. In HyperCard, each of its objects (stack, background, card, button, and field) can be an individual class.

object descriptor: Designation used to refer to an object. An object descriptor is formed by combining the name of the type of object with a specific name, number, or ID number. For example, `background button 3` is an object descriptor. Stacks do not have a number or ID number, so only the name can be used for a stack descriptor.

object properties: The properties that determine how HyperCard objects look and act. For example, the `location` property of a button determines where it appears on the screen.

object specifier: A specific data type that contains references to specific classes (objects) and their relating specifiers (such as names, indexes, or IDs). For HyperCard, the metaphor that chunk expressions describe is an example of an object specifier.

on-line help: Assistance you can get from an application program while it's running. In HyperCard, on-line help refers to the HyperCard disk-based Help system.

operator: A character or group of characters that causes a particular calculation or comparison to occur. In HyperTalk, operators operate on values. For example, the plus sign (+) is an arithmetic operator that adds numerical values.

Paint text: Text you type using the Paint Text tool. Paint text can appear anywhere, while regular text must appear in a field created with the Field tool. Paint text is part of a card or background picture.

paint tool: Any HyperCard tool you use to make pictures. Paint tools include Lasso, Brush, Spray, Eraser, and many others.

painting properties: The properties that control aspects of the HyperCard painting environment, which is invoked when you choose a Paint tool. For example, the `brush` property determines the shape of the Brush tool.

palette: A small window that displays icons or patterns you can select by clicking. You can see two of the HyperCard palettes, the Tools palette and the Patterns palette, simply by "tearing off" their respective menus. To see the navigator palette, type `palette "navigator"` in the message box. See also **tear-off menu**.

parameters: Values passed to a handler by a message or function call. Any expressions after the first word in a message are evaluated to yield the parameters; the parameters to a function call are enclosed in parentheses or, if there is only one, it can follow `of`.

parameter variables: Local variables in a handler that receive the values of parameters passed with the message or function call initiating the handler's execution.

picture: Any graphic or part of a graphic, created with a Paint tool or imported from an external file, that is part of a card or background.

pixel: Short for *picture element;* the smallest dot you can draw on the screen. The position of the pointer is often represented by two numbers separated by commas. These numbers are horizontal and vertical distances of the pointer from the left and upper edges of the card window, measured in pixels. The upper left corner of the screen has the coordinates 0, 0.

point: (1) A location on the screen described by two integers, separated by a comma, representing horizontal and vertical offsets, measured in pixels from the upper left corner of the card window or (in the case of the card window itself) of the screen. (2) In printing, the unit of measurement of the height of a text character; one point is about 1/72 of an inch. When you select a font, you can also select a point size, such as 10 point, 12 point, and so on.

power key: One of a number of keys on the Macintosh keyboard you can press to initiate a menu action when a Paint tool is active. Power keys are enabled when you choose Power Keys from the Options menu or you check Power Keys on the Preferences card in the Home stack.

properties: The defining characteristics of any HyperCard object and of the HyperCard environment. For example, setting the user level to Scripting changes the `userLevel` property of HyperCard to the value 5. Properties are often selected as options in dialog boxes or on palettes, or they can be set from handlers.

Recent: A special dialog box that holds pictorial representations of the last 42 unique cards viewed. Choose Recent from the Go menu to get the dialog box. Also, an adjective describing the card you were on immediately prior to the current card, as in `recent card`.

recursion: The repetition of an operation or group of operations. Recursion occurs when a handler calls itself.

regular text: Text you type in a field. You use the Browse tool to set an insertion point in a field and then type. Regular text is editable and searchable, while Paint text is not.

resource fork: The part of a file that contains resources such as fonts, icons, sounds, and so on.

script: A collection of handlers written in HyperTalk and associated with a particular object. You use the script editor to add to and revise an object's script. Every object has a script, even though some scripts are empty, that is, they contain nothing.

script editor: A window in which you can type and edit a script. The title bar of the script editor describes the object to which the script belongs. You can use the Edit menu, the Script menu, and keyboard commands to edit text in the script editor. See also **handler, object,** and **script.**

search path: When you open a file from within HyperCard, HyperCard attempts to locate the stack, document, or application you want by searching the folders listed on the appropriate Search Paths card in the Home stack. Each line on a Search Paths card indicates the location of a folder, including the disk name (and folder and subfolder names, if any). This information is called a *search path.* Items in a search path are separated by a colon, like this:

```
my disk:HyperCard folder:my stacks:
```

Search Path cards: Three cards in the Home stack used to store information about the location of stacks, documents, and applications that you open while HyperCard is running. See also **search path.**

selection: A container that holds the currently selected area of text. Note that text found by the `find` command is not selected.

shared text: Field text that appears on every card in a background. Shared text can be edited only from the background layer. Text in shared fields cannot be searched.

source of value: The most basic HyperTalk expressions; the language elements from which values can be derived: constants, containers, functions, literals, and properties.

stack: A type of HyperCard object that consists of a collection of cards; a HyperCard document.

statement: A line of HyperTalk code inside a handler. A handler can contain many statements. Statements within handlers are first sent as messages to the object containing the handler and then to succeeding objects in the message-passing hierarchy.

static path: The message-passing route defined by an object's own hierarchy. For example, the static path followed by a message sent to (but not handled by) a button would include the card to which the button belongs, the background associated with that card, and the stack containing them. Compare with **dynamic path.**

string: A sequence of characters. You can compare and combine strings in different ways by using operators. In HyperTalk, for example, `23 + 23` will result in `46`; but `23 & 23` will result in `2323`.

syntax: A description of the way in which language elements fit together to form meaningful phrases. A syntax statement for a command shows the command in its most generalized form, including placeholders (sometimes called metasymbols) for elements you must fill in as well as optional elements.

System file: Software your computer uses to perform its basic operations.

system message: A message sent by HyperCard to an object in response to an event such as a mouse click, keyboard action, or menu command. Examples of HyperCard system messages are `mouseUp`, `doMenu`, and `newCard`.

target: The object that first receives a message.

tear-off menu: A menu that you can convert to a palette by dragging the pointer beyond the menu's edge. HyperCard has two tear-off menus—Tools and Patterns. When torn off these menus are referred to as palettes.

text field: See **field.**

text property: A quality or attribute of a character's appearance. Text properties include style, font, and size.

tick: Approximately one-sixtieth (1/60) of a second. The Wait command assumes a value in ticks unless you specify seconds by adding `secs` or `seconds`.

tool: An implement you use to do work. HyperCard has tools for browsing through cards and stacks, creating text fields, editing text, making buttons, and creating and editing pictures.

user level: A property of HyperCard, ranging from 1 to 5, that determines which HyperCard capabilities are available. You can select the user level on the Preferences card in the Home stack. Each user level makes all the options from the lower levels available and also gives you additional capabilities. The five user levels are Browsing, Typing, Painting, Authoring, and Scripting.

value: A piece of information on which HyperCard operates. All HyperCard values can be treated as strings of characters—they are not formally separated into types. For example, a numeral could be interpreted as a number or as text, depending on what you do with it in a HyperTalk handler.

variable: A named container that can hold a value consisting of a character string of any length. You can create a variable to hold some value (either numbers or text) simply by using its name with the Put command and putting the value into it. HyperCard has local variables and global variables. Compare with **constant.**

window properties: The properties that determine how the message box and the Tools and Patterns palettes are displayed. For example, the `visible` property determines whether or not the specified window is displayed on the screen.

Index

D

F

G

T

U

V

W

X

Tools and Keyboard Modifiers

Tools	Click on tool	Double-click on tool	Drag with tool
Browse tool (turns to I-beam over unlocked fields)	selects Browse tool; used to click buttons, edit field text		selects field text
Button tool	selects Button tool; used to create, modify buttons		from middle moves button; from corner resizes button
Field tool	selects Field tool; used to create, modify fields		from middle moves field; from corner resizes field
Selection tool (marquee)	reveals paint menus	selects entire graphics layer	selects rectangular picture; moves selection
Lasso	reveals paint menus	selects all images in graphics layer	selects irregularly sized picture (shrink to fit); moves selection
Pencil	reveals paint menus	toggles FatBits on/off	draws fine line
Paintbrush	reveals paint menus	displays Brush Shapes dialog box	draws with selected pattern and brush shape
Eraser	reveals paint menus	erases entire graphics layer	erases graphics
Straight Line	reveals paint menus	displays Line Size dialog box	draws straight line
Spray Can	reveals paint menus		paints spray with selected pattern
Rectangle	reveals paint menus	toggles Draw Filled on/off	draws rectangle with selected line width
Rounded Rectangle	reveals paint menus	toggles Draw Filled on/off	draws rounded rectangle with selected line width
Oval	reveals paint menus	toggles Draw Filled on/off	draws oval with selected line width
Curve	reveals paint menus	toggles Draw Filled on/off	draws irregular curved shapes with selected line width
Regular Polygon	reveals paint menus	displays Polygon Sides dialog box	draws regular polygons with selected line width
Polygon	reveals paint menus	toggles Draw Filled on/off	draws irregular polygons with selected line width
Paint Bucket	reveals paint menus	toggles the display of the Patterns palette on/off	click to fill surrounded graphic area with pattern
Paint Text	reveals paint menus	reveals Paint Text Style dialog box	click to position pointer for typing paint text